The Asian Economy

The book is a key reading which provides a comprehensive and systematic overview of the contemporary Asian economy.

The book focuses on the structural changes that are rapidly transforming the regional economic landscape in the 21st century. It highlights the concomitant challenges that have arisen, and further discusses prospects and potentialities of the Asian economy given this new economic environment. The book also looks at broader social issues that are both the cause and result of these new and complex economic dynamism in Asia. Understanding the Asian economy cannot be achieved without understanding the new interrelationships and complexities that have evolved from this context, which continue to be driven by drastic changes in technological, demographic, and social structures, among others.

Each of the chapters are titled based on "issues" and are framed in present continuous tense, intended to capture and emphasize the progressiveness of this new dynamism that are transforming the region in a fundamental way.

Kenta Goto is Professor at the Faculty of Economics, Kansai University, and Senior Research Fellow at the Asia Pacific Institute of Research. His research interests include development, global value chains, and the informal economy. He obtained degrees from Keio University, Harvard University, and Kyoto University.

Tamaki Endo is Associate Professor at Graduate School of Humanities and Social Sciences at Saitama University. Her research interests include informal economy, urban development, inequality, and global value chain. She received her PhD in Economics from Kyoto University.

Asei Ito is Associate Professor at the Institute of Social Science, University of Tokyo. He obtained a PhD from the Graduate School of Economics, Keio University, Japan. His research covers Chinese industrial development, innovation, and outward FDI.

"Goto, et al. fill a gap between what has been documented decades ago and the current reality of the Asian economy in the context of development economics. The authors are a group of well-trained Japanese economists with rich experience in fieldworks. The book is ideal to use as a textbook or a discussion material in both undergraduate and graduate classes. Academic scholars who would like to update their understanding on Asia as well as businesspersons and government officials who are keen to comprehend current Asia will find the book concise and insightful. Another Asian miracle is there."
—*Fukunari Kimura, Professor, Faculty of Economics, Keio University, Japan, and Chief Economist, Economic Research Institute for ASEAN and East Asia (ERIA), Indonesia*

'*The Asian Economy* is an innovative and successful attempt to bring to a Western audience the results of extensive work by Japanese scholars on Southeast and East Asian development in the 21st century. Organised mainly in terms of regional themes, it draws on the expertise of eleven authors to cover topics including migration, global value chains, informalisation, innovation, and the role of China in Asia. As a textbook it will be valuable for graduate students and advanced undergraduates, and also will be exceptionally useful for policy makers and academics interested in the region.'
—*John Thoburn, School of International Development, University of East Anglia, Norwich, UK*

The Asian Economy

Contemporary Issues and Challenges

**Edited by Kenta Goto,
Tamaki Endo, and Asei Ito**

LONDON AND NEW YORK

First published 2021
by Routledge
2 Park Square, Milton Park, Abingdon, Oxon OX14 4RN

and by Routledge
52 Vanderbilt Avenue, New York, NY 10017

Routledge is an imprint of the Taylor & Francis Group, an informa business

© 2021 selection and editorial matter, Kenta Goto, Tamaki Endo, and Asei Ito; individual chapters, the contributors

The right of Kenta Goto, Tamaki Endo, and Asei Ito to be identified as the authors of the editorial material, and of the authors for their individual chapters, has been asserted in accordance with sections 77 and 78 of the Copyright, Designs and Patents Act 1988.

All rights reserved. No part of this book may be reprinted or reproduced or utilized in any form or by any electronic, mechanical, or other means, now known or hereafter invented, including photocopying and recording, or in any information storage or retrieval system, without permission in writing from the publishers.

Trademark notice: Product or corporate names may be trademarks or registered trademarks and are used only for identification and explanation without intent to infringe.

British Library Cataloguing-in-Publication Data
A catalogue record for this book is available from the British Library

Library of Congress Cataloging-in-Publication Data
Names: Gotō, Kenta, 1969– editor. | Endō, Tamaki, 1975– editor. | Itō, Asei, 1984– editor.
Title: The Asian economy: contemporary issues and challenges/ edited by Kenta Goto, Tamaki Endo, and Asei Ito.
Description: Abingdon, Oxon; New York, NY: Routledge, [2021] | Includes bibliographical references and index.
Identifiers: LCCN 2020012071 (print) | LCCN 2020012072 (ebook)
Subjects: LCSH: Economic development—Asia. | Asia—Economic policy. | Asia—Economic conditions—21st century.
Classification: LCC HC412.A7558 2021 (print) | LCC HC412 (ebook) | DDC 330.95—dc23
LC record available at https://lccn.loc.gov/2020012071
LC ebook record available at https://lccn.loc.gov/2020012072

ISBN: 978-0-367-20370-2 (hbk)
ISBN: 978-0-367-20371-9 (pbk)
ISBN: 978-0-429-26116-9 (ebk)

Typeset in Berling and Futura
by codeMantra

Visit the eResources: www.routledge.com/9780367203719

Contents

Map of Asia xiii
Book structure chart xiv
Preface and acknowledgements xvii
List of contributors xix
List of figures xxi
List of tables xxiii

Introduction: the Asian economy in the Asian century 1
Tamaki Endo, Asei Ito, Keiichiro Oizumi, and Kenta Goto

Introduction 1
I.1 Key characteristics of the Asian economy 2
I.2 Key features of this book 5
I.3 The structure of the book 6

Part I New dimensions of the Asian economy 11

1 Transforming Asia: how the Asian economy has been discussed 13
Asei Ito, Tamaki Endo, Keiichiro Oizumi, and Kenta Goto

Introduction 13
1.1 From stagnation to development 14
   1.1.1 The post-war reconstruction of Japan and Asia 14
   1.1.2 Underdevelopment and stagnation in Asia 15
   1.1.3 The emergence of a "growing Asia" 16
1.2 From the "East Asian Miracle" to the Asian Financial Crisis 18
   1.2.1 The success story of East Asia 18
   1.2.2 The Asian Financial Crisis and the neoclassical era 19
1.3 The rise of China, and towards an "emerging Asia" 20
   1.3.1 China, production networks, and regional economic integration 20
   1.3.2 Risks and opportunities in middle-income Asia 22

	Conclusion	23
	Box 1 Reviewing the Asian economy from a historical perspective *Takeshi Nishimura*	24
2	Asianizing Asia: the rise of intra-regional trade and economic integration *Kenta Goto and Keiichiro Oizumi*	28
	Introduction: what is "Asianizing Asia"?	28
	2.1 Breaking away from economic dependency	30
	2.1.1 Evolving Asia in global trade	30
	2.1.2 The rise of Asian NIEs	31
	2.1.3 The Plaza Accord and the Asian Miracle	32
	2.2 *De-facto* economic integration and global value chains	35
	2.2.1 The financial crisis and China's accession to the WTO	35
	2.2.2 China, regional division of labor in production, and horizontal trade	37
	2.2.3 The deepening of the vertical international division of labor	39
	2.2.4 Asia as a major regional market	40
	2.3 *De-jure* economic integration, opportunities, and challenges	41
	2.3.1 The centrality of ASEAN in Asian regional FTAs	41
	2.3.2 Changes in the trade policies of Japan, China, and Korea	42
	2.3.3 Diversified economic relationships and challenges for future growth	42
	Conclusion	44
	Box 2 Trade-related databases *Keiichiro Oizumi*	45
3	China reshaping Asia: economic transition and the rise of an economic superpower *Asei Ito*	48
	Introduction	48
	3.1 Reform and opening-up policy, and China's economic development: Asia changing China	50
	3.1.1 Characteristics and limitations of the planned economy	50
	3.1.2 Economic transition toward a market economy	52
	3.1.3 Opening-up policy	53
	3.2 China as the workshop of the world: China's integration into the Asian economy	54
	3.2.1 The Asian production network and China as the assembly factory	54
	3.2.2 Industrial development based on the domestic market	56
	3.2.3 The "Lewis turning point" argument	56

	3.3 China as an economic superpower: China changing Asia	57
	3.3.1 China in the Asian and global economy	57
	3.3.2 State capitalism and mass capitalism in China	59
	3.3.3 Quality of growth and the challenge of "getting old before getting rich"	60
	Conclusion	62
	Box 3 The Belt and Road Initiative (BRI) *Asei Ito*	63

Part II Borderless Asia — 67

4 Factory Asia: global value chains and local firm development — 69
Momoko Kawakami and Kenta Goto

Introduction — 69
4.1 Industrialization in Asia and the shifting engines of growth of the global economy — 70
  4.1.1 The era of international trade: to the 1970s — 70
  4.1.2 The era of foreign direct investment and diffusion of industrialization: from the 1980s — 71
  4.1.3 The era of global production networks: from the 2000s — 72
4.2 The global value chains perspective — 73
4.3 Local industries and firms in GVCs — 74
  4.3.1 The Vietnamese apparel industry: integration into GVCs and upgrading — 74
  4.3.2 The Taiwanese Notebook PC Industry: upgrading by subcontracting — 78
  4.3.3 The implications from the GVC framework — 81
Conclusion — 83

Box 4 GVCs and corporate social responsibility — 84
Kenta Goto

5 Capital Asia: growth and capital flows — 87
Fumiharu Mieno and Kenta Goto

Introduction — 87
5.1 International capital flows — 88
  5.1.1 Capital and growth — 88
  5.1.2 Capital flows and the balance of payments — 89
  5.1.3 Post-war monetary and financial order and capital mobility — 91
5.2 The Asian economy and capital: from the Asian financial crisis to the 21st century — 95
  5.2.1 The Asian financial crisis — 95
  5.2.2 Structural change in the 2000s — 97

viii Contents

        5.2.3 The drastic change in the global capital and financial environment and Asia   100
        5.2.4 New challenges   101
    5.3 Policy challenges for Asia and its financial sector   102
        5.3.1 Financial system reform after the Asian financial crisis   102
        5.3.2 Asian financial cooperation: Asian monetary cooperation and bond market development   103
    Conclusion   104

    Box 5 Emerging issues in the micro-organizational finance systems and the Asian economy   105
    Fumiharu Mieno

6 Migrating Asia: labor mobility in an interdependent and connected world   109
   Tomohiro Machikita

    Introduction   109
    6.1 Background and framework   111
        6.1.1 Trends in international migration in Asia   111
        6.1.2 Demand and supply of foreign labor in Asia   112
        6.1.3 Theoretical framework: the benefits and costs of migration   113
    6.2 Stylized facts on international migration in Asia   115
        6.2.1 An overview in the trends of foreign population in Asia   115
        6.2.2 The roles of distance and income disparity in migration in Asia   117
        6.2.3 Changes in labor demand: the feminization of international migration   117
    6.3 The roles of policy and institutional change   120
        6.3.1 Demand-driven *status-quo* policy: the case of Thailand   120
        6.3.2 Government as an intermediary: the case of South Korea   121
        6.3.3 Free movement of high-skilled workers: the case of ASEAN   122
    Conclusion   123

    Box 6 Brain circulation and Asian entrepreneurs in Silicon Valley   124
    Momoko Kawakami

Part III Dynamic Asia   127

7 Innovating Asia: growth pattern changes in post-middle-income economies   129
   Asei Ito

    Introduction   129
    7.1 The success of "catching-up" and the "middle-income trap"   130
        7.1.1 Asian NIEs and catch-up industrialization   130
        7.1.2 Growth accounting approach   131

	7.1.3 Can Asia sustain its growth?	133
7.2	Innovation and sources of growth	134
	7.2.1 Human capital and research and development (R&D)	134
	7.2.2 Investments in IT capital and digitalization	136
	7.2.3 Industrial clusters and networks	138
7.3	Innovation policies in Asia	140
	7.3.1 Theoretical foundations of innovation policy	140
	7.3.2 China: "Made in China 2025" and the US–China trade dispute	141
	7.3.3 Thailand: from "Thailand-ness" to promoting emerging industries?	142
Conclusion		144

Box 7 Unicorns in Asia 145
Asei Ito and Keiichiro Oizumi

8 Urbanizing Asia: cities transforming into mega-regions 147
Tamaki Endo and Keiichiro Oizumi

Introduction		147
8.1	The evolution of cities from "over-urbanization" to production centers	149
	8.1.1 Urbanization trends in Asia	149
	8.1.2 The focus on over-urbanization and primate cities	150
	8.1.3 Policies to address Asian over-urbanization	153
	8.1.4 Industrialization and cities as production centers	154
8.2	Asian urbanization in the globalization era: nodes in global value chains	155
	8.2.1 Mega-cities' function as global cities	155
	8.2.2 Industrial clusters and mega-cities as nodes in global value chains	156
	8.2.3 Urbanization in Asia and the evolving mega-regions	157
8.3	Challenges and prospects for Asian cities	158
	8.3.1 Mega-regions and inter-regional inequalities	158
	8.3.2 The challenges of Asian mega-cities	161
	8.3.3 The socio-political risks and policy dilemmas in the era of the mega-regions	162
Conclusion		163

Box 8 Consuming Asia 164
Keiichiro Oizumi

9 Informalizing Asia: the other dynamics of the Asian economy 169
Tamaki Endo and Kenta Goto

Introduction	169
9.1 The informal economy and its theoretical perspectives	170

    9.1.1 What is the informal economy?   170
    9.1.2 The birth of the concept, and the shift in views from negative to positive   171
    9.1.3 Beyond the dichotomy view   172
  9.2 The informal economy in Asia and its roles in the 21st century   174
    9.2.1 Redefining the informal economy under globalization   174
    9.2.2 The informal economy in Asia: its size and trends   175
    9.2.3 Globalization, urbanization, and the dynamism of the informal economy   177
    9.2.4 The roles and functions of the informal economy   178
  9.3 The future outlook for the informal economy and its dilemmas   180
    9.3.1 Informality and institutions: taxes, risks, and social protection   180
    9.3.2 The new dynamics in the 21st century (1) – the internationalization of the informal economy   181
    9.3.3 The new dynamics in the 21st century (2) – from formal to informal   182
  Conclusion   183

  Box 9 Informal residential areas: the functions of "slum" communities from the urban lower-class perspective   184
  Tamaki Endo

Part IV Asia at a crossroads 189

10 Ageing Asia: from demographic dividend to demographic tax   191
  Keiichiro Oizumi and Asei Ito

  Introduction   191
  10.1 Population growth and economic growth   192
    10.1.1 Rapid population growth   192
    10.1.2 The poverty trap and birth control policies   193
    10.1.3 Declining birth rates in Asia   194
  10.2 Demographic dividend and demographic tax   194
    10.2.1 What is a demographic dividend?   194
    10.2.2 The effects of the demographic dividend   195
    10.2.3 Economic policies that are consistent with the demographic transition   197
    10.2.4 From demographic dividend to demographic tax   199
  10.3 Ageing and social security   199
    10.3.1 The rapid increase of the ageing rate   199
    10.3.2 The current status of social security policies in Asia   202
    10.3.3 The agendas of promoting social security policies in Asia   204

	Conclusion	205
	Box 10 Who are the "elderly people"? *Keiichiro Oizumi*	206
11	Unequalizing Asia: from poverty to inequality *Kunio Urakawa and Tamaki Endo*	209
	Introduction	210
	11.1 From poverty to inequality	210
	11.1.1 "The East Asian Miracle" and poverty reduction in Asia up to the early 1990s	210
	11.1.2 Rising inequality in Asia	212
	11.1.3 The Kuznets hypothesis and Asia	212
	11.2 Background and causes of increased income inequality: cases from Asian countries	217
	11.2.1 Why is income inequality increasing in Asia?	217
	11.2.2 The case of Japan	217
	11.2.3 The case of China	220
	11.2.4 The case of ASEAN	221
	11.3 Policy responses of Asian countries and future outlook	224
	11.3.1 Growing public concern about Asian income inequality, and countermeasures	224
	11.3.2 Policy responses and prospects for middle-income countries	225
	11.3.3 Policy responses and prospects in a high-income country: case of Japan	226
	Conclusion	227
	Box 11 Inequality and democracy *Wataru Kusaka*	228
12	Environmentally challenged Asia: in the context of backwardness and diversity *Fumikazu Ubukata*	233
	Introduction	233
	12.1 Environmental problems in Asia and their characteristics	234
	12.1.1 The duality of backwardness and the diversity of environmental issues	234
	12.1.2 Environmental pollution and destruction: some examples	235
	12.2 Economic development and environmental problems	237
	12.2.1 The environmental Kuznets curve	237
	12.2.2 The environmental Kuznets curve in Asia	238
	12.2.3 The environmental Kuznets curve and issues of focus	240

12.3 The key arguments and the processes of change	242
12.3.1 The pulp and paper industry in Southeast Asia	242
12.3.2 Cross-borderization and the increasing complexity of the issue: haze pollution around Singapore	245
Conclusion	247

Box 12 The ambitious attempts of Asian governments to "internalize" externalities   248
Fumikazu Ubukata

Conclusion: competing Asia, co-existing Asia	250

Kenta Goto, Tamaki Endo, Asei Ito, and Keiichiro Oizumi

Introduction: is the 21st century an "Asian century?"	250
C.1 The Asian economy in an era of international connectivity	251
C.2 Compressed development and regional challenges	252
C.3 The future outlook for the Asian economy – competing and co-existing	253
Conclusion: Japan in the 21st century Asia	255

Index   *257*

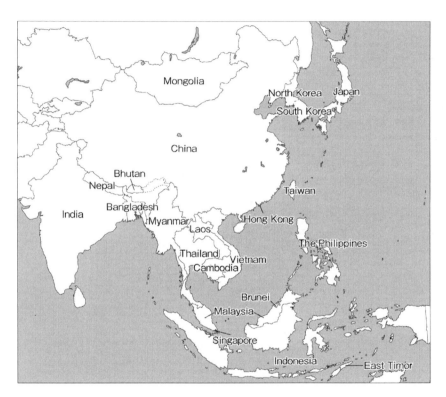

FIGURE 0.1 Map of Asia.

Book structure chart

The structure of the book and key contents

Part	Chapter	Theme
	Introduction	Overview of the contemporary Asian economy
Part I New Dimensions of the Asian Economy	Chapter 1 Transforming Asia	Review of the literature and overview of the past, present and the future
	Chapter 2 Asianizing Asia	Mutual interdependence
	Chapter 3 China reshaping Asia	China
Part II Borderless Asia	Chapter 4 Factory Asia	Global value chains (goods and value-added)
	Chapter 5 Capital Asia	International capital movement (money)
	Chapter 6 Migrating Asia	International human mobility (people)
Part III Dynamic Asia	Chapter 7 Innovating Asia	Innovation
	Chapter 8 Urbanizing Asia	Cities and megaregions
	Chapter 9 Informalizing Asia	Informal economy
Part IV Asia at a crossroads	Chapter 10 Ageing Asia	Demographic dynamics
	Chapter 11 Unequalizing Asia	Inequality
	Chapter 12 Environmentally challenged Asia	Environmental issues
	Conclusion: competing Asia, co-existing Asia	Future outlook

Note: MDGs (Millenium Development Goals), SDGs (Sustainable Development Goals), FTA (Free Trade Agreement), FDI (Foreign Direct Investment).

Earlier book's focus: (1) and (2)

This book's focus: (2) and (3)

(1) The post-war independence and development era (1945–1970s)	(2) The catch-up industrialization era (1980s–1990s)	(3) The post catch-up era (2000s–)
–	–	The "Asian Century" – the rising importance of Asia in the global economy, regional interdependence, and compressed development.
Post-war independence, from poverty and reconstruction to development, evolving NIEs, developmentalism.	Catch-up industrialization, the East Asian Miracle, post Cold-War era, the Asian Financial Crisis, MDGs.	Middle income status, post-catch up development, diversification of issues, and inclusive growth/SDGs.
Flying geese pattern of development.	FDI, GVCs, intra-regional division of labor in Asia, and *de-facto* integration.	Mega FTAs and *de-jure* integration.
Asia changing China, the transition from a planned economy to a market economy.	Asia and China co-existing. China becoming the global production hub, as the factory of the world.	China changing Asia. Economic superpower, and the hub for production, high-tech, investment, and consumption.
Inter-industry based international division of labor and trade.	Intra-industry based international division of labor, fragmentation, and product architecture.	Value addition in the post industrialization through information and digitalization.
Official financial flows, oil-money, and the accumulated debt problem.	From structural adjustment to major destination of FDI.	Emerging as a major credit exporter, and the increasing intra-regional circulation of funds.
Rural to urban migration.	Urbanization and international migration (to developed countries outside the region).	The dual structure of international migration (skilled and low-skilled), intra-regional migration patterns.
Developed country dominance.	Technology transfer through the catch-up process.	Middle income trap, from catch-up to innovation, promotion of R&D.
Rural-urban migration and over-urbanization.	Urbanization and the formation of mega-cities.	Mega-regions, globalization, and agglomeration.
The discovery of the informal sector, poverty and employment.	Informal sector and productivity.	Redefining informal economy and informality. Informality in the formal economy.
Poverty and population (birth) control.	Demographic dividend and economic growth.	Ageing population and demographic tax.
Poverty.	Economic growth and inequality.	Globalization, ageing, and rising inequality.
Resources and economic growth.	Environmental pollution as a major social issue.	Complexification and trans-border pollution. Emerging economies as major actors to preserve the environment.
The Cold War and a divided Asia.	Post-Cold War and *de-facto* integration.	Diversity and co-existence.

Source: Prepared by the authors.

Preface and acknowledgements

Kenta Goto

This is an English version of a book entitled *Asian Economy in the 21st Century* (*Gendai Ajia Keizai-ron*), published in Japanese by Yuhikaku Publishing Co., Ltd. of Tokyo, Japan in the spring of 2018. The four editors of this Japanese book; Tamaki Endo (Saitama University), Asei Ito (The University of Tokyo), Keiichiro Oizumi (Asia University), and Kenta Goto (Kansai University), gathered at Yuhikaku in the fall of 2015, with great ambitions to write a book that would serve university students who study the Asian economy, and the business community who interact with, and work in, Asia on a daily basis. We were extremely lucky to be able to invite six additional authors (plus two colleagues to each contribute to one of the short but important Boxes in the chapters), who are the leading experts in their respective fields.

The contents and data used in this English version are the same as in the original, but some of the Japanese references have been replaced by English-based literature whenever available. Because of its extensive focus on Japan, one chapter in the original Japanese version, discussing foreign aid, has not been included in this English version.

The primary motivation to write the book was based on a firm belief that the Asian economy has been going through significant and fundamental changes since the turn of this century. This is particularly pronounced in the deepening inter-connectedness, and the region-wide transformations, that are taking place at multiple levels across Asia. Japan is arguably one of the places in the world with the most extensive collections of works related to the Asian economy. Through our teaching and interactions with students at our universities, however, we have become acutely aware that a comprehensive textbook introducing and elaborating on the new dynamics of the Asian economy was, in fact, lacking, and urgently needed.

Books on the Asian economy have been typically structured on a country basis, with in-depth descriptions and cross-country comparisons. This book departs from this approach, and does not delve into country details per se. It does, however, focus more on the underlying dynamics of the interrelationships and the emerging cross-cutting issues that continue to shape regional development trajectories and redefine future prospects.

Being part of the Asian economy in the 21st century is exciting. It has evolved as the center of global production, as a major consumer, as a substantial investor, and as a leading innovator. Significant progress has also been made on poverty reduction and industrialization, and new opportunities are emerging almost everywhere. However, this has been accompanied by new challenges, which have been unfolding within new structural and technological contexts. Unless these are addressed adequately and effectively, they could compromise the sustainable development of the entire region. The original Japanese-language version of this book was written with the explicit intention of taking readers through these changes and the concomitant challenges and opportunities, in a way that was based on solid analytical frameworks. This book is truly the result of collaborative efforts by Japanese scholars who have spent most of their professional careers working on Asia. Our hope is that the book will trigger further discussions involving researchers and practitioners beyond Japan.

We are grateful to Eri Hasegawa from Yuhikaku Publishing Co., Ltd., who was our production editor, for overseeing the entire publication process of the original Japanese edition. If it were not for Eri, the Japanese book (and therefore *this* book) would never had come into existence. With great perseverance and integrity, she provided guidance and accommodated our requests for editorial meetings at Yuhikaku during the two and half years of writing and editing. Fifteen intensive meetings, involving editors and some of the authors, were held in Tokyo, which typically lasted from 10 am to 5 pm, with short lunch-breaks in-between. We also want to thank Yuhikaku Publishing Co., Ltd. for kindly granting permission to translate the original and for allowing the publication by Routledge of this English-language version.

We are highly indebted to John Thoburn (Emeritus Reader in Economics in the School of International Development at the University of East Anglia, UK, and former Professor at Ritsumeikan Asia Pacific University, Japan) for language-editing our manuscript. I have known John since we met first in Vietnam in the early 2000s, and was very lucky to have had the opportunity to conduct joint research with him and to co-author and publish articles in international academic journals (with another colleague) on Vietnam and Cambodia. In fact, John has published extensively on issues related to trade and development in Asia (and beyond), and I could not think of anyone more capable and trustworthy. The chapters are now in much better shape not just because of his elegant editing skills, but also because of his valuable advice on substance. However, the authors, of course, take responsibility for their own chapters and for any remaining errors.

Finally, we want to thank Yongling Lam, Samatha Phua, ShengBin Tan, and Cathy Hurren at Routledge and Assunta Petrone at codemantra for their support and advice extended to us during the production process, which were crucial for the publication of this book.

Kenta Goto, on behalf of the editors
December 2019

Contributors

Tamaki Endo is Associate Professor at Graduate School of Humanities and Social Sciences at Saitama University. Her research interests include informal economy, urban development, inequality, and global value chain. She received her PhD in Economics from Kyoto University.

Kenta Goto is Professor at the Faculty of Economics, Kansai University, and Senior Research Fellow at the Asia Pacific Institute of Research. His research interests include development, global value chains, and the informal economy. He obtained degrees from Keio University, Harvard University, and Kyoto University.

Asei Ito is Associate Professor at the Institute of Social Science, University of Tokyo. He obtained a PhD from the Graduate school of Economics, Keio University, Japan. His research covers Chinese industrial development, innovation, and outward FDI.

Momoko Kawakami is Deputy Director General of Area Studies Center at the Institute of Developing Economies, JETRO. She has been working on industrial development of Taiwan and East Asian economies. She received her PhD from The University of Tokyo.

Wataru Kusaka is Associate Professor at the Graduate School of International Development, Nagoya University.

Tomohiro Machikita is Associate Professor of the Center for Southeast Asian Studies (CSEAS), Kyoto University. His research covers labor economics, immigration, economic history, and industrial development. He was an economist of Institute of Developing Economies (IDE-JETRO) during 2006–2019. He obtained his PhD from Kyoto University.

Fumiharu Mieno has been professor of economics, Center for Southeast Asian Studies, Kyoto University. His major research areas are financial system in economic development and the economies of Southeast Asia. He obtained PhD at Hitotsubashi University. Before attaching the current position, he worked as faculties at Hosei University and Kobe University.

Takeshi Nishimura is Professor at the Faculty of Economics, Kansai University.

Keiichiro Oizumi is Professor at the Institute of Asian Studies, Asia University. He has previously been Senior Economist at the Japan Research Institute. He obtained his PhD from Kyoto University.

Fumikazu Ubukata is Professor of the Graduate School of Environmental and Life Science, Okayama University. His research interests include political economy of development and environment in Asia, especially the issues in natural resources and rural society. He obtained his PhD from Kyoto University.

Kunio Urakawa is Associate Professor of the Faculty of Economics at Kyushu University. His research interests include public economics, welfare policy, and poverty problem. He obtained degrees from Keio University (Bachelor of Commerce) and Kyoto University (Master's degree in Economics and PhD in Economics).

Figures

2.1	Export shares to the US	33
2.2	Share of industrial sector exports	34
2.3	The flying geese pattern	35
2.4	Share of Asia's exports to Asia	36
2.5A	Intra-regional trade in Asia	38
2.5B	Intra-regional trade in Asia, USMCA, and EU (2015)	38
2.6	Fragmentation	39
3.1	East and Southeast Asian GDP by economies	49
3.2	China's economic growth rate (1933–2015)	51
3.3	Industrial output by company ownership	53
3.4	Capital formation ratio and economic development (2015)	61
4.1	The production flow and value-added in the apparel industry	77
4.2	Notebook PC exports by Taiwanese firms (including overseas production)	79
4.3	Gross margins earned by selected value chain participants	82
5.1	Economic growth and capital accumulation	89
5.2	Capital flow based on balance of payment system	90
5.3	Net capital inflow into the Asia Pacific region	93
5.4	Gross financial accounts (inbound and outbound, Thailand)	99
6.1	Foreign population shares among different country income groups (1990 and 2015)	111
6.2	Changes in the sizes of foreign populations among the top five recipient countries in Asia	116
6.3	Changes in the sizes of foreign populations from Cambodia, Lao PDR, and Myanmar in Thailand	118
6.4	Changes in the sizes of foreign populations from China, Malaysia, and Indonesia in Singapore	119
6.5	Female share of foreign population	119
7.1	Per capita GDP in selected countries	133
7.2	Patent application and per capita GDP (2017)	136
7.3	Share of Internet connection speed above 4 Mbps (%, 2008Q1–2017Q1)	137
7.4	The relationships between innovation policy and the number of R&D projects	140
8.1	Urban population and urbanization rate, 1950–2050	149
8.2	Urban population in Asia, 1950–2050	150

8.3	Increase in population and number of communities for low-income groups in Bangkok	153
8.4	Per capita GDP in Bangkok and Shanghai (nominal exchange rate)	155
8.5	Gross regional products per capita of provinces in Thailand (2014)	159
8.6A	Population pyramid in Thailand (2010): Bangkok	160
8.6B	Population pyramid in Thailand (2010): Northeast region	160
8.7	Policy dilemma of mega cities in emerging countries	162
9.1	Informal employment and GDP in Southeast Asia	175
10.1	Demographic transition	193
10.2	Working-age and saving rate (2016)	196
10.3	Agricultural employment ratio and working-age population (1980–2015)	198
11.1	Poverty headcount ratio in East and Southeast Asia (2011 PPP)	211
11.2	Income share by quantile income class (around 2010)	215
11.3	Kuznets curve	216
11.4A	Income inequality in Japan (1961–2013)	218
11.4B	Gini coefficient by householder's age group (equivalent income)	218
11.5A	College enrollment rate by household income quartile	223
11.5B	Real hourly wage by educational group	223
12.1	Environmental Kuznets curve	237
12.2	Economic development and CO_2 emission per 100 US dollars of GDP in Asia (1993–2013)	239
12.3	Economic development and per capita CO_2 emission in Asia (1993–2013)	240
12.4	Economic development and annual exposure of PM2.5 (1995–2015)	241
12.5	Economic development and forest cover (1993–2013)	242

Tables

1.1	GDP (nominal) of Asian economies (US billion dollar, %)	2
1.2	GDP per capita (US dollar)	3
1.3	GDP growth rates (real), in local currency	4
2.1	Asia's imports and exports ($ million)	31
2.2	Japan's economic partnership agreements (EPAs) (as of July 2017)	43
3.1	Assembled locations of selected electronics products (2016)	55
4.1	Top 3 export and import products/commodities	71
4.2	Major apparel exporters in the world (unit: million $)	76
5.1	Changes in GDP expenditure compositions of Thailand and Indonesia	97
6.1	Changes in foreign population shares across regions	112
6.2	Changes in the total sizes of foreign populations, and foreign population shares, in Asia	116
6.3	Female share of foreign populations in Hong Kong and Singapore, by origins	120
7.1	Growth account in Asian economies (1970–2014)	132
7.2	Top ten universities in Asia (*The Times* higher education ranking)	135
8.1	Urbanization rate and growth of urban population in Asia (unit: %)	152
8.2	Increase of expectation toward commercial market (unit: %)	165
9.1	Share of informal employment (non-agricultural employment, %)	176
9.2	Contribution of the IE to GDP (estimation, %)	176
10.1	Total fertility rate (TFR) in Asia	195
10.2	Demographic dividend and ageing-population ratio in Asia	200
10.3	Top 10 regions with highest ageing ratio in China	202
10.4	Stages of social security in Asia	203
11.1	Changes in Gini coefficient of Asian countries	213

Introduction: the Asian economy in the Asian century

Tamaki Endo, Asei Ito, Keiichiro Oizumi, and Kenta Goto

INTRODUCTION

This book is about the economy of Asia in the 21st century. Drastic changes have taken place in the Asian economy in terms of its structure as new dynamics have evolved since the turn of the century. These are having profound effects on the livelihoods and outlook of its people. It has become more important than ever to have a good understanding of these new dimensions that characterize the contemporary Asian economy in order to correctly evaluate the opportunities and challenges that it faces as well as to think ahead and navigate into the future. While South Asia, particularly India, is undoubtedly important because of its evolving significance in the global economy, this book focuses on East and Southeast Asia, because of the strong interconnectedness that have shaped contemporary dynamics unfolding primarily in these two sub-regions. Such a geographical focus allows us to better highlight the emerging issues and concomitant challenges pertinent to regional integration, which are the book's main concerns.

When World War II ended, Asia was riddled with poverty and stagnation and was widely regarded as a region that was not expected to prosper much. However, this trend took a drastic turn in the 1950s when Japan regained its foothold in the international economy. In the 1970s Asia was already on a long-term growth trajectory, which led to region-wide industrialization based on outward orientation and export growth. This phenomenal economic performance was later highlighted as the "East Asian Miracle."

This regional and systemic growth was initially spearheaded by Japan, whose growth momentum stimulated the development of neighboring economies such as South Korea, Taiwan, Hong Kong, and Singapore (the so called Newly Industrializing Economies, NIEs). The wave of growth further spread to the "ASEAN 4" (Malaysia, Thailand, Indonesia, and the Philippines), subsequently to China and Vietnam, and eventually to the late-coming ASEAN countries of Cambodia, Laos, and Myanmar. The fact that inequality did not rise during the growth process has attracted as much significant attention as the extraordinary growth itself. This rapid and equitable development has been made possible by a developmentalist "catch-up" industrialization strategy, in which the state played a crucial role.

However, the Asian economy started exhibiting fundamental changes both quantitatively and qualitatively in the 21st century as globalization, the spread of information technology (IT), and the rise of China unfolded over a very short timeframe. The fact that Asia has become a global manufacturing hub, also referred to as "the world's factory," is already well known. In addition to this, as the size of the Asian economy has surpassed that of the US and Europe, it has also started to attract financial and human resources globally and became the prime destination for goods and services. Asia has also emerged as a major source of innovation that is having profound impacts on the global industrial landscape. Asia has evolved as the key driver of global growth, and this role will most likely increase in the future. Based on these observations, the Asian Development Bank (ADB) has pointed towards a possibility of an "Asian Century." However, whether Asia can sustain its growth momentum is dependent on multiple factors. One of these is its ability to manage and overcome the "middle-income trap," which is now one of the major issues for many of the emerging economies in Asia.

I.1 KEY CHARACTERISTICS OF THE ASIAN ECONOMY

To fully understand the evolving dynamics of the Asian economy, it is important at the outset to emphasize the following four key characteristics.

The first is the growing presence of Asia in the world economy. Table I.1 depicts the gross domestic product (GDP) share of selected countries and regions in the world. The share of East and Southeast Asia has grown from 16.0% in 1980 to 23.1% in 2000, and then to 27.9% in 2016. The economy of East and Southeast Asia is now larger than that of the US and the EU. The table also suggests that the country leading their growth has also changed over the past several decades: while Japan's share of Asia's GDP was more than 60% in 1980, this has declined to about 20% in 2016. Japan's falling share in the region's GDP is a consistent trend, while those of other Asian countries, notably China, have increased rapidly, and this trend may further accelerate in the future.

TABLE I.1 GDP (nominal) of Asian economies (US billion dollar, %)

Year	World (total)	East and Southeast Asia (total)	Japan	NIEs	China	ASEAN 5	US	EU
1980	11,137	1,778 (16.0)	1,100 (9.9)	148 (1.3)	305 (2.7)	223 (2.0)	2,862 (25.7)	3,799 (34.1)
1990	23,472	4,436 (18.9)	3,141 (13.4)	562 (2.4)	399 (1.7)	329 (1.4)	5,980 (25.5)	7,381 (31.4)
2000	33,820	7,804 (23.1)	4,887 (14.5)	1,161 (3.4)	1,215 (3.6)	519 (1.5)	10,285 (30.4)	8,914 (26.4)
2010	65,900	15,517 (23.5)	5,700 (8.6)	2,006 (3.0)	6.066 (9.2)	1,664 (2.5)	14,964 (22.7)	17,002 (25.8)
2016	75,278	20,967 (27.9)	4,939 (6.6)	2,557 (3.4)	11,218 (14.9)	2,142 (2.8)	18,569 (24.7)	16,408 (21.8)

Source: IMF, World Economic Outlook Database, April 2017.

Note: NIEs includes Korea, Taiwan, Hong Kong and Singapore. ASEAN5 includes Thailand, Malaysia, Indonesia, the Philippines and Vietnam.

TABLE I.2 GDP per capita (US dollar)

	1980	1990	2000	2010	2016	Population (million, 2016)
Japan	9,418	25,443	38,534	44,674	38,917	126.9
South Korea	1,711	6,513	11,947	22,087	27,539	51.2
Taiwan	2,367	8,178	14,877	19,262	22,453	23.5
Hong Kong	5,664	13,281	25,578	32,421	43,528	7.4
Singapore	5,004	12,766	23,793	46,569	52,961	5.6
Thailand	719	1,571	2,028	5,065	5,899	69.0
Malaysia	1,900	2,550	4,287	8,920	9,360	31.7
Indonesia	673	771	870	3,178	3,604	258.7
The Philippines	753	806	1,055	2,155	2,924	104.2
China	309	349	959	4,524	8,113	1,382.7
Vietnam	514	98	402	1,297	2,173	92.6
Cambodia	–	100	300	782	1,230	15.8
Laos	310	216	292	1,070	1,925	7.2
Myanmar	–	–	221	997	1,269	52.3
Brunei	–	15,423	20,511	35,437	26,424	0.4

Source: IMF, World Economic Outlook Database, April 2017 and World Development Indicator Database.

Note: According to the classification of the World Bank (July, 2016), 'low-income' economies are defined as those with a GNI per capita of $1,025 or less in 2015, 'lower-middle-income' economies are between $1,026 and $4,035, 'upper-middle-income' economies are between $4,036 and $12,475, and 'high-income' ecomomies are those of $12,476 or more.

Table I.2 provides a summary of per capita GDP and population of each of the economies in the region. This table shows that Singapore and Hong Kong's *per capita* income levels have already far exceeded that of Japan, joining the highest income group economies in the world. It also clearly indicates that the majority of the Asian economies are still in the middle-income group, while some have only just made it over the low-income group threshold by a very small margin. This illustrates the significant intra-regional diversity in terms of income levels.

While growth in real (inflation-adjusted) GDP, and the years in which each of the economies achieved their highest growth rates vary, Asia has registered higher growth rates overall than the world average, as shown in Table I.3.

The second of the region's key characteristics is that its development and growth have not been just a collection of events that occurred in each of the economies independently, but rather were achieved collectively as a region through intensifying intra-regional trade and investment relationships. Such a region-wide and systemic development was possible because most of the economies in Asia did promote, at one time or another, an outward-oriented policy to which multinational-enterprises (MNEs) responded quickly in establishing Asia as part of their international production and distribution networks. Such forms of Asian economic integration, which are one of its most important features in the 21st century, were also made possible by trade liberalization,

TABLE I.3 GDP growth rates (real), in local currency

	1980–1989	1990–1999	2000–2009	2010–2016
Japan	4.4	1.6	0.5	1.4
South Korea	8.7	7.0	4.7	3.5
Taiwan	6.7	6.6	3.8	3.5
Hong Kong	7.4	3.6	4.2	3.3
Singapore	7.7	7.2	5.2	5.3
Thailand	7.2	5.2	4.3	3.6
Malaysia	5.9	7.1	4.7	5.5
Indonesia	6.5	4.6	5.3	5.6
The Philippines	1.9	2.7	4.4	6.3
China	9.7	9.9	10.3	8.1
Vietnam	5.0	7.4	6.9	6.0
Cambodia	1.3	6.2	8.5	6.7
Laos	5.9	6.1	7.0	7.8
Myanmar	0.0	1.6	11.1	6.9
Brunei	−0.1	2.1	1.4	−0.2
Other regions				
India	5.5	5.7	6.9	7.3
US	3.1	3.2	1.8	2.1
EU	2.2	2.1	1.7	1.4
World	3.2	3.1	3.9	3.8

Source: IMF, World Economic Outlook Database, April 2017.

reductions in transportation costs, and by the rapid development and diffusion of IT-related technologies.

The third of the key characteristics highlights the drastic socio-economic changes that were induced and facilitated by rapid economic growth, in which changes in less-developed economies have been much faster than those experienced in the past by the now more-developed countries. Because such changes happen now within a much shorter time-frame, they are referred to here as "compressed development." As the sequences of these different stages of development now tend to happen within a much shorter time-horizon, some of the issues that were initially regarded as unique problems pertinent to developed countries have already appeared in much less-developed countries. This suggests that some economic and social challenges can now emerge regardless of the levels of development. For instance, employment in the informal economy, which typically operates outside formal public social security systems, has been regarded as a phenomenon observed in developing countries. However, there is increasing evidence that informalization is happening in more-developed countries. Likewise, the issue of declining birthrates, which ultimately leads to an ageing population, has also long been viewed as an issue specific to developed countries. However, similar trends are already becoming apparent in countries that are still at middle-income status. In short, social issues which in the past were associated with particular development stages are now appearing regardless of this.

The fourth of the characteristics is the change in the positions of Japan and its corporations amidst such new dynamics. The formation of the Asian economic order in the 20th century was primarily led by Japanese businesses. Japan still has a major role to play in the Asian economy today, particularly in manufacturing. However, the new dynamism that is evolving in Asia is not just driven by Japan or its corporations; different actors from different countries are emerging, taking on leadership roles which previously were mostly dominated by Japanese corporations.

The economic integration of Asia has been based on trade and investment relationships established by private corporations (*de-facto* based integration), whose momentum is augmented with an institution-led, or "*de-jure*" integration including arrangements such as the proliferation of Free Trade Agreements (FTAs). Japan is at a critical juncture at which it must reassess and re-evaluate its position within Asia, the challenges that lie ahead, and what kind of vision it can draw on while committing to the common future of the region.

1.2 KEY FEATURES OF THIS BOOK

Three important features of the book are worth mentioning. The first is its focus on the Asian economy *in the 21st century*. The book starts by classifying the latter half of the 20th century into the following three periods: (1) the period of post-war independence and economic recovery (1945 to the 1970s), (2) the period of catch-up industrialization (1980s and 1990s), and (3) the period of post-catch-up industrialization (2000 and thereafter). The primary focus is on the transition from the second period to the third. We attempt to highlight the ongoing region-wide structural changes and the concomitant challenges that have arisen, and to further discuss the prospects and potentialities, given this context. Each of the chapters is based on "issues" and is framed in the present continuous tense, intending to capture and emphasize the progressiveness of this new dynamism that are transforming the region in a fundamental way. The key issues which the book deals with are identified based on careful observation and assessment of the actual socio-economic changes in the region, and actively incorporate the latest research findings from relevant academic disciplines including development and international economic theories.

The second feature of the book is that it does not take a country-by-country approach, as many of the new issues that have evolved in the 21st century cannot be understood from such a "single country" point of view. One of the main reasons for this is the fact that a significant proportion of economic activities have become literally borderless and interconnected, where trade, investment, and non-equity-based inter-firm relationships have expanded beyond national borders and span right across Asia. An integrated production and distribution system within one country is now gradually being replaced by a fragmented, regional system where goods and services are produced in a very complex international division of labor. The only exception, however, is China, which has its own chapter because of its size, robust growth, and the resulting impact on the rest of Asia. The second reason is that the issues observed within one country have become common across countries in the region. One such issue is urbanization. Urbanization is proceeding at a global scale, but Asia is at the forefront of this trend, with mega-cities and mega-regions emerging. While such cities and regions have become engines of growth, which in turn are further attracting financial and human resources, the region has also undergone distinct demographic changes. These have sometimes played out in presenting new types of challenges, which are also observed across the region in different countries. Focusing on, and addressing the commonalities of such issues, is helpful in understanding these cross-cutting, new dimensions of Asia.

The third feature of this book is that it also takes into account the social changes which are both the cause and result of the new economic dynamism in Asia. Changes in the social and demographic structures have led to changes in how families are organized, while the evolving middle class due to rapid increases in income levels has also led to new and diverse values among its people. Understanding the contemporary Asian economy cannot be separated from its people and their livelihoods. Increases in incomes will generate greater demand for development that is equitable and sustainable. Growing income gaps, environmental degradation, and ageing population are already real and pressing issues for many, and people's views on those will alter priorities and the associated policy choices.

1.3 THE STRUCTURE OF THE BOOK

This book is organized into the following four parts:

Part I, New dimensions of the Asian economy, looks at both the past and present of Asia in order to provide a historical perspective.

Chapter 1 (Transforming Asia) discusses how Asia has been seen and treated from a theoretical point of view at different junctures during its post-war development process. The frameworks of analysis each reflect not just the changes that occur in the real economy, but also the policy concerns and trends, which are typically embedded in broader contexts that shape the discussions and paradigms at particular points of time. For instance, when poverty reduction was the key issue pertinent to Asia, it was mostly seen and analyzed from a development economics perspective. However, as Asia grew and evolved as the engine of global growth, different perspectives such as those from international economics, economic geography, finance, and manufacturing management have been applied in the analyses of the Asian economy. Asia is one of the regions that is at the forefront of the new economic dynamisms in the 21st century that has global implications, and thus has been attracting academic interest from many different disciplines.

Chapter 2 (Asianizing Asia) is primarily concerned with the economic integration that unfolded on a "*de-facto*" basis, resulting in strengthened relationships that can be characterized as co-dependency. The chapter highlights how economic integration in Asia is different from other regions – primarily North America and the European Union – by looking at various statistical data. Here the focus is on how this *de-facto*-based integration has proceeded and its relationship with the formal, institution-led "*de-jure*"-based integration.

Chapter 3 (China reshaping Asia) is devoted entirely to China. It first introduces the drastic changes that started from the "reform and opening-up" policy in the late 1970s. The chapter will then outline the process of China's integration into regional and global production networks, establishing itself as the central part of Asia's "world's factory." It further addresses the more recent dynamism in which China has literally become an economic powerhouse, whose influence goes well beyond Asia. The chapter closes by looking at some of the emerging issues, among which is a rapidly ageing population and the very recent slowing of the GDP growth rate.

Part II is entitled Borderless Asia. Cross-border flows of goods, people, money, and information are key characteristics of globalization, but the interrelationships between these flows at various levels are what makes this phenomenon new and dynamic.

Chapter 4 (Factory Asia) outlines the ongoing spread and intensification of international production and distribution networks that span Asia. The international division of labor involving different companies, countries, and regions is analyzed using the global value chain (GVC) framework. The GVC framework is then applied to look at specific sectors that are important for Asia, which include the apparel and notebook PC sectors. The chapter attempts to highlight how the organization of the production and distribution of goods and the associated services have changed from the past, and how these in turn have provided different upgrading prospects to industries and companies in emerging economies.

Chapter 5 (Capital Asia) explains how the globalization of capital and financial markets have promoted the development of Asia, as well as how it has at times contributed to crisis situations. It first provides a generic framework to understand how international capital flows affect and interact with economic growth, and further discusses how the Asian financial crisis erupted in the late 1990s. Then the chapter highlights the structural changes that were unfolding in Asia as it entered the 21st century and concludes with indicating the policy challenges and implications.

Chapter 6 (Migrating Asia) is devoted to international migration in Asia. People mobility in Asia is increasing as interdependency between countries is deepening and common challenges arising. As a diverse region, Asia comprises both migrant-sending and receiving countries. The issue of migration has become one of the most important policy concerns, and thus a good understanding of its realities and challenges is crucial. This chapter introduces readers to the framework through which the complex issue of international migration can be understood, primarily by looking at both pull and push factors, and then goes on to illustrate the reality and challenges of migration, particularly labor migration as it unfolds in Asia.

Part III is entitled Dynamic Asia. The "middle income trap" and economic stagnation have become major concerns for many countries in Asia, and the key to overcome this is through innovation.

Chapter 7 (Innovating Asia) addresses the current situation of innovation in Asia, with a particular focus on its sources and related policies. The innovative capacities of Asian companies, particularly those from emerging economies, have grown rapidly and they have become nontrivial players in the global innovation landscape, leading to the creation of new markets and products. This chapter particularly discusses the sources of innovation in Asia, including human capital and R&D, investment in IT capital and the ongoing digitalization, and the formation of industrial clusters. It also discusses the different policies to promote innovation in Asia.

Chapter 8 (Urbanizing Asia) discusses the rapid urbanization in Asia. While over-urbanization was among the main characteristics describing cities until the 1980s, they have now become literally the sources of growth where innovation occurs and are also the underlying factors in "compressed development." Some of these cities have further expanded to become the hub of a mega-region, which now also function as nodes that connect the production and distribution linkages of global value chains. It further outlines the challenges and prospects of Asian cities, such as the intensifying stratification within the cities and among regions.

Chapter 9 (Informalizing Asia) is about the informal economy, which highlights the other dynamics that drive the globalization process in Asia. As in many other regions, the informal economy is not just economically significant, but sometimes the major source of employment within a national economy. Trying to depict an economy simply in terms of the aggregate economic activities of formal, large companies can often be misleading. Development economics initially simply assumed that the informal economy would be replaced by the formal economy as a country starts to grow and develop. Nevertheless, the informal economy still remains a major part of the national economy for many countries in Asia, on which the livelihoods of the hundreds of millions are dependent.

Part IV, Asia at a crossroads, deals with new challenges that have emerged as a result of rapid socio-economic changes and diversification of values, including an ageing population, rising inequality, and environmental issues. Our ability to address these will define our future.

Chapter 10 (Ageing Asia) addresses the ageing population issue. Population growth has in the past been viewed as a source and manifestation of poverty and was subject to policies intended to control its growth. However, birthrates have been declining rapidly in Asia, and, based on this, the chapter goes on to discuss the ongoing shift from a population bonus (demographic dividend) to a population *onus* (demographic tax) as well as its implications. One of the key messages is that while this has archetypically been a challenge for developed economies, it has become an increasingly apparent and pressing issue for the developing economies as well. The chapter further discusses the current state of social security policies that can potentially mitigate the negative effects of the demographic changes.

Chapter 11 (Unequalizing Asia) focuses on the spread and deepening of income disparity across Asia. Asia's growth – the "East Asian Miracle" – has in the past been praised by others because of its equality; however, this no longer seems to hold valid. The chapter specifically takes up the cases of Japan, China, and a few ASEAN countries. This is an emerging but an urgent issue for many, which in some countries has even become highly political. The challenge for most of the emerging, middle-income countries is that the governments must address this even without proper and functioning social security policies in place.

Chapter 12 (Environmentally challenged Asia) provides an account and analysis of the ongoing environmental challenges in the region. Environmental issues are typically complex and diverse. The chapter first provides a framework to understand the different challenges regarding the environment, with concrete examples. These challenges have primarily risen because of the rapid economic development in the region. Environmental problems entail a wide range of issues, and they typically stem from different sources, affecting countries at every level of development. While no "one-size-fits-all" solution is available, addressing these problems is crucial for a sustainable future.

The concluding chapter of this book is titled Competing Asia, co-existing Asia. While economic integration is proceeding faster and deeper than anywhere else in the developing world, it also entails significant uncertainties, which is inevitable for a region with extensive cultural and political diversity. The challenges that this book has addressed are trans-boundary and common to all. How should we face them and prepare ourselves for a future that is sustainable and prosperous? This chapter proposes two pillars in relation to this – competition and coexisting. The time that one country or one company could win it all is over. Each of us should identify and play to our unique strengths and collaborate for coexistence.

The book was written initially for people who want to study the economy of Asia in universities at both undergraduate and graduate levels. However, all of the chapters have attempted to push the limits beyond the contents of traditional textbooks, in the sense that they do not stop at explaining conventional knowledge and what we know from history, but incorporate the latest dynamics that are continuously transforming the economy and society of Asia. These issues may not necessarily have been highlighted in similarly titled books. However, as these are the key dimensions of the 21st century, there is simply no way to omit these dimensions. As such, this book should be useful for a much wider readership including people in businesses and governments, other branches of research and academia, and in fact for whoever is interested in understanding the exciting frontier of the Asian economy at this pivotal time.

PART I
New dimensions of the Asian economy

1 Transforming Asia: how the Asian economy has been discussed

Asei Ito, Tamaki Endo, Keiichiro Oizumi, and Kenta Goto

Pudong New Area, Shanghai, China (left: 1995, right: 2016).
Source: Imaginechine.

LEARNING GOALS

- Understand the key literature on the Asian economy.
- Understand the post-war Asian economy from a historical perspective.
- Understand the evolving discussions on the Asian economy, and its current implications.

INTRODUCTION

Since the end of the Second World War, Asia has transformed itself dramatically from a region of widespread poverty and stagnation to one at the center of growth in the world economy. In the 1950s, per capita incomes in Asian economies were low, and the two main challenges were to overcome the causes of economic stagnation and to eliminate poverty. The wave of globalization and economic growth, however, soon reached the Newly Industrializing Economies (NIEs), including South Korea and Taiwan. This further spread to countries in Southeast Asia, and then eventually to China and also to Vietnam. Despite the Asian Financial Crisis of 1997 and the impact of the Global

Financial Crisis of 2008, Asia can be best characterized by the term "emerging," rather than "stagnant." Furthermore, with most of the countries in the region having achieved middle-income status, one of its challenges is now to seek avenues to realize inclusive and sustainable growth. This chapter will provide an overview of the post-war economic development trajectory of Asia, a period ranging from the 1950s to today. It will also look at how the relevant academic perspectives on the Asian economy have changed during this period.

1.1 FROM STAGNATION TO DEVELOPMENT

1.1.1 The post-war reconstruction of Japan and Asia

Right after the Second World War, the Japanese economy, which had been considered one of the most developed economies in Asia, was still agrarian. In 1950, five years after the end of the Second World War, 48% of employed Japanese workers were engaged in primary industries such as agriculture, forestry, and fishery (Yoshikawa, 2012). Only half the number of boys entered high school, while the ratio for girls who entered high school was as low as just one-third. The average per capita income was $124, one fourteenth of that in the United States (US). Because of the mounting problems due to wartime destruction, Japan had to focus first on stabilizing and reconstructing its domestic economy. As such, it took a while before Japan regained its position in the wider global economy, including expanding into and re-establishing, business relationships with other Asian economies.

This changed in 1950 when the "special demand" spurred by the Korean War triggered Japan's subsequent rapid economic growth. This induced investments in key sectors such as the material industries, and massive labor migration from rural to urban areas led to significant improvements in productivity. This accompanied increased demand for durable consumer goods, which placed the Japanese economy back on a growth trajectory.

Japan's efforts of post-war reconstruction started to bear fruit in the 1950s. When the Bandung Conference was held in Indonesia in 1955, Japan began to rebuild diplomatic relations with other Asian countries. In the 1960s, Japan was experiencing a construction boom in the preparation for the Tokyo Olympic Games in 1964, while already becoming an advanced economy.

For many other countries in Asia, the biggest challenge in the war's aftermath from 1945 to the 1950s was in relation to achieving political independence and national stability. A power struggle between the US, as the representative of the Western liberal camp, and the Soviet Union, which represented the Eastern socialist camp, emerged, and Asia became embedded into the so-called Cold War. As these Asian countries gradually achieved political independence from their former colonial regimes in the 1960s, the main goals for these Asian countries, in particular for those belonging to the Western camp, shifted from political independence towards economic development (Perkins, 2013; Miyagi, 2014).

As a result, two conditions underlying the regional economic and political structure emerged in the 1960s: Japan's ascendance and its return to Asian diplomacy on the one hand, and the increasing emphasis on the pursuit of economic development among Asian countries on the other. At that time, Japan viewed the rest of Asia as a region characterized by low levels of development and widespread poverty, and its involvement was primarily from a development assistance angle. Hara, one of the major Japanese scholars on Asian economics at the time, published a book on the same topic as this one, *Contemporary Asian Economy*, in 1967, which first sentence reads, "Asia, needless to say, is classified as a low-development area, economically and socially" (Hara, 1967). Moreover, the per capita GDP in East Asian countries remained remarkably low even in 1970. Although Japan's per capita GDP had reached $2,040 (40% of that in the US for the same year), Singapore's was $925 (18%), while South Korea's was only $286 (5.6%).

During the Cold War, the US also wanted Japan to become more deeply involved in the political and economic relationships of Asia. Walt Rostow, famous for his "economic takeoff" theory, stated that Asia could modernize its rural-based economies through international trade and industrialization. In this context, he wrote that "Japan has a major mission to perform; and we in the US are prepared to work side by side with you, assisting with resources, technical assistance, good will, and faith that a new, free and modern Asia shall emerge" (Japan Council for International Understanding, 1965). After Japan's accession to the Organization for Economic Co-operation and Development (OECD) in 1964, Japan's commitment to Asian economic development, was manifested clearly by its involvement in the establishment of the Asian Development Bank in 1966 (Okita, 1966).

1.1.2 Underdevelopment and stagnation in Asia

In the post-war years, the overwhelming economic disparity between developed and developing countries was a key global issue, the so-called North–South problem. As such, one of the crucial issues was understanding why Asia has been so poor. Development economists at the time looked at the factors of stagnation and poverty in Asia from a structuralist point of view, which emphasized the unbalanced structure of the economic relationships between developed and developing countries (Esho, 1997).

In connection with this, Raul Prebisch's "dependency theory" claimed that modernization of low-development areas in the world economy would proceed in a form dependent upon developed countries. The main reason for this was the deterioration of such areas' terms of trade. The terms of trade refer to the number of units of imports that could be exchanged for one unit of export. Developing countries typically exported resources and primary products. As the prices of those export items tend to increase less rapidly than manufacturing products, dependency theorists argued that the terms of trade tended to deteriorate for developing countries in the long run. Due to their history of colonization, the economies of Asian countries had been tailored to produce specific primary products by the old colonial powers, leading towards a monoculture. Under such initial conditions, an export pessimism perspective emerged. Curbing dependency on primary products became the objective of development policy, which led to widespread advocation of import-substitution industrialization strategies. This strategy aimed at substituting imported industrial products with domestic production, and the policy tools included higher tariffs and quantitative restrictions on imported goods.

Another issue was the relationship between population growth and the savings (investment) rate. Consider an economy with a high population growth rate and a relatively low savings/investment rate. If population growth rate outpaces per capita income growth, a "low-income equilibrium trap" can emerge (Hayami, 1997, Chapter 5). Additionally, in developing countries of Asia, there was "excess" population in rural areas. The "excess" refers to farmers who have zero marginal productivity of labor, which suggests that the agricultural sector can maintain its output even if the number of workers is reduced. Clifford Geertz, who examined rural villages in Indonesia, identified a phenomenon what he called "shared poverty." This is a situation where people in villages with excess workers tend to divide the total output among its members equally under high population growth, which leads to culminate in impoverishing everyone equally (Geertz, 1963). Gunnar Myrdal's book entitled *Asian Drama: An Inquiry into the Poverty of Nations* also discusses the lack of a productivity-improving mechanism in the agricultural sector due to the landowner system, as well as Asia's social norms (Myrdal, 1968). These discussions focused on the high population growth rate in rural areas and the resulting outcomes of low and stagnating per capita income.

1.1.3 The emergence of a "growing Asia"

The Asian economy has attracted global attention as a result of its rapid economic growth since the 1970s. In the 1970s, industrialization of developing countries started in Asia and Latin America, with these countries becoming known collectively as Newly Industrializing Countries (NICs). The OECD report *The Impacts of the Newly Industrializing Countries on Production and Trade in Manufactures* pointed to the fact that the rapid industrialization of Asian NICs was due to an "outward-looking growth policy" focusing on exporting labor-intensive products through active participation in the international division of labor (Secretary-General of the OECD, 1979).

Of the NICs, South Korea, Taiwan, Hong Kong, and Singapore continued their growth even after the Oil Crisis in 1973 and 1979. These economies came to be called the "Asian Newly Industrializing Economies (Asian NIEs)" reflecting upon the issues related to sovereignty of Hong Kong and Taiwan. These four economies were also often referred to as the "Asian Four Tigers" (Vogel, 1993). The rise of these four tigers was important because it provided evidence that it was possible for a developing country to achieve remarkable economic growth through industrialization. Unlike the protectionist import-substitution industrialization strategy proposed by the structuralists, the view which advocated achieving economic growth by participating in the international division of labor was quite innovative at that time.

Discussions continued until the 1990s over the factors that allowed the Asian NIEs to achieve industrialization, with South Korea and Taiwan as the typical cases. Three major points were discussed in this: the advantages of backwardness (or late-starting); social capabilities for industrialization; and the relationship between the market and the state (Watanabe, 1979).

The advantage of backwardness was proposed by the economic historian Alexander Gerschenkron (Gerschenkron, 1962). The less a country's industrial structure is developed at the beginning of industrialization, the more rapidly will industrialization occur in that country as a result of the introduction of technologies from developed countries. However, not every developing country can take advantages of its backwardness. Proper conditions, such as the capabilities of private corporate managers, the availability of engineers who can support the induction of advanced technology at the factory level, and the administrative capacity of governments to alter existing protectionist policies play key roles. These factors are referred to as the social capability of industrialization (Watanabe, 1979). Development in Asian NIEs was based on a well-functioning market mechanism, which was strengthened by connecting to the global economy through the international division of labor. However, governments had an essential role in reforming existing protectionist policies and in selective intervention to the market. In this sense, managing the tension inherent between the market mechanism and the role of the state was essential in realizing a "growing Asia."

The growth of the Asian NIEs has gradually changed the framework that had been underlying in the existing studies. Low productivity and excessive population problems in agriculture, which had been regarded as a problem in the 1960s, were suddenly recognized as part of their sources of comparative advantages, as they came to be recognized by foreign companies as "cheap labor." This was further amplified as industrialization took place and these countries became more open. However, a dependency view still remained. Helleiner, for example, pointed out that export products from developing to developed countries, as also in the case of South Korea and Taiwan during their earlier development, tend to be exports from local subsidiaries of multi-national enterprises (MNEs) from developed countries (Helleiner, 1981). The question of how to increase the domestic value-added content of exports from developing countries became an important issue. This debate emerged along with Asia's progression in export-oriented industrialization, which has become one of the key topics within the context of Global Value Chains (GVCs).

The issues mentioned above have significant relevance today. First, starting from the post-war "stagnating Asia," economists have observed a region-wide shift towards a "growing Asia." This has contributed to the recognition of potentially new growth patterns, which earlier theories could not explain. The term "emerging economies" has become the norm to characterize many countries in Asia, and terms such as "developing economies" and "the South" are much less used to denote the region. The experience of Asian NIEs captured early signs of a fundamental structural change in the world economy, including the significant rise of developing countries, which were in the past collectively referred to as "the rest."

Second, the export-oriented industrialization and outward economic growth strategies adopted by Asian NIEs have demonstrated new pathways to success in the world economy. As previously mentioned, the early post-war export pessimism theory had proposed a closed economy with restrictive trade policies. Therefore, the new type of growth observed in Asian NIEs through their participation in the international division of labor also had significant impact and was the cornerstone on which extensive regional economic integration would evolve.

1.2 FROM THE "EAST ASIAN MIRACLE" TO THE ASIAN FINANCIAL CRISIS

1.2.1 The success story of East Asia

The accumulation of country-based research on the phenomenal growth in economies including Japan, South Korea, and Taiwan has been impressive. With this, however, there has been increased interest in looking at growth issues from a more regional perspective, with emphasis on cross-country dynamics. The focus has thus become increasingly on "Asia as a region of growth," as opposed to separate and independent analyses of individual economies (see Chapter 2). In addition, as China became increasingly integrated into the regional and global economy in the 1990s, the significance of Asia's outward oriented growth pattern increased. Such strategies were fully compatible with globalization, which also unfolded rapidly in this decade (see Chapter 3).

Three major viewpoints are generally used to analyze industrialization patterns in Asian NIEs: a nationalist approach focusing on the role of the state and government; a neoclassical approach focusing on the role of market mechanisms; and an institutional/organizational approach focusing the role of policymakers, bureaucracy, and corporate management.

The nationalist approach focused on the fact that at the time of these countries' economic takeoff, their political systems tended to feature authoritarian regimes or dictatorships as a major part of the post-war independence movement. South Korea's Park Chung-hee, who became President via a military coup, is a case in point. Other examples include Taiwan's Chiang Kai-shek administration and Thailand's Sarit Thanarat administration, both of which seized power without elections. Such phenomena have been called developmentalism, in which economic development was set as the highest priority. Political dictatorship was justified as the most efficient system that could accelerate the process of industrialization. Related literature also focused on the role of bureaucrats in specific policy planning divisions, such as the Economic Planning Institute of South Korea, and argued for the positive role of a state-led economic intervention for rapid economic growth (Amsden, 1989; Chang, 2006).

The neoclassical approach, taken by scholars such as Bela Balassa, on the other hand, emphasized the role of the market mechanism. Among the most influential is the well-known World Bank report, *The East Asian Miracle* (World Bank, 1993). This report focused on eight economies in East Asia that had achieved rapid economic growth while successfully reducing domestic income disparities, a remarkable achievement in comparison with Latin America. The report characterized a series of policy packages in successful Asian economies as "a market-friendly approach" that included investments in human capital through primary education, establishment of a system to promote competition among private enterprises, openness of the economy, stable macroeconomic management, and high savings and investment rates. This approach was fundamentally different from the first approach because of its emphasis on both the roles of the market and the government.

The third – institutional/organizational – approach focuses on collective capability formation at different levels such as the firm or production system, and also included different organizations such as the firm, state, economic associations, and even non-government organizations (Aoki, 1997). In line with this, Akira Suehiro focused on industrialization patterns that embedded capability building of engineering skills in the manufacturing sector. This has been referred to as "catch-up industrialization," in which Asia took advantage of its backwardness to expedite technological upgrading (Suehiro, 2000, 2008). In addition to the roles of the government and market, this approach extended the research scope to cover private firms, including large industrial conglomerates such as the *chaebols* in South Korea.

Industrialization and economic growth in Asia were not independent events that just occurred at the individual country level. Systemic dynamics also were at play that had spillover effects for neighboring countries within the region. Based on the international division of labor, developed countries had come to specialize in more sophisticated capital-intensive industries while latecomer countries specialized in labor-intensive industries, where the final products were exported to the US and Europe. The Flying Geese Model attempted to capture this phenomenon that unfolded within the region, by looking at direct investment linkages from advanced to late-coming economies. The initial model was a one-country model that described the process of structural transformation of a specific industry, where it initially started by domestic production through import substitution policies, which would eventually be transformed into an export-oriented industry. The interpretation of this model has been extended to explain cross-country sectoral transformation spillovers, as increases in wages levels and significant capital accumulation in more advanced economies actually led to such regional dynamics (Kojima, 2003; also see Chapter 2 of this book).

1.2.2 The Asian Financial Crisis and the neoclassical era

Although each of the three approaches had discussed the factors underlying the success of export-oriented industrialization in Asia, the Asian Financial Crisis that occurred as a result of the crash of the Thai Baht in July 1997 inevitably prompted reconsiderations of the Asian economy. At the beginning of the Asian Financial Crisis, the collapse of exchange rates of Asian countries including the Thai Baht and the Indonesian Rupiah caused defaults of dollar-denominated external debt, which further spread to other economies in the region. In 1998, Thailand's economic growth rate was −10%, while Indonesia's was −13.7%, clearly indicating the occurrence of an economic crisis. In the short term, there were signs of financial panic, which has been observed historically quite frequently. However, this was in fact a structural issue, triggered by a capital account crisis based on international capital movements, rather than the traditional problems related to current account balances based on import and export of goods and services. The focus of analysis of the Asian economy quickly shifted from an attempt to understand its "miraculous" performance, into a search for the shortcomings in the Asian economy that had caused this region-wide financial crisis (World Bank, 1998; Stiglitz and Yusuf, 2001; Yoshitomi, 2003).

Three factors have been discussed as causes of the Asian Financial Crisis: financial factors, real economy factors, and institutional factors. The financial factors were related to the mismatch between domestic and international capital movements. This was linked to a structure in which domestic financial systems were dependent on long-term bank borrowing, whereas international lending tended to be short-term. The result was that domestic funds quickly became exhausted when international lending was suddenly withdrawn, which led to extensive defaults. The real-economy factors emphasized structural problems inherent in the export-oriented industrialization strategy. The industrialization approach adopted by the Asian countries was alleged to contain "import-inducing export structures," because of the high import intensity of key components to be used for their industrial products, which led to a trade deficit. In addition, improvements in productivity have also been very limited. The institutional factors were primarily concerned with the weak and the inefficient corporate governance systems particularly of the local enterprises, which were not conforming to global standards (Yoshitomi, 2003; Suehiro, 2008).

The Asian Financial Crisis caused a major shift in the analytical perspectives on the Asian economy. As the financial sector became a new focus for analysis, the Asian economy was now discussed from the international capital flows and financial globalization perspectives. When Asia and other developing countries were first discussed in relation to the international economy in the 1960s, the focus was on issues pertinent to the terms of trade. This was replaced by a need to understand the Asian economy within the context of a globalizing financial market, in which Asia had to be positioned vis-à-vis the others.

In addition, Asia's input-induced growth structure, as well as the limited improvements in productivity, were also seen as major problems, as strongly advocated by Paul Krugman (1994). The crisis frontloaded the importance of the financial sector in achieving sustained growth. It also made clear that it was important to evaluate the Asian economy within a generalized framework that is independent from region-specific attributes.

Both the "miracle" and "crisis" of the Asian economy during the 1990s attracted worldwide attention, resulting in an increase of studies with a broader perspective. One of such perspectives sought to understand the emerging benefits and risks of globalization. The Asian NIEs' export-oriented growth was realized by their active participation in the rapidly evolving international division of labor; however, this also exposed them to the risks stemming from international capital movement (see Chapter 5). The Chiang Mai Initiative, a regional financial cooperation framework, was agreed at the Association of Southeast Asian Nation (ASEAN)+3 (Japan, China, and South Korea) meeting in May 2000. The purpose was to control and mitigate financial risks posed by cross-border financial flows through joint efforts by guaranteeing short-term supply of foreign currencies among the members to avoid disruptions in external payments. This effort became the basis of the subsequent economic cooperation of ASEAN+1 or ASEAN+3 (Hirakawa, 2016). The financial crisis caused a great deal of damage, but at the same time, it also led to intensified regional cooperation.

1.3 THE RISE OF CHINA, AND TOWARDS AN "EMERGING ASIA"

1.3.1 China, production networks, and regional economic integration

Despite the severity of the economic crisis, growth trends in Asia showed no major slowdown in the 21st century. Capital account transactions stabilized, and exports quickly recovered largely due to the increasing FDI inflow to the region (see Chapter 5). More fundamentally, stable labor and capital supply as well as genuine increases in productivity supported continued economic growth. The countries in Asia recovered from the financial crisis, and they have also entered into a new era of fundamental structural change.

The first fundamental change that has occurred is the impact of the rise of China in the Asian and the world economy. China joined the World Trade Organization in 2001 after negotiations that lasted over ten years, and as a result, foreign investment rapidly increased in China, particularly in its coastal areas. As will be discussed in Chapter 3, investment in China during this period concentrated in the Pearl River Delta and Yangtze River Delta regions, which soon formulated major clusters of manufacturing industries, which also came to be known as "the world's factory" (Kuroda, 2001; Gao, 2012). Further opening up of the Chinese economy and full-scale participation in the international division of labor was viewed with caution by ASEAN countries, some of whom were still in the process of recovery from the financial crisis (Kimura et al., 2002). According to a questionnaire survey of Japanese companies carried out by the Japan Bank for International Cooperation (JBIC), China had consistently been regarded as the most promising country since the 1990s from a medium-term perspective (about three years); in the first half of the 2000s, more than 80% of respondent companies chose China as the most promising location to invest (JBIC, various years). Meanwhile, a sense of caution against China emerged among ASEAN countries, although the possibilities of export expansion to China were also discussed. Both the "China threat" view and the "China opportunity" view were observed during this period.

The second important change was the rise of intra-Asian trade that now included China, which was a result of a robust evolution and expansion of Asian production networks. Cross-border manufacturing through fragmentation dynamics has progressed extensively (Ando and Kimura, 2005). This accompanied a transformation in international trade structures from the being based on "inter-industry" trade to one based on "intra-industry" trade. The former sort was the one that underlies the Flying Geese Model, while the latter is typical where international production networks have progressed. The Asian production network is discussed in detail in Chapters 2 and 4.

This new division of labor was promoted by lower trade barriers and communication costs, as well as lower logistics costs. Trade in parts and components, particularly for machinery and electronics among Asian countries, has increased as a result. This new trade pattern necessarily required the improvement of trade rules, which led to the pursuit of trade agreements that embedded rules to promote deeper regional integration. Economic integration in Asia has so far been "*de-facto*" based, led by strategic investments and trade by MNEs (Urata, 2001). However, the need to support such *de-facto*-based integration by establishing complementary rules and institutions – a "*de-jure*" based integration mechanism – has increased in Asia, particularly through free trade agreements (FTAs) (Kawai, 2005; Urata, 2006; Urata and Kurita, 2012).

The expansion of production networks and further regional integration also implies that each of the countries has become more exposed to risks originating from other locations, which will be transferred through these networks. The severe flooding in Thailand as well as the Great East Japan Earthquake in 2011 disrupted supply chains, and the global financial crisis in 2008 highlighted new sources of demand side vulnerabilities.

In a globalized economy, negative shocks from a crisis in a remote place can easily be transmitted to Asia through production and financial networks.

1.3.2 Risks and opportunities in middle-income Asia

Most of the region's economies have now reached middle-income status, which inevitably has resulted in the end of their low-cost advantage. This is the other key structural change that is happening in Asia, where innovation has become important than ever.

The region is also prone to other types of new challenges (Gill and Kharas, 2007; Kohli et al., 2012; Suehiro, 2014). Among these new challenges, the demographic changes in the region are one of the major ones. The peaking of the working population and the accompanying ageing society in many countries give rise to the need for more comprehensive and more inclusive social security systems (see Chapter 10).

The middle-income trap is an emerging concern for many in Asia as well. Data suggest that while a significant number of developing countries have lifted themselves out of poverty and achieved respectable economic development over the past 50 years, only a limited number of those have managed to further develop from middle-income to high-income status. Innovation-centered growth, which requires improvements in higher education systems and stronger capabilities in R&D activities, has been central in many countries' policy agenda since the 2000s to avoid falling into this trap (Yusuf et al., 2003). In addition, the spread of mobile networks in Asia and the newly evolving digital economy has resulted in an acute need to devise and implement new industrial policies that are compatible with this, and different initiatives are being sought (see Chapter 7).

Sustained growth in Asia has led to the birth of a vibrant middle class, which further has led to the emergence of a mass-consumption society particularly in the metropolitan areas, some of which have further grown into massive mega-regions. While Asia's export competitiveness based on inexpensive labor is, to some extent, gone, the expansion of the domestic market though is offering new prospects for growth. This, and the development of the service sector, is shifting the sources of its growth dynamics from "factory Asia" to "market Asia."

Along with the maturation of Asian economies, the region must also incorporate new dimensions of development, such as sustainability both in economic and environmental dimensions. Mitigating income gaps, providing inclusive social security to all, including the informal economy, have become crucial. At the global level, the "Sustainable Development Goals (SDGs)" were unanimously adopted by the United Nations General Assembly in 2015, following on from the earlier "Millennium Development Goals (MDGs)." While Asia has made significant progress in many of the goals set in the MDGs and SDGs, some of the global challenges set out in these have also evolved in Asia ahead of other regions.

Leading economies' positions have changed greatly over the past decades. During the industrialization stage of the Asian NIEs, Japan played key roles in the region as an investor and a leader in advanced technology. Today, however, Japan is leading the region with newly emerging social challenges, such as an ageing society and a degrading natural environment. South Korea, and Taiwan are not far behind. As these challenges span national boundaries, a collective approach and a new relationship embedding "growing with Asia" as a key principle is needed (Suehiro, 2014).

CONCLUSION

The Asian economy has crossed several major turning points, which have required new analytical frameworks and academic perspectives. The structural changes that have taken place during the region's transformation phases of poverty and stagnation, rapid growth, and further into crisis, have been very rapid, and, as it were, "compressed." However, while some of the key terms representing each of the different eras have changed drastically due to these structural transformations, several perspectives have survived.

First, theories and discussions that have attempted to analyze and understand the characteristics of the Asian economy and its problems have in most cases positioned Asia within a wider global context. These include dependency theory, discussions on the Asian NIEs, and those related to the Asian Financial Crisis. Dependency theory presented a framework in which the contrasts between developed countries and developing countries were emphasized, with discussions on Asian NIEs which positioned Asia as underdeveloped. Subsequently, the latecomer's advantages in relation to more advanced countries were used to explain their high growth performance. Also, the Asian Financial Crisis highlighted the risks of Asian countries being incorporated into global financial systems.

Second, economic relations and interdependencies within Asia have remained a key issue as well, as discussed in the flying geese models and more recently in relation to regional economic integration. The third point is related to the role of the state. Markets play crucial roles in every economy in Asia. However, the roles of governments in economic development have and will remain central because of the rigidities in the political systems in Singapore and China and the re-emergence of authoritarian regimes due to the military coup in Thailand. The issue of government intervention in the economy will continue to be important in Asia.

Despite these significant structural transformations, the dynamics in the Asian economy during each of the different periods were shaped by the influences of both past structures and present conditions. In the 1960s, low agricultural productivity and excessive population size were regarded as "problems," but since the 1970s, the export-oriented industrialization strategy harnessed these traits to fuel rapid industrialization. On the other hand, while the export-oriented industrialization of Asian NIEs brought about rapid economic growth, the import-inducing export structure and integration into the international financial system also increased risks, which led to the Asian Financial Crisis in 1997. Furthermore, as globalization proceeded within the region, China became also integrated into the international division of labor, which led to drastic expansion of the regional production networks enforcing *de-facto* economic integration. Trade and investment across borders have increased accordingly, which in turn has induced the need for *de-jure*-based integration. China's economic rise and its capability for innovation have resulted in a serious trade dispute with the US in 2018 and onwards.

The future of the Asian economy evolves from its past and from the present. Therefore, we need to look back into the history, and at the same time take stock of the evolving events and structures of our time. The following chapters of this book will discuss more specific issues pertinent to the contemporary Asian economy and attempts to elucidate the underlying mechanisms with reference to our past. By undertaking such a task, this book will offer readers a new perspective on the Asian economies for the coming era.

BOX 1 Reviewing the Asian economy from a historical perspective

Takeshi Nishimura

Previously, within the research field of economic history, Asia was perceived as a backward continent in comparison to Europe. Asia's economic structure had been crippled as it was colonized and exploited by the European nations. Although the continent became decolonized and many Asian countries gained independence after the Second World War, it continued to be considered economically backward from a Western perspective. This viewpoint is a historical paradigm fostered in the period when modern historical study itself, which was predominant until recently, was developing in Europe. In recent historical study such perspectives have not been favored.

A series of studies on global history, which began in the London School of Economics and Political Sciences in the 1990s, criticized such Euro-centric historical views and proposed a new perspective instead. Employing the framework of long-term comparative history, emphasis has shifted to the history of the non-European world, particularly East Asia.

In his book *The Great Divergence: China, Europe, and the Making of the Modern World Economy* (2000), Kenneth Pomeranz recognizes that Europe was more developed than the rest of the world in the mid-19th century; however, prior to the 19th century, there was no mention of Europe's economic superiority (Pomeranz, 2000). According to Angus Maddison's estimates, China accounted for 32.9% of the world's GDP in 1820, India 16.0%, and the United Kingdom only 5.2%, supporting Pomeranz's argument (Maddison, 2001).

Pomeranz compared the Lower Yangtze Delta in China with England using various indicators pointing out that the per capita income and the standard of living of these two areas were approximately the same prior to the beginning of the 19th century. After the mid-19th century, Europe dramatically improved its productivity because of (a) the easy access it gained to high-quality coal and (b) the development of the North Atlantic trade with the US and Canada. Pomeranz's claims instigated an intense debate, with some saying that he ignored the unique role and identity of European institutions, which held distinct concepts of private ownership and the legal system of the state.

Sugihara (1996) examined the industrialization of Japan and India in the late 19th century when the "Western Impact," including European influence, first touched Asia economically. According to his estimation, intra-Asian trade grew by developing international divisions of labor within the region, with a higher growth rate than the world's growth rate at that time. In other words, he argued that Asia was certainly not stagnant on the trade front. Sugihara pointed out the importance of constructing a new historical perspective to view modern times by focusing on the relative independence of Asian economies.

Sugihara also explored the historical background of the "East Asian Miracle" after the Second World War. He argues that the industrialization achieved in Europe and the US during the "Industrial Revolution" and the post-war East Asian industrialization were qualitatively different. In the case of East Asia, the labor force was abundant compared to capital and land, and it was used efficiently to form economic society. The industrialization that emerged in Japan and India expanded to the Korean peninsula, Taiwan, and the Chinese mainland in the period between the two world wars. Sugihara depicts such Asian patterns as labor-intensive industrialization (Sugihara, 2007; Austin and Sugihara, 2013). After the Second World War, capital-intensive industrialization in Europe and America emerged, along with labor-intensive industrialization in the Asia–Pacific region. Subsequently, strikingly fast developments occurred under the US-led free trade, with the US dollar as the key currency.

Thus, global history studies have been evolving in a variety of different ways in recent years. A research group led by Sugihara at Kyoto University focuses on how "Human Society" has been developed based on the humanosphere in relation to the geosphere and the biosphere. The team, which pursues studies over a longer time horizon, has highlighted new issues regarding the relationship between securing a sustainable humanosphere and developing an economic society. There is hardly any doubt that this research will place a stronger emphasis on Asia as compared to previous studies. With such new research themes, Asia is the primary field of examination, and the concept, scope, and meaning of "Asia" are being rewritten within a new historical framework.

REFERENCES

Amsden, Alice [1989] *Asia's Next Giant: South Korea and Late Industrialization*. New York: Oxford University Press.

Ando, Mitsuyo, and Fukunari Kimura [2005] "The Formation of International Production and Distribution Networks in East Asia," in Takatoshi Ito and Andrew Rose ed., International Trade in East Asia, NBER-East Asia Seminar on Economics, pp. 177–216. Chicago: University of Chicago Press.

Aoki, Masahiko ed. [1997]. *The Role of Government in East Asian Economic Development: Comparative Institutional Analysis*. New York: Oxford University Press.

Austin, Gareth, and Kaoru Sugihara eds. [2013] *Labour-Intensive Industrialization in Global History*. London and New York: Routledge.

Chang, Ha-Joon [2006] *The East Asian Development Experience: The Miracle, the Crisis, and the Future*. New York: Zed Books.

Esho, Hideki [1997] *Kaijatsu no Seiji Keizaigaku* [*The Political Economy of Development*]. Tokyo: Nihon Hyoron Sya.

Gao, Yuning [2012] *China as the Workshop of the World: An Analysis at the National and Industrial Level of China in the International Division of Labor*. Oxon: Routledge.

Geertz, Clifford [1963] *Agricultural Involution: The Process of Ecological Change in Indonesia*. Berkeley: University of California Press.

Gerschenkron, Alexander [1962] *Economic Backwardness in Historical Perspective.* Cambridge: Harvard University Press.

Gill, Indermit and Homi Kharas [2007] *An East Asian Renaissance: Ideas for Economic Growth.* Washington: The World Bank.

Hara, Kakuten [1967] *Gendai Ajia Keizairon* [*Contemporay Asian Economy*]. Tokyo: Keiso Shobo.

Hayami, Yujiro [1997] *Development Economics: From the Poverty to the Wealth of Nations.* Oxford; New York: Clarendon Press.

Helleiner, Gerald [1981] *Intra-firm Trade and the Developing Countries.* London: Macmillan.

Hirakawa, Hitoshi et al. (eds.) [2016] *Shin Ajia Keizairon* [*New Asian Economics*]. Tokyo: Bunshindo.

Ito, Takatoshi, and Andrew Rose (eds.) [2005] *International Trade in East Asia.* Chicago: The University of Chicago Press.

Japan Bank for International Cooperation (JBIC). [various years] *Report on Overseas Business Operations by Japanese Manufacturing Companies.* Tokyo: JBIC.

Japan Council for International Understanding (ed.) [1965] *A Design for Asian Development by Walt W. Rostow.* Tokyo: Hara Shobo. [Both in English and Japanese.]

Kawai, Masahiro [2005] "East Asian Economic Regionalism: Progress and Challenges," *Journal of Asian Economics*, 16(1): pp. 29–55.

Kimura, Fukunari, Toyojiro Maruya, and Koichi Ishikawa (eds.) [2002] *Higashi Ajia Kokusai Bungyo to Cyugoku* [*International Division of Labor in East Asian and China*]. Tokyo: JETRO.

Kohli, Harinder et al. (eds). [2012] *Asia 2050: Realizing the Asian Century*, Manila: Asian Development Bank.

Kojima, Kiyoshi [2003] *Genkyo gata Keizai Hattenron: Dai Ikkan Nihon Keizai, Ajia Keizai, Sekai Keizai* [*Flying Geese Pattern Economic Development: Volume 1 Japanese Economy, Asian Economy, and the World Economy*]. Tokyo: Bunshindo.

Krugman, Paul [1994] "The Myth of Asia's Miracle," *Foreign Affairs*, 73(6): pp. 62–78.

Kuroda, Atsuro [2001] *Meido in Chaina* [*Made in China*]. Tokyo: Tokyo Keizai Shinposha.

Maddison, Angus [2001] *The World Economy: A Millennial Perspective.* Paris: OECD.

Miyagi, Taizo (ed.) [2014] *Sengo Ajia no Keisei to Nihon* [*Formation of the Post-war Asia and Japan*]. Tokyo: Chuo Koron Shinsya.

Myrdal, Gunnar [1968] *Asian Drama: An Inquiry into the Poverty of Nations.* New York: Twentieth Century Fund.

Okita, Saburo [1966] *Ajia no naka no Nihon Keizai* [*Japanese Economy in Asia*]. Tokyo: Daimondosya.

Perkins, Dwight [2013] *East Asian Development: Foundations and Strategies*, Cambridge: Harvard University Press.

Pomeranz, Kenneth. [2000] *The Great Divergence: China, Europe, and the Making of the Modern World Economy.* Princeton: Princeton University Press.

Secretary-General of the OECD [1979] *The Impact of the Newly Industrialising Countries on Production and Trade in Manufactures.* Paris: OECD Secretariat.

Stiglitz, Joseph, and Shahid Yusuf (eds.) [2001] *Rethinking the East Asian Miracle.* New York: Oxford University Press.

Suehiro, Akira [2000] *Kyacchi-appu gata Kougyoukaron: Ajia Keizai no Kiseki to Tenbo* [*Catch-Up Industrialization: The Trajectory and Prospects of East Asian Economies*]. Nagoya: Nagoya University Press.

Suehiro, Akira [2008] *Catch-Up Industrialization: The Trajectory and Prospects of East Asian Economies*. Singapore: National University of Singapore Press.

Suehiro, Akira [2014] *Shinko Asia Keizai Ron* [*Emerging Asian Economies*]. Tokyo: Iwanami Shoten.

Sugihara, Kaoru. [1996] *Ajiakan Boeki no Keisei to Kozo* [*Formation and Structure of Intra-Asia Trade*]. Kyoto: Minerva Shobo.

Sugihara, Kaoru. [2007] "The Second Noel Butlin Lecture: Labour-intensive Industrialisation in Global History." *Australian Economic History Review*, 47(2): pp. 121–154.

Urata, Shujiro [2001] "Emergence of an FDI-Trade Nexus and Economic Growth in East Asia," in Joseph Stiglitz and Shahid Yusuf ed., *Rethinking The East Asian Miracle*, pp. 409–459. Oxford: Oxford University Press.

Urata, Shujiro [2006] "The Changing Patterns of International Trade in East Asia," background paper for Indermit Gill and Homi Kharas eds. *An East Asian Renaissance: Ideas for Economic Growth*. Washington: World Bank.

Urata, Shujiro and Kyosuke Kurita [2012] *Ajia Chiiki Keizai Tougou* [*Introduction to Asian Economic Integration*]. Tokyo: Keisoshobo.

Vogel, Ezra [1993] *The Four Little Dragons: The Spread of Industrialization in East Asia*. Cambridge: Harvard University Press.

Watanabe, Toshio [1979] *Ajia Chushotoku-koku no Chosen: Oiage no jittai to nihon no kadai* [*The Challenges of Asian Middle-Income Countries: The Reality of "Catch-Up" and Issues for Japan*]. Tokyo: Nihon Hyoronsya.

World Bank [1993] *The East Asian Miracle: Economic Growth and Public Policy*. New York: Oxford University Press.

World Bank [1998] *East Asia: The Road to Recovery*. Washington: The International Bank for Reconstruction and Development/The World Bank.

Yoshikawa, Hiroshi [2012] *Koudo Seicyo: Nihon wo kaeta rokusenn nichi* [*The Period of Rapid Growth: Six Thousand Days that Changed Japan*]. Tokyo: Chuo Koron Shinsya.

Yoshitomi, Masaru [2003] *Ajia Keizai no Shinjitsu: Kiseki, kiki, seido no shinka* [*The Truth of Asian Economy: Miracle, Crisis, and Evolution of Institutions*]. Tokyo: Toyo Keizai Shinposya.

Yusuf, Shahid et al. [2003] *Innovative East Asia: The Future of Growth*. Washington: The World Bank and Oxford University Press.

2 Asianizing Asia: the rise of intra-regional trade and economic integration

Kenta Goto and Keiichiro Oizumi

Newly constructed deep-water port (Cai Mep – Thi Vai Port), Vietnam (2010, Photo By Kenta Goto)

LEARNING GOALS

- Understand the linkage between industrialization and trade in Asia.
- Understand the progressing intra-regional trade patterns and international division of labor, and the roles of institutions and multinational enterprises that promoted these.
- Understand that Asia has evolved as the world's factory, within which it has also emerged as a key player in the organization of global production and distribution networks.

INTRODUCTION: WHAT IS "ASIANIZING ASIA"?

The term "Asianizing Asia" was first introduced by Toshio Watanabe, who predicted, in the wake of the aftermath of the Asian Financial Crisis in 1997, that the future of the Asian economy would be characterized by regional economic integration

(Watanabe, 1999). Economic growth in post-war Asia has been strongly dependent on exports to developed countries in Europe, and particularly to the US. "When America sneezes, Japan catches cold" – this was how Japan was characterized in its relationship with the US during Japan's period of rapid economic growth.

As growth in the region continued, Asia started to attract attention from the rest of the world, particularly in the early 1990s. Asian countries' economic performance, starting with the rise of Japan, was heralded as a "miracle." However, this reputation soon came to an end when the Asian Financial Crisis erupted in Thailand in 1997, which then spread throughout the region with serious consequences. The crisis was seen as a result of the vulnerabilities and backwardness inherent in the Asian economy and its society. Structural reforms and productivity improvements were strongly advocated by domestic policy makers as well as by international organizations. The economic structures and governance mechanisms of the West, particularly those of the US, were regarded as the "role model" for Asia's reforms.

It was within such a context that Watanabe argued that a new Asia was emerging. He had acknowledged early symptoms of an emerging Asia, moving from the traditional perception of a region that was dependent on the US and European markets for its exports, which until then had underpinned its members' rapid economic growth. His view was of a new Asia where it was becoming important in itself as well, absorbing a larger and larger share of the industrial products it produced, making it less dependent on Europe and the US. "Asianizing Asia" (Watanabe, 1999) represented such a philosophical yet real change in Asia's position vis-à-vis the world.

When the economic performance of Europe and the US started to decline in the early 21st century, Asia began to show strong signs of recovery through the expansion of intra-regional trade. The sub-prime loan problem of 2008–2009 triggered a serious economic downturn in the US, which eventually evolved into a financial crisis with negative consequences for the wider global economy. This further lead to the so called "EU crisis" in the 2010s, which pushed countries such as Greece to the brink of default. This global economic recession prolonged economic stagnation in most of the developed countries. However, the Asian economy started to regain its growth momentum during this time, except for Japan.

At the heart of "Asianization" lies regional economic integration. Economic integration in Asia has been regarded as "*de-facto*" based, which proceeded ahead of the "*de-jure*" based integration, as typically seen in the European Union (EU). A *de-jure*-based path is where economic integration is promoted through institutional frameworks such as international trade agreements. *De-facto* integration, on the other hand, refers to economic integration that has unfolded even in the absence of an institutional framework, in which the strategic behavior of Multinational Enterprises (MNEs) played key roles. This is an outcome that reflects the economic, political, and cultural diversity of Asia, and is a key perspective in understanding Asian economic integration.

Institution-based integration has proceeded significantly in Asia as well. Asia's liberalization policies have traditionally been multilateral-based, primarily centering around General Agreement on Tariffs and Trade/World Trade Organization (GATT/WTO). However, in the 21st century, a number of Free Trade Agreements (FTAs) have been signed and put into effect in the region. The Association of Southeast Asian Nations (ASEAN) is leading this movement. Since 2010, it has, in principle, abolished all tariffs under the ASEAN Free Trade Area (AFTA), and the ASEAN Economic Community was established in 2015.[1] Japan, South Korea, and China followed suit, and established bilateral and regional FTAs both within and outside Asia. Currently, discussions and negotiations regarding the Regional Comprehensive Economic Partnership (RCEP), covering ASEAN and Japan, China, South Korea, India, Australia, and New Zealand are also underway.

To say that Asian economic integration was "*de-facto*" based means that, compared to the EU where the integration process was led by institutional frameworks, in Asia integration was led initially by the strategic motivations and actions of private corporations, ahead of institutional frameworks. Economic integration in Asia was spearheaded by private initiatives (primarily those of Japanese MNEs) and these initiatives were eventually supported and further facilitated by institutional frameworks that were highly complementary. As such, the notion that Asia's integration was "*de-facto*" based does not mean that such bilateral and regional frameworks have had no effects on Asia's economic integration. The point is that, compared to the North American Free Trade Agreement (NAFTA, currently the USMCA) and the EU, the private sector played more of a leading role and was more important as the driving force of economic integration in Asia. Understanding the importance of MNEs in progressively integrating Asia is essential to the understanding of its challenges and possibilities in the context of "Asianizing Asia" (Goto, 2014).

2.1 BREAKING AWAY FROM ECONOMIC DEPENDENCY

2.1.1 Evolving Asia in global trade

Asia's presence in global trade is on the rise. Table 2.1 summarizes the trends in international trade of Asia during the period 1950–2015 (see Box 2.1 for an introduction to different trade data sources and their key characteristics). Exports from Asia have increased from 5.8 billion dollars in 1950 to 5.4 trillion dollars in 2015. Likewise, its imports have also increased from 5.1 billion dollars to 4.7 trillion dollars during the same period. In terms of global shares, its exports have increased from 9.4% to 32.7%, and its imports from 8.0% to 28.0%. Asia has constantly recorded positive trade balance since the middle of the 1980s, and in 2015 it recorded a surplus of 730 billion dollars.

Intra-regional trade was limited in Asia (except Japan) in the early stages after World War II. Its trade structure was characterized by vertical trade in which it mainly exported primary products including agricultural products and natural resources and imported industrial products. The share of Asian exports, excluding those of Japan, were less than 1% of the global trade in 1965, and industrial goods comprised only 35.2% of the region's total exports.

Japan, on the other hand, constrained by the lack of resources, was dependent on the imports of primary products from other Asian countries, which were used as inputs for manufacturing industries, whose outputs were eventually exported. Japan's economic growth was achieved through such processing trade, thus practically embedding an export-orientated development trajectory from the early stages of development. Japan's industrialization strategy had always been strongly linked with export promotion, as manifested as early as 1949 when export promotion was regarded in the *White Paper on International Economy and Trade* published that year as essentially the only way to

TABLE 2.1 Asia's imports and exports ($ million)

	Export Value	Share (%)	Import Value	Share (%)	Balance value
1950	5,821	9.4	5,141	8.0	680
1960	12,083	9.3	13,160	9.6	▲1,077
1970	32,752	10.3	35,383	10.7	▲2,631
1980	279,435	13.6	293,665	14.0	▲14,230
1990	710,987	20.3	664,264	18.4	46,724
2000	1,686,253	26.1	1,502,640	22.6	183,613
2001	1,525,391	24.6	1,393,169	21.7	132,222
2010	4,544,709	29.7	4,168,291	27.0	376,418
2015	5,393,776	32.7	4,664,200	28.0	729,576

Source: UNCTADstat.

achieve economic growth. Asian NIEs subsequently also followed the same path of industrialization through expansions in exports, which later led to systematic intra-regional industrialization dynamics.

2.1.2 The rise of Asian NIEs

In the early stages of post-war development, however, Japan and the Asian NIEs (except Hong Kong) had pursued active import substitution industrialization (ISI) policies. This included a set of measures to protect their domestic firms through high import tariffs, quantitative restrictions (quotas), and exchange rate policies, essentially making it more difficult for competitive foreign products to penetrate into the domestic market. Restricting imports through such measures, however, would not automatically lead to industrialization and growth, because the expansion of the industries was limited to the size of the domestic market, which tended to be small. This was particularly true for most Asian NIEs, in which it was difficult for firms to gain competitiveness by capturing the benefits from increasing returns to scale.

The other was the lack of competitiveness of local firms. One of the reasons for the success of ISI in some of these economies was the competitive business environment within their own domestic economy, which was a precondition for industrial upgrading. The failure of similar policies in Latin America, on the other hand, probably can be attributed to the lack of such conditions.

In the late 1960s, the Asian NIEs switched their development strategy from import substitution to export orientation. One of the main characteristics of their export orientation strategies was the promotion of foreign direct investment (FDI) through the establishment of export processing zones (EPZs) or industrial parks in which key infrastructure was available. While Asian NIEs started to achieve growth through exports, many countries in Latin America maintained import substitution policies, which eventually led to a debt crisis. The success of industrialization and growth in Asian NIEs has highlighted the importance of an export orientation as a viable growth strategy for developing countries, as discussed in Chapter 1.

Changes in industrial structures in Japan have had significant effects on the economic growth dynamics of Asia. For example, Japan was in a serious trade dispute with the US regarding textile-related products in early 1970s. This had its origins in the late 1950s, when exports of Japanese textile products to the US grew rapidly. As a response, the US introduced a series of import restriction measures against Japanese textile products, and also required the Japanese government to impose so-called voluntary export restraints (VERs). Japan initially responded by incorporating these requests. However, in the late 1960s the US started to demand more comprehensive VERs that not just covered specific textile products (such as cotton products) but included all types of textile products. For the Japanese government, this became difficult to accommodate, and led to a serious bilateral trade dispute between the two countries, which was regarded as the most serious since the end of the war. However, in the early 1970s, Japan had already lost international comparative advantage in textiles. It was in such context that Japanese firms started to relocate some of their labor-intensive production bases to Asian NIEs, particularly to South Korea and Taiwan. This was also a time when these economies were actively implementing foreign investment promotion policies.

Export-oriented growth in Asia started with light industries; during the late 60s and early 1970s about 40% of exports from South Korea and Hong Kong consisted of textile products, primarily garments. There was active relocation in the Japanese labor-intensive garment sector towards Asian NIEs. However, the more capital and technology intensive upstream sectors, including the synthetic fiber sector, still remained in Japan. As such, the export of textile products such as synthetic fabrics from Japan to Asia increased significantly. This would then be processed into garments in Asian NIEs, which would be exported to markets such as the US. A triangular trade structure thus emerged in the region.

As shown in Figure 2.1, 32% of exports from Asian NIEs were oriented towards the US in 1970, which suggests that the structural dependency of Japanese exports on the US had further spread to Asia. The US has played a significant role in the economic growth of Asia by absorbing industrial products manufactured in Japan and the wider region. In addition, because of US commitment and presence with regard to international security in Asia, most economies in Asia, particularly Japan, were able to focus their efforts on economic growth.

2.1.3 The Plaza Accord and the Asian Miracle

Against such export-oriented growth strategies taken by Asian NIEs, policies implemented in ASEAN countries (except Singapore) were more mixed; depending on the industry: some were protected under import substitution-based policies, while others were promoted through export-oriented policies. Economic growth in most of the ASEAN countries, however, was viewed with skepticism until the first half of the 1980s. The majority of exports were still non-industrial products, and while foreign investments were sought for both import substitution and export-oriented sectors, industrialization progressed only slowly because of the lack of necessary infrastructure in their domestic economies.

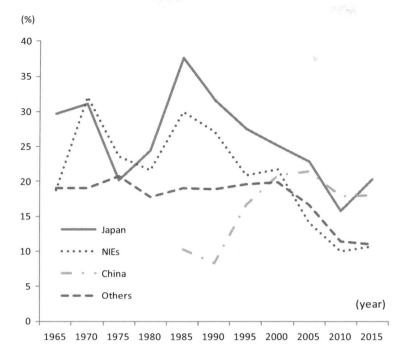

FIGURE 2.1 Export shares to the US.

Source: UN Comtrade.

Note: "Others" include ASEAN countries (except Singapore), North Korea, Mongolia, and Timor Leste.

This all changed with the G5 (US, UK, France, West Germany, and Japan) meeting in 1985 of finance ministers and central bank governors. As this meeting was held at the Plaza Hotel in New York, the agreement that emerged from it has become known as the Plaza Accord. One of the key outcomes of the Accord was the announcement of a common recognition that the value of the US dollar was consistently overvalued, and a willingness to take collective efforts to devalue the dollar. This triggered an acute depreciation of the dollar against the Japanese yen. For example, the dollar–yen exchange rate in 1985 was about 239 yen per dollar, under which the yen appreciated to 145 yen in 1990, and 94 yen in 1995. As a response, Japanese firms relocated and expanded their businesses in ASEAN countries in order to counteract the strong yen, and also to avoid further trade tensions with the US.

According to the Bank of Japan, FDI from Japan's manufacturing sector to ASEAN countries was 52 billion yen in 1985 and increased to 337 billion yen and 557 billion yen in 1990 and 1997, respectively. As firms in Asian NIEs started to face wage increases and appreciating local currencies, they followed suit in relocating some of their sectors into ASEAN as well. This has accelerated industrialization across Asia, altering their trade structures substantially. The shares of industrial products in total regional (ASEAN) exports has increased from 25.3% in 1985 to 49.7% in 1990, and further to 66.7% in 1997 (see Figure 2.2).

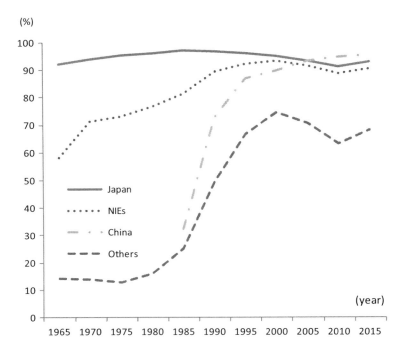

FIGURE 2.2 Share of industrial sector exports.

Source: UN Comtrade.

Note: "Others" include ASEAN countries (except Singapore), North Korea, Mongolia, and Timor Leste.

The ASEAN economy started to take off and move into a growth trajectory based on industrialization from the latter part of the 1980s. Countries that were performing particularly well, including Thailand, Malaysia, and Indonesia also became the subjects of study in the World Bank's "East Asian Miracle" report (World Bank, 1993).

Looking at Asia as a whole, the inclusion of ASEAN into the expanding regional triangular trade structure has further promoted intra-regional division of labor at the industry level. This division of labor was based on the differences in factor and technological endowments within an economy and allowed countries to specialize their exports accordingly. This intra-regional trade structure evolved through dynamic interlinkages of structural transformations among the countries in Asia. This is typically referred to as the flying-geese model of development, and also discussed extensively in relation to catch-up industrialization (Ohno and Sakurai, 1994; Kojima, 2003; Suehiro, 2008).

Figure 2.3 describes this dynamism. First, a labor-intensive industry such as the garment industry (industry A) emerges in a relatively advanced country such as Japan (left end of the horizontal axis) and starts to export its products to the world. Then as the Japanese economy starts to grow and accumulate capital, its wages will gradually increase. Eventually, the international competitiveness of Japan in industry A will decline, and its industrial structure will shift towards industry B, which is more

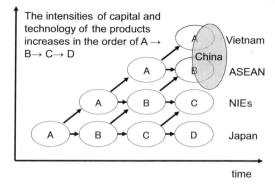

FIGURE 2.3 The flying geese pattern.
Source: Based on Suehiro (2008).

capital-intensive. Industry A will be transferred through, for example, foreign direct investment to lesser developed countries such as those of the Asian NIEs, which have stronger comparative advantages in labor-intensive industries. Japan, which used to be an exporter of industry A, will now become an importer of A. The continuation of this process would further spread into ASEAN countries such as Malaysia and Thailand, and eventually to countries such as China and the late-coming ASEAN countries such as Vietnam. This has led to a dynamic regional economic order with a clear industry-based division of labor.

Within this context, however, Asia's export share towards the US has been declining from 31.1% in 1985 to 22.3% in 2000. On the other hand, intra-regional export increased from 34.9% to 47.5% during the same period (Figure 2.4). This is the "Asianizing Asia" which Watanabe was referring to.

2.2 DE-FACTO ECONOMIC INTEGRATION AND GLOBAL VALUE CHAINS

2.2.1 The financial crisis and China's accession to the WTO

The financial crisis that erupted in Thailand in 1997 spread over the entire area of Asia. The World Bank, once heralding the growth experience of Asia in its *"East Asian Miracle"* changed its assessment towards the region by 180 degrees. For instance, "'efficient and stable financial institutions' became 'vulnerable systems with structural defects'," "selective market intervention by the government were distorting the functioning of markets," and "public administration that were once regarded highly" were downgraded to typical examples of "crony capitalism" which is characterized by collusion between politics, businesses, and government (Suehiro, 2014).

On the other hand, the Chinese economy, which was not affected much by the financial crisis, started to attract attention. Since the introduction of the opening-up

36 New dimensions of the Asian economy

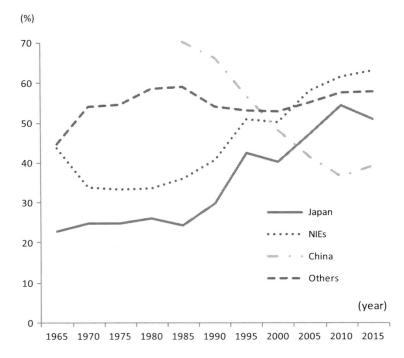

FIGURE 2.4 Share of Asia's exports to Asia.

Source: UN Comtrade.

Note: "Others" include ASEAN countries (except Singapore), North Korea, Mongolia, and Timor Leste.

policy in 1978, China's exports increased more than ten-fold during 1980–2000; from 18 billion dollars to 249 billion dollars. Its world shares of exports also increased from 0.9% to 3.9%. Given this, China's accession to the WTO in 2001 was seen as a major disturbance factor to Asia's flying geese pattern of economic development. This is the so-called "China threat" argument.

China has abundant cheap labor; however, it also has the technological capacity to launch satellites on their own. Concerns were raised too regarding possible Japanese investment diversion to China at the expense of other Asian economies. As a matter of fact, FDI into China grew from about 41 billion dollars in 2000 to 115 billion dollars in 2010. This accompanied a rapid increase of China's exports; from 249 billion dollars in 2000 to 1,578 billion dollars in 2010, and further to 2,275 billion dollars in 2015. These represent a world share of 3.9%, 10.3%, and 13.8%, respectively. China became the largest exporting country in the world from 2009. The investment boom into China has promoted its position as the "world's factory."

This rapid growth of the Chinese economy, however, turned out to be a positive factor for the Asian economy, rather than a threat. For example, China's exports to ASEAN expanded from 17 billion dollars in 2000 to 279 billion dollars in 2015, and its imports from ASEAN also increased from 22 billion dollars to 189 billion dollars during the same period. The trade relationships between China and ASEAN were much less substitutionary than initially anticipated and were actually further strengthened because of the complementarities in the intra-regional division of labor, which we will discuss in the next section. In 2015, the largest source country for China's imports was South Korea; however, China's total imports from ASEAN exceeded those of South Korea. As such, the "China threat" view has been gradually reshaped into a "mutual prosperity" view.

2.2.2 China, regional division of labor in production, and horizontal trade

The emergence of China has induced substantive changes in the production and distribution structure of Asia. This has been influenced by the proliferation of Information Technologies (IT) on a global scale, and the reductions in international logistic costs. The intra-regional trade patterns of the twentieth century could be explained in terms of the Heckscher-Ohlin model, which predicts that countries would specialize in the exports of industries in which their resource endowments allow them to realize comparative advantage. The model was, however, primarily used in the context of vertically integrated industries and products. In the 21st century, however, the international division of labor increasingly takes place within an industry or product, and the division of labor thus is process- or task-based. This is most evident in electronics-related industries, such as personal computers.

To see the extent of the international division of labor in processes, data compiled by the Research Institute of Economy, Trade and Industry (RIETI) of the Japanese Ministry of Economy, Trade and Industry (METI) is very useful (see Box 2 for a short discussion on the different sources and characteristics of trade data). The exports of electronics and machinery products from Asia increased from 406 billion dollars in 2000 to 1161 billion dollars in 2015. Asia's share of electronics and machineries out of the world total increased from 44.3% to 62.8% accordingly. Asia has evolved as the center of production for these products.

Out of total electronics and machinery exports from Asia, 61.9% were intermediate inputs (parts and components) while final products only constituted 38.1% in 2015. Exports from China in particular have been dominant in the exports of final products, with a regional share of 67.0%, while that of parts and components was only 27.4%. In addition, 82.6% of the electronics parts and components imports of China were from within the region. In short, China's electronics and machinery exports have been supported by intermediate inputs from its Asian neighbors.

Figure 2.5A depicts the changing trends of intra-regional trade in Asia between 1980 and 2015. It suggests that the share of intermediate inputs in intra-regional trade has steadily increased during this period; while their share was just 44% in 1980, this has increased to 65% in 2015.

Figure 2.5B compares the intra-regional trade structure of Asia with those of NAFTA and the EU. Asia's share (65%) is significantly higher than those of NAFTA and the EU (47% and 48%, respectively). On the other hand, final products play a much larger role in the intra-regional trade of NAFTA and particularly of the EU.

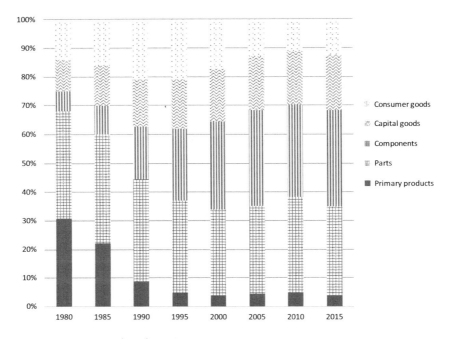

FIGURE 2.5A Intra-regional trade in Asia.
Source: RIETI Database.

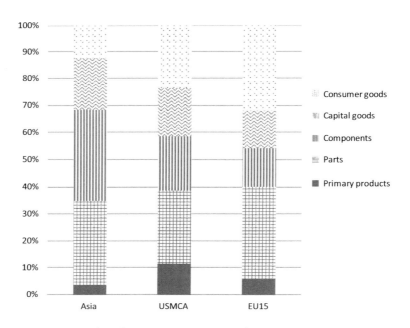

FIGURE 2.5B Intra-regional trade in Asia, USMCA, and EU (2015).
Source: RIETI Database.

2.2.3 The deepening of the vertical international division of labor

The international vertical division of labor, and the resulting production networks which span different countries, are often called global value chains (GVCs). Fragmentation theory is a key concept in GVCs. Fragmentation refers to a situation in which an integrated production structure is divided (fragmented) into different production blocks, and relocated in different offshore locations.

Prior to GVCs, production processes – from the procurement of resources to their transformation into final products – took place typically in one location (Figure 2.6). This integrated structure, however, is now fragmented into several production blocks. Each of those production blocks has been relocated offshore, where local resource endowments match the factor intensities of each of the production blocks. In other words, fragmentation allows corporations to optimize their production structures at the process level.

The forms of the actual production and distribution networks that emerge from such fragmentation dynamics are dependent on locational conditions (including wage levels, infrastructure, and the availability of natural resources) as well as the service links that connect the fragmented production blocks together, such as transportation costs, tariffs, and administrative procedures related to importing and exporting. Value chains are essentially networks in which those production blocks are connected, and when they cross borders, they are typically referred to as global value chains.

One of the industries where fragmentation has progressed most extensively is the electronics and machinery industry. This is partly because of the relative easiness and low costs in the transportation of the parts and components (hereafter, just parts). The other, which is more fundamental, is due to the increasing modularization of such parts.

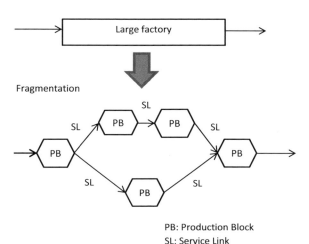

FIGURE 2.6 Fragmentation.

Source: Kimura (2003).

Modularized parts have common interfaces which allow connections of different parts that are not defined in terms of particular supplier–buyer relationships. As such, parts can easily be replaced by and combined with others, increasing flexibility in a highly generalized context of production. As such, modularization of parts has made the production of original electric products, such as monitors, much easier than before. The result is a boom in the number of electronics assemblers. Foxconn of Taiwan is one of such typical examples (see Chapter 4).

2.2.4 Asia as a major regional market

While the integration of production within Asia has been remarkable, the region has also emerged as a major global consumer. The GDP of Asia expanded from 7.8 trillion dollars in 2000 to 21.0 trillion dollars in 2016. Its global share has increased from 23.1% to 27.9% accordingly, which suggests that its market has also grown significantly.

Asia's consumer goods imports have increased from 229.9 billion dollars in 2000 to 566.8 billion dollars in 2015, with an increase in global share of 18.6% to 22.5% during the same period. Within these totals, the consumer goods imports of China increased drastically, from 9.4 billion dollar to 130.6 billion. China is no longer just the "world's factory," but also the "world's market." The main engine of growth is the evolving high-income groups in urban areas (see Chapter 8). The recent trends of increasing electronic commerce (EC) is expected to accelerate this trend.

The late-coming countries of ASEAN, including Myanmar, Laos, and Cambodia, are also becoming integrated into international production networks. While some of the trade statistics of these countries are not available, UNCTAD estimates that the export volumes of Myanmar, Laos, and Cambodia between 2000 and 2015 has increased from 5.3 billion dollars to 28.6 billion dollars, 0.8 billion dollars to 8 billion dollars, and 3.6 billion dollars to 26.1 billion dollars, respectively. Their dependence on Asia as an export destination has also been high, which in 2015 stood at 86.2%, 90.0%, and 61.9%, respectively. Among them, Cambodia has been importing textile related inputs from China, and exporting apparel products to the US market. Laos and Cambodia are catering for the production of industrial parts, as part of international subcontracting arrangements with their more advanced neighbor, Thailand.

This evolving international division of labor has also been promoted through increases in intra-regional investments. FDI into Asia was initially led by investments from Japan and Asian NIEs; however, the presence of China and ASEAN has increased rapidly. China's FDI in 2015 was 127.6 billion dollars, which was about the same as Japan's (128.7 billion dollars) in 2015. FDI from ASEAN (except from Singapore) rose from 2.2 billion dollars in 2000 to 31.2 billion dollars in 2015. Out of this, outward FDI from Malaysia and Thailand were 9.9 billion dollars and 7.7 billion dollars, respectively, which exceeded their inward FDI – both countries are shifting towards being net global investors. As investment funds have started to circulate within the region, this has strengthened the *de-facto* based "Asianizing Asia" phenomenon. In addition, countries such as China and Thailand have also emerged as international development donors to neighboring countries.

Development assistance and initiatives from multilateral organizations and developed countries have also played a role in reducing regional logistic costs in Asia. For example, the take-offs of Myanmar, Laos, and Cambodia were also supported by the infrastructure that was built by such support, including the Economic Corridors project led by the Asian Development Bank (ADB). These have contributed to reducing the service link costs between the different production blocks and have integrated the hinterlands into the Asian value chains.

2.3 *DE-JURE* ECONOMIC INTEGRATION, OPPORTUNITIES, AND CHALLENGES

2.3.1 The centrality of ASEAN in Asian regional FTAs

The post-war, export-led growth of Asia was based on trade policies crafted within the framework of the GATT, which came into effect in 1948. This global-level agreement on trade liberalization was based on the premises that free trade would allow countries to specialize in sectors in which they have comparative advantage. Such specialization would allow the total global output of goods and services to be maximized, and these later can be traded between countries, thereby maximizing the welfare of all. The GATT was succeeded by the WTO in 1995, which was also mandated to promote free trade on a multilateral level, based on the General Agreement on Trade in Services (GATS) and the Trade-Related Aspects of Intellectual Property Rights (TRIPS) principles, in addition to GATT. With the accession of Laos into the WTO in 2013, all economies in Asia, except North Korea, have become members of the WTO.

In conjunction to this, regional integration frameworks have evolved as well. The European Economic Community (EEC), which came into effect in 1958, was transformed into the EU in 1992. In North America, the US, Canada, and Mexico signed the North American Free Trade Agreement (NAFTA), established in 1994. In 2018 it has been decided to replace it with the United States–Mexico–Canada Agreement (USMCA) in the future upon ratification in the three countries concerned. It is worth mentioning too that such regional integration schemes do not contradict the GATT/WTO framework. These RTAs are in fact designed according to Article 24 of GATT, which ensures compatibility with the WTO principles, and are more progressively liberalized.

FTAs in Asia were led by ASEAN, which was established in 1967 to promote regional cooperation. One of its main objectives at the initial stage of establishment was political, expecting to play a role in halting the spread of communism in Southeast Asia.

With the end of the Cold War in the late 1980s and the dissolution of the Soviet Union in 1991, Vietnam (1995), Laos (1997), Myanmar (1997), and Cambodia (1999) joined ASEAN. With the current ten country membership, ASEAN practically covers the entire region, with the exception of East Timor.

In 1992, ASEAN set a goal to establish an ASEAN Free Trade Area (AFTA). The realization of AFTA was initially viewed with some doubt in terms of its feasibility. However, China's accession into the WTO in 2001 was an alarming event for ASEAN countries. This event accelerated the implementation of trade liberalization in this region; trade barriers were in principle abolished for six of ASEAN's more advanced countries (Brunei, Indonesia, Malaysia, Philippines, Singapore, and Thailand) in 2010, and the remaining ones were also integrated fully in 2018.

In 2015, the ASEAN Community was established, which is a more comprehensive framework encompassing security and socio-cultural aspects, in addition to economic and trade liberalization. In addition, opportunities to expand FTAs outside the region have been actively pursued. Some of those include FTAs with China (2005), South Korea (2007), Japan (2008), India (2010), and Australia/New Zealand (2010).

2.3.2 Changes in the trade policies of Japan, China, and Korea

In the 20th century, Japan's trade policies were centered on the multilateral-based, GATT/WTO framework. In the 21st century, however, it started to shift its emphasis in trade policies towards Economic Partnership Agreements (EPAs). EPAs are comprehensive bilateral trade agreements covering liberalization arrangements beyond trade in goods, including service trade, investment promotion, deregulation in international movements in people, protection of intellectual property rights, and the establishments of cooperation platforms for a wide range of issues pertinent to strengthening economic relationships. Since its first signing of the EPA with Singapore, Japan has concluded 15 EPAs with different countries and regions in July 2017 (Table 2.2).

Some take the view that such a fundamental shift in Japan's trade policy has affected trade policies of China and South Korea as well. China and ASEAN agreed to establish an FTA within the next ten years at a summit meeting in 2001. This has turned into the signing of the ASEAN-China economic cooperation framework in 2002, part of which was realized as the ASEAN-China Free Trade Agreement (ACFTA) in 2005. In 2010, tariffs for goods in the normal track were abolished; that is, excluding sensitive items (such as those that may cause significant economic loss or social unrest upon liberalization – the sensitive track). South Korea likewise signed the ASEAN-Korea Free Trade Agreement in 2007, and tariffs were abolished in 2010 as in the case of China.

As discussed earlier, regional economic integration in Asia was primarily *de-facto* based, which was led by the private sector. However, *de-jure*-based integration has been progressing in Asia, in which ASEAN is playing a central role.

2.3.3 Diversified economic relationships and challenges for future growth

The rapid economic growth of Asia in the post-war era has been based on international structural transformation dynamics, underlain by intensive intra-regional trade and investment relationships. In this, a "catch-up industrialization" structure had emerged, with a clear hierarchical structure at which Japan as the most industrialized country stood at the top.

In the 21st century, however, new phenomena have been observed in the region which cannot be fully explained by such a catch-up industrialization structure (Suehiro, 2014). The catch-up industrialization theory focused on the catch-up

TABLE 2.2 Japan's economic partnership agreements (EPAs) (as of July 2017)

Countries/regions	Date
In effect	
Singapore	November 2002
Mexico	April 2005
Malaysia	July 2006
Chile	September 2007
Thailand	November 2007
Brunei	July 2008
Indonesia	July 2008
The Philippines	December 2008
ASEAN	December 2008
Switzerland	September 2009
Vietnam	October 2009
India	October 2011
Peru	March 2012
Australia	January 2015
Mongolia	June 2016
Signed	
TPP	February 2016

Source: Ministry of Foreign Affairs, Japan.

processes of late-coming countries to more advanced economies. However, it did not anticipate late-coming countries surpassing more advanced countries. One of the major reasons for the increased prevalence of this leap-frogging of late-coming countries is due to the changes that have occurred in product architecture since late 1990s (see Chapter 4).

This suggests that new dynamisms are emerging in Asia, independent of, and quite different from, the older flying-geese pattern, which had a rather rigid and clear hierarchical structure. The rise of less developed countries in Asia, where the relationships between these countries have become much more diverse. This suggests that the mono-polar, post-war economic order with Japan at the top, has come to an end. Instead, a multi-polar structure has emerged. Changes in product architecture and the proliferating global value chains are behind this, and firms in Asia that were able to capture the growing opportunities within this evolving context are among the key players that have promoted the changes in the regional economic order.

The Asian economy, with such dynamic changes, is not without challenges. This book also addresses problems related to demography, inequality, and environmental issues. One of the challenges in relation to regional economic integration and sustainable development is the "middle-income trap." The middle-income trap refers to a phenomenon in which countries that have reached middle-income status (according to the World Bank classification) not being able to lift themselves up into the "high-income" status (Chapters 4 and 7). Global value chains have provided opportunities to firms in middle-income countries of Asia to connect to the global economy, and some of those have emerged as lead firms significantly impacting and altering the regional economic order. On the other hand, sustainable development of these countries is dependent on their ability to upgrade their economic structures from labor intensive, low value-added functions towards higher value-added functions which are typically of higher capital and knowledge intensity. This requires upgrading not just at individual firm levels, but more on a wider macro-economic level. A failure to meet this challenge will lead to significant risks related to the middle-income trap.

CONCLUSION

De-facto integration based on trade and investment relationships has strengthened the mutual dependency of the countries of Asia. In addition, progress in *de-jure* integration has further promoted regional integration. In this context, discussions have evolved on the possibility of establishing an East Asian Economic Community. However, such *de-jure*-based frameworks in Asia are still at their early stages in comparison with other regions. Bela Balassa classifies the forms of economic integration into the following five stages: (1) free trade area, (2) customs union, (3) common market, (4) economic union, and (5) complete economic integration, entailing substantial political coherence, where unification extends to monetary, fiscal, and social policies (Balassa, 1961). From this perspective, Asia's integration is still at the first stage. Movements in people are still highly restricted, and currency unions are currently not considered.

The focus of policy makers in Asia now is primarily on the geographical expansion of FTAs. For instance, one of the major pipeline projects is the Regional Comprehensive Economic Partnership (RCEP). Discussions on the RCEP were initiated by ASEAN, by involving the six countries where it had already established FTAs, namely Japan, China, Korea, India, Australia, and New Zealand. If the RCEP becomes a reality, then it would be a free trade area of 3.4 billion people, with a market size of 23.4 trillion dollars.

Higher levels of *de-jure*-based economic integration will progress only slowly in Asia. This is because of the wide variation between countries in their stages of economic development, political regimes, and other differences such as culture and religion. A too hasty approach to *de-jure* integration might in fact be detrimental and disruptive to the ongoing *de-facto*-based integration. The recent issues related to Brexit in the EU, and the policy stances taken by the Trump Administration in the US are examples.

Integration in Asia, in which ASEAN continues to play an important role, has so far been successful because of its gradualist approach, in which discussions and negotiations took place in a relative long timeframe, and where achievable issues were addressed first. However, globalization and further economic integration seems an irreversible trend, and governments including those from Asia, are increasingly pressured to better manage the challenges that arise from this.

BOX 2 Trade-related databases

Keiichiro Oizumi

An increasing number of trade-related databases have become available through various international organizations' websites. For those with an interest in international trade, getting data and tabulating figures can now be easily done. This box with introduce readers to the key characteristics of different trade databases and statistics.

The "UN Comtrade Database (https://comtrade.un.org/)" is one of the key databases for international trade and is particularly useful for longitudinal data. While availability is dependent on whether the data has been provided by member countries, the database includes export and import statistics of individual countries from as early as 1962 (availability depends on countries and classifications), which can be downloaded according to its trade partners. These trade statistics can also be extracted based on commodities, which are classified according to the Harmonized Commodity Description and Coding Systems (HS), the Standard International Trade Classification (SITC), and the Classification by Broad Economic Categories (BEC). A convergence and correspondence table has been provided for the three different classifications by the UN at the following link (https://unstats.un.org/unsd/tradekb/Knowledgebase/50020/HS-SITC-and-BEC-conversion-and-correspondence-tables).

Trade data in the HS classification can be obtained and downloaded at the two-, four-, and six-digit levels of the commodity codes. The level of commodity classification becomes more detailed as the code digit increases. The HS codes have been revised in 1992, 1996, 2002, 2007, and 2012, and import and export statistics are available for all of the different versions. However, as the availability of the data in this classification dates back only for a limited number of years prior to the revisions, the oldest data in this classification, based on the 1992 version, is 1988.

The SITC classification covers the longest duration of import and export statistics, which for some countries dates back to 1962. Data are available up to the five-digit level.

The BEC classification allows trade data to be analyzed by broad economic categories, such as food, capital equipment, and consumer durables. It is linked to both the HS and SITC classifications. Recent revisions also link the categories according to consumption goods, intermediate goods, capital goods, according to the System of National Accounts (SNA). However, not many countries report BEC statistics, and data are only available from 1988 and onwards.

While the UN Comtrade does provide detailed data, there are also substantial omissions in the database, and as such it may not be appropriate to calculate country or regional shares out of total world trade. The "UNCTADstat (https://unctadstat.unctad.org/EN/)" is more useful in this respect. While the database includes data from 1995, trade data can be extracted according to trade partners in terms of both countries and regions. Goods are classified according to the SITC classifications and UNCTAD's own commodity classifications. Regions are grouped into, for instance, EU15, ASEAN, G7, and OECD, and allows easy analysis of intra- and extra-regional trade patterns. Total trade values have also been recorded from 1948.

The "RIETI-TID (http://www.rieti-tid.com/)" of the Japanese METI is another useful database. It is particularly useful in looking at the levels of vertical (and horizontal) trade within particular regions. This is based on the SITC classifications, which are tabulated by RIETI. One of the shortcomings is in the country coverage and occasional omissions by years.

Finally, as will be discussed in Chapter 4, the proliferation of international production and distribution networks will lead to discrepancies between the gross export volumes and the actual value-addition that accrues within the domestic economy. For example, when country A carries out only labor-intensive assembly functions while all the inputs are imported, then the actual value that has been added by country A tends to be much smaller than its gross exports. To capture such differences, OECD and WTO provide Trade in Value Added data, which are estimated using the international input-output table. The database can be accessed via www.oecd.org/sti/ind/measuring-trade-in-value-added.htm#access.

NOTE

1 Myanmar. Cambodia, Laos, and Vietnam were given until 2018 to abolish intra ASEAN tariffs.

REFERENCES

Balassa, Bela. (1961). *The Theory of Economic Integration*. Homewood, IL: Richard D. Irwin.

Goto, Kenta. (2014). "Sengo Ajia no Kokusai Seisan Ryutsu Nettowaku no Keisei to Tenkai" ("The Development of Production and Distribution Networks in Post-War Asia"), Miyagi Taizo (hen) *Sengo Ajia no Keisei to Nihon* (in Miyagi, Taizo (ed) *The Formation of Post-War Asia and Japan*) Tokyo: Chuokoron-Shinsha, 167–205.

Kimura, Fukunari. (2003). "Kokusaiboueki-riron no Aratana Choryu to Higashi Ajia" (New Developments in International Trade Theory and East Asia), *Kaihatu-kinyu Kenkyu Shoho* (*Journal of JBIC Institute*), Kokusai-kaihatu Kyoryoku Ginko Kaihatsu Kinyu Kenkyusho (Research Institute for Development and Finance, Japan Bank for International Cooperation), 14, 106–116.

Kojima, Kiyoshi. (2003). *Gankou-gata Keizai Hattenron Dai 1 Kan – Nihon Keizai Ajia Keizai Sekai Keizai* (*Flying Geese Pattern Economic Development Vol. 1: The Japanese, Asian, and the World Economies*). Tokyo: Bunshindo.

Ministry of Economy, Trade, and Industry (METI). (Various Years). *Whitepaper on International Economy and Trade*. Tokyo: METI.

Ohno, Kenichi and Kojiro Sakurai. (1997). *Higashi Ajia no Kaihatu Keizaigaku (Development Economics of East Asia)*. Tokyo: Yuhikaku Publishing.

Suehiro, Akira. (2008). *Catch-up Industrialization: The Trajectory and Prospects of East Asian Economies*, Singapore: NUS Press.

Suehiro, Akira. (2014). *Emerging Asian Economies: Beyond the Catch-up Industrialization Approach (Shinko Ajia Keizairon: Kyacchi Appu wo Koete)*. Tokyo: Iwanami Shoten, Publishers.

Watanabe, Toshio. (1999). "Ajia-ka suru Ajia – Kiki no Mukou ni Mieru Mono" ("Asianizing Asia: Beyond the Crisis") in *Chuokoron* 114(6), 80–91.

World Bank. (1993). *The East Asian Miracle: Economic Growth and Public Policy*. New York: Oxford University Press.

3 China reshaping Asia: economic transition and the rise of an economic superpower

Asei Ito

Great Hall of the People, Beijing (2007, photo by Kenta Goto).

LEARNING GOALS

- Understand China's transition from economic planning to "reform and opening-up."
- Understand the effects of the structural changes in China's domestic economy on Asia and beyond.
- Understand the challenges of China's economy.

INTRODUCTION

The first chapter of this book opened with a short historical account of the postwar Asian economy. It reflected on this by looking at key literature and paradigms that had evolved at the time, such as the OECD report on Newly Industrializing Countries (NICs), the World Bank's *East Asian Miracle,* and the "developmentalism" argument.

Despite its undisputed role and influence in the Asian economy today, there was one country that was not included in these – China.

Why was China omitted from the "Asian economy" literature for so long? One of the reasons is related to the Cold War, which limited its economic relations with the West. The other is the fact that, despite being a large country with a population of one billion as of 1980, China's economy remained small until the 1990s. As shown in Figure 3.1, Japan accounted for 71% of East and Southeast Asian gross domestic product (GDP) in 1990, when Japan's bubble economy was at its peak. The dominance of the Japanese economy in the region at that time is best manifested by terms such as "Japan as Number One," which is the title of a major book by Harvard Professor Ezra Vogel, published in 1979. However, with the commencement of economic reforms in China in 1978, China has rapidly expanded its GDP share in the region, particularly since the 1990s. Its GDP surpassed that of Japan in 2010, accounting for 40% of regional GDP. This share is projected to reach 58% by 2020. China has historically been the world's largest and most prosperous economy since the Middle Ages (see Box 1). Since the 2010s, China has re-emerged as one of the largest and most powerful economic hubs in Asia and beyond.

China's extraordinary economic growth is due to its reform and opening-up policy launched in 1978. China maintains a socialist system which in principle aims for shared wealth. In reality, however, it has introduced market mechanisms in its economy, and adopted an opening-up strategy that encouraged active participation in the international division of labor. In this sense, China's economic policy since the 1980s has primarily followed the East Asian type of outward industrialization strategy, most typically observed in the experiences of Asian NIEs, as introduced in Chapter 1. In fact, the successful experiences of the Asian NIEs exerted a certain influence in the shifting of China's development strategy within the context of globalization. The 1980s was thus an era where "Asia changed China."

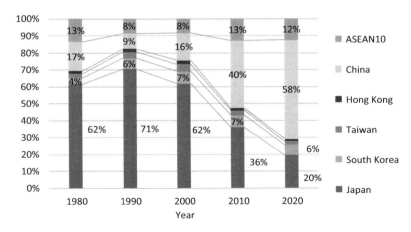

FIGURE 3.1 East and Southeast Asian GDP by economies.
Source: IMF's forecasting in 2017.

The substantial potentialities of the domestic market, as indicated by its significant population size, to some extent, contributed to its rapid economic development. This is a characteristic unique to China. However, China's rapid economic development through increased openness to the world was key, which further accelerated in the 2000s upon successful accession to the World Trade Organization (WTO). In the 2010s, China became the second largest economy in the world. With this, the policies of the Chinese government and actions of Chinese corporations started to make notable impacts on the Asian and the global economy.

3.1 REFORM AND OPENING-UP POLICY, AND CHINA'S ECONOMIC DEVELOPMENT: ASIA CHANGING CHINA

3.1.1 Characteristics and limitations of the planned economy

To understand China's recent economic performance, it is useful to look at the limitations and shortcomings of its planned economy of the past that led to the reform and opening-up policy of 1978. When the People's Republic of China (PRC) was established in 1949, the central government under the leadership of Mao Zedong installed a socialist economic planning system, whose implementation efforts intensified particularly from 1955. As China became part of the Eastern socialist bloc led by the Soviet Union, its investment relations with Western liberal democracies were cut off. While some trade relationships with the West still continued, they were extremely limited.

The central objective of China's planned economy at that time was to attain rapid heavy industrialization through a command economic system. In market economies, prices of most goods are determined through market transactions in which supply and demand play key roles. Scarcity of goods will lead to higher prices, which should then increase production and supply of those goods. In contrast, in a planned economy, the central government unilaterally decides upon the production output and prices of goods, replacing the market mechanism that would bring prices and quantities into equilibrium through the interaction of supply and demand. Under economic planning, surpluses generated by enterprises were re-invested by the Chinese government into specific sectors, particularly heavy industry. Private companies were nationalized or collectivized through socialist reforms that peaked in 1955. Prices of producer/intermediate goods such as steel, machinery, and cotton, were strictly controlled.

The government attempted to allocate resources efficiently by regulating production, prices, and sales destinations. However, incentives for enterprises and workers in terms of higher profits and wages were crucially lacking, leading to economic stagnation. Under a planned economy, enterprises usually do not have the autonomy to make key management decisions on issues related to price setting and product development. In urban areas, workers were assigned to units such as state-owned enterprises (SOEs) or collective enterprises, and farmers in rural areas were also collectivized into a socialist organization called "People's Communes." Ration tickets, issued by these units and organizations, were needed to buy goods including foodstuffs. "Free markets," where prices were determined privately were strictly regulated. Such control was most intense during the Cultural Revolution in 1966 – even selling farm-fresh eggs at rural markets would have been fiercely criticized as "capitalistic behavior," and faced ruthless crack downs by the authorities.

The second characteristic of China's intensive economic planning prior to 1978 is that it was punctuated by a series of political upheavals. The Great Leap Forward, launched in 1959 under Mao Zedong's leadership, aimed for China to surpass Britain's crude steel production. Massive targets of iron output were set and production was widely promoted in rural areas; however, the low-quality iron was useless, and this shift of economic resources including workers caused a famine, leaving an estimated 20 million people dead. As a response, planning controls were temporarily eased in the early 1960s to allow the economy to recover. This process, however, was disrupted by the Cultural Revolution, another political movement initiated by Mao Zedong. These political events not only caused serious fluctuations in economic growth rates, but also led to periods of negative growth, especially during the Great Leap Forward and the Cultural Revolution (Figure 3.2). Because Mao assumed that a third world war was inevitable, geographic concentration of heavy industries in the northeastern and coastal areas was considered a security risk. The coastal areas therefore faced under-investment, whereas investments in inland regions were prioritized. Such comparative advantage-defying strategies resulted in reduced efficiency and stagnant productivity growth throughout the planned economy period (Lin et al., 1997; Nakagane, 2012).

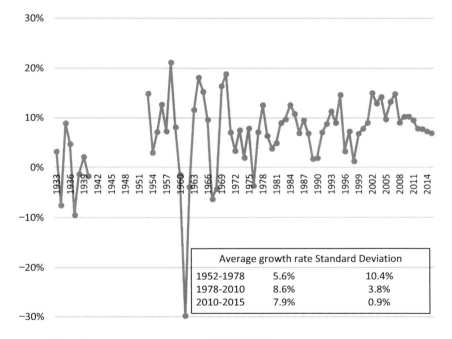

FIGURE 3.2 China's economic growth rate (1933–2015).

Source: Data from 1933 to 2010 is obtained from Minami and Makino ed. (2014, page 360), from 2011 to 2015 is obtained from China Statistical Yearbook (National Bureau of Statistics).

The reasons for Mao's radical heavy industrialization strategy can be explained by China's past. From the 1880s to the 1940s, China faced a series of political disturbances and foreign aggression. During the period following the collapse of the Qing Dynasty in 1912, and through the period of the Republic of China, there were increasing pressures from the expansion of Western powers. This also intensified trade relationships with these Western countries, which triggered the development of light industries in its coastal regions, especially in Shanghai. The experience of the Sino-Japanese war, the civil war, and the Korean War, however, strongly demonstrated the importance of heavy industries as these were more directly linked to military power. Although China's current robust economic development can mostly be understood by focusing on the period after the PRC's establishment, a longer historical perspective is highly useful to understanding the characteristics of the country's development trajectories (Kubo et al., 2016). From such a point of view, the legacy of China's socialist economy is not necessarily all negative. Instead, at the initial stages of its reform and opening-up policy, China already had higher levels of human capital than many low-income economies in terms of literacy rates and machinery and heavy chemical industries were present even in rural areas (Bramall, 2006). In contrast to the Soviet Union, China's planned economy was also much less strict in terms of government control, and economic planning was implemented for a much shorter period – for about 25 years from 1955 until the early 1980s (Naughton, 1995). Such a relatively short duration of economic planning allowed China to transform itself more easily into a market-based economy, following the 1978 reforms (Ito, 2017).

3.1.2 Economic transition toward a market economy

Figure 3.2 suggests substantially less fluctuations in growth rates since the 1980s. This is due to the reform and opening-up policies introduced by Deng Xiaoping, which led to institutional transitions toward a functional market economy.

These reforms started with the gradual introduction of market mechanisms by liberalizing prices and resource allocation in both urban and rural areas. This created stronger incentives for economic entities. As mentioned earlier, farmers had been organized into People's Communes during the economic planning period, and in the case of grains, the produce was required to be sold to state agencies at predetermined prices. Similarly, the levels of industrial outputs and their prices were also controlled by the state, leaving no room for enterprises to develop new products and markets. As a result, there were no incentives for companies and individuals to produce higher-quality products, or to develop new products and markets (Lin et al., 1997). When the Japanese economist Ryutaro Komiya visited Chinese factories during 1983–1984, he was struck by the level of restrictiveness firms faced in making decisions autonomously, prompting him to remark that "there are no entities in China that could be called a firm" (Komiya, 1987). This statement was received with shock by Chinese reformers and economists at the time (Wu, 2003).

Various types of enterprises were operating actively during the Republic of China era, including large business conglomerates. When the PRC was founded, however, all of the enterprises were nationalized or collectivized under the socialist economic planning regime in the 1950s, which eroded the essential characteristics of private corporations in its economy. As such, one of the focuses of marketization reforms has been to nurture and encourage private businesses to flourish as they did in the past. Figure 3.3

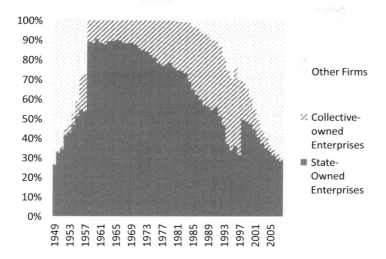

FIGURE 3.3 Industrial output by company ownership.

Source: Department of Comprehensive Statistics of the National Bureau of Statistics, China (2010), p. 40.

Note: Since 1998, all state-owned enterprises and the above scale of non-state enterprises (over 5 million RMB annual sales) are included.

shows the share of SOEs, collective-owned enterprises, and other types of firms (private enterprises and foreign-owned enterprises) in terms of their shares of industrial output. Private enterprises had accounted for 70% immediately following the establishment of the PRC. As socialization progressed, however, SOEs started to dominate the industry, reaching 90% in the late 1950s. Collective-owned enterprises (including township-village-owned enterprises) accounted for the rest, while private enterprises had essentially been eliminated. The share of "other firms" started to recover in the late 1970s as economic reforms began. Private enterprises have re-emerged due to the reform and opening-up policy.

3.1.3 Opening-up policy

Another feature of the reform package is the "opening-up" of its economy. For Asia and the world, such a policy shift meant that a vast country with a population of over a billion was suddenly participating in the international division of labor in which they are intricately embedded. To promote industrialization and economic development, China started attracting foreign direct investment (FDI) to fully participate in the international division of labor. China abandoned the previous comparative-advantage defying strategy, and instead adopted comparative-advantage following strategy that were consistent with these advantages (Cai et al., 2018). This also meant that such strategies were going to utilize its abundant cheap labor.

In this context, China set up Special Economic Zones (SEZs) in its southern coastal areas, initially in Guangdong and Fujian provinces. Departure from the previous inland-focused heavy industrialization strategy during the planned economy period became evident. Four SEZs were set up initially in Shenzhen, Zhuhai, Shantou, and Xiamen. Another SEZ in Hainan was established later. These SEZs were based on the export processing zones adopted in Taiwan and South Korea, offering tax exemptions for the importation of foreign materials and final goods export. This official permission for foreign companies to invest and trade, including companies from Hong Kong, further prompted the entry of foreign companies. All of the SEZs were set up in the coastal area because of the anticipation for foreign direct investment from Asian NIEs: Shenzhen is adjacent to Hong Kong; Zhuhai is adjacent to Macau, and Xiamen is close to Taiwan. In the case of Shenzhen, for example, it has experienced extremely rapid economic development over last four decades. Investments from Hong Kong poured in first, followed by investment from Taiwan, Japan, the US, and Europe. This triggered industrialization of the wider Pearl River Delta region in Southern China, which is today a key part of China as "the workshop of the world."

In 1988, the "Coastal Region Opening Strategy" was formulated, which aimed to attract direct investment from Asia after the Plaza Accord. However, the Tiananmen Square protests broke out in 1989, which led to a group of conservatives in China arguing for policy reversals with regards to the ongoing reform efforts, as they felt them to be a key factor making for political instability. However, Deng Xiaoping's speech during his "Southern Tour" in 1992, where he announced his commitment to economic liberalization, served to undermine these claims, and gave a strong boost to further economic reform.

China's implementation of its "Coastal Region Opening Strategy" clearly demonstrates that it was following the export-oriented industrialization strategies of the Asian NIEs. In other words, Asia's postwar economic success served to change China's position and strategy for economic development. The entry of a large country such as China, whose population size has grown from 980 million in 1980 to 1.27 billion in 2000, into the international economy has had substantial and wide-ranging repercussions, domestically, regionally, and internationally, which continue till date.

An economy's degree of openness is typically assessed by calculating the ratio of gross imports and exports divided by the GDP. The denominator, GDP, is the total value-added created within the country in a year, and the numerator reflects the gross value of total trade during that period. The degree of openness could exceed 1 in economies where with extensive trade relative to GDP, such as Hong Kong and Singapore. Looking at data from China, the degree of openness in 1980 was 12.4%. This rose to 24.3% in 1990, 39.4% in 2000, and 62.2% in 2005 (The World Bank Data). The reform and opening-up policy promoted China's openness up until the mid-2000s. After the late 2000s, however, the ratio has started to decline due to sluggish exports, while its domestic market started to expand because of rapidly evolving tertiary industries. Because tertiary industries tend to supply service goods, which are non-tradable, this led to the decline in the degree of openness, falling to 48.9% in 2010 and 37.8% in 2017.

3.2 CHINA AS THE WORKSHOP OF THE WORLD: CHINA'S INTEGRATION INTO THE ASIAN ECONOMY

3.2.1 The Asian production network and China as the assembly factory

As discussed, China's integration into the international economy had epoch-making impacts on Asian production networks, and more broadly on the Asian and global economy.

In addition to China's low wage levels and preferential policies for foreign investment, trade and investment were also spurred by China's accession to the WTO in 2001. This signaled that China had accepted the need to abide by relevant international rules with regard to foreign companies. Although China's economic relationship with the outside world started in the 1980s, its exports experienced a substantial boom in the 2000s, which were largely based on foreign companies' activities. This induced industrial upgrading in China over time. During the initial phases of opening-up, it was exporting mainly labor-intensive products such as apparel products and other miscellaneous goods. Eventually, however, Japanese and Taiwanese companies started producing capital-intensive products and components such copy machines and laptop computers, in mainland China. The coastal areas in China soon evolved as an export hub for such relatively high-tech products (see Chapter 2, Figure 2.3). Conventional trade data suggests that China has emerged as an exporter of a wide range of goods, from labor-intensive products to capital-intensive ones, indicating broad-based export competitiveness (Kuroda, 2001; Gao, 2012).

Table 3.1 provides a breakdown of the production locations for different electronic products. In 2016, for example, China accounted for 79.8% of the 1.48 billion smartphones and 91.5% of the 158 million laptop computers produced worldwide. However, it must be stressed that China merely serves as a location for assembly functions. Foreign companies play essential roles in the production process, particularly in product design, technological research and development (R&D), and core components production. As a result of the deepening international intra-industry division of labor (fragmentation) mentioned in Chapter 2, the fact that the products being assembled in China does not

TABLE 3.1 Assembled locations of selected electronics products (2016)

	Global production (thousand unit)	Asia total (%)	Japan (%)	China (%)	Rest of Asia (%)	North America (%)	Europe (%)	Other regions (%)
Smart phone	1,480,000	97.1	0.2	79.8	17.1	0.0	0.5	2.3
Desktop PC	123,000	76.2	1.9	66.6	7.7	9.5	8.9	5.4
Laptop PC	158,000	93.7	1.1	91.5	1.1	0.0	0.0	6.3
Tablet PC	200,000	96.4	0.2	79.8	16.4	0.0	0.4	3.3
Smart watch	84,000	99.6	0.6	96.2	2.9	0.4	0.0	0.0
Server	10,500	92.7	2.1	89.3	1.2	3.3	1.7	2.3
Copy machines	4,300	98.6	1.9	82.4	14.3	0.1	1.3	0.0
Automobile	92,730	54.9	9.9	30.4	14.5	15.6	20.6	9.0
Motor cycle	54,300	93.2	0.9	32.2	60.1	1.0	1.1	4.6
Drone	2,400	96.7	0.2	96.3	0.2	1.3	1.7	0.4
3D Printer	250	59.2	1.6	12.8	44.8	22.8	14.0	4.0
Monitoring camera	93,300	95.8	0.2	72.6	23.1	1.6	2.6	0.0

Source: Fuji Chimera Research Institute (2017).

mean that the value-added of the entire product originate from China. Instead, as in the case of high-end electronic products, core parts are typically imported from countries such as the US, Japan, or from Asian NIEs. Looking at China's import items, semiconductors and other electronic components occupy the top spots. According to China's official statistics, its trade structure is typically called "processing trade," which involves the importation of parts into China, assembling into final products in China, and the exportation of those final goods to other countries. This apparently accounted for the majority of China's total exports. In the early 2000s, when China had suddenly become a major player in the Asian economy, ASEAN countries saw it as a threat; however, such a view has gradually disappeared as intra Sino-ASEAN trade increased.

3.2.2 Industrial development based on the domestic market

As mentioned above, China has shifted towards a development strategy based on leveraging its comparative advantages, similar to that pursued by other Asian NIEs. However, there remain important differences between these economies and China. In the case of Asian NIEs, their pattern of industrialization was typically and inevitably based on exports, primarily to the US market, reflecting the limited size of their domestic markets. China, in contrast, has a vast domestic market with over one billion people, albeit many at low income levels. Nonetheless, many of the private companies in Figure 3.3 have grown by catering for low-end products for the domestic market since the 1980s. This is because the SOEs were not able to develop products according to the market's demand, while foreign companies lacked the know-how to manufacture and sell low-priced products suitable for the Chinese market. Thus, it was only the private domestic companies that could supply products to the vast low-end market segment in China (Ding, 2012; Watanabe, 2016).

Under such market conditions, a large number of industrial clusters, or local districts specializing in the production of specific products, have evolved in the coastal regions since the 1980s. While industrial development led by foreign companies was observed on the east side of the Pearl River Delta and in the northern part of the Yangtze River Delta, many local industrial clusters led by domestic private enterprises evolved on the west side of the Pearl River Delta and the south side of the Yangtze River Delta. A typical example of such a cluster is Wenzhou city in Zhejiang province, which specializes in products including glasses, leather shoes, sports shoes, buttons, and automotive parts (Ganne and Lecler, 2009). It is noteworthy that during China's economic planning phase, government control was relatively loose in these regions due to the limits of its managerial capacity. In addition, traditional entrepreneurial activities such as petty trading were preserved, which allowed these regions to rapidly revive private businesses immediately after the reforms were initiated.

3.2.3 The "Lewis turning point" argument

Another important change in the Chinese economy in the 2000s is the structural change in the labor market. At the beginning of full-scale industrialization in the coastal region of China in the early 2000s, its labor market was often regarded as a place with an "unlimited supply of labor." It was assumed that such a condition would last well into the future, given China's large population as well as the hundreds of millions of surplus workers in rural areas. Based on a model proposed by Arthur Lewis (1954), in an economy with unlimited supply of labor, wage levels in the urban sector will be set at the level of subsistence wages, which offer workers' wages equivalent to the minimum living cost as employers can hire any amount of labor from the rural sector. The urban wage levels will not rise until the supply of rural surplus workers is exhausted or urban living costs start to rise. In the early 2000s, wage levels in China's coastal area were stable.

However, the media started reporting on labor shortages as early as the end of the Chinese New Year (spring festival) of 2003. Debate arose over whether or not the supply of surplus workers from rural areas had been exhausted, or whether China had come to the so-called "Lewis turning point" (Minami and Ma, 2010; Cai, 2016). The abundance of labor force has long been the biggest strength of China's manufacturing sector. However, it became increasingly clear that this cost advantage was gradually eroding in the late 2000s due to rising wages especially in the coastal regions. Facing higher input costs, foreign-invested companies began to relocate their factories from China to other lower-cost countries such as Viet Nam, Indonesia, and Myanmar. In the case of Japanese companies, in addition to the cost issues, large-scale demonstrations carried out in China over the Senkaku/Diaoyu Islands issue in 2012 also raised concerns about investment risks, motivating them to undertake a risk-diversification strategy dubbed "China plus one." However, according to China's trade data up to 2015, there has been no clear downward trend in China's global export shares. One of the possible explanations is the positive effects of agglomeration in China, which may have become new sources of competitiveness, as well as its indispensable position in supply chains, offsetting the negative effects of wage increases. Factories in coastal areas have also started to relocate to the less-developed inlands where land and labor costs are low, a phenomenon often called the "domestic flying geese" pattern. Chinese manufacturing has also shifted to higher value-added and new industries such as robotics (see Chapter 7).

3.3 CHINA AS AN ECONOMIC SUPERPOWER: CHINA CHANGING ASIA

3.3.1 China in the Asian and global economy

The Chinese economy experienced multiple turning points in the 2010s, domestically and internationally. In addition to increasing wages, the domestic economy underwent a series of structural transformations. For example, the working-age population ratio peaked in 2010 at 74.5%, and domestic income inequality started to drop according to official statistics. Growth rates in inland regions started to exceed that of coastal regions. Likewise, significant issues emerged on the international front as well, especially in its relation to the wider Asian economy. This section will focus on such issues and discuss the growing impact of China and its implications on the Asian and the global economy.

The first structural change is related to the supply side. China is no longer just an assembly base for low-cost products but is in the process of transforming itself into an advanced manufacturing hub, which is also capable of carrying out its own R&D

activities and innovation. With the spread of trade in intermediate goods, China's exports typically contained many components imported from more developed countries. However, domestic value-added in China has risen in recent years. According to OECD data, domestic value-added contents of China's electrical machinery exports was only 35.3% in 2000, which means that the remaining 64.7% of the value-added came from abroad. By 2010, however, domestic value-added share of China in the same product category had risen to 53.9%, suggesting rapid upgrading of its domestic value-chain (OECD TiVA data).

China's R&D expenditure has increased even more rapidly. In the 1990s and 2000s, China was commonly regarded as a source of imitation products. In recent years, however, Chinese companies have demonstrated their R&D capabilities by releasing cutting-edge products in the market. In terms of the number of international patent applications acquired by companies in 2016 (the number of applications utilizing the Patent Cooperation Treaty system), three Chinese companies ranked among the world's top 10, which are Huawei, ZTE, and BOE. All three companies belong to the electronics industry, operating worldwide. The rise of China in high-tech industries, particularly in the development of next-generation communication technologies including the fifth generation of mobile telecommunication (5G) has become a serious concern to the US government, as we will discuss later.

The second structural change occurred on the demand-side: China is now the largest economy in East Asia in terms of the nominal GDP, surpassing that of Japan in 2010. Today, the Chinese are regarded as essential consumers for both companies in China and abroad. As of 2015, 7,900 Japanese-affiliated companies were established in China (including Hong Kong), accounting for 31.3% of Japan's 25,233 companies operating worldwide (Data from Ministry of Economy, Trade, and Industry, Japan). The expansion of business in China is exerting increased impacts on Japanese firms' overall performance. Reflecting this, Japan's *Nikkei* newspaper started publishing the "Nikkei China Related Stock 50" index in December 2010. The list includes major Japanese corporations in key industries related to materials, automobiles, and robotics such as Komatsu, FANUC, and Toyota, as well as a number of consumer product and service companies including Seven & i Holdings in retail, Ryohin Keikaku of MUJI brand, and Fast Retailing of UNIQLO.

The number of Chinese tourists traveling abroad is also increasing: from 11 million in 2000 to 128 million in 2015. This has been accompanied by increased spending during the same period: from $13.1 billion to $104.5 billion (China National Bureau of Statistics). The growth in the number of Chinese tourists visiting Japan had been particularly remarkable, increasing from 0.5 million in 2003 to eight million in 2018. The magnitude of tourists from China in the 2010s has been manifested in the extensive advertisements written in Chinese at major department stores in Tokyo, which also suggest that payment can be made with Chinese debit cards (Union Pay). Furthermore, options to make payments using new Chinese mobile payment systems, such as Alipay and WeChat Pay, are now being offered in most of the major shopping venues in metropolitan areas of Asia. The fact that such Chinese-oriented promotions and payment services were not even available in the early 2000s suggests that these changes unfolded rapidly within a very short timeframe. The massive number of Chinese tourists during the Chinese Lunar New Years in February and the National Day in October have become almost an annual event, signaling one of the peak-seasons for retail businesses in Asia.

The third issue occurred in the financial dimension. In the early stages of reform and opening-up, China lacked funds for the construction of infrastructure and large-scale industrial plants. China is, however, no longer short in capital, but enjoys a significant surplus. China's current account surplus increased rapidly in the 2000s along with the evolving of a full-fledged export sector, from $17.4 billion in 2001 to $420.6 billion in 2008. There was a short period of contraction due to the global financial crisis of 2008, but momentum was regained to reach $340.2 billion in 2015 (Data from State Administration of Foreign Exchange, China). This substantial current account surplus allowed China to accumulate foreign exchange reserves, which are one of the main components of foreign assets. The foreign currency reserves reached $212 billion at the end of 2001, grew to $1,946 billion at the end of 2008, and to a further $3,843 billion by the end of 2014.

Because most of China's external assets are in forms of foreign exchange reserves, it is taking steps to diversify its asset-base by encouraging outward foreign direct investment. Since such attempts were compatible with the needs of Chinese companies to acquire technological know-how, China's outward FDI has expanded rapidly since 2004. The Chinese government further implemented a "Going Global" program to promote outward FDI; typical cases include FDIs made by companies such as the electronics giant Haier group and the Chery group in automotives. FDI by Chinese companies caused some concern in host countries, particularly in the US. Potential leakages of advanced technology were considered to be a potential business risk, and in some cases were treated as a security issue (Nolan, 2012; Ohashi, 2016; Office of the United States Trade Representative, Executive Office of the President, 2018).

When Xi Jinping became the General Secretary of the Communist Party of China (CPC) as well as the country's president, his administration initiated a comprehensive development program called the "Belt and Road Initiative" (BRI) that consists of the "21st Century Maritime Silk Road" and the "Silk Road Economic Belt" (see Box 3). This initiative has a broad geographical and sectoral scope. From a geographic perspective, it extends into regions to cover South-East Asia, Central Asia, the Middle-East, Eastern and Western Europe, and even Africa. In terms of sectors, the initiative covers infrastructure development, financial cooperation, policy dialog, and cultural exchanges. It offers clear evidence that China is intending to become a global leader, not merely a regional economic power.

3.3.2 State capitalism and mass capitalism in China

Suspicions surrounding China's foreign investment and related initiatives have their roots in China's political and economic regimes. China is often regarded as practicing state capitalism (Bremmer, 2010). Article 1 of the constitution of the PRC, which was revised in March 2018, states that

> The People's Republic of China is a socialist State under the people's democratic dictatorship led by the working class and based on the alliance of workers and peasants. The socialist system is the basic system of the People's Republic of China. The defining feature of socialism with Chinese characteristics is the leadership of the Communist Party of China. Disruption of the socialist system by any organization or individual is prohibited.

The fact that economic development falls under the remit of the CPC clearly implies that China is essentially an authoritarian and developmental state regime. By the end of 2018, there were over 90 million CPC members in China, and Communist Party branches have been established inside both private enterprises and foreign-affiliated companies. Meanwhile, SOEs, especially "central enterprises" directly overseen by the central government, are formally managed by the State-owned Asset Supervision and Administration Commission (SASAC), a division of the State Council. In practice, the top executives of major SOEs are nominated by the Central Organization Department of the CPC. Top executives of state-owned electricity companies, oil companies, banks, automotive companies, and construction companies are nominated and "coordinated" by the CPC. This explicit Party control is one of the main causes of political concerns over Chinese investment in the US, especially those from SOEs (Ohashi, 2016).

During the reform and opening-up period, China witnessed a fall in the share of SOEs' industrial output, while that of the private-sector has risen continuously, as shown in Figure 3.3. In this sense, the reform and opening-up period was synonymous with privatization. However, since the 2008 global financial crisis, large-scale fiscal expenditures by both the central and local governments have been conducted to stimulate the economy. This has led to debates in China on the possibilities that it could lead to excessive expansion of the state-owned sector; the so called "state advances, and private retreats (*Guojin Mintui*)" controversy (Kato et al., 2013; Lardy, 2014). Official industrial statistics do not suggest any significant expansion in the overall share of the state-owned sector output since the 2000s. Nonetheless, some industries do have remarkably high proportions of SOEs outputs, including the power industry, the oil and gas industry, the tobacco industry, and most importantly, the financial sector. Also, a four trillion RMB stimulus package after the global financial crisis led to increases in local government debt and declines in investment efficiency (World Bank and DRC, China, 2019). Therefore, although the Xi Jinping administration repeatedly has been emphasizing the importance of the market mechanism and related reforms, some of foreign observers remain skeptical about the continuity of those reforms (Lardy, 2019).

Nevertheless, the Chinese economy is far from a pure state-led economy. Instead, it contains mixed ownership. Reforms in different periods has had different dynamics, exerting different influences on the balance and relationships between the state and private businesses (Huang, 2008). As mentioned earlier, Chinese private enterprises were catalysts to form domestic market oriented industrial clusters. Private internet companies have been growing, although financial support from the state banking sector was negligible at the growing process. Tomoo Marukawa, a Japanese economist, claims that China practices "mass capitalism," based on a fact that many of the successful entrepreneurs have started businesses with small amounts of capital (Marukawa, 2013). There is a similar argument that emphasizes the increasingly important roles of the private sector since the 2000s (Lardy, 2014).

3.3.3 Quality of growth and the challenge of "getting old before getting rich"

According to the IMF forecast cited in Figure 3.1, the Chinese economy will account for 58% of the GDP of East and Southeast Asia in 2020. China's growth or stagnation will both have significant effects on the region's economic outlook. The stability of China's economy has thus become an important issue for the Asian economy.

China's economy has been experiencing lower growth rates since 2010, clearly demonstrating the end of double-digit growth (see Figure 3.2). The annual growth rate has declined from 10.6% in 2010 to 6.1% in 2019, amidst newly evolving challenges. The first challenge is related to the "quality of growth." From an expenditure perspective, a country's GDP (Y) can be decomposed into consumption (C), government expenditure (G), investment (I), and net exports (NEX). The share of investment (I) was remarkably high during the 2000s, while that of consumption (C) tended to stagnate. Figure 3.4 shows per capita GDP on the horizontal axis and the ratio of investment (I) to GDP on the vertical axis (capital formation ratio). The size of each bubble indicates the relative size of GDP. China is located at the center of the figure, having reached a 45.4% capital formation ratio as of 2015. Although some countries' ratios are even higher than that of China, capital formation tends to decline with economic development. China's position is far from the global average, implying a potential risk to the sustainability of its development. Although capital investment is indispensable for economic growth, the return on investment will inevitably diminish. For this reason, the limitations of an investment-led growth have been identified for a long time, but the economic structure that encourages public investment has been continuing.

The Chinese government aims to shift the investment-led growth structure that has supported its phenomenal growth performance in the past into one stimulated

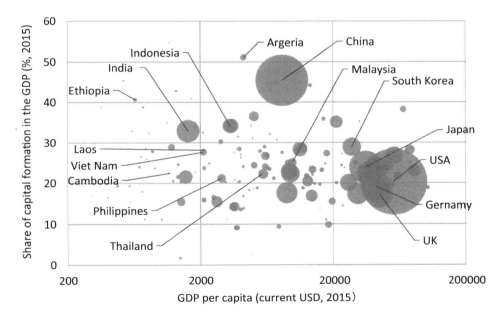

FIGURE 3.4 Capital formation ratio and economic development (2015).

Source: World Bank, World Development Indicators.

Note: The size of each bubble indicates the size of GDP.

by domestic consumption; a transformation towards the "new normal." However, underlying the investment-led growth model is a structural problem rooted in local government budget and revenue financing. In order to secure fiscal incomes at the local level, a conventional solution often taken by local governments has been to acquire state-owned land cheaply and sell it to real estate developers at a higher price. Such practices were often called "land finance." Such measures were not sustainable in the long term and led to rising property prices. They also caused environmental problems in some localities.

Finally, China's working-age population has also peaked in 2010. This will have significant impacts on the country's long-term growth trajectory. Given the fact that China's total fertility rate is far below that of other upper-middle-income economies, the country faces a serious risk of what is called the "getting old before getting rich" phenomenon, whereby per capita GDP would stagnate at the middle-income level (Cai, 2016). The ageing of its society is especially evident in rural areas, due to large-scale migration of the working-age population to urban areas. The average age of the overall population is predicted to rise rapidly in late 2020s. Establishing social safety nets and care services for the elderly will become urgent issues, which will also accompany increased social burden in the future (see Chapter 10). To avoid the potential risks of the "getting old before getting rich" phenomenon and the middle-income trap, improving productivity through innovation will be crucial for China (see Chapter 7).

CONCLUSION

China has promoted market mechanisms and openness since the late 1970s. Looking back on the past 40 years, China has also adopted the export-oriented industrialization strategies originally pioneered by Asian NIEs. In this sense, the 1980s–1990s marked the period when the Asian economy had changed China. In the 2000s, especially with China's accession to the WTO in 2001, Asia entered a new stage in which China became fully integrated into its regional economy. Although ASEAN countries initially considered increased economic links with China as a threat, the increase and deepening of intra-Asian trade, as discussed in Chapter 2, has played out in a win-win relationship in which both prospered.

China has become the largest economy in Asia since 2010 and started to exert strong influence on the Asian and world economy through trade, investment, and macro-regional initiatives. The growing presence of China in terms of production, consumption, and investment has led to new opportunities as well as challenges and risks. It used to be said that "If the US sneezes, the Japanese and Asian economy will catch cold." Nowadays, that saying might as well be updated to replace the US with China. The Asian economy has entered into an era where it is inevitably affected by the unfolding dynamics of the Chinese economy.

BOX 3 The Belt and Road Initiative (BRI)

Asei Ito

The BRI was proposed in 2013 by the Chinese government as a regional economic and diplomatic strategy covering the Eurasian continent and beyond. The Silk Road Fund and the Asian Infrastructure Investment Bank (AIIB) were established in 2014 to support the initiative. The BRI connects China and Europe through the "silk road economic belt" via Central Asia and Russia by land, and through the "21st Century Maritime Silk Road" via the Malacca Straits and the Suez Canal by sea. The geographical scope of the initiative has further expanded to cover Africa and Latin America in addition to Europe.

The outline of the BRI was first introduced in the "Vision and Actions on Jointly Building Silk Road Economic Belt and 21st-Century Maritime Silk Road," which was issued jointly by three divisions of the Chinese government in March 2015. The initiative included the promotion of policy dialog, the improvement of transport and energy infrastructure connectivity, the promotion of mutual trade, financial cooperation including internationalization of the RMB, and the promotion of mutual understanding through measures such as student exchanges. These initiatives were discussed and endorsed at major international conferences held in Beijing in May 2017 and April 2019, with representatives from Asia, Europe, and Africa.

This policy is based on the expectation that economic development in the target countries and deepening trade and investment relations with China would benefit both the host countries and China in realizing higher economic growth. However, according to data on foreign investment by Chinese companies, investment in emerging countries has been sluggish from 2013 to 2018. Instead, private enterprises in China are more focused on acquiring advanced technologies, know-how, and brands through investments in developed countries. At present, Chinese SOEs are leading investment in emerging countries, which is spurring controversies because of China's state-capitalist nature, as discussed in this chapter. Typically, a large amount of Chinese lending to developing economies is often criticized as "debt diplomacy."

Even if the real outcome is limited, however, the symbolic political implications of this China-led initiative are obvious. Central and Southeast Asian countries are making efforts to align their own economic development strategies to the BRI, through exchanges of Memorandum of Understandings (MOU). In addition to the construction of hard infrastructure such as highways, high-speed railways and ports, Chinese e-commerce giants such as Alibaba and Tencent are also accelerating their move into emerging countries particularly in Southeast Asia.

REFERENCES

Bramall, Chris. (2006). *The Industrialization of Rural China*. Oxford: Oxford University Press.
Bremmer, Ian. (2010). *The End of the Free Market: Who wins the war between states and corporations?* New York: Portfolio.
Cai, Fang. (2016). *China's Economic Growth Prospects: From Demographic Dividend to Reform Dividend*. Cheltenham, UK: Edward Elgar.
Cai, Fang, Ross Garnaut, and Ligang Song. (2018). "40 Years of China's Reform and Development: How Reform Captured China's Demographic Dividend," in Ross Garnaut, Ligang Song, and Cai Fang eds. *China's 40 Years of Reform and Development; 1978–2018*, pp. 5–25. Acton: Australian National University Press.
Department of Comprehensive Statistics of National Bureau of Statistics, China. (2010). *China Compendium of Statistics 1949–2008* [*Xin Zhongguo Liushinian Tongji Ziliao Huibian*]. Beijing: China Statistics Press [in Chinese].
Ding, Ke. (2012). *Market Platforms, Industrial Clusters and Small Business Dynamics: Specialized Markets in China*. Cheltenham, UK: Edward Elgar.
Fuji Chimera Research Institute. (2017). *World-wide Electronics Market Report 2017*. [*Warudo Waido Electoronikusu Shijo Sochousa 2017*]. Tokyo: Fuji Keizai Group [in Japanese].
Gao, Yuning. (2012). *China as the Workshop of the World: An Analysis at the National and Industrial Level of China in the International Division of Labor*. Oxon: Routledge.
Ganne, Bernard and Yveline Lecler eds. (2009). *Asian Industrial Clusters, Global Competitiveness and New Policy Initiatives*. Singapore: World Scientific.
Huang, Yasheng. (2008). *Capitalism with Chinese Characteristics: Entrepreneurship and the state*. Cambridge, UK: Cambridge University Press.
Ito, Asei. (2017). "Bottom-up Industrialization in the People's Republic of China: A Case Study of Industries Producing Small Things in Zhejiang," in Kazuko Furuta and Linda Grove eds. *Imitation, Counterfeiting and the Quality of Goods in Modern Asian History*, pp. 245–281. Singapore: Springer.
Kato, Hiroyuki, Mariko Watanabe, and Hideo Ohashi. (2013). *China in 21st Century: Light and Shadow of the State Capitalism* [*21 Seiki no Chugoku: Kokka Shihonsyugi no Hikari to Kage*]. Tokyo: Asahi Shinbun Publishing [in Japanese].
Komiya, Ryutaro. (1987). "Japanese Firms, Chinese Firms: Problems for Economic Reform in China," *Journal of the Japanese and International Economies*, Volume 1, Issue 1, pp. 31–61.
Kubo, Toru, Jun Kajima, and Yoshinori Kigoshi. (2016). *Economic History of Modern China: An Approach based on Statistical Data* [*Toukei de Miru Chugoku Kingendai Keizaishi*]. Tokyo: University of Tokyo Press [in Japanese].
Kuroda, Atsuro. (2001). *Made in China* [*Meido in Chaina*]. Tokyo: Toyo Keizai Publishing [in Japanese].
Lardy, Nicholas. (2014). *Markets over Mao: The Rise of Private Business in China*. Washington: Peterson Institute for International Economics.
Lardy, Nicholas. (2019). *The State Strikes Back: The End of Economic Reform in China?* Washington: Peterson Institute for International Economics.

Lewis, W. Arthur. (1954). "Economic Development with Unlimited Supplies of Labour," *The Manchester School*, Volume 22, pp. 139–191.

Lin, Justin Yifu, Fang Cai and Zhou Li. (1997). *The China Miracle: Development Strategy and Economic Reform*. Hong Kong: The Chinese University Press.

Marukawa, Tomoo. (2013). *Chinese Dream: Mass Capitalism Which Change the World* [*Cyainizu Dorimu: Taishu Shihonshugi ga Sekai wo Kaeru*]. Tokyo: Chikuma Press [in Japanese].

Minami, Ryoshin, and Xinxin Ma. (2010). "The Lewis Turning Point of Chinese Economy: Comparison with Japanese Exprerience," *China Economic Journal*, Volume 3, Issue 2, pp. 163–179.

Minami, Ryoshin, and Fumio Makino eds. (2014). *Asian Historical Statistics: China* [*Ajia Cyoki Keizai Tokei 3 Cyugoku*]. Tokyo: Toyo Keizai Press.

Nakagane, Katsuji. (2012). *Development Economics and Modern China* [*Kaihatsu Keizaigaku to Gendai Cyugoku*]. Nagoya: Nagoya University Press.

Naughton, Barry. (1995). *Growing Out of the Plan: Chinese Economic Reform, 1978–1993*. Cambridge: Cambridge University Press.

Nolan, Peter. (2012). *Is China Buying the World?* Cambridge, UK: Polity.

Ohashi, Hideo. (2016). "Chinese Company's Investment in the United States: What Is the Ooint of Dispute? [Chugoku Kigyo no Taibei Toushi: Masatsu Atsureki no Soten ha Nanika]," in Hiroyuki Kato and Kai Kajitani eds. *The Chinese Capitalism beyond Two Traps* [*Nizhu no Wana wo Koete Susumu Chugoku gata Shihon Shugi*]. Kyoto: Minerva Press.

Office of the United States Trade Representative, Executive Office of the President. (2018). "Findings of the Investigation into China's Acts, Policies, and Practices Related to Technology Transfer, Intellectual Property, and Innovation under Section 301 of the Trade Act of 1974," March 22.

Watanabe, Yukio. (2016). *An Inquiry into the Industrial Development in Modern China: Logic of Development based on Field Survey on Manufacturing Sector*. Tokyo: Keio University Press.

World Bank and Developing Research Center, China. (2019). *Innovative China: New drivers of growth*. Washington: World Bank.

Wu, Jinglian. (2003). *Economic Reform in Contemporary China* [*Dangdai Zhongguo Jingji Gaige*]. Shanghai: Shanghai Yuandong Press [in Chinese].

PART II
Borderless Asia

4 Factory Asia: global value chains and local firm development

Momoko Kawakami and Kenta Goto

A garment factory in Hung Yen Province, Vietnam, catering for exports to the EU and US markets (2008, Photo by Kenta Goto).

LEARNING GOALS

- Understand the industrialization process in Asia, and the evolution of international production networks in Asia.
- Understand the Global Value Chains perspective.
- Understand the prospect of local firms in Asia within this structure of international division of labor.

INTRODUCTION

Over the past few decades, Asia has attained phenomenal economic growth and emerged into a global manufacturing hub, often referred to as "the world's factory" or "Factory Asia." In 1985, Asia accounted for 28% of the world's total exports of machinery and transportation equipment (SITC 7), and for iron and steel (SITC 67) as well. By 2015, these shares had risen to 44% and 36%, respectively. Exports of digital hardware products are even more heavily concentrated on East Asia, especially in China, South Korea, and Taiwan: the three economies together accounted for 50% of the world's total exports of HS 8471 (automatic data processing machines) and 63% of HS 8542 (electronic integrated circuits), respectively (Global Trade Atlas database).

The rise of Asia as the world's factory took place as the process of globalization and economic integration started to accelerate in the mid-1980s and spread to late-coming ASEAN countries after the 2000s. To understand the dynamism that gave rise to "Factory Asia," we must explore the driving forces behind the process, which were crucial in the formation and development of global production and distribution networks that cut across country borders. In so doing, this chapter employs the global value chain (GVC) framework. The term GVC refers to a string of activities that are required to bring a good or service from product planning through the different phases of production, to delivery to final consumers (Cattaneo et al., 2010). The GVC framework helps us understand how global production networks are organized and how the strategies of powerful firms from industrial economies (or lead firms) shape the growth opportunities of local firms from developing economies.

This chapter is organized as follows. We will first look at the history of the changing drivers of industrialization in the region since the 1970s through to the 2000s. We will then explore how the dynamism of GVCs has shaped growth trajectories of local firms and industries in Asian countries. We will further turn to industry cases as examples, particularly the Vietnamese apparel industry and the Taiwanese notebook PC industry and explore how the dynamics of GVCs have shaped trajectories of local firm development.

4.1 INDUSTRIALIZATION IN ASIA AND THE SHIFTING ENGINES OF GROWTH OF THE GLOBAL ECONOMY

4.1.1 The era of international trade: to the 1970s

From the early to the mid-20th century, the main forces that drove the industrialization of Asia and its integration into the world economy were expansions of international trade. The major pattern of international trade in this phase was the traditional North-South trade, in which industrialized economies of the "North" produced and exported capital intensive manufacturing goods while importing labor intensive products and agricultural commodities from developing economies of the "South."

Table 4.1 summarizes the top three export commodities of Taiwan and South Korea in 1962, and of (Peninsula) Malaysia and Thailand in 1970. The trade structures of Asian economies in those years reflected classical patterns of international division of labor, as is predicted by the Heckscher-Ohlin model, which postulates that trade between countries with different relative endowments of factors of production can improve economic efficiency.

Since the mid-1960s, this trade pattern started to change. Asian economies have undergone transformations and evolved from exporters of primary commodities and labor-intensive industrial products to producers of a wide range of more advanced industrial goods, including technology-oriented, high-tech products, and components. This was triggered by rapid expansion of foreign direct investment in the region.

TABLE 4.1 Top 3 export and import products/commodities

1962

	South Korea				Taiwan			
	Export		Import		Export		Import	
1	Raw silk	7%	Ginned cotton	8%	Sugar	21%	Machinery and tools	16%
2	Fresh fish	6%	Textile yarn and threat	6%	Textile products	16%	Ores, metals, and products	14%
3	Tangsten ores	6%	Wheat	6%	Chemicals	9%	Raw cotton	11%

1970

	Thailand				Malaysia (Peninsula only)			
	Export		Import		Export		Import	
1	Cereals	31%	Boilers, machinery and mechanical appliances	16%	Rubber	49%	Road motor vehicles	10%
2	Rubber and synthetic rubbers	16%	Mineral fuels, oils and waxes	9%	Tin and tin-in-concentrates	30%	Petroleum and petroleum products	6%
3	Tin and articles thereof	11%	Electrical machinery and equipment	7%	Palm oil	7%	Iron and sttel and alloys of steels	5%

Source: Major Statistics of Korean Economy, Taiwan Statistical Data Book, Statistical Yearbook Thailand, Statistical Handbook of Peninsular Malaysia, various years.

4.1.2 The era of foreign direct investment and diffusion of industrialization: from the 1980s

Foreign direct investment (FDI) refers to cross-border investment in which an investor in one economy establishes a lasting interest in, and a significant degree of influence over, an enterprise in another economy (OECD iLibrary[1]). The establishment of new factories by Japanese automobile manufacturers in China, or the acquisition of local banking institutions by American financial corporations in Thailand, are typical examples of FDI. Inflows of FDI, especially those by manufacturing companies, are expected to trigger the economic growth of recipient countries, as FDI generates employment and sources of foreign currency earning. And more importantly, foreign investments accompany cross-border diffusion of technologies and managerial knowledge, which are scarce resources in developing economies.

FDI became a central engine of industrialization in Asia after the mid-1960s, when South Korea, Taiwan, Hong Kong and Singapore – the economies referred to as Asian "NIEs" (Newly Industrializing Economies) – launched export-oriented, outward-looking industrial policies. In this process, governments encouraged inward foreign direct investments, bonded processing, and other export-oriented manufacturing activities. These economies imported manufacturing equipment and machinery, components and other intermediate goods from industrialized countries including the US and Japan, while exporting labor intensive products to these economies. Major exporters in these countries were foreign investors in the early phase, which were later replaced by local firms, which emerged as the main pillar of their exporting sectors.

The historic Plaza Accord, which was signed in 1985, prompted rapid appreciation of the Japanese yen and other currencies of Asian NIEs against the US dollar. Together with the rise of wages that had unfolded in these countries over years, the rapid appreciation of currencies affected the export sectors of Japan and Asian NIEs negatively, leading to massive outflows of investments to Thailand, Malaysia and other ASEAN countries. Socialist economies such as China and Vietnam had launched market-oriented economic reforms in the late 1970s and mid-80s, respectively, and soon became major recipients of FDI as well. In the early to mid-2000s, the wave of FDIs reached late-industrializing ASEAN economies, i.e. Cambodia, Laos and Myanmar.

Relocation of manufacturing sites by multinational enterprises (MNEs) contributed to the expansion of cross-border trade of equipment and components, leading to the formation of region-wide production networks. This resulted in changes in the regional trade structure. The share of intermediate goods in total trade rose from 44% in 1980 to 65% in 2015, accelerating the phenomena that is referred to as "Asianizing Asia" (see Chapter 2). Trade patterns of Asian countries shifted from traditional inter-industry and inter-regional trade as formulated in the North-South trade model and Heckscher-Ohlin model to a more horizontal one in which intra-industry and intra-regional trade have become dominant.

Relocation of manufacturing activities across borders typically is accompanied by international diffusion of technologies. Suppose a Japanese motorcycle manufacturer J invests in Thailand. After the launch of production in Thailand, Firm J assembles motorcycles using equipment, components and materials imported from Japan to meet its quality standards. As its operation matures, Firm J will start searching for local suppliers and train them in order to avoid currency risks and delivery costs. Along with Firm J's efforts to train the employees of their subsidiary, its commitment to help local suppliers would also lead to develop capabilities of the local manufacturing sector in Thailand. In this way, Firm J's foreign investment in Thailand generates not only employment opportunities, but would also spread advanced technologies and managerial resources across borders. The growth of FDI thus will fuel economic growth in the host country, which in turn results in the expansion of domestic markets in these economies.

4.1.3 The era of global production networks: from the 2000s

FDI has continued to play a pivotal role as an engine of industrialization and expansion of intra-industry trade after the turn of the 21st century. In addition, international trade among independent firms has expanded significantly, becoming another central pillar of economic development and global integration in the 2000s. Especially noteworthy is the growth of international outsourcing. Typical examples of this include outsourcing practices in the production of iPhones and iPads by Apple to one of the gigantic EMS (electronics manufacturing service) firms based in Taiwan, Hon Hai (Foxconn). Another is the subcontracting arrangements in footwear, between brand-owners such as Nike and Taiwanese and Korean footwear subcontractors that operate in countries such as China, Vietnam, and Indonesia.

The growth of international outsourcing is often associated with the phenomena called "fragmentation." Fragmentation refers to a splitting up of a previously integrated production processes into two or more segments ("fragments") that may enter international trade (Jones and Kierzkowski, 2001). Factors that have contributed to the increasing fragmentation over the past few decades include the following. First, advanced technology and lower costs of services have enabled businesses to disperse the production process geographically (Arndt and Kierzkowski, 2001). Second, increasing modularity of product architecture, especially in the electronics sector, has lowered cross-border trade costs and accelerated the "slicing up" of production processes on a global basis. Third, the rise in technological capabilities of Asian firms due to massive inflows of FDI, and investments in education and human training made by Asian governments over past decades, have enhanced the technological capabilities of local firms, and made international subcontracting arrangements that save fixed investment costs and lock-in costs more attractive.

All these factors have contributed to the expansion of global outsourcing, leading to further inclusion and integration of late-industrializing economies into global production networks. The next section will introduce the GVCs perspective, a framework that helps to understand how the progressive fragmentation of production has shaped the growth trajectories of local firms in Asia, and has changed the industrial landscape of the Asian economy.

4.2 THE GLOBAL VALUE CHAINS PERSPECTIVE[2]

The GVC perspective, an analytical framework proposed by an inter-disciplinary group of scholars in the early 2000s, investigates the global organization of "value chains," i.e. the vertical sequence of value-adding activities that are required to bring a product or service from conception through to production, and delivery to final producer (Gereffi et al., 2001).

One of the central concepts of the GVC perspective is the *governance* of value chains by *lead firms*. Very often, GVCs are coordinated by powerful firms that tend to emanate from developed economies and set product strategy, place orders, and take financial responsibility for the goods and services delivered to consumers (Sturgeon, 2009). Lead firms set and enforce the parameters under which others in the chains operate. These parameters include: what to be produced (product definition), how it is to be produced (definition of production process), when it is to be produced (delivery), and how much is to be produced (quantity) (Humphrey and Schmitz, 2001). In addition to these, lead firms may also set the price under which suppliers operate. The action of setting and enforcing these parameters is referred to as value chain governance by lead firms.

Lead firms can be global buyers with or without production of their own, or global producers. Gereffi (1994) calls the chains governed by the former type of lead firms "buyer-driven" value chains, while those coordinated by the latter "producer-driven" value chains.

The former chains are common in consumer-oriented industries such as apparel and footwear, while the latter are found more in technology-and capital-intensive manufacturing sectors such as the automobile and aircraft industries. Regardless of the type of chain governance, lead firms have the power to shape growth trajectories of supplier firms.

Another key concept of the GVC perspective is *upgrading*. Gereffi et al. (2001) define "upgrading" as several kinds of shifts that firms undertake to improve their positions in GVCs. While the particular classifications of upgrading differ according to scholars and literature, four types of upgrading are typically identified; (1) process upgrading (upgrading by transforming inputs into outputs more efficiently), (2) product upgrading (upgrading by shifting to more sophisticated product lines), (3) intra-chain upgrading (upgrading by acquiring new functions in the chain), and (4) inter-chain upgrading (upgrading by applying the competence to a new sector) (Gerefffi et al., 2001; Goto, 2014).

With these key concepts, the GVC framework helps to analyze how global industries are organized and coordinated. It is also useful to determine how asymmetric power relationships between lead firms and suppliers, and the strategies of lead firms, can affect the growth trajectories of local firms in Asia. In the next section, we will look at two cases – the Vietnamese apparel industry and the Taiwanese PC industry – and examine the experiences of those local firms in GVCs, with respect to integration into these chains as well as upgrading.

4.3 LOCAL INDUSTRIES AND FIRMS IN GVCs

4.3.1 The Vietnamese apparel industry: integration into GVCs and upgrading

4.3.1.1 Developing countries and the apparel industry

The GVCs of the apparel industry are typically buyer-driven, coordinated by retailers, brand owners, and trading companies. These chains tend to be organized through non-equity based inter-firm relationships, similar to footwear as mentioned earlier.

The apparel industry is an archetypal industry in which developing countries with abundant labor have international comparative advantage, and serve as a springboard for industrial development. In the apparel industry, the assembly function, which is often referred to as Cut, Make and Trim (CMT), is highly labor intensive. As such, these functions are usually carried out by garment companies in developing countries that are richly endowed with relatively cheap labor.

The apparel industry was one of the key industries which spearheaded Japan's post-war economic development, primarily through exports to the US, and to a smaller extent, to the European market during the 1950s and 60s. Japan's apparel sector became integrated into the global economy through value chains led by buyers from these developed countries. This induced significant technological transfer from American and European buyers to Japanese garment manufacturing companies, which further allowed them to upgrade in terms of process and products within the labor intensive CMT function.

The Japanese apparel sector, however, started losing international competitiveness in the mid-1960s as wage levels started to increase. This prompted Japanese garment and trading companies to relocate the labor intensive CMT processes to Asian NIEs, where wage levels were much lower. As development took place and wage levels in these Asian NIEs also rose, similar relocation happened to China and ASEAN countries including Thailand and Malaysia, and eventually to late-coming ASEAN countries such as Vietnam and Cambodia. The so-called flying geese pattern was at work, as discussed in Chapter 2.

During this phase, the Japanese apparel industry experienced a fundamental change: the Japanese apparel companies started to shift their market orientation from exports to domestic sales. While it had become difficult for Japanese apparel firms to compete in the labor intensive assembly functions in exports, its domestic market became increasingly attractive as economic development pushed up the purchasing power of its population, creating a significant consumer base. Japanese apparel firms started targeting their own market, by undertaking other functions such as designing, branding and marketing of the products. The labor intensive CMT functions were offshored to neighboring countries in Asia. It was in such a context that Japanese apparel firms evolved as *lead firms* coordinating production networks in Asia.

4.3.1.2 Vietnam's integration into the global economy through the apparel industry

The case of Vietnam's apparel industry provides a good example of how developing countries in Asia have been integrated into the wider regional and global economy; what this implies to economic upgrading; and the concomitant challenges as well as prospects. Table 4.2 presents an overview of the top ten apparel exporters in the world since 2000. The table suggests that China has been the world's largest exporter of apparel throughout. If we add the apparel exports from Bangladesh, India, and Sri Lanka to that of total ASEAN and China (including Hong Kong and Macao), then this area accounted for 62% of the world apparel exports in 2015. Even when excluding the three South Asian countries, it accounted for 51%, suggesting the importance of Asia as the main supplier in the global apparel market. Within this, Vietnam's share of apparel exports has also been rising significantly; it became the third largest exporter in the world in 2015, after China and Bangladesh.

The foundation of Vietnam's export-oriented apparel industry was established when the country's *Doi Moi* (renovation) policy was introduced in 1986. Prior to *Doi Moi*, Vietnam already had an extensive production base of textiles and garments which primarily supplied to the Soviet Union and Eastern European economic block under the Council of Mutual Economic Assistance (COMECON) framework. The industry was, however, lagging far behind its Western counterparts in terms of quality and productivity. Substantial changes started to occur as business linkages were established with Japanese buyers in the early 1990s, who coordinated value chains to the Japanese market. Orders for the CMT functions in Japanese market-oriented GVCs were taken up by state-owned garment companies, where transfer of technology from Japanese buyers has been significant. This contributed to the process and product upgrading of the Vietnamese garment companies (Goto et al., 2011).

The development of Vietnam's export-oriented apparel industry gained momentum as its diplomatic relationship with the US was improving in the late 1990s. When

TABLE 4.2 Major apparel exporters in the world (unit: million $)

	2000			2005			2010			2015		
1	China	32,290	17.6%	China	65,902	24.6%	China	121,072	34.9%	China	162,349	37.4%
2	Hong Kong (China)	22,696	12.3%	Hong Kong (China)	25,569	9.6%	Hong Kong (China)	22,884	6.6%	Bangladesh	26,532	6.1%
3	Italy	12,453	6.8%	Italy	17,656	6.6%	Italy	18,567	5.4%	Vietnam	21,434	4.9%
4	Mexico	8,432	4.6%	Germany	11,720	4.4%	Germany	16,944	4.9%	Italy	19,400	4.5%
5	US	8,128	4.4%	Turkey	11,453	4.3%	Bangladesh	14,845	4.3%	Hong Kong (China)	17,446	4.0%
6	Germany	6,456	3.5%	India	8,201	3.1%	Turkey	12,367	3.6%	India	17,131	3.9%
7	Turkey	6,183	3.4%	France	7,826	2.9%	India	10,604	3.1%	Germany	16,657	3.8%
8	India	5,465	3.0%	Mexico	7,163	2.7%	Vietnam	10,119	2.9%	Turkey	14,845	3.4%
9	France	5,019	2.7%	Bangladesh	6,846	2.6%	France	9,221	2.7%	Spain	11,874	2.7%
10	Indonesia	4,562	2.5%	Belgium	6,393	2.4%	Spain	7,450	2.1%	France	9,775	2.3%
	Asia	85,303	46.4%	Asia	131,186	49.1%	Asia	197,655	57.0%	Asia	269,339	62.0%
	Total	183,918		Total	267,368		Total	346,527		Total	434,134	

Source: Prepared by the author using UN Comtrade.
Note: Asia in this table includes ASEAN, China (including Hong Kong, Macao), and India, Bangladesh, and Sri Lanka.

the US–Vietnam Bilateral Trade Agreement (BTA) was signed, and came into effect in 2001, exports to the US surged. The US soon replaced Japan as the largest importer of Vietnam's apparel. Vietnam also initiated state-owned enterprise (SOE) reforms, which led to diversification of export-oriented garment companies. Private and foreign invested companies emerged, stimulating further growth of the industry. As apparel exports continued to grow, they overtook the positions of previous key export items, mostly those in the primary sector such as crude oil, and garments soon became the largest export industry of Vietnam. This reflected the fact that Vietnam's overall export structure was undergoing substantial changes; from the primary and resource-based sectors towards one based on manufacturing.

It is important to note that not all processes in the apparel industry are labor intensive, in which developing countries exhibit comparative advantage. While the labor intensive CMT function is suitable for countries endowed with abundant and cheap labor, others are of different factor intensities, where *lead firms* in developed countries play crucial roles. Figure 4.1 describes the production flow of apparel on the horizontal axis, and their relative value-added on the vertical axis. The processes and functions that come at the beginning and end of the production flow are typically of the highest value-added. On the other hand, the labor intensive assembly functions (CMT) tend to be of the lowest value-added, and input material supply and sourcing come somewhere in-between. As such, the figure depicts a U-shaped curve, which is often referred to as the "smile curve."

In the apparel industry, knowledge-intensive functions including product specification, branding, and marketing, are key. Such functions entail significant risks stemming from market uncertainties, and managing these require significant amount of

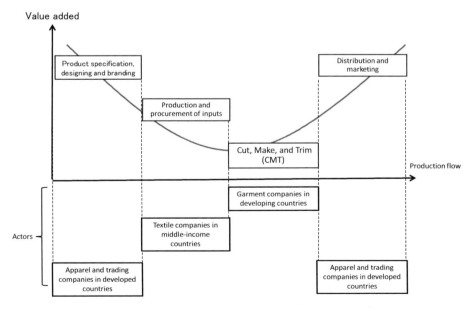

FIGURE 4.1 The production flow and value-added in the apparel industry.
Source: Goto (2014).

knowledge. As such, those functions are normally undertaken by *lead firms* in developed countries. The production processes of fabrics, on the other hand, are more capital intensive, where middle-income countries such as China and Thailand have comparative advantages. The labor intensive CMT function depends on workers with generic skills, and therefore entry barriers are the lowest. Vietnam's competitiveness has been confined almost entirely within this particular function.

4.3.1.3 Future opportunities and challenges of the Vietnamese apparel industry

Vietnam has achieved considerable economic development in the 21st century, in which the apparel sector has played a pivotal role. This however has been accompanied by increases in wage levels, which have eroded Vietnam's competitiveness in the labor intensive CMT functions. While the negative effects of such wage increases could be offset by process and product upgrading, this becomes increasingly difficult as such prospects diminish with the levels of upgrading achieved. In 2011, apparel was replaced by electronics as Vietnam's top foreign currency earner.

Such a situation has led to new challenges for the Vietnamese apparel industry. The evolving question is how to achieve functional upgrading of the domestic industry. Vietnam is currently in a difficult position because new apparel exporting countries such as Bangladesh and Cambodia have the advantages of lower wage levels, and as such have become competitive rivals in the labor intensive CMT function. On the other hand, most of the apparel firms in Vietnam have not yet accumulated enough knowledge and skills to compete in the higher value-added function such as designing and marketing to compete with firms in developed countries. This is a classic case of a middle-income trap. The challenge is therefore to find a way to successfully upgrade functionally, and in this respect, a reorientation from export to the domestic market is one potential option (Goto, 2014).

4.3.2 The Taiwanese Notebook PC Industry: upgrading by subcontracting[3]

4.3.2.1 Case selection

The history of the Taiwanese notebook PC industry is a good example that illustrates how integration of local firms into global production networks helps them to upgrade in high-tech value chains.

The achievements of Taiwanese notebook PC manufacturers are conspicuous in two respects. First, as Figure 4.2 shows, the industry has attained exponential growth in terms of worldwide shipments. The quantity of notebook PCs produced by Taiwanese firms, and Taiwan's share in the world total, grew from 2.6 million sets (27%) in 1995, to 12.7 million sets (52%) in 2000, and to 174.8 million sets (89%) in 2011.[4] Taiwanese firms achieved this growth mainly by acting as subcontractors for brand-holding firms from developed economies: the share of OEM contracts (where the customer provides the design), and ODM contracts (where the contractor carries out some or all of the

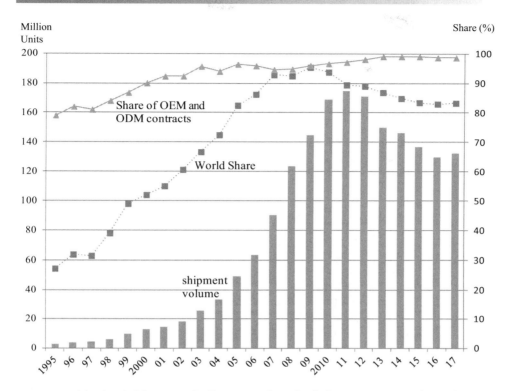

FIGURE 4.2 Notebook PC exports by Taiwanese firms (including overseas production).

Source: Prepared by author, from Market Intelligence & Consulting Institute, various years.

Note: Data from 2011 include mini PCs.

design work), together accounted for over 95% of total production by Taiwanese firms in the 2000s and 2010s.

Second, the functions that Taiwanese subcontractors assume in GVCs have evolved over time. As their production swelled drastically, Taiwanese contract manufacturers started to provide not only manufacturing services but also product design and logistics-related services for their customers, or *lead firms*. After the mid-2000s, they even started to provide design inputs for their customers and the latter started to rely on the former for product planning. Clearly, Taiwanese firms attained remarkable growth both in terms of quantity (a high percentage share in the world's production volume), and quality (successful upgrading in the value chains). Below we present a brief history of the Taiwanese notebook PC industry.

4.3.2.2 Technological changes and emergence of latecomer firms

Notebook PCs were first developed and mass-produced by Japanese electronics firms, i.e. Toshiba and NEC, in 1989. In the early years, PCs' product architecture was highly integral. Designing a portable computer that is light, thin, and solid required superior technological capabilities compared to desk-top computers. Enclosing heat-emitting CPUs and heat-sensitive electronics parts in a small chassis was a tough challenge that required close coordination and integration of a wide range of components, including semiconductors, software, hard disk drives. As a result, vertically-integrated Japanese electronics firms that produce proprietary parts and components in-house, and possessed market channels with established brand names, dominated the market until the mid-1990s.

Starting from the mid-1990s, however, the entry barriers to the industry began to decline and new entrants started to emerge. The main trigger of this change was the strategic actions by Intel, the major supplier of central processing units (CPUs). Intel was motivated to remove technology hurdles facing potential manufacturers of notebook PCs and to lower product prices, and by so doing expand the market for their CPUs. The company was also eager to capture more of the value-added created in the value chains. As a part of its strategy, Intel started to integrate its CPUs with chip-sets to provide turnkey solutions to latecomer firms, encapsulating an increasing range of key product functions and technological knowledge within its chip-sets. This led to the modularization of the notebook PC product. Intel also began to provide "reference guides" to its customers that helped their product development and supported them in dealing with various engineering problems.

All these developments lowered the technological entry barriers which latecomer firms faced. American PC firms like Dell, Compaq and Gateway began to increase outsourcing to reduce costs, and their competitors from Japan and Europe followed suite. Among firms from Asia, Taiwanese firms were best-positioned to tap into the opportunities created by the massive inflow of outsourcing orders. Taiwan has a history in the manufacturing of electronics products and components dating back to the late-1960s, and had accumulated a pool of engineering talents and parts suppliers. Since the early 1980s, Taiwan has developed a large number of OEM/ODM suppliers of desktop PCs and motherboards. These firms naturally tapped into these assets and entered the GVCs led by American and Japanese brand firms.

Under subcontracting arrangements, brand-holding firms often dispatched groups of engineers and managers to train their subcontractors. This led to successful process upgrading and product upgrading by Taiwanese subcontractors. As their manufacturing capabilities were enhanced, the shares of shipments of related products by Taiwanese firms to the world total rose drastically, reaching 49% in 1999.

Over time, Taiwanese firms came to assume more value chain functions. Starting from being OEM suppliers, they began to provide product design services (thereby upgrading into ODM suppliers). They also incorporated more functions over time such as logistic services, product planning and marketing, including the development of new models. Taiwanese firms are successful cases of functional upgrading in the notebook PC value chains.

4.3.2.3 Upgrading in value chains

The spread of high-speed wireless networks in the 21st century boosted demand for mobile computing products. Rapid expansion of the product market associated with intense price competition led to an industry shakeout that gave rise to a small number of gigantic subcontractors such as Quanta and Compal.

The consolidation in the subcontracting market made trading relationships between brand-holding firms and their subcontractors more stable. This also encouraged bi-directional exchange of in-depth information between the two parties. In this process, as brand firms came to share more details about their product strategies and market observations with their subcontractors, Taiwanese subcontractors began to accumulate knowledge about the requirements and preferences of customers and consumers. In addition to this, Intel and other key part suppliers started to share technological and market information with top-tier subcontractors, who came to possess rich engineering resources. Tapping into this knowledge, Taiwanese firms began to develop new models tailored to individual customers (especially for top-priority customers). In this way, Taiwanese subcontractors achieved further functional upgrading in the value chains.

4.3.2.4 Distribution of value added across value chains

While the Taiwanese notebook PC subcontractors have achieved phenomenal growth and attained upgrading in product, process and functions in these value chains, the distribution of value-added across the chains reveals a different picture. Based on seminal work by Dedrick et al. (2009), Figure 4.3 summarizes the gross margins earned by different firms in the value chain of a specific notebook PC launched by Hewlett-Packard (HP) in 2005. As this figure indicates, while HP (the brand firm or *lead firm*), Intel (CPU supplier) and Microsoft (OS vendor) earned 333 USD, 205 USD and 100 USD respectively from this chain, the gross margin of Taiwanese subcontractors was only 24 USD. Xing and Detert (2010) show a similar pattern of value distribution in the case of iPhones. Despite their successful upgrading in value chains and dominant position in the subcontracting market, Taiwanese firms still remain in the position of "suppliers," where profits are competed away by potential entrants and the commoditization of products. In contrast, American firms with powerful technology and market leaderships appropriate larger gross margins in GVCs.[5]

4.3.3 The implications from the GVC framework

The above two cases have each illustrated the potentials of local industrial development through their participation in the evolving international division of labor. The implications from these are as follows.

First, the roles of lead firms in technology transfer to local firms, particularly during their initial stages of integration, have been crucial. Upgrading of local firms of both Vietnam's apparel industry and Taiwan's notebook PC industry were possible because of such technology transfer from Japanese and US buyers and lead producers. Growth trajectories of local firms are thus highly dependent on the capabilities of lead firms.

Second, the patterns of upgrading and the development of local firms depend on their relationships with lead firms. Consider, for example, the case in which a Japanese apparel company establishes a garment factory in Vietnam. As this represents an intra-firm based international division of labor, the Japanese headquarters may have incentives to transfer some of the key technology and knowledge that are related to their core-competence areas to these units in Vietnam. However, such incentives may not arise when

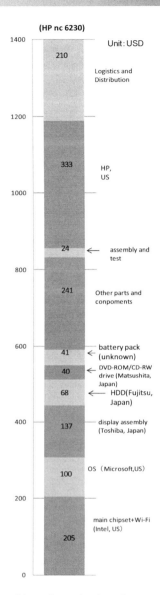

FIGURE 4.3 Gross margins earned by selected value chain participants.
Source: Prepared by author using data from Dedrick et al. (2009).

the relationship is more flexible and does not involve any equity and ownership, as this may in the future threaten the core competencies of the Japanese lead firms. The diffusion of information and technology in GVCs occurs through highly asymmetric power relationships between lead and local firms, where interests are not necessarily aligned particularly in non-equity based inter-firm (buyer–supplier) relationships.

Third, the cases also indicate that suppliers in Asian countries were not always passive in terms of the instructions stemming from strategic decisions of lead firms. During its phenomenal growth, the Taiwanese notebook PC industry was very proactive in accessing and absorbing information and knowledge that were transmitted through value chains. The key was to establish and maintain business relationships with multiple lead firms, and actively apply these new resources to further strengthen its competitiveness. Similarly, the development of the Vietnamese apparel industry was due to the ability of local garment companies to adopt to the rapidly changing economic environment since the implementation of the *Doi Moi* policy as well as the diversification of firm characteristics, particularly in ownership structures, within the industry. The potentials for growth are therefore also dependent on the policies in the local economy, as well as on the strategies of local firms.

The proliferation of GVCs has also induced fundamental changes in the patterns of industrial development of developing countries. As the cases of the apparel and notebook PC industries indicate, local economies and firms were integrated into GVCs by undertaking highly fragmented processes and functions, of which factor intensities and technological attributes matched the factor endowments of those localities. These fragmentation dynamics are occurring across industries, and, as such, local economies tend to be connected to GVCs through processes and functions with similar factor intensities and technological requirements, in different industries. For example, while apparel had been the major export item for Vietnam, it was overtaken by electronics products exports in 2011, whose export volume came to occupy about 30% of the country's total exports in 2015. Because electronics products contain higher technological contents than apparel, it almost looks as if the industrial structure of Vietnam has upgraded to the extent similar to those in high income countries such as Japan or the US. However, the point is that in either sector (electronics or apparel), the processes that Vietnam undertakes in GVCs are labor intensive assembly functions that are of low-skills and technology intensity. Neither of the sectors cater for the knowledge intensive functions including research and development (R&D), product design, and marketing, which are still retained by lead firms in developed countries. Thus, from Vietnam's development point of view, one of the key issues for its future is to attain functional upgrading within their respective value chains, in which local and regional markets could play important roles.

CONCLUSION

This chapter has taken stock of Asia's economic development and integration processes as well as their key drivers since the 1960s. "Factory Asia" has evolved through the following three phases. The first is the expansion of vertical trade relationships with developed countries, in which Asia exported labor intensive industrial goods and primary products and imported capital-intensive manufacturing goods. The second is a rapidly intensifying intra-regional trade structure led by foreign direct investment, which resulted in the establishment of a region-wide production base of industrial products, and the third is the emergence of complex production networks made up of independent firms through various types of interfirm relationships and governance structures. These three phases were, however, not strictly in sequential order; there were significant overlaps, and they often unfolded simultaneously. Foreign direct investment involving the establishment of offshore manufacturing units, or mergers and acquisitions of foreign firms, continues to expand, which in many cases led to generating new employment opportunities as well as transferring technology to local industries. The spread of GVCs that incorporated local firms in the highly fragmented international division of labor has also contributed significantly to the growth of local firms in Asia.

This chapter has shed light on the international dynamics of "Factory Asia" from a rather dichotomic perspective of a "developing Asia" and "developed countries." However, as discussed in Chapter 2 (Asianizing Asia), intra-regional economic interdependence has grown strong particularly in terms of investment. In addition, as discussed in Chapter 7 (Innovating Asia), considering the increasing importance of Asia as a rapidly evolving region of innovation, Asian firms have also emerged to lead and coordinate GVCs alongside their counterparts in developed countries such as Japan and the US. Chapter 8 (Urbanizing Asia) further discusses the pivotal roles Asian cities are playing, particularly as key nodes in GVCs. Asia seem to have embarked into a new era that is bound to new relationships and partnerships in the global economy.

BOX 4 GVCs and corporate social responsibility

Kenta Goto

One of the key issues that was discussed during the 105th session of the International Labour Conference of the International Labour Organization (ILO) was on "Global Supply Chains and Decent Work." The ILO is one of the specialized agencies of the United Nations (UN) system, which takes a unique governance structure involving not just the government, but also the workers' and employers' organizations. The ILO currently has 187 member countries, and major labor and employment-related legislation are in principle set through dialogue within this tripartite structure in each of the countries.

Issues related to Corporate Social Responsibility (CSR) have also been typically addressed through such country-level tripartite structures. Prior to the evolving of GVCs, the production of goods and services was more or less integrated within national and corporate boundaries. As such, country-based tripartite dialogue might have been effective in discussing the various social issues, including labor and employment. As fragmentation dynamics started to take effect, however, such production processes and functions became increasingly disintegrated, leading to geographical dispersion in which various types of firms from different countries were connected through different inter-firm relationships and governance structures, as discussed in this chapter. This is posing new challenges with respect to promoting Decent Work in those value chains.

The Tripartite Declaration of Principles concerning Multinational Enterprises and Social Policy (MNE Declaration) is ILO's key instrument on policies and practices to promote Decent Work in operations of MNEs. It is an instrument to provide direct guidance on enterprise practices. However, in production organized through the evolving GVCs, its efficacy through the traditional country-based tripartite structure is limited. For example, consider a case where children below working ages have been engaged in precarious work in one of the processes in GVCs coordinated by a Japanese MNE at suppliers in offshore locations with no ownership relationship. Dialogues through national-level tripartite structures may not be optimal platforms to discuss effective measures to address such child labor issues because they do not involve the Japanese MNE (lead firm), which are typically the most powerful in exercising control over how their supply chains should operate and how each of the firms involved be managed. This is an important issue given the increased presence of MNEs in Asia.

The author was involved in one of the ILO projects a few years ago called "More and Better Jobs through Socially Responsible Labour Practices in Asia." This Japanese government funded project looked at the Vietnamese electronics sector, which is one of the typical industries where fragmentation dynamics is at play, connecting various firms from different countries through complex interfirm relationships.

In this, data collected through the tripartite structure in Vietnam suggested interesting features; while there were about 1,100 registered firms operating in the industry, 99 firms out of the largest 100 were in fact foreign invested companies (the only Vietnamese firm ranked exactly 100th). These 100 firms employed more than 80% of the total number of workers in the sector, which indicates the dominant positions of foreign firms in this industry. Given this, discussing the labor and employment issues of this sector without the engagement of MNEs that drive the chain will prove ineffective.

As GVCs in the electronics and many other industries have in recent years proliferated to a significant extent, discussions on CSR to promote Decent Work in the contemporary global economy require new mechanisms of dialogue. There should be an extended framework ("tripartite-plus") that goes beyond the traditional, country-based structures. In this, it is crucial to involve headquarters and the home governments of the MNEs (Goto and Arai, 2018).

NOTES

1. https://www.oecd-ilibrary.org.
2. Part of this section is based on Kawakami (2011)
3. Part of this section is based on Kawakami (2011).
4. Starting from 2012, the volume started to decline rapidly partly due to erosion of the notebook PC market by tablets, smartphones, and other high-tech gadgets.
5. Ali-Yrkko et al. (2011) and Xing and Detert (2010) investigated the distribution of financial value across the handset value chain participants and elucidated that platform leaders and lead firms – mostly based in US and Europe at the time – were appropriating large shares of the value, while contract manufacturers based in Asia earned only small shares of the industry's value-added.

REFERENCES

Ali-Yrkkö, Jyrki, Petri Rouvinen, Timo Seppälä, Pekka Ylä-Anttila. (2011). "Who Captures Value in Global Supply Chains? Case Nokia N95 Smartphone." *Journal of Industry, Competition and Trade*, 11(3): 263–278.

Arndt, Sven W. and Henryk Kierzkowski (eds.). (2001). *Fragmentation: New Production Patterns in the World Economy*. Oxford: Oxford University Press.

Cattaneo, Olivier, Gary Gereffi, and Cornelia Staritz. (2010). "Global Value Chains in a Postcrisis World: Resilience, Consolidation, and Shifting End Markets," in Olivier Cattaneo, Gary Gereffi, and Cornelia Staritz (eds.) *Global Value Chains in a Postcrisis World: A Development Perspective*. Washington, DC: The International Bank for Reconstruction and Development/The World Bank.

Dedrick, Jason, Kenneth L. Kraemer and Greg Linden. (2009). "Who Profits from Innovation in Global Value Chains? A Study of the iPod and Notebook PCs." *Industrial and Corporate Change*, 19(1): 81–116.

Gereffi, Gary. (1994). "The Organisation of Buyer-Driven Global Commodity Chains: How U.S. Retailers Shape Overseas Production Networks," in Gary Gereffi and Miguel Korzeniewicz (eds.) *Commodity Chains and Global Capitalism*, Westport, CT: Praeger, 95–122.

Gereffi, Gary, John Humphrey, Raphael Kaplinsky and Timothy J. Sturgeon. (2001). "Introduction: Globalisation, Value Chains and Development." *IDS Bulletin*, 32(3): 1–8.

Goto, Kenta. (2014). "Vietnam: Upgrading from the Export to the Domestic Market," in Takahiro Fukunishi and Tatsufumi Yamagata (eds.) *The Garment Industry in Low-Income Countries: An Entry Point of Industrialization*. Basingstoke and New York: Palgrave Macmillan, 105–131.

Goto, Kenta, Kaoru Natsuda, and John Thoburn. (2011). "Meeting the Challenge of China: The Vietnamese Garment Industry in the Post MFA Era." *Global Networks*, 11(3): 355–379.

Goto, Kenta and Yukiko Arai. (2018). *More and Better Jobs through Socially Responsible Labour and Business Practices in the Electronics Sector of Viet Nam*. Geneva: ILO.

Humphrey, John and Hubert Schmitz. (2001). "Governance in Global Value Chains." *IDS Bulletin*, 32(3): 19–29.

Jones, Ronald W. and Henryk Kierzkowski. (2001). "A Framework for Fragmentation," in Sven W. Arndt and Henryk Kierzkowski (eds.) *Fragmentation: New Production Patterns in the World Economy*. Oxford: Oxford University Press.

Kawakami, Momoko. (2011). "Value Chain Dynamics and Capability Formation by Latecomer Firms in East Asia," in Momoko Kawakami and Timothy J. Sturgeon (eds.) *The Dynamics of Local Learning in Global Value Chains: Experiences from East Asia*. Basingstoke and New York: Palgrave Macmillan, 16–42.

Market Intelligence & Consulting Institute. (various years). *Information Industry Yearbook*. Taipei: Institute for Information Industry.

Sturgeon, Timothy J. (2009). "From Commodity Chains to Value Chains: Interdisciplinary Theory Building in an Age of Globalization," in Jennifer Bair (ed.) *Frontier of Commodity Chain Research*. Stanford, CA: Stanford University Press.

Xing, Yuqing and Neal Detert. (2010). "How the iPhone Widens the United States Trade Deficit with the People's Republic of China." *ADBI Working Paper Series*. No. 257, Asian Development Bank Institute.

5 Capital Asia: growth and capital flows

Fumiharu Mieno and Kenta Goto

Merlion in front of the financial center of Singapore (2016, Photo by Fumiharu Mieno).

LEARNING GOALS

- Understand the mechanisms of investment/re-investment, and the role of foreign capital in economic growth.
- Understand the Asian economy and its relationship with the two financial crises within the context of post-war international capital flows.
- Understand the policies pertinent to the Asian financial system and its future directions.

INTRODUCTION

The Asian financial crisis that erupted in 1997 was a key turning point that triggered awareness of the importance of capital flows and the financial environment in the Asian economy, probably for the first time. As such, these issues are still relatively new and evolving within the Asian economy literature. Nevertheless, it has become practically difficult to understand the emerging issues pertinent to the Asian economy without addressing capital flows and finance.

The "Asian financial crisis" that struck Southeast Asia in 1997 was primarily due to a significant influx of capital into a rapidly growing region. Increased international capital mobility in the 1990s, and the resulting confusion that led to a regional financial crisis was, in fact, a prelude for the subsequent intensive debates on capital control. Meanwhile, a major financial crisis also erupted in the US in the late 2000s, which spilled over to Europe leading to severe fiscal crisis in several countries. This continued well into the late 2010s, culminating almost in a full-fledged Euro crisis. This time, however, Asia had already recovered from its own crisis, and had again picked up growth momentum in its real economy. Unlike its position in the late 1990s, it had also evolved as a global net capital exporter.

Given this context, this chapter will look at the Asian economy from the capital flow and financial points of view. Specifically, it will attempt to understand the dynamics of the Asian economy, using basic conceptual and theoretical frameworks that underpin past, current, and future issues related to capital flows and finance in Asia, while emphasizing the evolving context of the post-war global financial environment.

5.1 INTERNATIONAL CAPITAL FLOWS

5.1.1 Capital and growth

Foreign capital plays increasingly important roles in the accumulation of capital in developing countries, including those in Asia. Compared to the rather traditional savings-investment channels, the inflows of foreign capital allow these countries to accumulate capital at a much faster speed. Most of the Asian economies have been largely successful in this. However, controlling global capital flows has always been difficult. There have been several cases in Asia and elsewhere where such attempts have failed, resulting in wide-spread financial crises. This has often further led to global financial turmoil. In order to fully understand what exactly happened, this chapter starts by reviewing the basic key concepts of capital accumulation and the balance of payments statements.

Figure 5.1 summarizes the role of capital in economic growth. Firms use factors of production such as labor and capital as inputs to produce outputs. The products produced incorporate the values of labor and capital, and the value that has been generated and added through this process. This value-added will be distributed as income from wages, interests, or dividends to households, who are the owners of labor and capital. Households spend part of their income for consumption, and the rest will be saved. These savings are then mobilized for investment. Investment in this context means, for example, the purchase of additional machines used for the production of more industrial outputs. In general, household savings are the basic sources of corporate investment, which are intermediated through financial markets.

Investments will lead to increases in capital stock, which will in turn lead to increased production. As developing countries tend to be much better endowed with labor compared to capital, labor is more intensively used in the production process. On the other hand, a certain proportion of the value-added created through this process is also directed towards capital investment, contributing to increased capital stock. As such, the

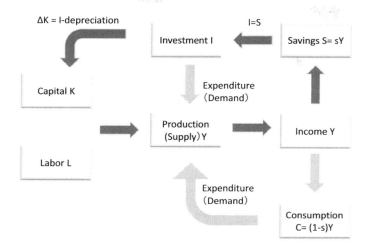

FIGURE 5.1 Economic growth and capital accumulation.
Source: Prepared by author.

process of economic growth, particularly at the initial stages of economic development, can also be interpreted as a conversion of the value-added generated through the labor-intensive production processes into capital. This is the essence that characterizes the relationship between economic growth and capital accumulation.

Modern economic growth theories, however, consider other factors as even more important sources of growth. For example, improvements in productivity through the accumulation of human capital and knowledge is seen as key in "endogenous growth theory." The other is the role of foreign financial resources (capital), which this chapter focuses on.

5.1.2 Capital flows and the balance of payments

The balance of payments table provides a summary of foreign trade and financial transactions for a given country. Figure 5.2 describes how the different types of financial flows are related to each other accordingly. International transactions can be divided into current transactions and capital transactions. Current transactions include general transactions such as trade in goods and services as well as international remittances. Broadly speaking, exports will induce an inflow of funds, and imports will lead to an outflow of funds.

Capital transactions, on the other hand, are the inflow and outflow of capital mainly for the purposes of investment, which is summarized in "financial account." Within capital transactions, flows can be classified into (1) foreign direct investment (FDI), (2) portfolio investment, and (3) others (mainly bank credits and deposits). Within this, the differences in the direction of capital flows; from foreign investors to the domestic economy (inbound), and those from domestic residents to overseas markets (outbound), are important to understand what has underpinned the dynamics of the Asian economy.

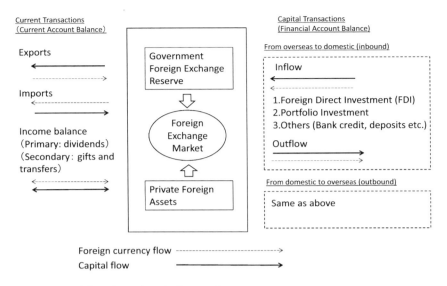

FIGURE 5.2 Capital flow based on balance of payment system.
Source: Prepared by author.

The inflow and outflow of foreign funds by current and capital transactions always accompany currency issues. For example, when foreign funds flow into the domestic economy, foreign currency (which in most cases is the US dollar) must be converted into local currencies. This will generate demand for the local currency. Conversely, to mobilize domestic assets to overseas markets, local currencies must be converted into foreign currencies, leading to increased demand for those foreign currencies (US dollar). The supply and demand of currencies are typically adjusted in foreign exchange markets, where foreign exchange rates are determined as market clearing prices. However, governments often intervene in foreign exchange markets to stabilize exchange rate fluctuations. For example, when the outflow of assets is greater than the inflow, this will increase demand for foreign currency. If the government wants to stabilize and keep the exchange rate at a certain level, then it can sell foreign currencies in the foreign exchange market, which will sterilize depreciation pressures on the local currency. The funds being held by governments, used to intervene into foreign exchange markets are called foreign exchange reserves.

Because foreign currencies cannot be issued domestically, they need to be brought in from abroad. If the current account balance is recording a surplus, then there will be an inflow of foreign currencies. Even when there is a current account deficit, foreign currencies may still flow in when there is a surplus in capital transactions. In such a case, governments can still build up foreign exchange reserves by purchasing those foreign currencies in the domestic market. On the other hand, however, when current account deficits and net outflow in capital account transactions continue, foreign exchange reserves will eventually be depleted.

Sustainability of growth based on foreign capital is thus dependent on whether it can further evolve to generate a vibrant export sector to earn foreign currency in the long run, rather than whether the investment promotes growth of the domestic economy. This is crucial as repayment for the investment has to be made in foreign currencies. For example, if the borrowed funds are allocated for government consumption or to domestic infrastructure construction with low economic returns, then the country may become insolvent in the long run. This is referred to as the solvency problem.

What makes the issue difficult is the fact that drastic short-term fluctuations in capital inflows and outflows can lead to crisis situations, even when the particular country is not in an insolvent condition in the long run. This can happen when there is a sudden, unexpected, and significant capital flight, that exceeds the government's capacities for effective intervention with foreign exchange reserves. When foreign exchange reserves are depleted, government cannot intervene to stabilize and maintain exchange rates, and corporations in the private sector may become insolvent because of the lack of foreign currency. This is exactly what triggered the Asian financial crisis.

5.1.3 Post-war monetary and financial order and capital mobility

5.1.3.1 The Bretton Woods system and currency management

Since the 1990s, international capital flows have significantly impacted the Asian economy. To understand the basic context of this problem, it is useful to take stock of how international currency management systems and capital flow since World War II have changed and evolved over time.

The post war fixed-exchange rate system under the Bretton Woods regime started with the signing and the establishment of the International Monetary Fund (IMF) in December 1945. The US guaranteed full convertibility of the US dollar and gold at a fixed rate, and other countries had to peg their currencies to the US dollar and maintain a fixed exchange rate. Article 8 of the IMF Agreement requires member countries not to impose any foreign exchange restrictions on current account transactions, and to stabilize exchange rates through government interventions (developing countries were provisionally exempted from this rule). The flow of capital was regarded as the vital mechanism to bring international balance of payments into an equilibrium. Liberalization of capital movement accelerated during the 1960s and 1970s.

Under the gold-dollar dual standard regime, market exchange rates between the US dollar and gold needed to be maintained in equilibrium with the official exchange rate, which restricted America's economic policy space. Capital movements increased from the 1960s at a time when the US government debt was also increasing, which led to depreciationary pressures on the US dollar. This made it difficult for the US to maintain the value of the dollar and the entire international monetary system. In August 1971, the US suddenly made an announcement that it would suspend full convertibility of the dollar and gold, and by 1975 most developed countries had shifted to a floating exchange rate system. Even under such changing conditions, however, most developing countries had been allowed to implement current account controls and fixed exchange rate policies.

5.1.3.2 The changes in international capital flows

Maintaining fixed exchange rate systems has become increasingly difficult in developing countries including those in Asia as well, when capital flows have also expanded in these countries. Here, let us first review the trends of capital flows towards developing countries.

The earlier stages of post-war international capital flows to developing countries were predominantly public based. Large-scale aid programs such as the Marshall Plan of the US or loans from institutions such as the World Bank and the Asian Development Bank (established in 1966) flowed not only into Europe and Japan, where national capital stocks had been severely damaged by the war but also into developing countries that just gained independence and were aspiring to build a strong economic base as independent and sovereign countries, on very favorable terms and conditions.

Figure 5.3 summarizes the trends of capital inflow into developing countries in the Asia Pacific region from 1970 and onwards. As there was a sudden increase in capital flows in the 1990s, the figure is divided into two; note that the upper and lower vertical axes are on one-digit different scales. The average share of public funds in total inflows during 1970–1973 was 29.5%, rising to 42.4% when FDI and debt financing instruments are included.

This drastically changed in the first part of the 1970s when there was a rapid expansion of oil money. The funds of oil exporting countries that were gained during the oil crisis were deposited at commercial banks in Europe and the US, which were then channeled into developing countries. Figure 5.3 suggests that while the influx of public funds in the 1970s was still significant, private debt financing instruments (such as bank credit and bonds) increased much faster. When the second oil shock broke out in the late 1970s, developed countries turned towards monetary tightening policies to curb inflation, which led to a global recession. This triggered a financial crisis in developing countries in Latin America, which had significant outstanding bank debt financed by oil money. The crisis in Poland in 1981 and that of Mexico in 1982 were just the beginnings of wide-spread defaults in the world. This is usually referred to as the "Accumulated-Debt Problem of the 1980s."

In response, the US took initiatives to address and coordinate this debt problem, and at the same time to arrange for the implementation of macroeconomic "structural adjustment programs" in those defaulting countries. "Structural adjustment" refers to sets of interventions to adjust economic policies, through leverages such as price deregulation and fiscal austerity. The main logic for this was to address the inefficiencies in the allocation of foreign funds to private and government spending, or the inefficiencies of public investment projects. These were perceived as the root causes of the accumulated debt problem. These programs, however, had serious side effects because of the austerity measures, typically leading to reduced public spending and services, increasing social burdens to the general public. As shown in the figures, during the structural adjustment phase, the inflow of private debt financing instruments into the Asia Pacific region also declined significantly.

When the accumulated debt problem was to some extent contained in the 1990s, new elements in international capital movement emerged. The first was the increase of FDI, including in Asia. FDIs are typically the results of increased overseas business by

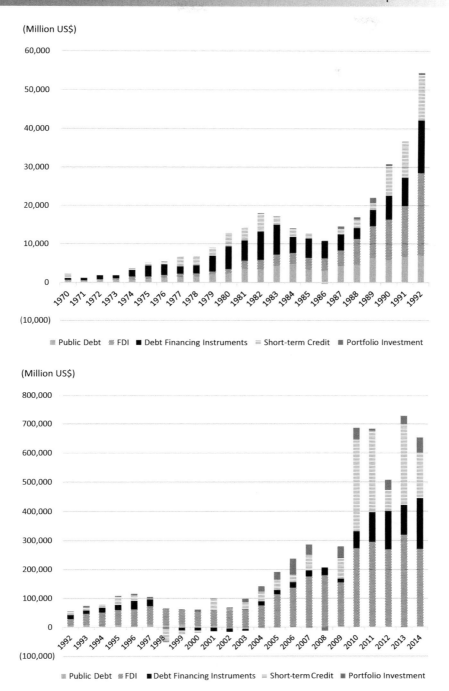

FIGURE 5.3 Net capital inflow into the Asia Pacific region.

Source: World Bank, World Debt Table, compiled by author.

Note: Debt financing instruments are mainly private debts and commercial bank credit (including government guaranteed bonds).

multinational enterprises and are thus underpinned by real economic activities. As such, they tend to be less volatile and more stable, and have become increasingly important as a form of investment in the region. The second is the expansion of short-term capital and portfolio investment. The expansion in the transactions of short-term capital has in particular become apparent since the 1990s. The ability to effectively manage those market-based financial transactions has become increasingly crucial.

While there were occasional declines in international capital flows, particularly during the Asian financial crisis and the Lehman shock, the overall trend of international investment flows has nevertheless been expanding on a global scale.

5.1.3.3 Foreign capital and Asia

Asia has been in the midst of such post-war currency regime and capital movement dynamics. During this period, some of the countries have gained independence, others have experienced civil wars, while even others struggled to break free from the colonial economic structure that still characterized their domestic economy. Until the 1960s, economic policies tended to be rather suppressive and autarkic, partially influenced by moderate socialist ideology. In the middle of the 1960s, however, non-communist countries in Asia shifted their economic management towards giving the private sector higher priority. This led to increases in foreign capital inflows, particularly from public sources such as loans from the World Bank, and development assistance from Japan originating from its war reparations.

Asia was also greatly affected by the structural changes in international capital flows that took place from the 1970s. The recession that followed the second oil shock put South Korea and the ASEAN countries into debt difficulties similar to those observed in Latin America. Foreign currency debt increased rapidly while the pace of industrialization was relatively lagging. The formation of competitive export-oriented industries happened only slowly, which created structural current account deficits. Inflow of foreign currency occurred through capital account transactions, not through current account channels. Given this situation, the second oil-shock led to serious fiscal and current account deficits in Asia in the late 1970s. As a result, many countries such as Thailand, Indonesia, South Korea, and the Philippines, had to accept and implement structural adjustment programs. The Philippines announced a debt moratorium in 1983.

This phase of confusion, however, underwent a radical change with the appreciation of the Japanese yen against the US dollar following the Plaza Accord in 1985. In the late 1980s Asian currencies having been pegged to the dollar (particularly those of Southeast Asian countries) depreciated against the Yen. This led to increased export competitiveness of those countries vis-à-vis Japan, which attracted large inflows of FDI from the Japanese manufacturing sector (see Chapters 2 and 4). Asia's rapid industrialization-based growth was essentially driven by this inflow of foreign investment. Alongside the expansion of FDI inflows, governments in Asia also started to deregulate their capital markets. For example, Indonesia, Thailand, and the Philippines adopted IMF Article 8 in 1988, 1990, and 1995, respectively, and terminated all foreign exchange restrictions on current account transactions. Deregulation also took place for capital account transactions.

The inflow of foreign capital played a significant role in the economic development of Asian countries. However, this growth was also linked to a cyclical structure of domestic capital accumulation. Since the 1960s, local enterprises have evolved by adjusting themselves to the changing socio-economic environments in countries such as Thailand, Indonesia, and South Korea, leading to the emergence of big corporations and powerful business groups (see, for instance, Suehiro [1989] for the case of Thailand). It is these companies that are still leading these Asian economies in the 21st century.

5.2 THE ASIAN ECONOMY AND CAPITAL: FROM THE ASIAN FINANCIAL CRISIS TO THE 21ST CENTURY

5.2.1 The Asian financial crisis

The Asian financial crisis occurred amidst these dynamic changes in the international financial environment. The Thai economy, which so far had been performing exceptionally well, suddenly turned into chaos on July 2, 1997. Thailand was under acute pressure from foreign speculators that were selling their currency, the Baht. The Thai government responded by intervening in the foreign exchange market in order to maintain and stabilize the exchange rate, through large expenditures of foreign reserves. However, the magnitude of the currency movements was beyond the government's capacity to defend their currency, and soon their foreign exchange reserve was depleted. The exchange rate, which was 24–25 baht per dollar, dropped to 56 baht per dollar in January the next year. This triggered large-scale bankruptcies among commercial banks and big corporations, which had significant foreign currency denominated debts in their portfolios. The turmoil spilled over to the wider economy, and the annual growth rate dropped below −10% in 1999. Countries that had been maintaining similar fixed-exchange rate regimes such as Indonesia and South Korea were also affected in a similar way, and within a year the crisis had further destabilized the currencies of Brazil and Russia as well.

Asian countries soon learned the lesson that fixed exchange rates could not be maintained in the face of increased international capital mobility, and therefore shifted to a floating exchange rate system.[1] The currencies of those countries inevitably experienced devaluation particularly in the initial phases of this transition. This transmitted a shock into their domestic economy, which in turn caused their real sector to stagnate. Thailand, Indonesia, and South Korea were particularly hard-hit.

Here, the framework of balance of payment table, presented earlier is useful to interpret and understand this crisis. All the countries were having current account deficits until the mid-90s, and thus there were basically outflows of foreign currency through current account transactions. Nevertheless, foreign exchange reserves were maintained because of the continuous inflow through capital transactions including FDI, bank credit, and portfolio investment. When there is a stable inflow of foreign currency that matches the outflow through the current account, there will be no pressures to the foreign exchange market, and the monetary authorities just have to utilize foreign reserves to control minor exchange rate fluctuations. Inflows of capital can happen despite current account deficits, when foreign investors expect with confidence that eventually the current account will turn into a surplus through continuous economic development. This is actually quite normal.

However, inflow of capital accelerated towards the mid-1990s, and compared to FDI, short-term capital including bank credit and portfolio investment constituted its majority. The crisis that hit Thailand in 1997 was due to the inability of the government to sustain the exchange rate with its foreign reserves, because of a sudden outflow of short-term, footloose funds. Speculative selling of the Baht by hedge funds, in anticipation that the fixed exchange rate could not be maintained, was what triggered this event. Yet, the root of this problems was structural; the government had allowed the influx of capital without any control, which eventually went beyond their capacity to defend the currency. The rapid selling and outflow of funds was based on an implicit consensus among the speculators at large that the balance between capital inflow and outflow has been crucially lost.

In relation to the question of the root cause of the crisis, there have been various discussions in the aftermath of the crisis. The arguments can be classified according to the following two perspectives. The first is the argument about the discrepancies between the increasing trends of capital inflow, and the policy leverages and capacities to manage capital flows and exchange rate regimes. In the 1990s, the global financial market had largely recovered from the previously accumulated debt problem. Various types of innovation in the financial sector by investment banks and hedge funds took place during the US's economic recovery, which led to expansions in short-term capital movements. On the other hand, financial liberalization was in progress in Asia, and Thailand and South Korea were progressively pursuing capital flow deregulation. The foreign exchange regimes of many countries in Asia could not catch up with such quantitative and qualitative changes, and fixed exchange rate policies were maintained.[2] Risks related to foreign debt were not recognized appropriately by banks and corporations, and measures to hedge exchange rate-related risks were typically not taken. Based on this story, the problem therefore is attributed to the sudden expansion of the inflow of foreign capital and to the mismanagement of these flows. Thus, the cause of, and responsibility for, this problem, from this perspective, essentially boils down to the lack of capacity in foreign exchange management of each of the countries; excessive capital flow deregulation; and the overoptimistic views and advices of developed countries and international financial institutions.

On the other hand, the second perspective is related to the sustainability of Asian countries' foreign debt positions, or the solvency problem. This view attributes the cause of the problem to the fact that allocation of foreign capital was directed inefficiently to domestic sectors such as real estate, construction, and consumption. This, according to this view, had negatively affected the competitiveness of the manufacturing-based export sector, which should have been the main foreign currency earner. As such, questions regarding the credibility of its long-term debt solvency were raised, which later triggered capital outflows.

This view is often associated with a logic that lays responsibility for the financial crisis at the doors of the pre-modern domestic financial institutions and corporate governance mechanisms. The governance and ownerships structures of business groups and banks were criticized, and the need for sectoral reforms as well as the strengthening of the dysfunctional stock markets were advocated. All these were seen as issues related to the pre-modern structural suppression that prevailed in these Asian economies. This led to the conclusions that increased protective measures for shareholders and creditors were needed, as well as institutional reforms to create a more conducive and enabling environment for investors, including those from abroad.

The prescriptions provided by the IMF and the World Bank in the aftermath of the crisis were based on the latter view. In South Korea, Thailand, and Indonesia, where the effects of the crisis were most severe, large scale reforms of the financial and corporate sector were implemented, which involved the restructuring of commercial banks with substantial non-performing loans.

5.2.2 Structural change in the 2000s

5.2.2.1 Returning to the growth trajectory, and changes in the real economy

Asia had recovered from the crisis and was back on a stable growth trajectory by around 2003. During the previous five years, each of the affected countries worked on non-performing loan issues, financial sector restructuring, and corporate governance reform, as suggested by the international financial institutions. However, the actual changes that took place during this process was somewhat different from what was initially intended. Thailand and Indonesia provide good examples in this respect.

Table 5.1 outlines the GDP composition in terms of expenditure of Thailand and Indonesia. According to this, the growth prior to the Asian financial crisis was primarily led through investment (fixed capital formation), while net exports were sometimes

TABLE 5.1 Changes in GDP expenditure compositions of Thailand and Indonesia

	Private consumption	Government consumption	Fixed capital formation	Net exports	Others
Thailand (Unit: %)					
1990	53.3	10.0	41.6	−7.5	2.5
1995	51.2	11.3	42.9	−6.7	1.3
2000	54.1	13.6	22.3	8.4	1.6
2005	55.8	13.7	30.4	−1.0	1.1
2010	52.1	15.8	25.4	5.5	1.1
2015	51.6	17.2	24.1	11.3	−4.2
Indonesia (Unit: %)					
1990	58.9	8.8	30.7	1.5	0.0
1995	61.6	7.8	31.9	−1.3	0.0
2000	61.7	6.5	22.2	10.5	−0.9
2005	64.4	8.1	25.1	4.1	−1.7
2010	56.2	9.0	32.9	1.9	−0.0
2015	57.1	9.8	34.6	0.2	−1.6

Source: Asian Development Bank, Statistical Database System, compiled by author.

negative. In contrast, the shares of investments after the crisis have declined significantly, while net export have turned positive. The drivers of growth have thus shifted from investment to exports.

At first glance, this may seem to suggest that the recovery was based on the view advocated by the solvency problem perspective. This is, however, not entirely correct. Thailand has made great efforts in restructuring its financial sector through means including nationalization of private banks and promotions of acquisitions with foreign banks. However, it was not able to solve the non-performing loan problem until 2002, and bank operations had been very unstable. Meanwhile some of the major domestic corporations and business groups faced bankruptcy, and those that survived had to face drastic restructuring. It took some time for those domestic corporations to completely regain competitiveness.

It was FDI-based foreign companies that led economic growth through manufacturing exports, particular those in the automobile and the electronics industries. FDI actually increased continuously after the financial crisis in these countries. Automobile-related FDI businesses were already operating in Thailand even before the crisis, although their contributions to current account surpluses were limited because of their operations' high import intensity of intermediate goods (parts and components). After the crisis, agglomeration of these supporting industries started to occur basically because of currency depreciation, and the industrial parks in the Eastern Seaboard turned into a major automobile cluster, which eventually has become the "Detroit of the East." This structural transformation enabled Thailand to turn its trade balance into a surplus. This induced the recovery of its macroeconomy, which in turn supported the disposal of non-performing loans, stabilizing the operations of domestic businesses.

In Indonesia, corporations that were connected to the Suharto family and the regime were affected the most, which eventually led to the fall of the regime. Mega-conglomerates which grew under protection from the previous government, such as the Salim Group, had to downsize its business, and the founding family had to withdraw from key management positions. The political environment continued to be unstable until Yudhoyono became the president in 2004. It was the mining sector, including coal, that led the economic recovery from 2004. Its economy shifted from an investment-led growth structure to one based on the export of natural resources. In this process, new business groups such as the Bakrie Group evolved, which earned concessional rights for natural resource development, and are now increasingly exerting political influence.

As such, even if the financial crisis was intrinsically due to an insolvency problem rooted in an "inefficient economic system," the recovery process was not led through modernization of financial institutions and corporate systems, that was initially aspired to after the crisis. Recovery was based on the deepening of industrialization and increased exports by FDI companies, without fundamental changes in domestic economic structures and conditions.

5.2.2.2 The structural changes of capital flows in Asia

While financial and corporate reform did not proceed as initially planned, it remains true that Asia has regained its sustainability in growth from a macroeconomic point of view. In fact, this has induced structural changes in the flow of capital in Asia in the 2000s. Figure 5.4 summarizes the trends of capital flows for Thailand since 1993. The

Capital Asia 99

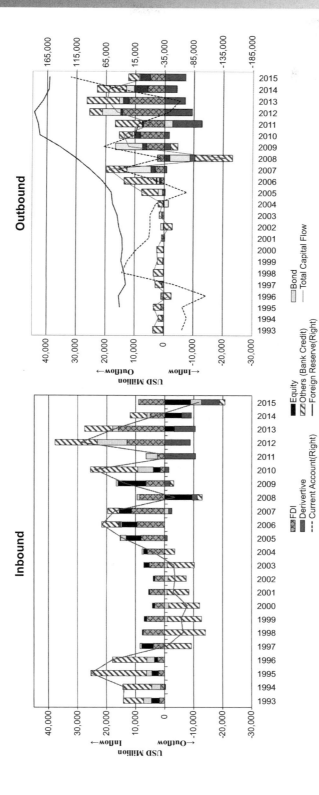

FIGURE 5.4 Gross financial accounts (inbound and outbound, Thailand).

upper diagram depicts inflows/outflows from foreign countries (from overseas residents to the domestic economy: inbound), and the lower diagram inflows/outflows to foreign countries (from domestic residents to markets overseas). The lower diagram also summarizes trends in current account balances and foreign exchange reserves.

Looking at the flows from overseas residents to the domestic economy (inbound, upper diagram), the inflow of bank credit and portfolio investment that was significant prior to the crisis has declined drastically since the outbreak of the crisis, whose outflow continued well into mid-2000s. On the other hand, there has been an increase in FDI, which suggests that this was what has driven the growth of exports.

The flows originating from domestic residents to markets overseas (outbound, lower diagram), suggests that the current account balance has in general been positive throughout the post-crisis period. A current account surplus means an increase of foreign assets, which increases foreign exchange holdings in the domestic economy. This is represented by an increase of foreign reserves. This figure also suggests that the increase of foreign assets holdings has been manifested in increased foreign investments since the latter half of 2000s. Inflow of foreign capital has also recovered in the middle of 2000s (upper diagram). However, when one compares Thailand's inbound investments and their outbound investments, these had become about equal by the end of 2000s.

The share of FDI in Thailand's total outbound investment is still limited; however, some notable cases have already emerged. In Japan, sample cases include the purchasing of the "Kiroro Resort" in Hokkaido by a Thai real estate company in 2012, and the acquisition of a Japanese major automobiles molding and metal sheet pressing company "Ogihara" by a Thai manufacturing company. These evolving trends seem to be common across countries in Asia. In ASEAN, Malaysia has progressed much faster as an exporter of capital than Thailand, and outbound investment are increasing in Indonesia and the Philippines as well. The fact that China has become an even more active investor compared to ASEAN is already well known (see Chapter 3). During the recovery phase of the 2000s, Asia has transformed itself from a mere recipient to a provider of capital. This is a long-term, structural change that is rooted on the development of the real sector.

5.2.3 The drastic change in the global capital and financial environment and Asia

One of the important and fundamental trends that occurred in global capital and finance during this period is the progress made in financial technology and the associated changes in the financial sector in the US. As the recession during the 1980s, due to the decline of the manufacturing sector, came to an end, the US entered into a new long-term growth path by evolving as the leader in the IT sector. In the financial sector, which used to play a supporting role for industry, new players such as investment banks utilizing sophisticated securitization technologies, and speculative hedge funds aiming for high returns, have emerged (Johnson and Kwak, 2010). These financial institutions played a key role in promoting global capital deregulation and were also major players behind the speculative selling triggering the Asian financial crisis in 1997.

This trend in global capital flows and finance did not change and continued even after the Asian financial crisis. The rapid progress in new financial technologies, such as securitization, suggested that the security market was going to overtake commercial banks in their financial functions. On the other hand, progressive consolidation of commercial banks in developed countries through mergers and acquisitions was promoted as a survival strategy to enable taking on larger risks. This created an oligopolistic market structure (World Bank, 2001). Commercial bank consolidation also progressed in Asia, particularly in Malaysia, Indonesia, and South Korea.

The Lehman shock and the global financial crisis that erupted in 2008 can be seen as negative responses to these technological changes in the financial sector. This all started when BNP Paribas, a large investment bank, decided to suspend redemptions of funds that were exposed to US subprime mortgages, in August 2007. This raised concerns about the systemic risks inherent in securitized products due to issues such as subprime loans, leading to significant contraction of the market. This particularly caused shrinkage and confusion in risk-money markets, which eventually led to the Lehman shock; the bankruptcy of a major investment bank on September of 2008. The global financial market contracted accordingly, which led to a global recession (the global financial crisis). This crisis further exposed fiscal problems in a number of European countries, which were the results of the burdens with bank rescue packages. This has destabilized the Euro system (Euro crisis).

The global financial crisis which originated in the US had long-term effects in Europe. The impact of the crisis on Asia was not trivial, but it remained short-term and indirect. From a financial point of view, the private sector in Asian economies was already holding enough foreign assets, and governments had accumulated significant foreign reserves. In Thailand, for example, domestic residents withdrew their foreign investments according to the contracting capital market, as is manifested in the reverse inflow of foreign investments depicted in Figure 5.4.[3] The financial sector also refrained from making aggressive foreign investments, because of the poor performance in the aftermath of the Asian financial crisis. As such, there had been almost no cases of bankruptcies because of this.

The Asian economy was mostly affected by this crisis through the real economy. In the process of economic recovery in the 2000s, exports, instead of investments, played a major role. In these circumstances, the contraction of the global economy has led to significantly reduced exports. In ASEAN, for example, countries with high trade dependency such as Thailand and Malaysia, recorded negative growth rates in 2009. During this period of trade contraction, Asian countries shifted their export orientations from Europe and the US towards Asia, particularly China.

5.2.4 New challenges

The global financial crisis pointed regulators' attention towards the need to manage capital flows and the financial sector at large. In the US and Europe, where governments intervened to rescue financial institutions, strong capital adequacy requirements were introduced. Banks were also restricted in operating in security investments, particularly those associated with high risks (Johnson and Kwak, 2010). There was also increasing recognition of the need to regulate short-term capital flows.

On the other hand, countries in the Europe and US initiated large scale monetary easing after October 2008, which led to the sharp appreciation of the US dollar, the key currency in the global market. At around 2013, the US started to seek exit strategies from these monetary easing policies. Roughly speaking, the situation as of the end of 2010s was such that the market was watching what this backward flow of the dollar implied for vulnerable emerging economies.

In this context, new developments have been observed in Asia, which suggests long-term structural changes to come. The dollar standard of the world's financial and currency order is under challenge from a capital-rich Asia, backed by its strong real economy. China, for example, has been requesting increasing representation in the IMF and ADB as its economy has continued to grow. As soon as it observed that the responses to these requests have been slow, China decided to set up its own multilateral organization, the "Asian Infrastructure Investment Bank (AIIB)." This was established in December 2015, with participation from countries including some from Europe (Japan and the US were not members as of August 2019). Moreover, China announced the implementation of the Belt and Road Initiative, which aims to develop infrastructure and trade relationships in the wider region. China has been providing loans to neighboring countries through this initiative. In addition, China has been advocating an "internationalization of the Yuan (Renminbi)" since 2016, which is essentially aiming for wider dissemination of the Renminbi in Asia, replacing the position of the US dollar as a key currency.

While there have been no similar initiatives from the ASEAN countries, there are growing interests in utilizing capital flows from China to further promote economic development. These countries nevertheless have also transformed themselves into capital rich countries like China. Asia had been dependent on capital inflows from outside the region, particularly from developed countries. This has, however, ended, and now capital is flowing from within the region. Asia has also become a significant exporter of capital. These changes are historic and probably irreversible.

There have been numerous discussions on the most desirable financial system in Asia since the Asian financial crisis. We will review some of the major arguments and policies in relation to this and identify challenges for these in the next section.

5.3 POLICY CHALLENGES FOR ASIA AND ITS FINANCIAL SECTOR

5.3.1 Financial system reform after the Asian financial crisis

As discussed earlier, there are two types of perspective on why the Asian financial crisis occurred. The key economic reforms advised and agreed with the IMF and the World Bank, that were also actually implemented in the aftermath of the crisis, were the ones that were primarily based on the domestic capacity to enable repayment of the capital that flowed in. Therefore, the argument was not based on how to regulate the excessive liquidity of capital flows, but rather on how to upgrade the inefficient and backward domestic financial and corporate sectors. The reforms were implemented as part of agreed conditionality imposed by the IMF and the World Bank. The basic direction was to prevent concentration of corporate ownership, to have improved protection of investors and creditors, and to a shift away from an overdependency on debt towards an active functioning of equity markets.

In South Korea, fundamental reform on corporate governance was pursued. The limitations of the traditional business groups (chaebols) have also been highlighted in the memorandum of understanding between the IMF. The Kim Dea-jung government set a goal to reduce the debt ratio (debt/equity) of the 30 major corporations of those chaebols to below 200% by the end of 1999, which had reached 519% during the crisis. In 1998, the "big deal policy," which was a program to swap and consolidate businesses of major chaebols was implemented. In addition, increased regulations on cross-shareholdings, deregulations on rules related to foreign investors, and strengthened requirements on corporate information disclosure were implemented.

In Thailand, a plan was drawn up for closures and restructuring of financial institutions in 1997 after the crisis. Medium size banks were nationalized and put under government control, and mergers and acquisitions were promoted for the smaller banks. Stock market reforms were also implemented in order to protect the minority shareholders' rights and to promote disclosure of information, revisions in the public limited company law, and strengthening of the functions of the stock exchange and stock exchange commission were implemented in this occasion.

In Indonesia, government efforts, with the support of the IMF, in restructuring ailing banks have achieved positive results. The bankruptcy law was introduced as early as 1998, and regulations related to corporate governance (independent auditors and auditing committees) were also institutionalized.

While governments of those affected countries pursued both financial and corporate sector reforms after the financial crisis, remarkably positive results were observed only in the financial sector restructuring. In most of the cases, the influence of big business groups on the financial sector was weakened significantly, and foreign banks have also entered into these countries. On the other hand, reforms related to the governance and ownership structures of large corporations did not generate the expected results. In South Korea, for example, the "big deal" policy led to the reshuffling of leading chaebol corporations. However, there has been no fundamental change in the concentration of ownership structure in the economy, and frequent violations of corporate governance regulations have been reported. It has also been pointed out that there has been no change at all in the skewed ownership patterns in Thailand. In Indonesia, while there has been increased representation of foreign businesses, there have also been delays in debt adjustments of business groups. In addition, new connections between businesses and new political groups, with new players that are different from those under the past Suharto government, seem to have emerged.[4]

5.3.2 Asian financial cooperation: Asian monetary cooperation and bond market development

As a response to the financial crisis, regional financial cooperation in Asia has been promoted since 2000 under the leadership of Japan, separately from the IMF and the World Bank regime. These include the following two Asian Financial Cooperation schemes under the ASEAN+3 framework. The first is the Chiang Mai Initiative (CMI), signed in 2000, which is a currency cooperation scheme to allow currency swaps in emergency situations. The second is the initiative to promote the development of the bond markets in the region (Asia Bond Market Initiative, ABMI).

The key justification for an Asian Financial Cooperation scheme is based on a perception called the "double mismatch" (Yoshitomi, 2003). Prior to the financial crisis, the US dollar was used as the standard currency, even when intra-regional trade was expanding rapidly. This is referred to as the "currency mismatch." In Asia, the inflow of capital was predominantly short-term through bank financing, while demand for long-term capital was also increasing due to rapid economic growth. This is the second one, referred to as the "maturity mismatch." Introduction of capital flows into Asia has always been based on the US dollar, despite the fact that there have been sufficient savings within the region. This forced governments in Asia to intervene in the foreign exchange markets to stabilize exchange rates vis-à-vis the dollar, which was one of the main reasons for the Asian financial crisis. These views are based on the perspectives of capital flow controls, rather than on the solvency problem.

The currency cooperation framework (CMI) was initially proposed and promoted under a bilateral swap arrangement. However, it has been shifting towards a multilateral drawing arrangement of the US dollar in emergency situations since 2010 (CMI Multilateralization, CMIM). The arrangement so far in terms of contribution of each of the member countries is as follows: Japan and China will bear one-third, South Korea one-tenth, and the remaining portion will be divided among the ASEAN countries. In contrast, the drawing rights are designed to favor ASEAN countries, disproportionately. The scheme has been designed so that the foreign reserves of Japan and China will be disbursed to regional members in cases of emergencies.

During the Lehman shock, activation of the CMI instruments was considered among some of the countries, but this was not resorted to. This experience led to several adjustments to the rules to operationalize these regional cooperation frameworks. As one example, the relaxing of the coordination rules with the IMF ("IMF delink") was introduced to allow more flexible and mobile invocation. Another is the establishment of the AMRO (ASEAN+3 Macroeconomic Research Office) in Singapore. The effort to strengthen practical operational relevance in Asian Financial Cooperation has continued.

Regarding the development of the bond market (ABMI), domestic institution building, and regional institutional cooperation is underway. In addition, a credit guarantee mechanism (Credit Guarantee and Investment Facility, CGIF) has been set up within the Asian Development Bank in 2010.

CONCLUSION

This chapter has focused on the fundamental roles that capital has played in economic development in Asia, by looking at foreign capital flows in relation to the evolving Asian economy in the post war era. Foreign capital has flowed into Asia since the end of World War II in the process of economic development. These have been crucial to the accumulation of capital in Asia. On the other hand, global capital dynamics have been changing drastically during this period, and sometimes have run completely out of control, having devastating impacts on economies at a global scale. The Asian financial crisis is one such example.

However, Asia is no longer merely a recipient of foreign capital, and it has started to become the provider of capital to the regional and the global economy. The capital circulation is now bi-directional in Asia. There have been increasing momentum towards a fundamental change of the dollar-based regional capital and currency order, which have been created and maintained in the post war era, due to new regional dynamics.

From a micro-perspective, local financial systems in Asia still retain many of the non-institutional elements in financial intermediation trajectories to the real economy. The Asian financial sector is still halfway in terms of financial intermediation and stock market functions, and investment demand have so far primarily been met by informal interfirm credit or self-financing (Mieno, 2015). There is still a significant gap in the Asian financial sector between the macroeconomic aspects of capital flows due to international capital movements, and the micro-level functions related to the efficient allocation of investments to corporations (see Box 5).

Financial reform and regional financial cooperation are all efforts to regulate and utilize capital flows appropriately, as well as to allocate them stably to the domestic sector. In order to successfully close the abovementioned gaps, financial systems must be reformed and developed in line with future development trajectories of the real sector, consistent with the characteristics of financial demand. These are the key issues that must be taken into account for designing the future of the financial systems in Asia.

BOX 5 Emerging issues in the micro-organizational finance systems and the Asian economy

Fumiharu Mieno

This chapter has focused on international capital flows; however, it has not engaged in discussions on the problems related to domestic financial systems. The capacity of financial systems to allocate resources efficiently is another important aspect of the Asian economy, in particular in relation to the arguments on financial and corporate sector reform.

The key channels for the allocation of financial resources can be divided into the following: on the one hand are the indirect financing channels (1) financial intermediation through banks; and on the other is direct financing channels through security markets (stocks and bonds). The former is a relationship-based transaction, characterized by regular contacts between banks and corporations, while the latter is based on "arms-length" relationships in relevant financial markets. Within security market transactions, however, (2) bond financing is different from (3) equity financing as it basically takes the same form of credit as bank-based financial intermediation. Equity financing works through direct ownership structures. In addition, in many Asian economies, and in developing countries in general, (4) self-financing plays important roles as well.

These four different financial channels each are functionally different. The first is related to the costs of processing information. The problem of information asymmetry can get very serious in financial markets, which can impede business transactions. Given this, one of the important functions of financial markets is to reduce this asymmetric information structure by processing and providing the necessarily information to the market (Diamond, 1984; Leland and Pyle, 1977). The cost of processing such information is low in banks' financial intermediation, and higher in security markets. This is because banks usually pool financial resources from a large number of small depositors, and process related information through their daily business transactions with each of the corporations.

The second is related to the enforcement of contracts and the protection of the rights of shareholders and creditors. In financial intermediation, negotiations and adjustments can take place through private interfirm-relationships between the corporations in the event of default. On the other hand, monitoring of corporations is typically difficult in cases of stocks and bonds, and thus this typically require legal solutions. Therefore, for securities market to function, legal, and institutional frameworks that can protect the rights of shareholders and creditors are necessary, particular those related to bankruptcies.

In this context, financial intermediation by banks tends to be formulated much earlier because of the lower information costs, and because it can function even when related legal frameworks are still not fully developed. On the other hand, equity and bond financing have an advantage first in terms of their ability to provide long-term finance, and second their ability to take on higher risks because of the much larger number of investors. When security markets functions, it allows the addressing of financial demand that is large scale, long-term, and high risk.

In the Asian economy, financial intermediation was much more common than the other channels. Notable examples include the high dependency on financial intermediation in the high growth era of Japan and South Korea. The industrialization patterns of these countries were essentially a catching-up process to advanced technologies of more advanced countries, which entailed technological learning through the introduction of licensed technologies and technical cooperation. In such cases, the information on the particular technology that was going to be introduced was already widely known, and as such, the risks associated were low. Therefore, renewals of short-term financing were sufficient for the purpose of technological catch-up, which made bank credit highly useful.

Also, the development of new technology contains higher risks and requires much larger financial resources and longer time spans. Equity financing is typically based on various motivations on the part of multiple stakeholders and is more capable of addressing these types of financial demand. A typical example can be seen in the cases of venture capitalists financing startups in the US.

A shift from financial intermediation towards security markets has been emphasized in the aftermath of the Asian financial crisis. However, the new realities of the middle-income countries of ASEAN and China, aiming to climb up into the ranks of high-income economies, seem to suggest that such a dichotomous view may not be most suitable to address some of the emerging issues. For example, ASEAN has been known as a region where a significant proportion of financing is based on self-financing. Technological upgrading of the manufacturing sector in this region as achieved through direct investment, which is essentially self-financing without any channeling through either financial intermediation or markets (McMillan and Woodruff, 1999; Mieno, 2015). In China, short-term credit transactions (trade credit) based on interfirm relationships complemented the shortcomings of banks' lending abilities. This has been viewed as one of the important financial mechanisms that have supported its rapid economic growth in the 2000s (Allen et al. 2005).

It is highly possible that these informal financial channels, through reducing information asymmetry and ensuring contract enforcement, have contributed to technological catch-up and development during the recovery of the Asian economy. Financial institutions should be designed to be compatible with the technological attributes of the manufacturing sector in Asia, which is also an important aspect to understand the economic development of Asia. What kind of financial system will emerge attention should be paid to the type of financial system that will emerge as Asia gains its position in the global innovation space.

NOTES

1 Malaysia, however, insisted on maintaining its fixed exchange rate policy by implementing strict rules to regulate foreign capital flows. Similarly, China also implemented strong capital regulations to prevent the spread of the crisis domestically.
2 Financial regulators in Southeast Asia were strongly in favor for fixed exchange rates because of the risks associated with exchange rate fluctuations for exporting companies.
3 The possibilities for a foreign exchange reserve crisis have been pointed for only a few countries such as South Korea and Vietnam, and therefore no rescue package has been mobilized.
4 The details of the financial sector reform in Thailand, for example, can be found in Khanthanavit et al. (2003).

REFERENCES

Allen, Franklin, Jun Qian and Meijun Qian. (2005). "Law, Finance, and Economic Growth in China," *Journal of Financial Economics*, 77, 57–116.
Diamond, Douglas. (1984). "Financial Intermediation and Delegated Monitoring," *The Review of Economic Studies*, 55(3), 393–414.
Johnson, Simon, and James Kwak. (2010). *13 Bankers: The Wall Street Takeover and the Next Financial Meltdown*. New York: Pantheon Books.
Khanthanavit, Anya, Piruna Polsiri and Yupana Wiwattanakantang. (2003). *Did Families Lose or Gain Control after the East Asian Financial Crisis?* CEI Working Paper Series, No. 2003-1 Tokyo: Center for Economic Institutions, Hitotsubashi University.

Leland, Hayne, and David Pyle. (1977). "Information Asymmetries, Financial Structure, and Financial Intermediation." *Journal of Finance*, 32, 371–387.

McMillan, John and Christopher Woodruff. (1999). "Interfirm Relationships and Informal Credit in Vietnam." *The Quarterly Journal of Economics*, 114(4), 1285–1320.

Mieno, Fumiharu. (2015). *Financial Reform and Southeast Asia: Analyzing Regional Long-term Trends and Corporate Finance* (*Kinyu Shisutemu Kaikaku to Tounan Ajia – Kaihatu Keizaigaku no Chousen*). Tokyo: Keiso Shobo.

Suehiro, Akira. (1989). *Capital Accumulation in Thailand 1855–1985*. Tokyo: UNESCO (The Centre for East Asian Cultural Studies).

World Bank. (2001). *Finance for Growth: Policy Choices in a Volatile World*. Oxford: World Bank and Oxford University Press.

Yoshitomi, Masaru. (2003). The Truth of the Asian Economy (Ajia Keizai no Shinjitu). Tokyo: Toyokeizai Shimposha.

6 Migrating Asia: labor mobility in an interdependent and connected world

Tomohiro Machikita

Passport control at Maesai, Thailand (Border between Thailand and Myanmar, 2013).
Source: Photo library.

LEARNING GOALS

- Understand the migration patterns in Asia over the past two decades through looking at key statistics.
- Understand the framework for analyzing the causes and consequences of international migration for sending and recipient countries.
- Understand the recent changes in institutional and policy frameworks for international migration in Asia.

INTRODUCTION

This chapter deals with international migration in Asia. Over the past 20 years, labor migration has grown rapidly across regions and countries in Asia. There have also been movements of capital, intermediate goods, and final goods. Given this, this chapter explores the following two issues. First, how does international migration in Asia relate to economic development in East and Southeast Asia? Second, why do people move across countries, and how does this affect labor markets in destination and origin countries? Looking at those questions will provide in-depth understanding about the changes in wages, employment patterns, labor markets, and industrial structures in Asia. This chapter will also provide an overview of the recent institutional changes regarding international migration in relation to both origin and destination countries in Asia.

There are three important reasons to study international migration in Asia. First, international migration has doubled in Asia in the past three decades. According to World Development Indicators of the World Bank, it has been growing in Asia at a higher rate during the same period compared to other regions such as North America. Since such rapid influxes of people have most likely impacted the economies of both the origin and destination countries, this dynamic merits attention. Second, some of the richer economies in Asia face a rapidly ageing population, in particular Japan, South Korea, Taiwan and Thailand. This has led to quantitative and qualitative (skills) changes in the demand and supply of labor in both the origin and destination countries. As such, it is important to understand international migration within the context of such demographic change. In fact, ageing and labor shortages have become increasingly evident even in labor-abundant countries, which would further induce transformation of demographic structures in both the sending and receiving countries in much shorter timeframes.

Third, Asia as a whole will nevertheless witness significant population growth in the next decade or two. According to the United Nations (2016), 4.4 billion (60%) of the world's 7.2 billion lived in Asia in 2016. Of these, 60% (2.6 billion) were living in China and India. Asia's population is estimated to further grow to 4.6 billion in the 2020s, and to 4.9 billion in the 2030s. Population growth will induce substantial demographic changes and increase the supply of labor. It is therefore essential to understand the relationship between demographic changes and international migration in Asia.

Furthermore, a focus on skills would help understand how cross-border movements of people influence economic development from the resource re-allocation perspective. Economic efficiency and welfare gains will be achieved by promoting international migration through the reduction of various barriers, as it will facilitate re-allocation of labor across countries. Wages will increase if labor moves from labor-abundant to labor-scarce countries. Such an influx of labor would also lead to more productive use of capital in those capital-abundant countries. While such movements of people will contribute to increasing global efficiencies, it would also lead to social welfare gains in Asia. Asia's demographic dynamics are key foundations that drive international migration in Asia.

Section 6.1 of this chapter provides an overview of relevant data on international migration in Asia. It also provides a simple theoretical framework to understand and interpret the data. Section 6.2 introduces an analysis of migration behavior and patterns by focusing on geographic distance and income disparities between origin and destination countries. Section 6.3 offers three case studies covering recent institutional changes related to unskilled migration in Thailand and South Korea, and on skilled migration in Southeast Asia. We derive basic policy implications from combining case studies with statistical data related to migration behavior and patterns.

6.1 BACKGROUND AND FRAMEWORK

6.1.1 Trends in international migration in Asia

From an income perspective, the world is not "flat." Substantial income disparity exists across countries within and between regions such as Africa, America, Asia-Pacific, and Europe. These income gaps are one of the main driving forces of international migration. Diversity of income levels are also significant within Asia – while it has some of the world's highest income economies such as Singapore, Hong Kong, or Japan, it is also home to the poorest that have barely made it out of the low-income categories. This chapter examines how income disparities within the region drive international migration.

Figure 6.1 provides an overview of the share of residents from abroad out of total population in countries in different income groups for 1990 and 2015, based on the World Bank classification of 2015. This figure suggests three interesting features. First, countries in the high income group have the highest ratio of foreign population among all income groups. The ratio has also increased over time. While it was 7.7% in 1990, it almost doubled to 13.6% in 2015. Second, countries in middle- and low-income groups had lower shares of foreign population. Third, while two of the highest income groups have increased their shares of foreign population between 1990 and 2015, the shares of the remaining income groups have all decreased during the past 25 years. The fact that high income countries were able to disproportionately attract foreigners compared to lower income countries suggests that international migration has become more income elastic.

Next, let us take a look at the geographical differences in the shares of foreign population across regions. Table 6.1 shows the changes in these shares of each of the regions for 1990, 2000, 2010, and 2015. Table 6.1 also highlights three interesting points.

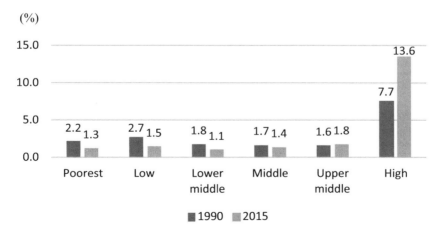

FIGURE 6.1 Foreign population shares among different country income groups (1990 and 2015).

Source: World Development Indicators (2015).

TABLE 6.1 Changes in foreign population shares across regions

Region	1990	2000	2010	2015	Change (%)
North America	9.8	12.9	14.9	15.2	54.6
European Union	5.7	7.1	10.2	10.7	88.8
Middle East and Northern Africa	7.1	6.4	8.4	9.3	29.7
Sub-Sahara Africa	2.8	2.0	1.7	1.9	−33.5
Latin America and Caribbean	1.6	1.2	1.3	1.4	−9.7
Asia and Pacific	0.6	0.8	1.0	1.1	77.3
World average	2.9	2.8	3.2	3.3	15.4

Source: World Development Indicators (2015).

First, the shares of foreign population are higher for North America and Europe (EU) than others. The shares are more than 10% points higher compared to Asia, where it is only about 1% of the total population. Second, the shares of Sub-Sahara Africa, Latin America, and Asia-Pacific are all lower than the world average. Furthermore, the shares in Sub-Sahara Africa and Latin America have been decreasing over time. Third, the Asia-Pacific region, which includes populous countries such as China, has the lowest share of foreign population; the overall share increased, however, by more than 70% between 1990 and 2015. This is almost on par with the European Union (EU) with an 88% growth, where regional integration has practically eliminated borders. These figures nevertheless suggest significant regional differences in international migration trends.

6.1.2 Demand and supply of foreign labor in Asia

Given the importance of income variability and regional differences for international migration, we now focus on Asia with particular emphasis on member countries of ASEAN, where international migration patterns changed drastically between the 1990s and 2000s. In the 1990s, ASEAN countries encouraged their citizens to migrate to more developed economies in the Middle East, and to Newly Industrializing Economies (NIEs) in Asia such as Hong Kong, Singapore, and Taiwan. In fact, 80% of the migration patterns were long-range based, with a clear orientation towards such developed economies. This was supported by increased demand for labor in these economies during the 1990s, which was catered for by labor migration from ASEAN.

The World Bank *Migration and Remittances Fact Book* provides interesting insights of the recent trends. Since the 2000s, there has been a decline in the share of such long-range based international migration in Asia. In 2013, more than one-third of migrants from ASEAN countries moved within the ASEAN region (34%). The shares of ASEAN-born migrants out of the total number of migrants in ASEAN increased from 48% to 69% between 1990 and 2013. Such changes in international migration patterns of ASEAN have become evident over the past 20 years. Clear trends have been observed in both continental and archipelago/island Southeast Asia. The former is represented by the substantial influx of labor into Thailand from its three neighboring countries:

Myanmar, Laos, and Cambodia. It has been estimated that there are about three million migrants from ASEAN, primarily from these countries, in Thailand. Likewise, a significant influx of labor from Malaysia to Singapore, and from Indonesia to Malaysia is also observed. It is estimated that there are more than 1.3 million migrants from ASEAN countries (primarily from Malaysia) in Singapore, while Malaysia has also attracted more than 2.1 million migrants also from ASEAN, mainly from Indonesia. The main reason for this is the shortage of unskilled labor in Thailand, Singapore, and Malaysia, all of which experienced rapid industrial development during the past 20 years.

6.1.3 Theoretical framework: the benefits and costs of migration

This section discusses the causes and consequences of international migration between origin and destination countries, in relation to the basic theoretical framework. This framework is based on two important factors: the push factor (labor supply) and the pull factor (labor demand). First, the following dimensions of the two push factors are discussed; (1) income disparity between the origin and destination countries and (2) geographic distance between the origin and destination countries. These are important because they determine the benefits and costs associated with cross-border migration.

Second, the role of labor demand is also important. Labor demand drives the expected benefits of migration across borders, which is also driven by larger-income disparities and lower-moving costs between countries.

Take the case of Singapore. Singapore is the richest country in ASEAN, with a GDP per capita of US $52,000 in 2015. Cambodia, on the other hand, is the poorest in the region. In per capita terms, Singapore is 44 times higher than that of Cambodia. Such substantial income gap affects migration decision and behavior – people tend to move from Cambodia to Singapore with the expectation of higher incomes.

Geographic distance also plays a significant role in migration patterns as well. The difference of income levels between Singapore, Malaysia, and Indonesia is significant; the per capita income of Singapore is five times higher than that of Malaysia, and Malaysia's is 1.4 times higher than that of its neighboring country, Indonesia. Migration tends to be most intensive within these three ASEAN countries, because of geographical proximity.

The case of Thailand provides clear evidence of how income gaps and geographic distance with its neighboring countries play out in migration patterns. Because the income level of Thailand is much higher than those of Myanmar, Laos, and Cambodia, it attracts significant migrant workers from them, which are also neighboring countries. Thailand's GDP per capita is 4.6 times that of Myanmar, 4.8 times that of Cambodia, and 3 times that of Laos. The pattern is similar to the relationships of Singapore, Malaysia, and Indonesia.

Geographic distance is also closely related to differences in cultural dimensions, including religion, language, and lifestyle. If larger differences in such cultural aspects would be a source of disutility for migrants, then geographic distance could increase the costs of migration, which could further influence migration decisions and patterns. In essence, individuals will choose their destinations to maximize their expected utility (benefits), subject to the constraints, and costs of migration.

Pull factors (particularly labor demand) are other drivers of international migration. While there are regular push factors for migration to neighboring countries that are more advanced, labor demand plays a pivotal role in actual migration outcomes. Aspects such as the number of vacancies, wage levels offered, and the required quality of labor (skills) in local labor markets all determine expected utilities of migrant workers. Differences in these three aspects across potential destination countries affect migration patterns through workers' skill levels.

As such, heterogeneity in skills will most likely lead to different outcomes for migrant workers. Workers with higher skill sets, including foreign students at higher educational institutions in developed countries, may find jobs in enterprises and contribute to innovation in the future. Workers with lower skills, on the other hand, are typically absorbed in labor-intensive jobs in agriculture, manufacturing, and service sectors.

Migration will also impact labor markets of recipient countries. Standard labor economic theory suggests that wage levels in labor markets will become lower along with the influx of immigrants (Borjas 2014, 2016; Lewis, 2013). This is based on two assumptions: immigrants have lower reservation wages, and migrant and local workers are substitutable. On the other hand, theory also suggests that wage levels could increase if there is complementarity between migrant and local workers. This is because the demand for labor for local workers will increase along with the inflow of migrant workers.

International migration will also impact the labor and capital shares of income. Firms will determine the level of capital investment according to levels of labor supply. Thus, if an inflow of migrant workers will lead to increased availability of labor at lower cost, this will affect labor and capital inputs. If labor and capital are substitutable, firms will increase labor demand by reducing capital investment. Demand for capital will decrease, leading to lower returns to capital (rent). On the other hand, when labor and capital are complementary, the returns to capital will increase because of the increase in demand, along with an influx of labor.

Finally, from the government's perspective, proper policy design and implementation can lead to improved economic welfare. Theory suggests that there would be overall economic welfare gains as long as there is income re-distribution between those gaining from returns on capital to those that lose by reduced wage levels.

In sum, the key drivers of international migration in this theoretical framework can be summarized as follows. The impact of international migration on labor markets of recipient countries depends on the following three fundamental parameters: (1) the degree of complementarity and substitutability between migrant and local workers; (2) the degree of complementarity and substitutability between labor and capital; and (3) the quality and success of redistribution policies in recipient countries.

It would be useful to note that this static framework can be further extended into a dynamic analytical framework. In a more dynamic setting, firms will optimize production technologies by adjusting capital investments along with changes in the number of migrant workers. If migrant workers and capital are substitutable, firms are more likely to hire migrant workers, and less likely to upgrade their production technologies to save capital. Such dynamic firm-level adjustments could determine the trajectories of industry-level upgrading with respect to production technologies (Lewis, 2013).

6.2 STYLIZED FACTS ON INTERNATIONAL MIGRATION IN ASIA

This section provides some of the stylized facts on recent international migration in Asia from a theoretical perspective, with a focus on geographical distance and income difference between origin and destination countries, as discussed in the previous section.

The changes in the past 30 years since 1990 have revealed three vital facts. First, the number of migrants has increased in Asia, as the statistics suggest. It is important to understand that this is caused by the changes in foreign labor demand in Asia. Second, conditions related to the demand and supply of migrant workers have changed. Finally, demand for male in relation to female migrant workers has also changed since 1990. This is due to changes that have occurred in the industrial structures of recipient countries – a shift from manufacturing to services (for details up to 2000, see Ananta and Ariffin, 2004).

6.2.1 An overview in the trends of foreign population in Asia

Table 6.2 presents the number of resident foreigners, and their shares out of total population in different countries in Asia for 1990, 2000, 2010, and 2015. The last column of Table 6.2 shows the changes in foreign population shares between 1990 and 2015. The table suggests that the presence of foreign population is most significant in Singapore and Hong Kong. Their shares were high in 1990, and still high in 2015. More than one-third of their populations are foreign nationals. Their trends, however, have been quite different. While Hong Kong has experienced no substantial changes in foreign population share, that of Singapore has almost doubled in the past 25 years.

This table shows that other countries such as South Korea, Thailand, and Malaysia have also experienced large increases in foreign population shares. South Korea had almost no foreign residents in 1990 but experienced a 26-fold increase in its share in the past 25 years (2.6% in 2015). Similarly, Thailand has also experienced a rapid increase in foreign population share – by six-fold – during the same period, reaching a share of 5.8% in 2015. Meanwhile Malaysia has doubled its foreign population share between 1990 and 2015, with a share of 8.3% in 2015. The foreign population shares of Thailand and Malaysia follow those of Singapore and Hong Kong, and are relatively high in terms of Asia (see also Figure 6.2). Japan is also one of major countries in terms of the size of its foreign population, which has also increased in the past 25 years. These were the top five countries in terms of foreign population in 2015 in Asia. On the other hand, because the population growth rates of the Philippines and Indonesia have been higher than their respective foreign population growth rates, this has led to declining foreign population shares in both countries.

If the sizes of foreign population in each of the countries in Table 6.2 are added up, the total number amounted to 6.3 million in 1990. This had grown 2.6 times to 16.8 million by 2015. Similar trends are observed in the top five countries, which collectively account for 82% of the total foreign population increase in Asia during this period.

TABLE 6.2 Changes in the total sizes of foreign populations, and foreign population shares, in Asia

Country	Total number of foreign population (ten thousand)				Foreign population share (%)				Changes (2015/1990)
	1990	2000	2010	2015	1990	2000	2010	2015	
Japan	107.6	168.7	213.4	204.4	0.9	1.3	1.7	1.6	1.8
South Korea	4.3	24.4	91.9	132.7	0.1	0.5	1.9	2.6	26.4
Hong Kong	221.8	266.9	278.0	283.9	38.3	39.3	39.8	38.9	1.0
Singapore	72.7	135.2	216.5	254.4	24.1	34.5	42.6	45.4	1.9
Indonesia	46.6	29.2	30.5	32.9	0.3	0.1	0.1	0.1	0.5
Thailand	52.9	125.8	322.4	391.3	0.9	2.0	4.8	5.8	6.2
The Philippines	15.4	31.8	20.9	21.2	0.2	0.4	0.2	0.2	0.8
Malaysia	69.6	127.7	240.6	251.4	3.8	5.5	8.6	8.3	2.2
China	37.6	50.8	85.0	97.8	0.0	0.0	0.1	0.1	2.2
Vietnam	2.8	5.7	6.2	7.3	0.0	0.1	0.1	0.1	1.9
Lao PDR	2.3	2.2	2.1	2.2	0.5	0.4	0.3	0.3	0.6
Cambodia	3.8	14.6	8.2	7.4	0.4	1.2	0.6	0.5	1.1

Source: World Development Indicators (2015).

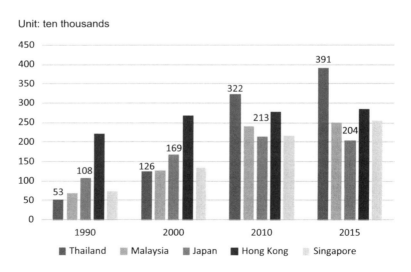

FIGURE 6.2 Changes in the sizes of foreign populations among the top five recipient countries in Asia.
Source: World Development Indicators (2015).

Figure 6.2 describes the changes in the sizes of the foreign population among the top five countries. A rapid increase in the size of the foreign population in Thailand and Malaysia is evident. Thailand had the highest foreign population in Asia since 2010. Their number in Malaysia also increased rapidly, surpassing that of Japan, and catching almost up with Hong Kong and Singapore.

6.2.2 The roles of distance and income disparity in migration in Asia

This section further discusses the roles of geographic distance and income disparity between origin and destination countries, by picking up the cases of Thailand and Singapore. Thailand's three neighboring countries (Myanmar, Laos, and Cambodia) account for 95% of the total foreign population in Thailand. Thailand is the largest recipient country of migrants in Asia, and the number reached 3.9 million in 2015.

This section looks at why this number has rapidly increased in Thailand. Figure 6.3 describes the number of migrants in Thailand between 1990 and 2013 from these neighboring countries, Myanmar, Laos, and Cambodia. The nominal per capita GDP in Thailand has been three to five times higher compared to these three countries for the past 20 years. These income disparities have been the key drivers, which were further strengthened along with robust economic growth of Thailand. Among these three neighboring countries, Myanmar contributes the largest share (about half) of the foreign population in Thailand. The actual number of migrants from Myanmar in Thailand also increased by more than six times (from 0.2 million to 1.6 million) between 1990 and 2010. This is also evident in Figure 6.3, which suggests sizeable movements of people from Myanmar to Thailand over the past 20 years.

In the case of Singapore, migration from neighboring Indonesia and Malaysia is significant, as shown in Figure 6.4. Singapore is the richest country in Asia and exhibits a significant income disparity with these two neighboring countries. The Singaporean cultural and language dimensions are very close to those of China, and as such, this proximity should affect migration patterns from China. As Figure 6.4 shows, Malaysia and China together occupied about 50% of the foreign population in Singapore in 1990. This has gradually increased to 60% in 2013.

In 1990, there were 0.2 million migrants from Malaysia, while that number was 0.15 million for China. In 2013, however, while there were more than 1 million migrants from Malaysia in Singapore, the number for Chinese was less than 0.4 million. This could imply that geographic proximity may be more important than similarities in culture or language to explain the patterns of international migration to Singapore.

6.2.3 Changes in labor demand: the feminization of international migration

The importance of costs associated with moving in relation to migration patterns is also highlighted by looking at the cases in Thailand, Singapore, and their neighboring countries over the past 20 years. Geographic distance, income disparity, and cultural or language similarities between origin and destination countries are key variables. Changes in

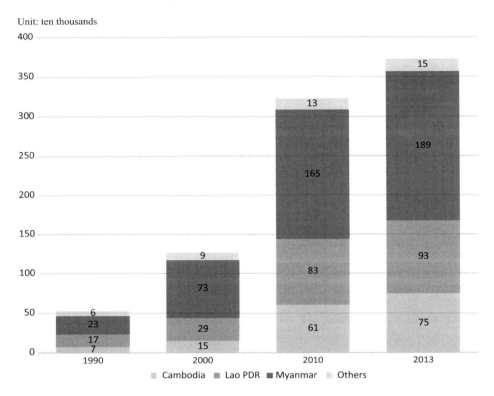

FIGURE 6.3 Changes in the sizes of foreign populations from Cambodia, Lao PDR, and Myanmar in Thailand.

Source: Trends in International Migrant Stock: Migrants by Destination and Origin (2013).

labor demand in local labor markets determine migration patterns as well, particularly in the changes observed with respect to the proportion of female and male workers.

Figure 6.5 shows the change in the share of females among foreign residents of the top five countries in 1990, 2000, 2010, and 2013. According to this, the shares for Thailand, Malaysia, Japan, and Hong Kong were less than 50% in 1990. However, all countries except Malaysia experienced increases in their shares of female migrants. In particular, Hong Kong's share has increased by 10 percentage points in 2013 to 59.2%. The shares for Thailand and Japan have also gradually increased. These trends suggest that richer economies in Asia, in particular Singapore and Hong Kong, have attracted disproportionately more female migrants than males.

Table 6.3 summarizes the female proportions of foreign residents in Hong Kong and Singapore. The shares of female migrants from China are roughly the same for Hong Kong and Singapore, at around 50%. However, while the total numbers of migrants from Indonesia and the Philippines are smaller than that from China, their female shares are much higher, at around 90%. One of the possible reasons for this could be related to the fact that female migrants in Hong Kong tend to be often engaged in domestic work in local households. In Singapore, on the other hand, no such concentration is observed: the shares of female migrants from Indonesia and Malaysia were at similar rates as that for Chinese.

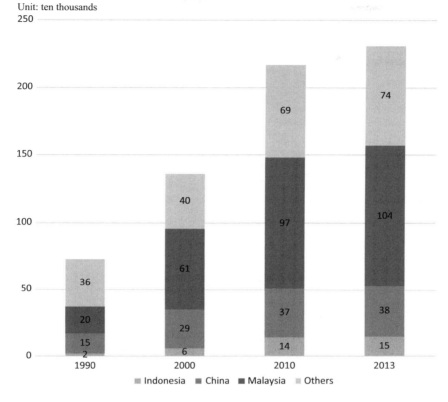

FIGURE 6.4 Changes in the sizes of foreign populations from China, Malaysia, and Indonesia in Singapore.

Source: Trends in International Migrant Stock: Migrants by Destination and Origin (2013).

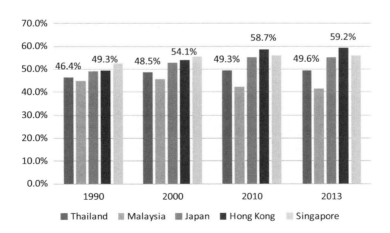

FIGURE 6.5 Female share of foreign population.

Source: Trends in International Migrant Stock: Migrants by Destination and Origin (2013).

TABLE 6.3 Female share of foreign populations in Hong Kong and Singapore, by origins

(%)	1990	2000	2010	2013
Destination: Hong Kong				
China	44.5	48.2	55.4	55.8
Indonesia	81.2	82.2	89.8	90.5
The Philippines	88.2	89.3	97.5	98.3
Destination: Singapore				
China	53.2	57.4	58.8	59.0
Indonesia	36.1	43.5	42.4	41.5
Malaysia	54.6	58.9	56.7	56.4

Source: Trends in International Migrant Stock: Migrants by Destination and Origin (2013).

6.3 THE ROLES OF POLICY AND INSTITUTIONAL CHANGE

6.3.1 Demand-driven *status-quo* policy: the case of Thailand

As discussed earlier, Thailand has become a major destination and recipient of foreign workers from neighboring countries in the past 20 years. Its migration policy is essentially driven by the needs of businesses, where the ongoing realities of migrant inflows from Myanmar, Laos, and Cambodia, and the related employment practices, are approved tacitly, ex-post. We will refer to such practices as *status-quo* policies.

When the Thai economy was growing rapidly through an export-oriented industrialization strategy in the early 1990s, shortages of unskilled labor became apparent. Demand for foreign workers started to rise. In response, the government extended the application of work permits, which were initially introduced for workers from Myanmar in 1992, to workers from Laos and Cambodia as well. Such decisions were casually approved by the cabinet and did not go through the legislative system. It was basically a policy response that allowed issuing work permits to migrants already in Thailand, who had not gone through formal entry procedures and thus were not registered. Such ad-hoc extensions of work-permit systems were often inconsistent and contradicted immigration control law and the foreign labor law of Thailand. Such practices, however, have been repeated to allow employment from the three neighboring countries on a temporary basis, and for specific targeted industries. The majority of unskilled migrant workers in Thailand were thus illegal in terms of immigration control, but as they were provided work permits, they were given a "semi-legal" status, conditional on registration (Yamada, 2015).

In 2008, the Foreign Labor Act of 1978 was abolished, and a new Foreign Labor Act of 2008 was promulgated. This Act required foreign workers who were granted work permits, to obtain nationality certificates and official travel documents from the respective governments of their countries of origin. It attempted to legalize the illegal and semi-legal migrant workers in Thailand. The new legal framework also intended to deport workers that could not meet the legalization procedures under the new legislation as illegal migrants.

This new legalization policy was, however, very costly for workers from the three neighboring countries, especially for those from Myanmar. This was also true for their Thai employers, because of the significant transaction costs involved. Exploitative agents and intermediaries emerged as well, and opportunity costs became high for employers who lost workers, even temporarily.

Given this, the government was under strong pressure to address the increasing labor demand in the domestic economy. *Ad-hoc status-quo* policy responses were repeated, which involved the extension of old work permits. This is a typical example of a business-driven *status-quo* policy.

6.3.2 Government as an intermediary: the case of South Korea

South Korea provides an interesting case, whose employment permit system is based on a policy that is almost completely the opposite to that of Thailand. In South Korea, there had been a technical intern training system similar to that of Japan. This was, however, abolished and a new employment permit system was established in 2004. The inflow of foreign workers accelerated after that (Imaizumi, 2014).

This system works as follows. First, labor shortages are estimated for each of the industries. Then, the government mediates the placement of migrant workers and the operations of recruiting enterprises. This is based on bilateral agreements between South Korea and sending country governments, where job matching is done through intergovernmental arrangements. A standardized contract is then exchanged between the governments of the sending country and South Korea. The main receiving partners are small and medium enterprises (SMEs) in South Korea. To qualify for this program, recruiting Korean SMEs must have had at least engaged in local recruitment activities for two weeks and found that the job positions could not be filled by local workers. Language training is also offered to migrant workers. Migrant workers can move from one company to another as long as they operate within the same industry. The Korean system is an elaborate system, which is designed relatively meticulously (Takayasu 2017).

This employment permit system in South Korea is based on the "brotherhood visa" and general visa acceptance procedures. Brotherhood visas are mainly for Korean-Chinese who share common languages. General visas mainly cover migrants from ASEAN countries. Migrant workers under brotherhood visas work in the manufacturing, nursing, and construction sectors. In addition, South Korea has signed an agreement with Thailand and Vietnam, where migrant workers under the general visa system are accepted into the manufacturing sector. South Korea's employment permits are valid for three years but can be extended for another year and ten months. Since Korean law requires the granting of permanent residence status to migrants after five years, the government typically sends workers back to their home countries in about four years and ten months. As described, the South Korean government plays a unique and pivotal role of an intermediary coordinating demand and supply of foreign labor.

Thus far, the section has described pull factors in Thailand and South Korea for migrant labor. They see migration issues in terms of compensating for the shortages of unskilled labor in their labor-intensive domestic industries, and their positions favoring temporary labor over full-fledged migration are similar. However, they differ significantly in terms of the involvement of the government and the institutional setup to manage international migration. Such differences ultimately play out in differences in payoffs for migrant workers, employers, agents, affecting the overall economic welfare of the society.

6.3.3 Free movement of high-skilled workers: the case of ASEAN

This section will finally look at the labor mobility of highly skilled workers, or "global talents" (Kerr 2019), within the context of the economic integration of ASEAN.

The economic integration of ASEAN is manifested by the establishment of the "ASEAN Economic Community (AEC)." The AEC was launched with the aim of eventually establishing a similar type of integration to that of the EU. Given this, this section explores the aspirations behind the liberalization of human movement in the region, and the extent and progress of institutionalization to achieve these.

AEC is an economic community consisting of the ten ASEAN member states. It was launched at the end of December 2015 with the goal of integrating the region with following four key objectives: (1) to achieve a single market and a single production base; (2) to realize a competitive economic area through infrastructure development; (3) to realize fair economic development; and (4) to promote integration into the global economy through trade and investment. Concrete measures include the abolition of tariffs, streamlined cross-border transactions by introducing electronic systems, promotion of service-trade, and liberalization of international aviation. The expectation was that these would turn ASEAN into a regional hub for trade and investment, which would be further facilitated by FTAs with countries outside the region (Fukunaga and Isono 2015).

Because of its focus on the liberalization of trade and investment of goods and services, liberalization in labor migration is limited to highly skilled personnel only, who directly work in trade and investment, as well as to international tourists who consume the services offered in the region. It does not yet deal with movements of unskilled and low-skilled workers (Yamada 2015).

Because the AEC was only launched quite recently, it is still difficult to assess the impacts of increased labor mobility of high-skilled workers on recipient and sending countries. Theoretically, however, if the those high-skilled workers substitute for local workers, increased supply of such migrant workers would reduce the wage levels of workers in host countries as well. On the contrary, if they are complementary, this would lead to increased demand for local workers in host countries, and thus wage levels of those workers in host countries would not decrease. Furthermore, if high-skilled migrant workers are complementary to both unskilled and low-skilled workers in the host country, wages of both types of workers in the host country will also not decrease.

What would be the effects on the sending country? One of the key concerns is the possibility of a serious brain-drain. This could happen when high-skilled workers do not return to their home countries. However, there is also a possibility that such liberalization could bring benefits to the sending countries through the following two routes, that do not require the return of those high-skilled workers to their home countries. The first is the potential related to the transfer of knowledge and technology from host to home countries, and that of capital through remittances. The second is that liberalization of international labor migration could increase future wage incomes, encourage human capital investments in sending countries, and create positive externalities. How could this happen?

Take the case of Singapore, where the share of resident foreigners is higher than 30%, and also has the highest income level in the region. With the launch of the AEC, workers with high skills from neighboring lower income countries, such as Cambodia, will move to Singapore. Even if they do not return to Cambodia, there is still a possibility that the latest knowledge and technology acquired by those workers will flow back into Cambodia. This could happen because the knowledge and technology embedded in these Cambodian workers will always be updated and reflect Singapore's standards, and when they become key nodes of both formal or informal networks, connecting the Cambodian community in Singapore. Furthermore, as opportunities of moving to Singapore grow, this could induce investments in education in Cambodia. This could in turn promote increased inflows of foreign knowledge into Cambodia. It could also lead to more active diffusion and creation of knowledge. There is a possibility that such benefits from increased liberalization in the regional labor market could outweigh the losses from brain-drain (see Box 6).

CONCLUSION

This chapter has discussed the pull (demand) and push (supply) factors that lead to international labor migration, which are determined by the degree of regional income disparity and geographic distance. First, the significant income disparities in Asia are the primary causes of labor movement across borders. The extent of the disparity influences the extent of benefits of international labor migration. Regarding the second point, if the distance between sending and receiving countries is short, the cost incurred for movement would be small, which could trigger international migration even when the income gap is not as large.

As such, the expected income and cost of migrating would determine the flow and patterns of international labor migration. In addition, historical migration patterns would also increase network effects of migration, and it could thus affect migration patterns through changes in the cost structures of migration.

Would there be any disadvantages associated with international migration, in terms of economic welfare in both the sending and recipient countries? This ultimately depends on the conditions of the pull factors (demand) and the push factors (supply). If the working conditions in recipient countries are better and more decent, workers will be happy to move. Under rapid economic development, however, demand for migrant workers often increases in sectors with poor working conditions (Peters 2017). Such cases have been reported in Japan, within the context of the Industrial Training and Technical Internship Program (Kamibayashi 2015). This happen when workers in the recipient country avoid employment in sectors with bad working conditions, and this creates demand for migrant workers. The issue of working conditions and international migration is not necessarily straightforward and requires further research. Similarly, more research on issues such as the effects of migrant workers leaving their children at their home country is needed (see Cortes, 2015).

For Asia to maintain and further promote its position as an attractive market and competitive production base, its labor markets must be efficient, and with decent working conditions too. International labor migration could alleviate labor market mismatches and could contribute to upgrading working conditions. These issues are particularly important for Asia, because of its significant population size, and its potential to realize

BOX 6 Brain circulation and Asian entrepreneurs in Silicon Valley

Momoko Kawakami

Recent trends in international labor migration are characterized by the rising number of those with high skills and educational backgrounds, as well as by a concentration in destinations to only a few developed countries (Docquier and Rapoport, 2012; Kerr et al., 2016). The outmigration of the highly educated from developing countries to developed countries has long been viewed negatively as a "brain drain," detrimental to the economic development of their home countries, further contributing to increased inequality at the international level. Empirical evidence since the mid-2000s, however, suggests that such international movement of highly skilled individuals has had, in fact – and under certain conditions – positive effects on the economic development of such developing countries.

How could brain drains affect sending countries positively? One of the primary reasons is because of the connections migrant workers often continue to maintain with their home countries after moving abroad. These relationships contribute to economic development as the highly skilled migrants transmit knowledge and information through these networks and provide local industries access to global business networks. The diffusion of knowledge and information through international movement of people is captured by the concept of "brain circulation."

The case of Asian migrant entrepreneurs in Silicon Valley provides a good example that suggests strong relationships between "brain circulation" and the rise of high-tech industries in Asia. Silicon Valley, located in California to the south of San Francisco, is known as the home of leading high-tech companies such as Google, Facebook, and Tesla. It is also renowned as the birthplace of high-tech startups. Silicon Valley has always been a global innovation hub, in semiconductors and computers in the 1970s and 80s, and in new technologies such as Internet of Things (IoT), Artificial Intelligence (AI), and autonomous driving in the 2010s.

Asian entrepreneurs and engineers play key roles in this global high-tech community. Of the start-ups established between 1995 and 2005, 16% had an Indian founder, while immigrants from China and Taiwan were key founders in 13% of them (Wadhwa et al., 2007). Many high-tech companies, such as Google, have key board members from Asia as well.

Among Asian entrepreneurs in Silicon Valley, quite a few came to the US as science and engineering students and found jobs in the US after graduation. Take the case of Taiwan, in which a significant number of its "best and brightest" students have eventually emerged as global entrepreneurs. In Taiwan, from the 1970s to the 1990s, many science and engineering graduates from prestigious universities departed for the United States for graduate study and future job opportunities (Chang, 1992). Many of them stayed in the US after graduation, and landed jobs with high-tech companies and research institutions. Some of them went on to establish their own businesses with their peers and have become successful entrepreneurs in Silicon Valley.

These immigrants bridged the high-tech communities in the US and Taiwan and contributed to the rise of the Taiwanese high-tech industries by playing the following roles. First, they provided key advice and inputs into Taiwan's science and technology policy through various international fora and conferences as well as personal connections. For example, the roles of Taiwanese scientists and engineers in the US were crucial in the establishment of the Taiwanese semiconductor industry in the 1970s (Sato, 2007). Second, when Taiwan's electronics industry began to grow in the mid-1980s, an increasing number of people started to return from Silicon Valley to assume key positions in high-tech companies or established their own businesses in Taiwan. These people brought back not only technologies but also management know-how, market knowledge, and personal networks from the American high-tech industry, which all contributed to the development of Taiwan's high-tech industry (Hsu and Saxenian, 2000; Saxenian, 2006). Third, those who have remained in the US have also contributed to the advancement of the high-tech industry in Taiwan by establishing R&D bases and promoting collaboration with Taiwanese companies. Similar mechanisms of brain circulation have also been at play in India and China.

In this way, these individuals who migrated to the US for high education have been contributing to the industrial development of their home countries in various ways over decades. At the same time, they were also pivotal in connecting the innovative capabilities of Silicon Valley with the growing production capacities and market potentials in Asia, keeping Silicon Valley dynamic. Whether the outmigration of highly educated people will play out as a net "brain drain" or as a net "brain gain" contributing to diffusing advanced managerial and technological knowledge to their home countries can only be evaluated from a longer time-perspective.

REFERENCES

Ananta, Aris and Evi Nurvidya Ariffin (eds.). (2004). *International Migration in Southeast Asia*, Singapore: ISEAS.
Borjas, George J. (2014). *Immigration Economics*, Chicago: Harvard University Press.
Borjas, George J. (2016). *We Wanted Workers: Unraveling the Immigration Narrative*, New York: Norton.

Chang, Shujen Lee. (1992). "Causes of Brain Drain and Solutions: The Taiwan Experience," *Studies in Comparative International Development*, 27(1): 27–43.

Cortes, Patricia. (2015). "The Feminization of International Migration and its effects on the Families Left behind: Evidence from the Philippines," *World Development*, 65: 62–78.

Docquier, F. and H. Rapoport. (2012). "Globalization, Brain Drain, and Development," *Journal of Economic Literature*, 50(3): 681–730.

Fukunaga, Yoshifumi and Ikumo Isono. (2015). "AEC Sousetsu to ha Nanika" [What Is a Foundation of AEC (ASEAN Economic Community)?], *Ajiken World Trend*, 242: 4–7.

Hsu, Jinn-Yuh and AnnaLee Saxenian. (2000). "The Limits of Guanxi Capitalism: Transnational Collaboration between Taiwan and the USA," *Environment and Planning A*, 32: 1991–2005.

Imaizumi, Shinya. (2014). "Higashi Ajia ni okeru Gaikokujin Koyou Hosei no Kosatsu" [An Investigation of Foreign Labor Laws in East Asia], in Miwa Yamada (ed.), *Ajia ni okeru Iminrodosha no Hoseido: Okuridashikoku to Ukeirekoku no Kyotsukiban no Kochiku ni Mukete* [*Laws and Labour Migration Policies in East Asia: Seeking a Common Platform of Sending and Receiving Countries*]. No. 611. Chiba: IDE-JETRO.

Kamibayashi, Chieko. (2015). *Gaikokujin Roudousha Ukeire to Nihon Shakai – Ginou Jisshyu Seido no Tenkai to Jiremma* [*Demanding Foreign Labour Forces and Japanese Society—Expansions and Dilemmas of Industrial Training and Technical Internship Program*]. Tokyo: The University of Tokyo Press.

Kerr, S. P., W. Kerr, Ç. Özden and C. Parsons. 2016. "Global Talent Flows," *Journal of Economic Perspectives*, 30(4): 83–106.

Kerr, William R. (2019). *The Gift of Global Talent: How Migration Shapes Business, Economy & Society*, Stanford: Stanford University Press.

Lewis, Ethan. (2013). "Immigration and Production Technology," *Annual Review of Economics*, 5: 165–191.

Peters, Margaret. (2017). *Trading Barriers: Immigration and the Remaking of Globalization*, Princeton: Princeton University Press.

Sato, Yukihito. (2007). *The emergence and development of Taiwan's high-tech industry* (*Taiwan Haiteku Sangyo no Seisei to Tenkai*), Tokyo: Iwanami Publishers.

Saxenian, A. (2006). *The New Argonauts: Regional Advantage in a Global Economy*, Chicago: Harvard University Press.

Takayasu, Yuichi. (2017). "Kankoku ni okeru Gaikokujin Roudousha Ukeire Seisaku ni Kansuru Kousatsu—Koyou Kyoka Sei wo Chushin ni" [An Investigation of Policy of Foreign Labour Forces in Korea—Looking at Employment Permit System], *Daito Bunka Daigaku Keizai Ronshu* [*Economic Journal*], No. 108. Tokyo: Daito Bunka University.

Wadhwa, V., A. Saxenian, B. Rissing and G. Gereffi. (2007). *America's New Immigrant Entrepreneurs*, Master of Engineering Management Program, School of Engineering, Duke University.

Yamada, Miwa. (2015). "ASEAN ni Okeru Roudousha no Idou—2015 ni Ukeirekoku to Okuridashikoku ha Goui Dekiru no ka" [Labour Movement in ASEAN—Can Sending and Receiving Countries Make an Agreement?], *Ajiken World Trend*, 242: 24–27.

PART III
Dynamic Asia

7 Innovating Asia: growth pattern changes in post-middle-income economies

Asei Ito

Emerging center of increasing international patents applications, Nanshan District, Shenzhen, China (2017, Photo by Asei Ito).

LEARNING GOALS

- Understand the changing patterns of economic growth in Asia.
- Understand the sources of innovation.
- Understand the development initiatives of Asian countries and the underlying principles involved.

INTRODUCTION

The third part of this book, entitled *Dynamic Asia*, takes a look at the Asian economy in terms of the following three dimensions. The first is innovation as a critical factor underlying contemporary economic growth (Chapter 7). The second is urbanization as the driver of global production networks and the robust domestic consumption in the rapidly emerging mega-cities and regions of Asia (Chapter 8). The third are the important roles and contribution of the informal economy to the Asian economy (Chapter 9). These are dimensions that have vital implications for the prosperity, inclusiveness, and sustainability of Asia in its endeavor to realize the "Asian century."

This chapter focuses on innovation, which is increasingly gaining momentum in the Asian economy. Half a century ago, new products and services were invented in developed countries, and then introduced to Asia with significant time lags. Economic growth in Asia during the past half-century has lifted many Asian countries from poverty to middle-income levels. As a result, conventional economic growth patterns that depended on low-cost advantages are reaching their limits.

In this context, the first objective of this chapter is to understand the mechanisms of economic growth at different stages of economic development, the main sources of innovation and productivity improvement, and the common challenges that Asian countries face as a result. The second objective is to understand the various efforts of Asian countries in relation to innovation, by focusing on their different economic conditions and advantages to solve common challenges.

7.1 THE SUCCESS OF "CATCHING-UP" AND THE "MIDDLE-INCOME TRAP"

7.1.1 Asian NIEs and catch-up industrialization

As outlined in Chapter 1, the Newly Industrializing Economies (NIEs) of Asia share a common growth pattern. Their phenomenal economic growth in the 1970s and onwards was achieved through export-oriented industrialization strategies, attained through underlying mechanisms. The first was increased productivity that can be attributed to the migration of agricultural workers to urban and industrial sectors, backed by the expansion of primary education and an increase in the working-age population. Second, the introduction of advanced equipment (particularly machinery) from developed countries was also essential, especially in the manufacturing sector. This led to improvements in productivity within a short period, which were based on the "advantage of backwardness" as discussed in Chapter 1. However, the availability of local human resources with sufficient technical and engineering knowledge became increasingly important for operating the advanced equipment, and to accumulate knowledge through reverse-engineering to build internal capacity in mechanical design and manufacturing methods. Each economy needed to internalize capabilities and realize the potential advantages and opportunities of their backwardness relative to advanced economies in Europe, the US, and Japan.

In the Asian NIEs, such advanced technologies were first introduced in specific geographical areas, often called export processing or special economic zones, or at large plants. Noteworthy is that manufacturing and business knowledge had significant spillover effects, spreading beyond specific companies and plants as people deepened their technological capabilities through product reverse-engineering and spin-offs. Through these mechanisms, small- and medium-sized enterprises gradually evolved around large export-oriented factories, which led to the formation of sizeable supporting industries through backward linkages. In such industrial clusters, geographical proximity allowed manufacturing and marketing know-how to be shared more quickly, which contributed to improving productivity.

7.1.2 Growth accounting approach

The sources of economic growth can be understood by decomposing the increase in gross domestic product (GDP) during a certain period. In growth accounting, GDP can be broken down in three different ways: production-based decomposition by industry; expenditure-based by consumption, government spending, investment, and foreign trade; and distribution-based by household income, corporate revenue, and government revenue. In addition, by assuming a specific form of production function, we can separately estimate the contribution to growth by capital input (K), labor input (L), and other unexplained efficiency improvements, called "total factor productivity (TFP)." Each decomposition approach is useful for understanding economic growth. However, the production function approach, rooted in neoclassical growth theory, is regarded as essential to evaluating economic growth performance.

Table 7.1 provides a breakdown of the contributions of the different input factors to the growth of Asian economies since 1970. From 1970 to 1985, the growth in Asian NIEs (Singapore, Taiwan, South Korea, and Hong Kong) was primarily led by capital inputs. In the case of South Korea, for example, 7% points out of the average annual growth rate of 8.5% was due to capital inputs. This figure indicates that 82% of South Korea's economic growth during this period was based on capital inputs, such as investments in fixed-assets and new machinery. Another important characteristic of this period was the positive and substantial contribution from labor input of approximately 1–2 percentage points in all countries except Japan. Large numbers of workers entered the labor market, supported by the favorable demographic dynamics of a rapidly increasing working-age population. This effect, often called the demographic dividend, is discussed in Chapter 10. On the other hand, the contribution of the TFP has been quite limited. Capital input was probably the most important driver of growth, which was supported by labor inputs. A similar pattern persisted during the period 1985–2000.

However, the table suggests a significant structural change in Asia's growth mechanisms since 2000. Although the contributions of capital input to growth continues to be large, it has dropped to 3% points or less in Asian NIEs, which is about half of what it was in the 1970s. The effects of labor inputs also declined to somewhere between 0.1% and 0.4% except for Singapore, where population growth continues through active immigration policies. In Japan, where the workforce has started to decline, the effects of labor inputs were negative, while the contribution of TFP to economic growth has been increasing. Similar trends have been observed in Asian NIEs as well; the rate of TFP increased to 1.1%–1.8%. In the case of South Korea, for example, out of the total average growth rate of 4.0%, 1.5 percentage points were due to TFP growth during 2000–2014. In other words, TFP was responsible for approximately 37.5% of South Korea's growth during this period.

In 1993, Paul Krugman published an article entitled, "The Myth of the Asian Miracle," which emphasized the low contributions of TFP growth in Asian countries, and argued that such growth based on injection of labor and capital could not be sustained

TABLE 7.1 Growth account in Asian economies (1970–2014)

	1970–1985						1985–2000						2000–2014					
	GDP growth rate (ΔY) (%)	Contribution by capital input (ΔK)			Contribution by labor input (ΔL) (%)	Contribution by TFP (ΔA) (%)	GDP growth rate (ΔY) (%)	Contribution by Capital Input (ΔK)			Contribution by labor input (ΔL) (%)	Contribution by TFP (ΔA) (%)	GDP growth rate (ΔY) (%)	Contribution by Capital Input (ΔK)			Contribution by labor input (ΔL) (%)	Contribution by TFP (ΔA) (%)
		Sub-total (%)	Non-IT capital (%)	IT capital (%)				Sub-total (%)	Non-IT capital (%)	IT capital (%)				Sub-total (%)	Non-IT capital (%)	IT capital (%)		
Japan	4.3	3.3	3.1	0.3	0.2	0.8	2.4	1.9	1.6	0.4	-0.2	0.7	0.7	0.3	0.1	0.2	-0.2	0.6
Singapore	7.9	6.5	5.9	0.5	2.1	-0.6	7.3	4.2	3.4	0.8	1.8	1.3	5.2	2.7	2.1	0.6	1.4	1.1
Taiwan	8.9	5.7	5.3	0.4	1.7	1.5	7.3	3.7	3.2	0.4	0.9	2.7	3.7	1.9	1.7	0.3	0.4	1.4
South Korea	8.5	7.0	6.6	0.4	1.4	0.1	7.7	5.0	4.4	0.6	0.9	1.8	4.0	2.4	2.1	0.3	0.1	1.5
Hong Kong	7.5	3.8	3.6	0.2	1.4	2.3	5.0	3.6	3.1	0.5	0.7	0.6	3.7	1.6	1.2	0.4	0.3	1.8
China	7.3	3.9	3.9	0.0	1.6	1.8	9.1	4.1	4.0	0.1	1.1	3.9	9.4	5.4	4.9	0.5	0.5	3.5
Malaysia	7.0	6.2	6.1	0.1	1.2	-0.6	6.9	5.5	5.2	0.3	1.2	0.1	5.1	3.0	2.4	0.6	0.9	1.2
Philippines	3.3	3.8	3.7	0.2	1.6	-2.2	4.0	2.3	2.0	0.2	0.7	1.0	4.9	2.3	1.9	0.4	0.7	1.9
Thailand	6.1	3.3	3.1	0.2	1.8	0.9	6.1	4.1	3.7	0.4	0.9	1.1	4.0	1.4	1.1	0.3	0.1	2.6
Vietnam	3.7	0.8	0.7	0.1	1.7	1.2	6.6	4.4	4.1	0.3	0.3	1.1	6.7	5.7	5.2	0.5	0.8	0.2
Indonesia	6.9	5.0	4.9	0.1	1.5	0.4	5.1	4.2	4.0	0.2	1.2	-0.3	5.5	2.9	2.7	0.2	1.0	1.7
Mongolia	6.1	5.7	5.6	0.1	0.8	-0.4	1.1	1.7	1.6	0.1	0.6	-1.2	7.8	2.7	2.4	0.3	0.9	4.2
Bangladesh	1.6	1.0	0.9	0.0	1.0	-0.3	4.8	3.6	3.4	0.1	1.6	-0.4	5.6	4.9	4.7	0.2	0.9	-0.2
India	3.6	1.5	1.5	0.0	1.6	0.5	5.5	1.8	1.8	0.1	1.2	2.4	6.7	3.4	3.2	0.2	0.8	2.6

Source: Asian Productivity Organization (APO), Productivity Database 2016.

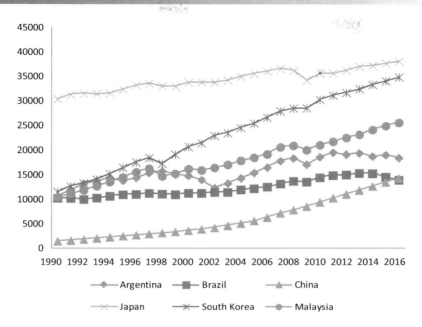

FIGURE 7.1 Per capita GDP in selected countries.

Source: The World Bank, World Development Indicators.

Note: Per capita GDP is in purchasing power parity (PPP) and 2011 constant US dollar.

(Krugman, 1993). This attracted significant attention and sparked debates among academics and policymakers, which were further fueled by the outbreak of the Asian financial crisis in 1997, which had detrimental effects on countries particularly Indonesia and Thailand. However, many of those countries recovered shortly after this event, as indicated in Figure 7.1; while some of the Asian countries recorded negative growth from 1997 to 1999, they started to gain momentum again in the 2000s. In contrast, economic stagnation became evident in other regions, such as Latin America. Because many of the Asian economies were still of middle- and low-income status in the 1990s, there remained significant space for economic catching-up with developed countries through growth induced by increased inputs of capital and labor. The point Krugman made on the need to improve TFP is theoretically correct, but most of the Asian economies were at a place where input-driven growth was still effective (Ohno, 2013).

7.1.3 Can Asia sustain its growth?

Asia's economic growth continued even after the Asian financial crisis. According to the World Bank, China and Thailand ascended to the upper-middle-income group in the 2000s, and Vietnam and India to the lower-middle-income group. Such region-wide increases in income levels triggered a debate as to whether such robust growth could be sustained in the future. Growth from low- to middle-income status can be achieved through export-oriented industrialization supported by low wage levels and a demographic dividend. However, when an economy reaches the middle-income level, further shifting from middle- to high-income status requires different growth strategies. Achieving further growth into the high-income group is by no means simple, considering the fact that only a handful of economies had been successful at doing so, including the Asian NIEs. This phenomenon is often called "the middle-income trap" (Gill and Kharas, 2007). As indicated in Figure 7.1, South Korea's growth trajectory has been remarkable and the country has developed into the high-income category, while the GDP per capita of Argentina and Brazil in the 2000s remained stagnant at the level of the 1990s.

The reasons for the stagnating, or declining, growth rates can also be understood using the growth accounting framework. Capital inputs (K) and labor inputs (L) had been the main drivers of growth during the catching-up stage. Since the 1990s, however, the contribution of capital investments started to decline as their marginal returns diminished. In addition, economic development induced changes in demographic factors particularly in terms of declining birthrates and increased life expectancies, which led to the emergence of an ageing society (see Chapter 10). This transition in demographic structures resulted in decreased labor inputs (L), and as such, the expansion of labor-supply could not be the source of further growth. Despite the differences in the stages of economic development, many countries in Asia have already entered such phases of declining workforce and reduced efficiency of capital inputs. To effectively address such common challenges, improvements in productivity are becoming particularly important for the region.

7.2 INNOVATION AND SOURCES OF GROWTH

7.2.1 Human capital and research and development (R&D)

Improving macro-level productivity can be achieved through different avenues such as the promotion of urbanization, upgrading of the industrial structure, institutional reform, and opening-up of the economy. This section will, however, focus specifically on the role of innovation within this context. Particular attention will be given to issues such as human capital accumulation, research and development (R&D), progress in digitalization, and the effects of agglomeration and networks.

First, human capital has long been the focus of attention as a source of economic growth and innovation. During the phase of industrialization and catching-up, the importance of primary and secondary education was emphasized in relation to the basic skills and knowledge needed to undertake work in modern factories. In 1970, the Asian NIEs including South Korea, Taiwan, and Hong Kong, achieved universal primary education, and likewise significant progress were also made in secondary education coverage, as highlighted in the *East Asian Miracle* report (World Bank, 1993). Similar progress was seen in latecomer countries such as Malaysia and Thailand, where 80% of their populations received primary education in the 1970s. Regarding secondary education, this picked up momentum in the 1990s as well, reaching about 80% of their populations in 2015. While countries such as Cambodia and Myanmar are still in the process of making such progress, for most countries in Asia, the remaining challenges are mainly related to achieving increased opportunities for higher education.

While these quantitative dimensions of growing educational opportunities are impressive, Asia has also made improvements in the quality of education. This is evident from the results of various international academic examinations, and in the changing positions in global rankings of leading Asian universities. Table 7.2 lists the top 10 universities in Asia, adopted from the World University Ranking published by *The Times*. In addition to former Asian NIEs, several universities from mainland China are also among the top. In contrast, universities in ASEAN countries are not yet in these rankings, except for Singapore. This suggests that universities in NIEs and China are now in a position to cater for the supply of competitive human resources at the global level.

As improvements in education typically contribute to productivity by raising human capital, R&D by firms in the private sector and public research institutions also contributes to innovation through the development of new technologies and products. To assess

TABLE 7.2 Top ten universities in Asia (*The Times* higher education ranking)

The world rank	Name of university	Location	Overall score	Teaching	Research	Citations	Industry income	International outlook
22	Tsinghua University	China	82.9	87.7	94.1	74.8	99.8	45.8
23	National University of Singapore	Singapore	82.4	77.3	88.8	78.9	67.6	95.5
31	Peking University	China	79.3	88.8	80.4	76.7	48.3	57.5
36	University of Hong Kong	Hong Kong	76.3	72.6	78.4	73.7	56.5	99.7
41	The Hong Kong University of Science and Technology	Hong Kong	74.5	56.8	67.6	93.9	65.8	98.0
42	The University of Tokyo	Japan	74.1	84	87.2	61.3	67.2	35.9
51	Nanyang Technological University, Singapore	Singapore	72.2	55.4	65.8	88.6	83.1	95.4
53	Chinese University of Hong Kong	Hong Kong	71.4	59.3	64.9	84.5	54.1	98.6
63	Seoul National University	South Korea	67.5	74.6	71.1	64.2	77.2	35.1
65	Kyoto University	Japan	67.3	75.9	77.5	55	95.6	31.1

Source: The Times Higher Education World University Rankings 2019 (Accessed in July 3rd, 2019).

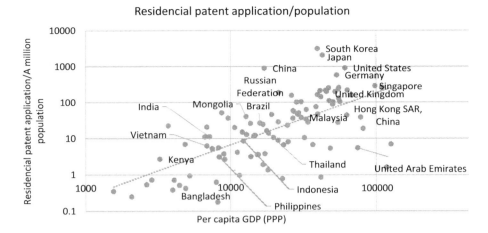

FIGURE 7.2 Patent application and per capita GDP (2017).
Source: The World Bank World Development Indicators.

the degree of investments in R&D, the ratio of R&D expenditures to GDP is often used. According to the World Bank and OECD, Japan increased its R&D to GDP ratio from 3.00% to 3.58% between 2000 and 2014, reaching 3.26% in 2018, to become one of the highest ratios in the world. South Korea had an even higher ratio, 4.29% in 2014, and 4.52% in 2018. China's R&D to GDP ratio is also increasing rapidly, reaching 2.04% in 2014, while that of Malaysia was 1.26% in the same year.

One of the outcomes of such R&D spending is the acquisition of patents and trademarks. In general, knowledge and know-how are nonexcludable, meaning that it is difficult to exclude those who did not invent them from using and benefitting from this knowledge and know-how. Because of this, when the benefits of cost-intensive R&D are easily secured by others, firms will have less incentives to undertake R&D at optimal levels. To address this issue, the patent system typically was introduced to guarantee royalty payments to the inventor for a certain period. The horizontal axis in Figure 7.2 indicates the per capita GDP of 102 countries, and the vertical axis the number of patent and trademark applications per million people in 2017 for different countries. The number of patent and trademark applications is clearly associated with the level of economic development, where countries such as South Korea, Japan, and China are positioned higher than the global average, indicating intensive applications for patents in these countries, while those in ASEAN are still at the global average.

7.2.2 Investments in IT capital and digitalization

The second issue is related to improving the efficiency of capital investments. In recent years, the Internet has spread in Asia and throughout the world, and the digitalization of the economy has progressed rapidly accordingly. There have been significant increases in efficiency levels through the application of IT in the manufacturing as well as the service sector. As indicated in the framework of growth accounting, the returns from capital investments tend to diminish over time. However, investments in IT and related equipment typically exhibit spillover effects, and do not diminish as fast as investment in capital.

Table 7.1 indicates the different contributions of capital inputs: the contribution of non-IT capital investments and that of IT capital investments. The latter refers to investments in computers, copy machines, communication devices, and software. To date, the contribution of IT capital in each country has not exceeded 1%, and the effect of traditional fixed-asset investments (non-IT capital) is still substantial. However, the contribution of IT capital investments is increasing as the economic growth rate is gradually declining. In the cases of Singapore and Hong Kong, the contribution of IT capital accounted for only 6% and 3% of overall economic growth (ΔY), respectively, during the period 1970–1985. This rate has increased to 11% for both countries during the period 2000–2014. In other Asian countries, the contributions of IT capital to growth are also increasing gradually; between 2000 and 2014, they contributed 6% of overall growth in China, 12% in Malaysia, 8% in Thailand, and 7% in Vietnam.

Investments in IT equipment have promoted the digitalization of the economy. Figure 7.3 summarizes the coverage of Internet connection with a speed of 4 Mbps (megabit per second) or faster for selected countries. A total of 4 Mbps is a speed sufficient for browsing general websites and watching videos on the Internet. In Thailand, fourth-generation mobile network services (4G services) started in 2012, and the speed of the network has rapidly improved. In Vietnam, the penetration rate of the 4 Mbps network exceeded 80% in the first quarter of 2017. According to the World Bank, mobile phone subscriptions in Singapore, South Korea, and Japan in the 2000s were already at approximately 50 per 100 people. However, penetration rates rapidly improved for other countries in Asia over the period 2005 to 2010, reaching 108 per 100 people in Thailand and 125 in Vietnam in 2010. Because the economy of Myanmar was in isolation for many years, and reforms and opening-up of its economy started only recently, the same figure in 2010 was just 1.1 units, although this rapidly increased to 75.7 units in 2015.

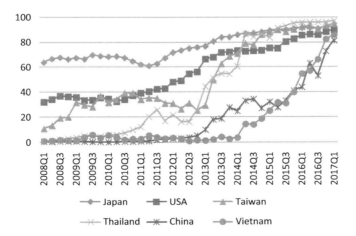

FIGURE 7.3 Share of Internet connection speed above 4 Mbps (%, 2008Q1–2017Q1).
Source: Akamai Technologies Database.

In the past, mobile phones were used to exchange text messages, in addition to voice calls. Today, the fourth-generation (4G) communication infrastructure allows us to access the Internet and exchange photos and electronic files on those hand-sets at any time. As a result, new services have evolved including, for example, those that match demand and supply for taxi services through applications on smartphones, equipped with Global Positioning Systems (GPS), which have become technically feasible. These digital technologies can better allocate scare resources and improve productivity in both developed and developing economies. In the past, developing countries were regarded as highly disadvantaged in terms of access to such advanced digital technology. This was referred to as "digital divide." However, the application of IT and related technology may also lead to productivity gains for developing countries as well, which are now referred to as "digital dividends" (World Bank, 2016).

7.2.3 Industrial clusters and networks

The third issue related to innovation is geographical proximity and networks. There have been increasing discussions regarding the importance of particular localities and regions in economic development and innovation in recent years (Sonobe and Otsuka, 2006; Yusuf et al., 2003). When companies in related industries and workers with specialized talent gather in a specific geographical area, the production of key parts and components of an industry become more efficient due to scale effects, and the diffusion of relevant productive knowledge is also promoted. Such benefits are referred to as "agglomeration economies." When there is concentration of population, or in general economic activities, these locations will be called "urban areas"; likewise, concentration of specific economic activities pertaining to specific industries are called "industrial clusters." However, such concentrations of economic activities will increase dis-utilities stemming from increased costs related to congestion (including traffic) and property prices. Spatial economics emphasizes the role of local demand, especially in urban areas, for diversified and differentiated goods, which in turn will result in promoting concentration of economic activity in a particular locality (the home-market effect). In Asia, however, industrial clusters were formulated primarily within export-oriented development strategies, and as such those clusters have had relatively weaker connections with local demand.

In Japan, the Keihin Industrial Zone between Tokyo and Yokohama, and the East-Osaka region, are among the main manufacturing clusters. Taiwan's Hsinchu area is also well known for the agglomeration of the electronics industry, led by a large semiconductor manufacturing foundry, Taiwan Semiconductor Manufacturing Company (TSMC). In Southeast Asia, large-scale investments of major foreign companies have promoted the formation of an extensive parts-supplier base, leading to a significant supporting industry cluster. One such example is the largest automobile manufacturing bases in Southeast Asia in the Eastern Seaboard Industrial Estate, located on the outskirts of Bangkok in Thailand, the formation of which has been led by foreign direct investment from major automotive manufacturing companies of the US and Japan. In mainland China, hundreds of industrial clusters exist in the

Yangtze Delta region centered around Shanghai, and in the Pearl River Delta region including Shenzhen, Guangzhou, and Dongguan (Fujita and Tabuchi, 1997; Ganne and Lecler, 2009).

Industrial clusters play an essential role in the production of knowledge and the promotion of innovation. According to data on international patent application published by the World Intellectual Property Organization (WIPO), Asia has the largest number of international patent applications globally. In particular, Japan's Tokyo-Yokohama area ranked first in the world, while in the second spot came China's Shenzhen-Hong Kong area, third the San Jose–San Francisco area in the US, followed by the Seoul area in South Korea (Cornell University, INSEAD, and WIPO, 2017). In China's Shenzhen and Hong Kong area, several globally competitive companies' headquarters are located, including Huawei Technology, Tencent, and DJI. In South Korea, LG Group and Samsung Electronics Corporation, both of whose headquarters are located in the Seoul mega region, lead R&D in their respective fields of businesses.

In addition to the role of geographical concentration on innovation, that of networks has also been widely recognized today, connecting local economies to leading industrial clusters and research institutes outside the region. According to recent studies, firms with diverse networks tend to perform better in product development and innovation (Beers and Zand, 2014). Looking back at the experiences of Asia, the growth of Taiwan's electronics industry is the result of its close relationships with Silicon Valley in the US, as demonstrated by the success case of the Acer Group, in which entrepreneurs formed personal cross-border networks that led to new business models in Asia (Saxenian, 2008). For research institutions, subsequent success in the commercialization of the inventions and innovation is dependent on collaborative relationships with companies.

In recent years, so-called "unicorn companies" have also been attracting significant attention, particularly those in Asia. A unicorn company is an unlisted company worth more than $1 billion in corporate value (see Box 7). These companies tend to emerge in the IT and other new industries, such as businesses in the "sharing economy," or those using evolving technologies including artificial intelligence. The concomitant challenge is to create an enabling environment for those potential entrepreneurs to quickly start their own businesses in these fields.

The presence of young entrepreneurs who graduated from Asian universities has also become prominent in the dynamic start-up scene in Asia. Some of those have not just been successful as entrepreneurs but have also emerged as pioneers of new goods and services. For example, DJI, the world's largest commercial unmanned aerial vehicle (UAV or drone) developer was established in Shenzhen, China, by young entrepreneur Frank Wang upon graduation from the Hong Kong University of Science and Technology in 2006 (listed in Table 7.2). New business models provoking startups and nurturing venture businesses is spreading in Asia, stimulated by such dynamic entrepreneurs. Such business models were initially imported from Silicon Valley, which also accompanied the emergence of angel investors, incubation centers, accelerators, and co-working spaces that provided low-cost startup environments. However, each of those ecosystems is now increasingly adopting and localizing through different local policies and conditions.

7.3 INNOVATION POLICIES IN ASIA

7.3.1 Theoretical foundations of innovation policy

As discussed in Chapter 4, Asian companies have mainly been engaged in low value-added processes within global value chains. This is particularly exemplified in the electronics manufacturing services, where many local companies are still struggling to catch-up with those in developed countries. Without a doubt, human capital, R&D, clusters, and networks have played important roles in improving productivity. However, an increasing number of these companies as well as governments in Asia are making efforts attempting to accelerate innovation.

Policies are crucial in promoting and supporting innovation. Governments, particularly those of Asian NIEs and China, are prioritizing and emphasizing the fostering of the development of new industries by formulating such innovation policies. Typical policy levers include funding for priority research areas and subsidies for corporate R&D activities. The rationale for such policy interventions is the presence of positive externalities of knowledge and innovation – the creation of new knowledge and the development of new products and services having spillover effects to other companies and individuals in the wider society. Therefore, one of the roles of policy is to make sure, for a certain period of time, that private returns to R&D are protected from free riders taking advantage of them, as discussed earlier. Otherwise, resources and efforts invested in innovation-related activities would be far below the socially optimal levels.

Let us take a look at the relationship between individual companies' R&D projects and innovation assistance policies, using a simple model (see Figure 7.4). The number of R&D projects of a company is determined by where the expected gains and associated costs from the R&D are in equilibrium. Assuming that promising fields for R&D are limited, the cost of R&D per project increases as the number of implemented projects increases, particularly for lower priority projects. In contrast, although the expected profit from the first project, which is most promising, is high, it is expected that the returns to R&D would decrease as the number of implemented projects increases. The horizontal axis represents the number

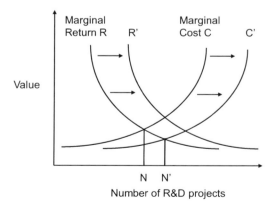

FIGURE 7.4 The relationships between innovation policy and the number of R&D projects.
Source: Made by the author based on David et al. (2000).

of projects implemented, and the vertical axis indicates the monetary value of the return and costs. As such, the marginal cost curve for R&D (curve C) has an upward slope, whereas the marginal return schedule (curve R) has a downward slope. Under this, promotion of R&D activities can be achieved by reducing the associated costs through government subsidies for R&D expenses. This would result in shifting the marginal cost curve C to C'. Such policies could shift the number of R&D projects from N to N', as figure 7.4 depicts. On the demand side, increasing the returns of R&D by boosting demand for those emerging technologies is possible by providing subsidies, which shift the marginal profit curve R to R'. For instance, governments can subsidize consumers with the purchase of new energy vehicles, which would promote R&D in related technologies.

7.3.2 China: "Made in China 2025" and the US–China trade dispute

Currently, the growth strategies of many Asian countries include elements that emphasize innovation. Here we discuss the cases of China and Thailand.

The global financial crisis in 2008, which started with the real estate sector in the US, affected Asian countries through a sharp decline in external demand. The crisis severely damaged China's export-oriented industry clustered in the coastal regions. Although the sharp decline in external demand was a short-term problem, because of the labor shortages which had already become apparent in the late 2000s in China, continuous wage increases eroded China's cost competitiveness. The need to be proactive to avoid the middle-income trap, and the importance of maintaining growth and productivity improvements by promoting marketing and structural reform, were acutely acknowledged as policy priorities in China accordingly (World Bank and Development Research Center of the Review Commission, PRC, 2013). As Table 7.1 indicates, China's economy had achieved an astonishing 9.4% annual growth rate from 2000 to 2014, of which 3.5 percentage points were due to productivity improvements.

To avoid the middle-income trap, the Chinese government has formulated a series of policies related to innovation. The "Made in China 2025" plan announced in 2015, assesses the current state of China's manufacturing industry as large but uncompetitive (The State Council, China, 2015). This plan aspires for China to become a globally competitive manufacturing country by 2049, which will mark the 100th anniversary of the founding of the People's Republic of China. To achieve that goal, China aims to incubate companies with indigenous R&D capabilities and globally acknowledged brand names. With specific numerical targets, the plan intends to double from 2013 to 2025 the number of R&D expenditures per unit of manufacturing companies' income and the number of patents per unit of operating income.

The plan is influenced by Germany's "Industry 4.0" plan and aims to combine the Internet and manufacturing industries. Currently, in addition to factory automation, Chinese companies suffering from soaring labor costs are actively looking for ways of applying the evolving technology for automation. Furthermore, a policy was announced in 2017 that targeted the promotion of artificial intelligence (AI) and related industries, which include technologies pertaining to language processing, voice and image recognition, and geographical data processing, as well as the applications of smart appliances, autonomous driving, and robotics using AI (The State Council, China, 2017).

The Chinese government is also supporting startups to promote innovation. The "mass entrepreneurship and innovation initiative" was launched in 2013 to support and emphasize innovation through a new generation of young entrepreneurs. Innovation policies of China's central government, however, tend to cover a wide range of sectors, lacking clarity in focus, resulting in ambiguous outcomes or making space for corruption among local bureaucrats. Using a firm-level dataset on renewable energy from 2009 to 2014, Yu et al. (2016) found negative and significant effects of government subsidies on firms' R&D investments. Such negative effects are also reported by Hong et al. (2016), who used an industry-level dataset for the high-tech sectors from 2001 to 2011, and suggested that government subsidies, particularly direct financing, have no causal effect on innovation.

When considering innovations from China, attention must be paid not only to central government plans but also to the initiatives of private companies and the role of clusters. In addition to Beijing and Shanghai, two cities are worth noting as innovation-driven clusters: Shenzhen in Guangdong Province in southern China, and Hangzhou in Zhejiang Province in eastern China. In terms of the number of international patent applications, Shenzhen is the most rapidly emerging city in the world because of the presence of Huawei and ZTE, which are both telecommunications equipment manufacturers. Tencent, the Chinese Internet giant, is also headquartered in Nanshan, Shenzhen. As of the first quarter of 2017, WeChat, Tencent's flagship application, had 928 million monthly active users. Hangzhou, another leading city in China, houses the e-commerce giant Alibaba, which developed an electronic payment network called Alipay. Today, Alibaba is already expanding into the Southeast Asian market and beyond and is expected to be a global tech giant in the 2020s.

The US–China trade dispute, or more broadly, the US–China confrontation which evolved after 2018, is intrinsically related to the fact that China has been reaching the technological frontier while maintaining its authoritarian regime. According to a report by the US government, China has surpassed the United States in two of nine emerging technological fields, which are exascale computing and commercial drones. China also has close competitive capabilities in another three fields – AI, quantum information science, and high-performance computing (US–China Economic and Security Review Commission, 2017). In relation to this, the Trump administration has harshly criticized China for unfair practices including subsidies, forced technology transfers, and technological theft, while the Chinese government denies such practices (The White House Office of Trade and Manufacturing Policy, 2018; The State Council, China, 2018). In particular, the "Made in China 2025" is one of the policies that is looked upon with vigilance and suspicion by the US government and the international business community, including the European Chamber of Commerce, because of unfair subsidies through various channels.

7.3.3 Thailand: from "Thailand-ness" to promoting emerging industries?

In Thailand, the risk of "the middle-income trap" has been widely acknowledged, and a major policy shift has been observed in recent years accordingly. Since the collapse of the Thaksin administration as a result of a military coup in 2006, Thailand had been unstable politically. Table 7.1 indicates an average growth rate of 4.0% over the period 2000–2014, which was the lowest among the ASEAN countries. The sources of growth during this period were attributed as follows; the contribution of capital input was 1.4% points, that of labor input 0.1% points, and TFP growth was 2.6% points. It is interesting to note that improvement in productivity itself has actually been relatively steady. However, large-scale infrastructure development plans were postponed during this period, which is reflected in the low contribution of capital input, leading to low growth.

The need for a long-term development strategy has also been recognized in Thailand but has not materialized because of the political disturbance. Since 2014, a military administration by the Prayut interim government has been in place. Interestingly, efforts exist to reorganize the state with a long-term perspective. The "20-year National Strategy" created by the Prayut administration is a plan based on the new constitution, and the concept of "Thailand 4.0" represents its vision. According to the Prayut administration, version 1.0 of the Thai economy – the first stage – represents the pre-industrialization stage before the war, with keywords such as "rural society" and "cottage industry." Post-war industrialization shifted Thailand to the second stage, described with keywords including "light industry," "import substitution," "natural resources," and "cheap labor." After the Plaza Accord agreement in 1985 when Thailand experienced an influx of foreign direct investment, it entered into the third stage with keywords such as "heavy industry," "export orientation," and "introduction of foreign capital." This was the stage when it followed the export-oriented industrial pattern of Asian NIEs. As a result, industrialization took roots in Thailand, turning it into the world's second largest producer of hard disk drives, the sixth largest rubber tire producer, the seventh largest producer of computer products, and the 12th largest producer of automobiles.

The fourth stage is specifically termed "Thailand 4.0," where a goal is set for the coming 20 years, aiming to transform itself into an industrial society that continuously creates value-added through innovation, including promotion of trade in services and further increases in productivity. Under this vision, the country aspires to become an advanced economy, and is structured in line with its national strategies.

The previous National Economic and Social Development Plan of Thailand (2001–2006), formulated by the National Economic and Social Development Board (NESDB) was based in principle on the vision of the "sufficiency economy," proposed by the late King Bhumibol Adulyadej. During this period, industries with "Thailand-ness" were prioritized, such as the cultivation of energy plants (including cassava, sugar cane, and palm oil) to fuel bio-energy power generation, and natural herbs for cosmetic use.

Although the "sufficiency economy" remains a keyword to date, the 12th Development Plan launched under the Prayut administration aims to transform Thailand into an advanced, modern economy (NESDB, and Office of the Prime Minister, Thailand, 2017). This new plan in fact represents a significant departure from Thailand's previous development concept. "Thailand 4.0" is also influenced by Germany's "Industry 4.0," as in the case of China, which aims to upgrade its economic structure through the introduction of advanced, digital technology, by attracting foreign investments. Priority sectors include next-generation vehicles, smart electronics, medical and health tourism, agricultural biotechnology, future food industries, robotic industries, aviation and logistics, biofuels and biochemistry, digital industries, and medical industries.

Whether these plans will be implemented and play out successfully remains unclear, as the country moves from a military administration to a civil government. However, the conflicts that may exist between the efforts to preserving "Thailand-ness," and the aspiration to "become an advanced country" are potential sources of challenges that are more or less common for other middle-income countries in Asia too.

CONCLUSION

Significant potential still exists in Asia to drive further growth through investments in basic infrastructure and productive facilities. As discussed in Chapter 4, expanding domestic added value is not easy in the face of intense competition under the global division of labor. While catch-up industrialization still remains as one of the key catalysts of Asia's economic development, Asian countries are gradually accumulating capabilities to realize innovation-driven growth. Various policy efforts based on different development stages and economic conditions have been observed in Asia, where improvements in productivity and economic digitalization have evolved as common challenges.

This chapter discussed policy initiatives related to innovation in China and Thailand only. Other countries in Asia, however, have formulated similar policies. In Malaysia, a digital free-trade zone was launched in March 2017 under the Najib administration to create Southeast Asia's largest hub for e-commerce and IT companies near Kuala Lumpur. In Singapore, the most advanced economy in Asia, Prime Minister Lee Hsien Loong launched the "smart nation vision" in August 2014. This plan is a national strategy to improve the overall efficiency of the economy by promoting the Internet of Things throughout the city-state, and by the utilizing its global-leading Internet technology in upgrading transportation infrastructure, healthcare, environmentally friendly technology; and to improve administrative efficiency. In relation to this, Singapore has already embarked on initiatives such as autonomous car experiments, and the provision of data science training for its bureaucrats.

While digitalization of the economy, and the adaptation of mobile-Internet technology cuts across policy priorities among countries in Asia, each of the individual countries' responses differs depending on their particular industrial structures. However, it is important to note that policies related to issues including robotics and AI are no longer issues just for advanced economies such as Germany or Japan but have become relevant and important for less-developed countries in Asia as well. In fact, new services that are based on mobile technology are being used more intensively in emerging Asian countries than in some high-income economies, such as Japan. Innovation in Asia can happen regardless of the stages of development, which will create new conditions for competition and collaboration. Innovation policies and digital economy-related initiatives in Asia will have significant implications on the wider economy, and for this reason, careful monitoring of how the outcomes will play out warrants attention.

BOX 7 Unicorns in Asia

Asei Ito and Keiichiro Oizumi

A company not publicly listed, with a value exceeding $1 billion, and less than ten years of history since its establishment is called a "unicorn." Although the name seems to reflect their rarity, unicorn companies have not, in fact, been rare in recent years. According to CB Insights data, as of August 2017, 215 unicorn companies existed worldwide. Although half of them – 106 – were based in the United States, unicorn companies have also emerged in Asia. Behind the rise of unicorn companies, the rapid expansion of mobile networks has created new business opportunities globally. In addition, an environment has been formed, particularly in Silicon Valley, where such investments take place, and where advice from third parties to promising ventures is available.

China has the largest number of unicorn companies, second only to the United States, with 57 companies in 2017. For example, Xiaomi, which was founded in 2010, is in the development and manufacturing business of smartphones. Today, the company has developed a variety of electronics products, and has recorded a corporate value of $45 billion. Likewise, a variety of web-based service companies is evolving rapidly in the Chinese domestic market, such as Didi, which has developed the largest rideshare application in China.

It is noteworthy that Xiaomi also invests in a large number of venture companies that focus on so-called "smart hardware," which refers to home appliances connected to the Internet. This has led to the formation of a business group, which is referred to as the "Xiaomi ecosystem." China has far overtaken Japan and South Korea in terms of the numbers of unicorn companies, of which each had only one and three, respectively, in 2017. In addition to its much larger domestic market, China's ecosystem has nurtured the growth of such unicorn companies, and the lack of such an environment in Japan and South Korea seems to explain these differences.

Unicorn companies have also emerged in South Asia and Southeast Asia. Indonesia-based Go-Jek is expanding its business as a local IT platformer in the Southeast Asian market. Founded in 2010, Go-Jek currently has contracts with more than 200,000 drivers, and had a mark-to-market value of $1.3 billion as of 2016. In addition to mobility, Go-Jek offers other services, such as food and small item deliveries and payments.

It may be the case that the local application you download when traveling in Asia is a service from a locally born unicorn company.

REFERENCES

Beers, Cees van, and Fardad Zand. (2014). "R&D Cooperation, Partner Diversity, and Innovation Performance: An Empirical Analysis," *The Journal of Product Innovation Management*, Vol. 31 No. 920, pp. 292–312.

Cornell University, INSEAD, and WIPO. (2017). *Global Innovation Index 2017: Innovation Feeding the World*. http://www.wipo.int/edocs/pubdocs/en/wipo_pub_gii_2017.pdf

David, A. Paul, Bronwyn H. Hall, and Andrew A. Toole. (2000). "Is Public R&D a Complement or Substitute for Private R&D? A Review of the Econometric Evidence," *Research Policy*, Vol. 29 No. (4–5), pp. 497–529.

Fujita, Masahisa, and Takatoshi Tabuchi. (1997). "Regional Growth in Postwar Japan," *Regional Science and Urban Economics*, Vol. 27 No. (6), pp. 643–670.

Ganne, Bernard and Yveline Lecler (ed.). (2009). *Asian Industrial Clusters, Global Competitiveness and New Policy Initiatives*, Singapore: World Scientific.

Gill, Indermit and Homi Kharas. (2007). *An East Asian Renaissance: Ideas for Economic Growth*. Washington: The World Bank.

Hong, Jin, Bing Feng, Yanrui Wu, and Liangbing Wang. (2016). "Do Government Grants Promote Innovation Efficiency in China's High-Tech Industries?," *Technovation*, Vol. 57, pp. 4–13.

Krugman, Paul. (1994). "The Myth of Asia's Miracle," *Foreign Affairs*, Vol. 73 No. (6), pp. 62–78.

National Economic and Social Development Board (NESDB), and Office of the Prime Minister, Thailand. (2017). *The Twelfth National Economic and Social Development Plan (2017–2022)*. http://www.nesdb.go.th/nesdb_en/ewt_dl_link.php?nid=4345.

Ohno, Kenichi. (2013). *Learning to Industrialize: From Given Growth to Policy-aided Value Creation*. Oxon: Routledge.

Saxenian, AnnaLee. (2007). *The New Argonauts: Regional Advantage in a Global Economy*. Cambridge: Harvard University Press.

Sonobe, Tetsushi, and Keijiro Otsuka. (2006). *Cluster-Based Industrial Development: An East Asian Model*. Basingstoke: Palgrave Macmillan.

The State Council, China. (2015). *Made in China 2025 [Zhongguo Zhizao 2025]*. May 8th. http://www.gov.cn/zhengce/content/2015-05/19/content_9784.htm [in Chinese].

The State Council, China. (2017). *Development Plan for New Generation Artificial Intelligence. [Xinyidai Rengong Zhineng Fazhan Guihua]* July 8th. http://www.gov.cn/zhengce/content/2017-07/20/content_5211996.htm [in Chinese].

The State Council, China. (2018). "The Facts and China's Position on China-US Trade Friction," September. [Both in Chinese and English].

The White House Office of Trade and Manufacturing Policy. (2018). "How China's Economic Aggression Threatens the Technologies and Intellectual Property of the United States and the World," June.

US-China Economic and Security Review Commission. (2017). *2017 Annual Report*. November 15. https://www.uscc.gov/Annual_Reports/2017-annual-report.

World Bank. (1993). *The East Asian Miracle: Economic Growth and Public Policy*. New York: Oxford University Press.

World Bank. (2016). *World Development Report 2016: Digital Dividends*. Washington: The World Bank.

World Bank and Development Research Center of the State Council, the People's Republic of China. (2013). *China 2030: Building a Modern Harmonious, and Creative Society*. Washington: The World Bank.

Yusuf, Shahid, et al. (2003). *Innovative East Asia: The Future of Growth*. Washington: The World Bank and Oxford University Press.

Yu, Feifei, Yue Guo, Khuong Le-Nguyen, Stuart J. Barnes, and Weiting Zhang. (2016). "The Impact of Government Subsidies and Enterprises' R&D Investment: A Panel Data Study from Renewable Energy in China," *Energy Policy*, Vol. 89, pp. 106–113.

8 Urbanizing Asia: cities transforming into mega-regions

Tamaki Endo and Keiichiro Oizumi

Siam Paragon, high-end department store in Bangkok, Thailand (2017, Photo by Tamaki Endo).

LEARNING GOALS

- Understanding the relationship between economic development and urbanization in Asia.
- Understanding the driving forces of urbanization, formation of mega-cities and mega-regions, and their function in Asia.
- Understanding the new challenges and problems faced by Asian cities.

INTRODUCTION

The 21st century is called not only the "Asian century," but also the "Urban Century." The world's urban population exceeded 50% in 2008 and became larger than the rural population. The increase of urban population in Asia has been remarkable. In the 2000s, more than 50% of the world's urban population was concentrated in Asia. Future expansions of urban population are expected mainly in Asia and Africa.

The urbanization rate (ratio of urban to total population) of East and Southeast Asia in 1950 was only 17.4%. Most societies were rural-based, and many people lived in villages practicing agricultural activities. After World War II, most countries in these regions experienced rapid urbanization of their capital cities, while other regions remained rural, keeping the overall urbanization rate low. However, urbanization at the country level accelerated in the late 20th century, exceeding 50% in 2007 and reaching 56.5% in 2015 (see Figure 8.1). The transition from a rural-based society to an urban-based one was very rapid in Asia.

Three factors account for the increase in the urbanization rate: (1) the natural increase of urban population; (2) migration to cities (social increase); and (3) changes in the definition of the urban–rural border. Except for city states, such as Singapore and Hong Kong, we can distinguish between three different features of urbanization in Asia, according to their timing and characteristics. Japan and South Korea were the first countries to experience rapid urbanization, which peaked immediately after the World War II. Primate cities started to appear in countries such as Thailand and Malaysia during the 1980s and 1990s, mainly due to the social increase channel. This was followed by rapid urbanization in China in the 1990s, during which several mega-cities emerged. Mega-cities in Asia, which are often also capital cities, have in most cases also been the main drivers of economic development, producing disproportionately higher ratios of value-added in their domestic economies.

Meanwhile, the focus of academic discussions on the urbanization process has changed over time, as urbanization has further progressed. In Asia, the rapid urbanization after World War II was initially caused by migration (social increase). The large influx of rural population to the cities started well before their economies were able to accommodate them, because employment opportunities and infrastructure were still crucially lacking. This was perceived as a phenomenon unique to Asia, in comparison to the experiences in Western countries, and was referred to as the "over-urbanization" problem. However, by the end of the 1980s, the concept of over-urbanization to characterize Asian cities became less acceptable, because of cities' increasingly apparent roles in driving economic development, as in developed countries of the West. As such, positive assessments became dominant with respect to urbanization. Asian mega-cities and their surrounding areas were thus regarded as contributors to industrialization. Export processing zones and industrial estates were established around mega-cities, and employment of young people accelerated in these areas. Furthermore, once the mega-cities started to function as hubs of global value chains, their centers were transformed into global service centers, and became the most developed areas within those cities. Such evolving mega-cities gradually expanded their economic boundaries, transforming themselves into larger geographical units, "mega-regions," which included the surrounding suburban areas. Currently, such mega-regions are home to headquarters of major domestic companies as well as the regional bases of multinational enterprises (MNEs), and are attracting highly educated and skilled workers, locally and internationally.

Since the late 2010s, the core of growth strategy has been strengthening the competitiveness of mega-regions and further developing infrastructures to deal with multiple risks such as natural disasters. However, at the same time, the disparities within the cities and among regions have attracted public attention as critical social problems to be addressed.

This chapter first reviews the steps of the urbanization process, and then discusses how this urban dynamism has become the key driver of economic development and social change in Asia. We will also discuss some of the complex social challenges that mega-cities and mega-regions are currently facing, including the increase in regional inequalities and the lack of adequate infrastructure. Finally, the chapter will discuss future prospects.

8.1 THE EVOLUTION OF CITIES FROM "OVER-URBANIZATION" TO PRODUCTION CENTERS

8.1.1 Urbanization trends in Asia

The urbanization process in Asia has some specific features. First, the Asian urbanization rate for many years was below the world's average (Figure 8.1). East and Southeast Asia, however, started to show rapid growth in their urbanization rates from the 1990s. As a result, the average urbanization rate had exceeded the world average by 2010. By 2005, Asia's total urban population, including South Asia, exceeded 50% of the world's urban population. Figure 8.2 shows the countries and regions contributing to

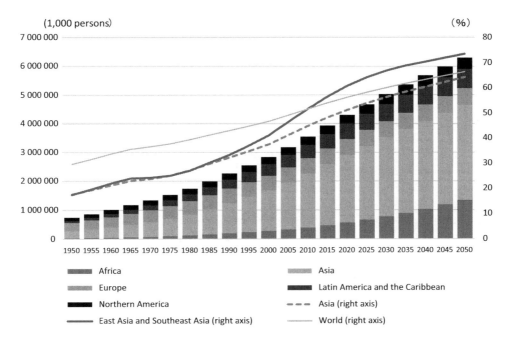

FIGURE 8.1 Urban population and urbanization rate, 1950–2050.

Note: "Asia" in this figure includes not only East and Southeast Asia but also South and Central Asia.

Source: Tabulated from World urbanization prospects: the 2014 revisions.

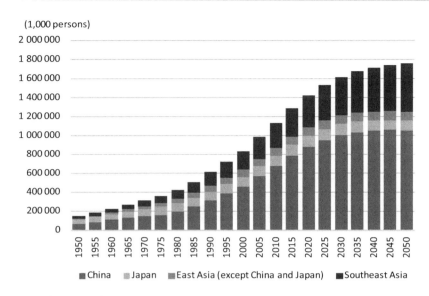

FIGURE 8.2 Urban population in Asia, 1950–2050.
Source: Tabulated from World urbanization prospects: the 2014 revisions.

the growth of the urbanization rate in East and Southeast Asia. China's urbanization is clearly one of the major drivers of Asian urbanization.

The second characteristic is the development of primate cities (mainly capital cities) into mega-cities[1] and the concentration of economic power in these mega-cities (see Section 8.2). In Asia, primate cities have shown rapid population growth since the 1960s, even when the overall urbanization rates were still low. The urbanization of developing countries in Asia was different from that of developed countries. Some defined it as "compressed urbanization," in which urbanization proceeded while the ratio of the rural population was still high (Tasaka, 1998). These mega-cities accumulated significant economic power as the concentration of population intensified. In recent years, the expansion of urban functions has been gradually permeating into surrounding regions, creating geographically connected mega-regions. The third feature is the extremely high population density of Asian cities compared to other regions in the world. Their population densities range between 10,000 and 20,000 persons per km^2, which is double that of cities in Latin America, triple that of Europe, and ten times that of US cities (UN Habitat, 2010).

Asian cities grew rapidly through compressed economic development, fueled by rapid industrialization. In the next sections, we will review the process of urbanization since World War II.

8.1.2 The focus on over-urbanization and primate cities

As discussed above, the urbanization rate in Asia was low for many years in the post-war period, and the region was predominantly rural. Except for Japan, which urbanized at an early stage, and city states such as Singapore and Hong Kong, research on the Asian economy mainly focused on agricultural productivity and the changes in rural economies. The "two-sector model" introduced by Arthur Lewis (1965) captures the relationship between rural-urban migration and economic growth. In this, the rural economy was characterized as a traditional and agriculturally oriented sector, and the urban economy a modern industrial sector. Economic development, therefore, was defined as

> the process of the evolution of a productive modern urban economy within an economy in which the traditional rural sector with a significant surplus of low productivity labor is dominant. The growth of the modern sector will take place by absorbing the surplus labor of the traditional rural sector.
>
> *(Watanabe, 1986)*

The leading factors making for rural–urban migration, such as rural poverty, were seen as the causes of urbanization. As the migration inflows from rural areas were often beyond the urban areas' capacity to absorb, this often led to increased unemployment and the emergence of slum communities. As such, the urbanization of developing countries in Asia was often seen as an "over-urbanization" issue, which was defined as "urbanization proceeding without industrialization (economic development)" (Hayase, 2004). The seminal paper of Kingsley Davis that conceptualized the notion of over-urbanization looked at the correlation between the degree of urbanization (the ratio of urban population in cities with or over 100,000 residents, to the total population) and the degree of industrialization (the ratio of non-agricultural male employment to total employment). It pointed out that, compared to advanced countries, developing countries were far more urbanized than required by their levels of industrial development (Davis and Golden, 1954; Tasaka, 1998). Theoretical frameworks such as the Harris-Todaro model further evolved to study the over-urbanization issue (see Chapter 9) and assess the relationship between migration and the urban labor market in the urbanization process.

The first typical feature of these early discussions was that they attempted to explain urbanization based on the push factors in rural areas. Second, rapid urbanization was discussed mainly from the perspective of urban problems such as urban poverty, slums, and the informal economy. Third, the discussion focused on primate cities because the urbanization of local cities was still limited.

Table 8.1 shows the urbanization and urban population growth rates of Asian cities in 2014. Excluding city states such as Singapore and Hong Kong, Japan, and South Korea were the ones reaching an 80–90% urbanization ratio, while those in the ASEAN-4 (Malaysia, Thailand, Indonesia, and the Philippines) and China were around 50%. The least developed in Asia were still at around 30%. As mentioned earlier, the peak of rapid urbanization occurred in the 1960s in Japan, 1970s in South Korea, 1980s–1990s for the ASEAN-4, and 1990s for China.

A monopolar concentration of population in primate cities is also often observed in Asia. For example, Figure 8.3 shows an increase in population and slum communities in Bangkok, Thailand. The rapid population increase in Bangkok continued until the 1990s, and it was mainly due to social increase. The "over-urbanization" debate captured and focused on the effects this regional trend of rapid population increase had. In recent years, the expansion of Bangkok has slowed down but the urbanization of its surrounding areas is proceeding at a drastic speed. For example, Bangkok's population

TABLE 8.1 Urbanization rate and growth of urban population in Asia (unit: %)

	Urbanization rate (2014)	Growth rate of urban population 1965–1970	1990–1995	2010–2015
ASIA	47.5	3.18	3.12	2.50
East Asia	58.9	2.50	3.28	2.53
Japan	93.0	2.42	0.54	0.56
South Korea	82.4	6.63	1.92	0.66
China, Hong Kong SAR	100.0	1.11	1.27	0.74
China, Macao SAR	100.0	4.04	2.07	1.78
China	54.4	1.93	4.36	3.05
Mongolia	71.2	4.23	0.94	2.78
North Korea	60.7	6.45	1.71	0.75
Other non-specified areas	76.5	6.42	1.52	0.82
Southeast Asia	47.0	4.16	3.63	2.53
Singapore	100.0	1.97	2.87	2.02
Malaysia	74.0	4.86	4.82	2.66
Thailand	49.2	3.60	1.40	2.97
Indonesia	53.0	4.13	4.96	2.69
Philippines	44.5	3.79	2.21	1.32
Viet Nam	33.0	4.91	3.79	2.95
Cambodia	20.5	9.42	5.61	2.65
Lao People's Democratic Republic	37.6	5.31	5.12	4.93
Myanmar	33.6	4.16	2.23	2.49
Timor-Leste	32.1	4.50	4.41	3.75
Brunei Darussalam	76.9	7.88	3.60	1.79
World	53.6	2.63	2.34	2.05

Source: World Urbanization Prospects: the 2014 Revisions.
Note: "Asia" also includes South Asia and Central Asia.

was only 10% of the total country's in 1990, while it constituted about 58% of the total urban population. In 2000, Bangkok's population remained around 10% of that of Thailand, but the ratio of Bangkok's population to total urban population decreased to about 34% (NSO, 1993, 1994, 2001, 2002). Still, Bangkok's primacy in size is remarkable as it is boasting a population of 10 million,[2] while secondary cities only have populations of around 400,000. Similar primate cities in other countries also show high population concentrations. For example, Tokyo's population was 32% of the total urban population in 2010, and the ratio was 25% for Seoul, 29% for Kuala Lumpur, and 28% for Manila. In contrast, China has several urban centers; indeed, it has 398 cities

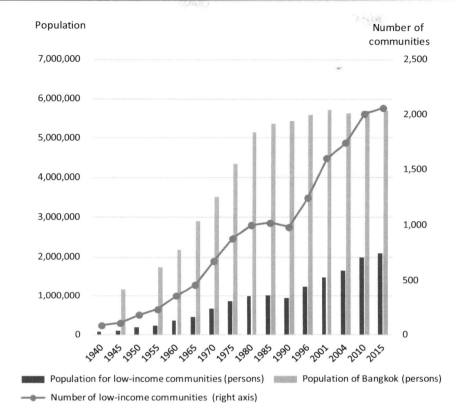

FIGURE 8.3 Increase in population and number of communities for low-income groups in Bangkok.

Source: Endo (2014, p. 40) and statistical profile of BMA.

Note: "Number of low-income communities" from 2004 partly include "distributive village community" for middle class (around 200).

with populations exceeding 300,000. Beijing's population share of the total urban population is about 2.4%, and Shanghai, with more than 10 million residents, accounts for only 3.0% (United Nations, 2014).

8.1.3 Policies to address Asian over-urbanization

In the early stages of urbanization, some countries took measures to mitigate the rapid inflow of population to urban areas. For example, in 1958 China introduced the "household registration system." This system distinguished between rural registration (agriculture registration) and urban registration (non-agricultural registration) and decreed that "those who have rural registration are not allowed to move to cities except for those who are already employed or entering schools in those cities" (Marukawa, 2013).

In Thailand, economic disparities were seen as driving forces of migration and, therefore, policies to de-centralize and promote investment in local provinces were introduced. The 3rd National Economic and Social Development Plan (1972–1976) clearly stated that the rapid urbanization of Bangkok was problematic, and that it was important to suppress the increase of urban population by providing incentives, such as tax reductions, to factories to relocate out of Bangkok. In Indonesia, no direct mitigating policy was promoted, but there was an attempt to move urban population to other areas by encouraging migration. Vietnam also had a migration control policy to restrict rapid urban expansion.

As it turned out, however, none of these policies was successful in slowing down the rural to urban migration flows. Furthermore, the concept of over-urbanization lost popularity, for the following reasons. First, when many mega-cities emerged not only in Asia but also in other developing countries, the ambiguities related to the defining and assessing the "limitation" of urban "capacity" came to be recognized as a problem. Second, during the rapid economic development of Asian NIEs and ASEAN countries, cities started to be recognized positively as the growth centers and driving forces of development. The idea that rural poverty was the source of urban expansion was questioned. Furthermore, Asian economic development patterns, whose dynamics were progressively interlinked with that of the global economy, made increasingly clear the limitations of a one-country perspective to explain the causes of urban expansion in terms of domestic migration. The urban problems identified in the over-urbanization perspective were also more likely to be solved, or at least mitigated, by the development of urban infrastructures, economic growth, and the out-bounded expansion of the city to the surrounding areas. Yet, many challenges still remain unsolved, and urban expansion keeps accelerating.

According to a UN survey, there were only two Asian cities with more than 5 million residents in 1950 (Tokyo and Shanghai) but the number had increased to 28 by 2015 (22 cities in East Asia, and six in Southeast Asia) (United Nations, 2014). The same survey showed that there were 29 cities with more than 10 million residents in the world, and ten of them were in East and Southeast Asia (16 cities, including South Asia).

8.1.4 Industrialization and cities as production centers

Economic development, rather than policies to control migration, attenuated urban problems. As economic globalization progressed, migrants to cities were seen as a source of cheap and abundant labor by the MNEs. Most governments also implemented tax benefits (reduction of corporate income tax and of import tariffs) to attract investments from MNEs, and established export processing zones and industrial estates. In these industrial estates, the necessary infrastructure, such as electricity, roads, and ports, was prepared beforehand, as well as offices to manage administrative issues and to recruit workers.

The spread of investments from MNEs accelerated rural-urban migration. Even in China, where the urban inflow was limited by the strict household registration systems, local authorities in the coastal areas tolerated the increase of urban migration to overcome the shortage of workers. The number of rural migrant workers in China was close to 200 million by the early 2000s. For example, Shenzhen, located in Guangdong Province across from Hong Kong, was a small city of 60,000 residents in 1980. However, the area became one of the main destinations of foreign direct investment (FDI) from MNEs after the start of the opening-up policies. Its population expanded to 6.6 million inhabitants by 2000, and 10.8 million by 2015. Shenzhen is an example of a mega city formed by migration.

These mega-cities transitioned from export-oriented production bases to specialized industrial clusters led by MNEs. Given this trend, debates on urbanization started to focus on pull factors rather than on push factors (see Chapter 6). At the same time, urbanization started attracting interest not only in population and development studies, but also in other fields of study in economics.

8.2 ASIAN URBANIZATION IN THE GLOBALIZATION ERA: NODES IN GLOBAL VALUE CHAINS

8.2.1 Mega-cities' function as global cities

Mega-cities in Asia have benefited from globalization in terms of achieving outstanding economic growth. Figure 8.4 summarizes the Gross Regional Product (GRP) per capita for Bangkok and Shanghai. Both cities showed soaring GRP per capita, which in 2015 were $14,991 and $16,753, respectively. In the same year, GRP per capita for Thailand

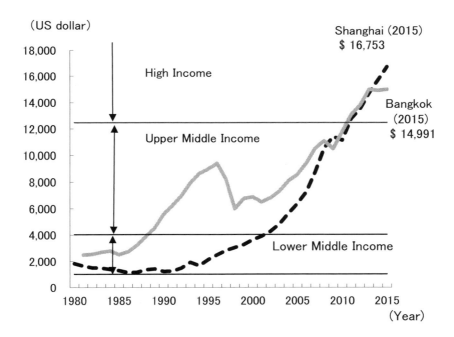

FIGURE 8.4 Per capita GDP in Bangkok and Shanghai (nominal exchange rate).

Source: Made by author from Shanghai Statistical Yearbook for Shanghai, and NESDB, Gross Regional and Provincial Products for Bangkok.

Note: The definition of 2015 is as follows: High-income country is 12,476 dollar and above, Upper-middle-income country is between 4,036 and 12,475 dollars, Lower-middle-income country is 1,025 and 4,035 dollars (World Development Indicators 2016).

and China were $5,799 and $8,167, respectively. GRP per capita for both cities were more than double that of the national average. While Thailand and China are still in the "middle income" group according to the classification of the World Bank, both Bangkok and Shanghai had already achieved income levels of countries in the "high-income" categories. This indicates the importance of such mega-cities as drivers of growth, playing key roles as global production centers and financial hubs.

Saskia Sassen (1991) introduced a distinction between "global cities" and other international cities. She defined global cities as those characterized by (1) the provision of key command services to support global operations of MNEs; (2) the provision of professional services such as in finance; (3) the ability to promote innovation; and (4) availability of a sizeable market for the goods and services produced. Examples of such cities include New York, London, Tokyo, and Paris.

While Asian mega-cities such as Bangkok and Shanghai do not yet qualify in terms of all the characteristics, they already cater for some. These cities already function as nodes in global value chains, undertaking management, and administrative functions. The mega-regions that spread around these cities also generate most of the value-added in their respective economies, in which several industrial clusters have been formed.

8.2.2 Industrial clusters and mega-cities as nodes in global value chains

As we have seen in Chapters 2 and 4, the fragmentation of the production process led to the development of global value chains, where agglomeration dynamics were also important (Kimura 2003). Functions with similar factor intensities such as labor and capital tend to agglomerate in the same location. This agglomeration effect integrates cities into global value chains as important nodes, which further increase their roles. Some of the examples include the automobile and supporting industry clusters in the Bangkok mega-region, and the electronic industrial clusters in the Pearl River Delta Region (see also Chapter 7).

The concept of increasing returns to scale (particularly *external* economies of scale, i.e., those external to the firm) is useful to understand the mechanism underlying the formation and functions of agglomeration in cities in relation to their functions within global value chains. Such economies of scale mean that an increase in total production will lead to reductions in average cost. As this happens in a specific region, it will increase productivity of cities. This mechanism is based on positive externalities, conditional that the companies in the city, or region, operate with similar functions in the value chains, as this makes it easier to capture relevant knowledge and skills as well as workers with such knowledge/skills. Once these *economies of agglomeration* start to kick in, the role of the city as a node in the global value chain will increase.

For many Asian mega-cities, the driving force of economic growth has been their connections to the global economy through the international division of labor. In this, the mega-cities and the areas in their vicinity became connected to such globalized networks. Economic concentration on the mega-cities and regions has been particularly high in recent years. For example, Tokyo and its metropolitan area (Tokyo, Kanagawa, Chiba, and Saitama) produced 18.4% and 32.4% of Japan's GDP, respectively, in 2010; Beijing alone accounted for 3.5% of China's, while the Yangtze River Delta mega-regions (Shanghai,

Jiangsu Province, and Zhejiang province) produced 21.5% of the GDP. Similarly, shares for Seoul and its mega-region were 23.2% and 47.8%, respectively, of that of South Korea; Bangkok and its mega-regions were 29.1% and 66.2%, respectively, of Thailand's; and for Manila and its mega-regions were 23.5% and 51.1%, respectively, of the GDP of the Philippines (IDE-JETRO 2015).

Given this, the governments of developing countries considered that it was not enough merely to invite the MNEs, but it was also important to plan strategies to become part of the global value chains (see also Chapter 4). The mega-cities became the targets of these strategies in order to strengthen countries' economic competitiveness. The policies were targeting not only individual enterprises but also promoting the formation of industrial clusters and strengthening urban competitiveness.

The "cluster theory" (or "diamond theory") put forward by Michael Porter (1990) at Harvard University, which outlines strategy for building a nation's competitiveness, received much attention, and influenced the policies to increase urban competitiveness in Asia. Following Porter's cluster theory, policies such as human capital development, promotion of supporting industries, and the creation of an enabling environment to foster competition (deregulation) were implemented. International organizations also revised their views on the roles of cities. For example, the Asian Development Bank (ADB) published a report called *City Cluster Development* in 2008 (ADB 2008). There has also been a trend of relocating central management and administrative functions to mega-cities. Tax reductions and infrastructure developments were promoted to attract some of the higher value-added functions of global value chains from abroad, including headquarters functions of MNEs and research and development (R&D) activities.

Mega-cities are growing rapidly as globalization and rapid development in IT is taking place, particularly in Asia. As such, Asian cities are attracting attention from researchers from various branches of economics, such as development economics and spatial economics, specifically looking at transfer costs and clusters. The connectivity between these cities is further promoting growth, accelerated by the development of cross-border transport infrastructures. Examples include the Kunming-Bangkok (South-North) economic corridor, the Eastern, and the Southern economic corridors within the Greater Mekong Region.

8.2.3 Urbanization in Asia and the evolving mega-regions

The formation of industrial clusters in mega-cities and their surrounding areas, discussed above, led to spatial expansion of the cities. Michael Douglass (1995) looked at the spatial expansion of Southeast Asian cities in the 1990s, and concluded that its key features lay in the strong concentration dynamics leading to polarization of development in "mega cities" and emergence of a mega-region, which accompany the establishment of industrial estates in cities' outskirts. Douglass notes that "industrial location and corporate decision making linked to international markets and worldwide systems of production accentuates these trends." This is because, first,

> modern production requires sophisticated transportation and communication systems usually found only in the core regions of medium-and lower-income

countries. Second, these regions also provide key amenities-schools, sports, and other leisure facilities, and even steady supplies of electricity-which other regions can rarely offer.

(Douglass, 1995, p. 50)

As mentioned earlier, primate cities in Asia have become important nodes in global value chains, which accompanied spatial decentralization of manufacturing industries. Pushing them outwards to neighboring areas, while it also induced concentration of management and administration functions in inner cities (Tasaka, 1998; Endo 2016).

Richard Florida of the University of Toronto and his co-researcher Timothy Gulden illustrated the geographical/functional scope of mega-regions that go beyond administrative borders, utilizing data from the US Defense Meteorological Satellite Program and the National Oceanic and Atmospheric Administration, to capture satellite images of lightening in cities during night time. They concluded that the global economy is led by about 20–30 mega-regions. While the total population of these mega-regions is just about one-fifth of the world population, yet two-thirds of all economic activities take place in these mega-regions, and they generate about 80% of the innovation. The top 10 mega-regions account for only 6.5% of the world's population but generate more than 40% of world economic activities, and about 57% of patented innovation (Florida 2008; Florida, Gulden and Mellander 2008). Their list includes 12 mega-regions from Asia,[3] which continue to expand today (Suehiro and Oizumi, 2017).

8.3 CHALLENGES AND PROSPECTS FOR ASIAN CITIES

8.3.1 Mega-regions and inter-regional inequalities

Asian cities experienced compressed development and urbanization. Economic development has been phenomenal; however, they also face various challenges, including rising inequality and increased vulnerability to natural disasters. Among these challenges is the issue of inter-regional inequality.

The sets of rules or variables normally used to define and classify regions may not be helpful in understanding inequality today. Classifying regions and grouping them into either "urban" or "rural" has been widely used. However, such a dichotomic view may not be optimal in assessing evolving inequalities. There are significant differences between cities, for example between primate and local cities. Likewise, the difference between villages in rural areas has become significant as well. For example, villages close to mega-cities are totally different today compared to those in remote areas.

For instance, let us look at and compare mega-regions with other regions. Figure 8.5 depicts the GRPs per-capita of the different provinces of Thailand in 2014. Surprisingly, Bangkok and another seven provinces in the Bangkok mega-region, with a population of 16 million, had a per capita GRP exceeding $10,000.[4] Thailand is a middle-income country, but as far as those 16 million people are concerned, they have been living in a society which has attained the status of "high-income," at least in terms of income statistics. On the other hand, per-capita GRPs for many provinces still remain below $3,000, in which 27 million people live.

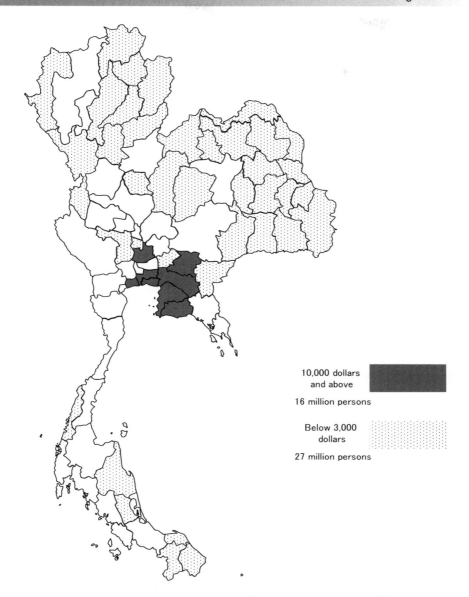

FIGURE 8.5 Gross regional products per capita of provinces in Thailand (2014).

Source: Made by author from NESDB, Gross regional products, each year.

Such inter-regional economic disparities are manifested in the fact that the middle and upper classes are mainly concentrated in cities, because of the availability of high-skilled, and thus high-paid jobs. Asian cities, therefore, have also become important consumer markets, particularly in the 21st century (see also Box 8).

These mega-cities and regions also attract young people, which will, on the other hand, also promote the ageing of the rural and remote areas (also see Chapter 10). Figure 8.6A and B compares the population pyramid of Bangkok with that of Northeast

160 Dynamic Asia

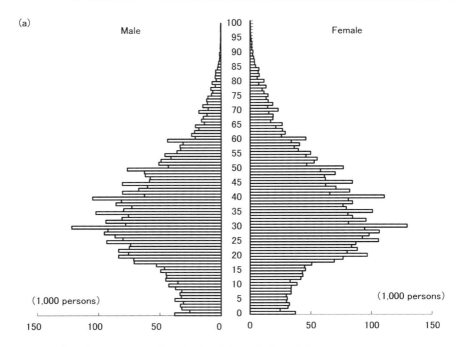

FIGURE 8.6A Population pyramid in Thailand (2010): Bangkok.
Source: Tabulated from population census of Thailand 2010.

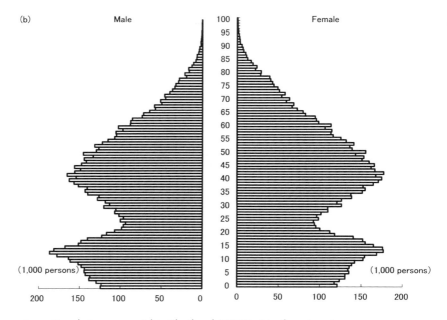

FIGURE 8.6B Population pyramid in Thailand (2010): Northeast region.
Source: Tabulated from population census of Thailand 2010.

Thailand of 2010. The difference is striking, even within the same country. Bangkok has a rich layer of young people aged between 20 and 30, whereas in the Northeast region, there are fewer youths than any other age groups. This reflects the result of massive migration of youth to urban areas.

While the ageing of the overall population will proceed, mega-cities will keep growing. In contrast, growth potentials of rural areas will be weakened because of the population effect. This disparity between mega-cities and others continues to grow, which could further lead to rural areas "disappearing" as is currently happening in Japan. This could occur in many of the other Asian countries in the future as well.

This increase of inter-regional inequality is not just due to the changing population structures. Another factor is the uneven inter-regional distribution of human capital. Universities and other forms of institutions for higher education and research tend to be located in mega-regions. The graduates of these universities and colleges tend to find jobs in these urban areas and are not likely to go back to their hometowns. For example, in Bangkok's labor market, 2.2 million workers have graduated from universities and technical schools, accounting for 27.7% of all such graduates of Thailand. This suggests that high-skilled workers have been concentrated in Bangkok. Policy measures are needed to mitigate the impact of these phenomena to avoid further increases in inequality.

8.3.2 The challenges of Asian mega-cities

Mega-cities and mega-regions are the places where economic power and resources concentrate. However, compressed urbanization has also contributed to increasing the economic and social risks of these cities. For example, mega-cities are the main sources of environmental pollution and, therefore, taking proper measures is crucial for their sustainability (see Chapter 12). Here we focus on growing urban inequality and on the lack of adequate infrastructure. These are important because these problems relate to the challenges and dilemmas of issues pertinent to urban governance.

Intra-regional inequality is becoming more serious than inter-regional inequality in many countries (see Chapter 11). Despite economic prosperity, "slum communities" are still widespread (see Figure 8.3), and the problem of urban poverty has not been solved yet. In 2014, 26.2% of those in East Asian cities and 28.4% of those in Southeast Asian cities were slum dwellers. In Cambodia, this percentage reached 55.1%, and was 41.0% and 38.3% in Myanmar and the Philippines, respectively (UN Habitat, 2016).

As economic activities and services concentrate in cities, this will also generate demand for low-paid jobs to sustain urban functions. Such jobs include, for example, service work at restaurants and hotels, construction, and domestic work for wealthy households. This creates demand for infrastructure to provide basic services to such low-income groups. However, because priority is given to the development of infrastructure for industrial purposes, there are often no adequate efforts being made to develop such infrastructure necessary to sustain urban livelihoods (see Box 9). As the backdrop to urban inequality, there is the problem of housing shortages for lower income groups amidst soaring real estate prices, and the redevelopment of low-income areas leading to the replacement of low-income classes with higher classes (gentrification), which can be sources of new political conflicts. In recent years, foreign migrant workers have also increased, who are typically in the lowest layer of the urban labor market and can easily become the target of social exclusion.

Another issue of relevance is the vulnerability of the infrastructure. For example, traffic jams are still a serious problem along with the inadequacy of public transport, and ad-hoc road development without a comprehensive plan. Preparation for natural disasters is also important. The 2011 Thai flooding, which was as severe as happens only once in 100 years, caused major disruption of supply chains. The typhoons that often hit the Philippines also have been an obstacle to the economic development of the country. As cities play pivotal roles in economic development, there are increased needs to handle these new risks adequately. Infrastructure has to be developed to minimize risks and the potential damage from natural disasters, as inadequate infrastructure can often worsen such damage.

8.3.3 The socio-political risks and policy dilemmas in the era of the mega-regions

Mega-cities and regions were seen as particularly strategic for China and ASEAN countries with respect to the "middle-income trap." In the 2010s, many Asian countries clearly shifted their policy orientation from addressing inter-regional inequality to prioritizing mega-regions. However, if the governments neglect the problem of inequality and other related social issues, political and social risks could increase, possibly causing further political instability in the country.

Infrastructure developments require large investments and financial resources. However, in middle-income countries, prioritizing resource allocation to the cities is likely to be a controversial political issue given the large regional disparities and lack of public finance. Figure 8.7 shows the policy dilemma of middle-income countries. On the one hand, governments aim at enforcing policies to increase competitiveness by prioritizing urban infrastructure development or corporate tax reductions for MNEs, under budget

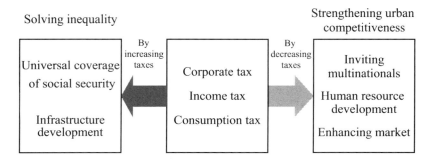

FIGURE 8.7 Policy dilemma of mega cities in emerging countries.
Source: Made by author.

constraints. On the other hand, problems related to social issues are mounting, such as the inequalities among regions and within the cities. In order to spread the benefits of development to other regions, it is important to secure the budgets for development infrastructure for rural areas. Social security systems to support the rapidly ageing society also need to be planned and implemented. In middle-income countries such as China, Thailand, and Malaysia, medical and pension systems for rural residents and the urban poor remain very basic and are of low standard in quality and coverage (see also Chapters 10 and 11). Increased taxes and adequate redistribution are needed for better social security systems, and to ensure social stability.

Middle-income countries in Asia thus have to deal simultaneously with the need to elaborate a strategy to strengthen competitiveness and avoid the middle-income trap. At the same time, they also need to build better social security systems to decrease income inequalities. This double requirement involves two different policy orientations because the former leads governments to reduce taxes, while the latter requires further tax collection. Taxes on property, assets, and inheritance should be introduced, or increased, to gain tax revenue. However, the residents of mega-regions are likely to disagree with policies that propose higher tax rates. Any tax policy should also consider business strategies for the country's competitiveness. The government also needs to consult with the business sector to achieve social consensus for tax reform. The key challenges for Asian countries lie in balancing these two policy targets. How policymakers will address these issues concerning mega-regions will define the future of Asia.

CONCLUSION

Rapid and compressed economic development has been accompanied by "compressed urbanization" in Asia. Mega-cities and mega-regions in middle-income countries developed through enhanced connectivity to the global economy. Their urban landscapes often are not distinguishable from those of cities in developed countries.

MNEs and global investors look globally when making decisions about location strategies and new foreign investments. They often compare Tokyo, Singapore, Shanghai, Bangkok, and Jakarta. Given that industry clusters are mostly located around mega-regions, they form strong production networks across and beyond country borders. With further digitalization and reduction of mobility costs, urban networks might be even strengthened, which will accelerate the further concentration of human capital towards the mega-cities and regions.

This chapter reviewed the dynamics of the Asian economy from a regional and country perspective. In the era of economic interdependency, the factors that influence the regional economy of one country are not limited to domestic factors and policies. External factors have a significant impact on a wide range of economic decisions and outcomes, from the reorganization of the domestic industrial structure and labor market to the spatial allocation of different economic functions. Mega-regions are centers of activities not only for local residents, workers, and domestic enterprises, but also for global actors, and their interests are sometimes conflicting. The dynamics of global economy seem elusive, but they shape regional economies through spatial reformation of these economies and allocation of functions of the global value chain. At the same time, despite the progress of globalization, the regions are the foundation of productive activities and daily life for local enterprises and residents. The regional socioeconomic structure and its characteristics directly affect the competitiveness of enterprises and people's quality of life. However, the means to respond to the social challenges faced by the regions depend on the socioeconomic features of each region and country, and their policy consensus formation process.

As shown by the dilemma of the middle-income countries, mega-cities are somehow miniatures of the world in which the social issues faced by developing and developed countries co-exist. For example, in the urban labor market there are white-collar workers, including global actors at the top of the ladder, while there are also many informal economy workers, irregular workers, and foreign migrants who work at the bottom of the labor market. Social issues such as inter-regional inequalities, urban inequality, and shortage of economic and life infrastructures represent complex policy challenges for many countries. Addressing these social challenges will be the key for a better and sustainable future for Asian countries.

BOX 8 Consuming Asia

Keiichiro Oizumi

The *White Paper on International Economy and Trade 2008* of the Ministry of Economy, Trade and Industry of Japan focused on Japan's challenges as an international trade-based country and encouraged the creation of new markets. The document described the world market as a market of 5 billion people: 1 billion people in developed countries and 4 billion in the emerging and developing countries. Since 2008, the white paper has carefully analyzed the markets of such emerging and developing countries. The media, especially after the world financial crisis in 2008, also started to publish special issues on emerging consumer markets. Japanese enterprises also shifted their targets to such emerging markets, particularly in Asia, because the ageing and declining population in Japan limits the future expansion of its market.

For Japanese companies, developing countries in Asia were providers of natural resources until the 1980s. They soon started to see these regions also as providers of cheap labor force. In the 21st century, however, they started considering Asia as an attractive consumer market. The sale of cars has rapidly increased in China, from 5.8 million units in 2005 to 28 million in 2016. ASEAN also saw an increase in domestic sales from 1.9 million to 3.1 million during the same period.

The expectations of Japanese companies towards the Asian consumer markets are reflected in the survey conducted by the Japan Bank for International Cooperation (JBIC). Table 8.2 shows the results of questionnaire surveys conducted with Japanese companies from 2003 to 2016. The table reports the frequencies for two

TABLE 8.2 Increase of expectation toward commercial market (unit: %)

	China		Indonesia		Thailand		Vietnam	
	Cheap labor	Current Market Scale	Cheap labor	Current Market Scale	Cheap labor	Current Market Scale	Cheap labor	Current Market Scale
2003	74.9	19.7	67.7	17.7	57.4	17.0	74.1	5.9
2004	66.1	23.9	68.9	20.0	49.3	20.5	75.9	6.5
2005	62.8	27.0	68.9	28.9	50.3	20.7	81.7	4.0
2006	57.2	24.9	54.1	27.0	45.9	24.1	71.4	5.2
2007	50.3	30.1	55.6	26.7	48.5	28.5	71.0	6.8
2008	44.9	37.1	56.1	39.0	38.7	25.8	61.3	6.0
2009	44.0	32.8	46.0	22.0	41.7	25.0	57.7	9.4
2010	35.3	38.1	51.4	24.8	44.7	22.0	61.2	10.3
2011	32.8	46.4	46.1	27.7	41.5	25.2	63.1	13.4
2012	26.6	46.8	40.4	26.0	36.3	27.5	58.8	10.0
2013	16.9	61.2	38.1	30.7	32.4	34.6	57.5	12.3
2014	17.8	57.0	28.6	37.3	28.3	42.2	53.0	17.9
2015	13.0	67.9	35.0	38.7	36.7	35.9	49.0	15.5
2016	12.7	62.4	30.5	43.3	26.1	37.7	42.2	19.5

Source: JBIC, Research report on oversea advancement of Japanese manufacturing companies (each year).

particular answers in the questionnaire regarding the reasons for overseas investment, which are "cheap labor" and domestic "current market size."

The frequencies for the answers "cheap labor" has been decreasing in all countries, whereas "current market size" has increased. For example, in the case of China, 74.9% of the Japanese companies chose "cheap labor" as the reason for their advancement into China in 2003 but in 2016 this response was selected by only 12.7%. Also, the choice of the answer "current market size" increased from 19.7% to 62.4%. Therefore, it seems that companies' reason for starting business activities in China has already shifted from the utilization of cheap labor to the possibility of investing in developing and expanding new markets. Other countries show the same trend; for Thailand and Indonesia the "current market size" was already selected more frequently than the "cheap labor." For Vietnam, "cheap labor" was still the predominant answer, but the trend is the same.

This is because of the increase in the income level of these countries. More precisely, high-income groups in urban population show a rapid increase. According to the national statistics of China, the average of the top 20% in terms of income in the urban population (disposable income) is 70,348 yuan per capita ($10,595) in 2016. If the household has three members, then its disposable income exceeds $30,000.

Considering the fact that China's urbanization rate in 2016 was more than 50%, the top 20% of urban population is equivalent to more than 150 million persons. That means that the number of people in the high-income group in China is equivalent, or is even exceeding, that of Japan's total population.

Given this, we can understand why Chinese tourists with strong purchasing power are rapidly increasing in number. In Japan, this phenomenon is associated with *Bakugai*, that is, explosive buying. Tourists from Asian countries to Japan increased from 6.5 million in 2010 to 20.4 million in 2016. The total expenditure of these tourists has been estimated to around 3 trillion yen, and it is considered a significant source of revenue for the Japanese economy.

At the same time, the shopping style of the Asian population is rapidly shifting from buying at physical shops to E-commerce via the Internet. "Alibaba," one of the biggest Internet shopping websites in China, established that November 11th is "single's day," promoting prices reductions for mega bargaining sales. In 2016, the sales of Alibaba on November 11th accounted for 12.07 million yuan ($1 trillion, 90 million) in a single day. E-pay on smartphones is widespread too. Some might have an image that market transactions in Asia still take place in traditional markets, where there is active negotiation between the buyer and the seller. However, this traditional image no longer captures the current practices of those in middle-income countries in Asia. Rather, the momentum of e-pay almost replacing cash payment seems to be in place in some of these countries. There are cases where one can make payments to street vendors using QR (Quick Response) codes.

NOTES

1 Mega cities are defined by UN as those cities with more than 10 million inhabitants. However, some researchers and policy papers sometimes use this term to refer to cities with large populations, even though they do not reach 10 million people.
2 Bangkok's population in official statistics of the BMA is around 6 million persons. However, many people have not moved their household registration, and Government estimates that the actual population is around 10 million. For example, the population census in 2010 reported 8.3 million people in Bangkok.
3 The first is the Greater Tokyo metropolitan region; Osaka-Nagoya mega-region occupies the fifth position; Seoul-Busan mega-region is 13rd; North Kyushu region is 16th; Hong Kong-Shenzhen region is 23rd; Greater Sapporo region is 24th; Shanghai city is 31st; Taipei is 32nd; Greater Beijing region is 34th; Delhi-Lahore mega-region is 35th; Singapore is 38th; and Bangkok is 40th.
4 The population of Thailand in 2014 was about 68 million persons.

REFERENCES

ADB, Asian Development Bank. (2008). *City Cluster Development: Toward an Urban-Led Development Strategy for Asia*, Asian Development Bank.

Davis, K. and H. Golden. (1954). "Urbanization and the Development of Pre-Industrial Areas", *Economic Development and Cultural Change*, Vol. 3. No. 1, pp. 6–26.

Douglass, M. (1995). "Global Interdependence and Urbanization: Planning for the Bangkok Mega-Region", in T.G. McGee and Ira M. Robinson (eds), *The Mega-Urban Regions of Southeast Asia*, UBC Press.

Endo, Tamaki. (2014). *Living with Risk: Precarity & Bangkok's Urban Poor*, NUS Press in association with Kyoto University Press.

Endo, Tamaki. (2016). "'Asianization of Asia' and restructuring of regional economics: Formation of Mega-Region and Changes in Urban Function in Thailand [Ajiaka suru ajia to chiikikeizaino saihen: taini okeru megarijyon no keisei to toshikinou no henka]", *Chiikikeizaigaku kenkyuu*, Vol. 31, pp. 2–18 [in Japanese].

Florida, Richard. (2008). *Who's Your City? How the Creative Economy Is Making Where to Live the Most Important Decision of Your Life*, Basic Books.

Florida, Richard, T. Gulden, and C. Mellander. (2008). "Rise of the Mega-Region", CESIS, Electronic Working Paper Series, No.129.

Hayase, Noriko. (2004). *Population in Asia: In the Wave of Globalization [Ajia no jinkou: gurobarukano nami no nakade]*, Institute of Development Economics [in Japanese].

IDE-JETRO. (2015). *IDE World Trend: Social Transformation of Asia from Population Census [Ajiken warudo torendo: Tokusyu jinkou sensasu kara miru higashiajia no syakaidaihendou]*, No. 238 (August), IDE-JETRO.

Kimura, Fukunari. (2003). "FDI as the Industrialization Strategy [Kougyouka senryaku toshiteno chokusetsu tousi]", in K. Ono and N. Kawabata (eds) *Industrialization Strategy of Viet Nam [Betonamu no kougyouka senryaku]*, Nihonhyouronsya, pp. 67–97 [in Japanese].

Lewis, W. A. (1954). "Economic Development with Unlimited Supplies of Labour", *The Manchester School*, Vol. 22, No. 2, pp. 139–191.

Marukawa, Tomoo. (2013). *Contemporary Chinese Economy [Gendai Chugoku Keizai]*, Yuhikaku [in Japanese].

NSO. (1993). *The 1990 Population and Housing Census/Bangkok*, NSO.

NSO. (1994). *The 1990 Population and Housing Census/Whole Kingdom*, NSO.

NSO. (2001). *The 2000 Population and Housing Census/Bangkok*, NSO.

NSO. (2002). *The 2000 Population and Housing Census/Whole Kingdom*, NSO.

Porter, Michael. E. (1990). *The Competitive Advantage of Nations*, Jossey Bass.

Sassen, Saskia. (1991). *The Global City: New York, London, Tokyo*, Princeton University Press.

Suehiro, Akira and K. Oizumi (eds.). (2017). *Social Transformation of East Asia: The World from Population Census [Higashi ajia no syakaihendou: jinkou sensasu ga kataru sekai]*, Nagoya University Press [in Japanese].

Tasaka, Toshio (ed.). (1998). *Asian Mega City [1] Bangkok* [*Ajia no mega toshi[1] Bankoku*], Nihonhyouronsya [in Japanese].

UN Habitat. (2010). *The State of Asian Cities 2010/2011*, UN Habitat.

UN Habitat. (2016). *World Cities Report 2016: Urbanization and Development: Emerging Futures*, UN Habitat.

United Nations. (2014). *World Urbanization Prospects: The 2014 Revision*, United Nations.

Watanabe, Toshio. (1986). *Development Economics: Economics and Contemporary Asia* [Kaihatsukeizaigaku: Keizaigaku to gendai ajia], Nihonhyouronsya [in Japanese].

9 Informalizing Asia: the other dynamics of the Asian economy

Tamaki Endo and Kenta Goto

Street vendor selling sweets in Ho Chi Minh City (2003, Photo by Kenta Goto).

LEARNING GOALS

- Understand what the informal economy is, and its roles in terms of peoples' livelihoods.
- Understand what role the informal economy plays in the Asian economy.
- Understand the future challenges and prospects of the informal economy.

INTRODUCTION

Street vendors, motorbike taxis, scrap collectors, and small repair shops – the streets of major Asian cities are full of such colorful, vibrant economic activities. A busy office worker enjoying her bowl of noodle for lunch at a small stall on the corner of the central business district in Bangkok; or a retired man getting his hair cut from a barber on a street in a quiet neighborhood in Hanoi. Scenes like these characterize a normal day of ordinary people in Asia.

Such activities are often referred to as the informal economy, and are not captured by official statistics, yet informal activities constitute a significant part of the economy in Asia, particularly from a livelihoods perspective.

The rapid economic development of Asia has been driven by industrialization, based on large, formal enterprises. While the focus of attention has therefore been on these segments of the economy, people involved in formal enterprises are, for many countries, the minority. A significant number of people in the world make their living in the informal economy, especially in Asia.

In the early theories of development economics, the informal economy was regarded as a temporary feature associated with under-development, which was supposed to disappear along with economic development. It was assumed that workers in this sector would eventually be absorbed into the modern, formal economy. Against such optimistic predictions, however, the informal economy remains widespread. In fact, informality seems to have crept into the formal economy in developed countries as well.

Informal jobs are wide-ranging, including various types of occupations. The definition of the informal economy has also changed over time, along with the shifting policy concerns at each of these junctures. The informal economy was regarded as a pre-modern economic sector in the context of post-war Asian development and was neglected for a long time. The informal economy, however, remains important for a large number of people living in Asia, and its contribution to the macro-economy is significant. This chapter looks at these other dynamics of the Asian economy.

9.1 THE INFORMAL ECONOMY AND ITS THEORETICAL PERSPECTIVES

9.1.1 What is the informal economy?

The informal economy is broadly defined as economic activities, jobs, and livelihoods that are not subject to social security or taxation, and typically not officially registered. Most of it is, therefore, not captured in official statistics. Traditionally, the types of occupations in this sector were assumed to include peddlers and street vendors, shoe polishers, and domestic workers, among others. These were the ones that were not found in, and considered unfit for, the formal, modern economy.

The International Labour Organization (ILO) categorizes the informal economy into the following three groups of occupations (excluding agricultural workers). The first are self-employed workers, including those in non-registered, micro and small enterprises. The second are wage workers with no employment contracts and social security coverage, and the third are home-based workers (ILO, 2002). In some cases, these activities are regarded as unlawful as they tend to operate outside the legal framework. However, it is important to make clear at the outset that the informal economy that we discuss should be differentiated from illegal acts, such as human trafficking and drug smuggling. The focus of this chapter is on economic activities that produce and supply goods and services that are of themselves legal.

9.1.2 The birth of the concept, and the shift in views from negative to positive

The perception of the informal economy has in recent years shifted from a negative to a positive one. The "informal sector"[1] arguments in traditional development economics were based on a linear view of modernization, in which it was treated as a waiting place for the potentially unemployed (disguised unemployment). This backward sector was expected to shrink, and eventually dissipate as economic development progressed. The main characteristics of these discussions were, firstly that they were based on a dichotomic view of the economy, which could be classified into either formal or informal sectors. Another was that the birth and growth of the informal sector was due to labor migration into urban areas from the rural areas. Finally, the discussions implicitly assumed that development was synonymous with the formalization of this sector.

One of the pioneer theoretical frameworks on disguised unemployment is Arthur Lewis' two-sector model (Lewis, 1954). This looks at rural–urban labor migration in an economy in which a modern urban sector with competitive labor markets and profit maximizing firms, and a traditional rural sector, where community principles dominate economic organization, coexist. A crucial assumption of this model is that the rural sector is endowed with abundant labor to the extent that the marginal product of labor is virtually zero, which can provide, at least for some time, an unlimited supply of labor to the evolving urban sector. Workers in the rural sector are also assumed to be receiving subsistence wages, which are essentially the average product of labor, typically higher than the marginal product of labor. Economic development through the expansion of the urban sector could occur by tapping into this vast labor supply base of the rural sector, without affecting the agricultural output of the rural sector. As such, this essentially suggests that such abundance of workers in fact represents disguised unemployment.

The informal economy in the urban sector, in relation to rural–urban migration, can be best explained by another well-known framework, the Harris–Todaro model (Todaro, 1969; Harris and Todaro, 1970). This model assumes that rural–urban migration occurs because of the difference in expected income. As a result of this movement of people between the two sectors, the expected incomes in the two sectors should become equal (in equilibrium), providing no incentives for further migration. However, because the urban labor market tends to be regulated by legislation such as minimum wages, this would result in downward rigidities of wage levels, keeping wage levels in this sector artificially high. The number of jobs available in the urban sector will be fixed because of this, but workers in rural areas will nevertheless opt to move to cities in the expectation that they would be able to get the higher-paying jobs. The new equilibrium will be where the expected income in the urban areas will become equal to that of rural income, in which those that will end up unemployed will form an urban informal economy.

From a policy perspective, the "informal sector" has been viewed negatively, if not with hostility, and has also been often associated with urban problems such as slums and crime. However, the ILO Employment mission to Kenya in the early 1970s turned a positive spin on this, by recognizing its role in employment creation to sustain the livelihoods of the poor. In the early days in developed countries after World War II, unemployment was almost synonymous with poverty. However, the poor in developing countries did not have the luxury to remain unemployed, and so had to be proactively involved in any kind of work available in the informal sector. The focus of the ILO thus was on the "working poor," and argued that the problem was not unemployment per se, but more on the forms of employment (ILO, 1972; Hart, 1973).

ILO's definition of the informal economy has recently experienced a fundamental change. However, its initial version has had significant influence on related policies in Southeast Asia. Three attributes are worth mentioning. The first is the dichotomy view as had become dominant in the 1960s, dividing the two sectors – formal and informal – and emphasizing their discontinuity and their differences. The second is the fact that the informal sector was defined as a residue that did not fit the formal sector. Third, the informal sector was assumed to be perfectly competitive because of the lack of, or freedom from, regulations. Also, an underlying idea was that while efficiency could be achieved and profits generated in the informal sector, this has been restricted because of the various constraints embedded in its economic and social structures, leading to employment problems.

While such a definition triggered criticism, the "discovery" of the informal sector by the ILO nevertheless contributed to raising awareness on this issue. Occupations that were previously neglected were recognized as informal sector activities, making them potential recipients for policy support. However, policy priorities and targets have changed over time. In the 1970s, the priority was to support the self-employed micro entities from a poverty alleviation perspective. However, this shifted towards the provision of support to improving productivity in micro and small enterprises with high growth potential.

9.1.3 Beyond the dichotomy view

As the informal economy comprises a wide variety of occupations and types of jobs, defining it always presents challenges. New jobs in the informal economy are also emerging on a daily base, making it difficult to design effective institutional mechanisms to address associated problems. These new jobs were in many cases also available in developed countries. The theoretical frameworks to understand the informal economy have shifted according to the policy priorities and targets that evolve out of dynamic contexts, and its definition has also changed along with these shifts.

One of the main criticisms of ILO's dichotomy approach is to view the informal sector as perfectly competitive and dismiss the inherent diversity of actors and occupations in it. From his study of slums in Manila, Nakanishi (1991), for example, argues that migrants from rural areas do not necessarily migrate to large cities for jobs in the modern, formal sector, but often actually aim for the urban informal sector. The urban informal sector, however, presents significant entry barriers, contrary to the beliefs of a neoclassical competitive market assumption. The informal sector entails substantial diversity, in which high productivity sectors co-exist alongside low productivity ones. In some cases, patron–client relationships make for non-competitive environments, in which market entry is neither free nor easy. Pasuk and Itoga also find similar results from their research in Bangkok (Pasuk and Itoga, 1992). While these research findings were important, they were nevertheless still of the same lineage as the old school, as they were still based on the postulation that the rural sector was traditional, putting it in stark contrast to the urban economy.

In the 1990s, with the progressing of globalization under the increased influence of neo-liberalism, different views on the informal sector/informal economy started to emerge. According to a global research and policy network Women in Informal Employment: Globalizing & Organizing (WIEGO),[2] it can broadly be classified into three distinct groups.

These three groups approach the informal economy from an urban perspective. The first are the structuralists, represented by people such as Manuel Castells and Saskia Sassen. Castells attributes the formation and expansion of the informal economy to globalization, intensifying competition, and the changes in industrial structures that are thereby induced, rather than as a result of individual decisions on rural-urban migration caused by rural poverty (Portes et al., 1989). As such, the informal economy is defined as an unregulated, specific form of production relationship. In this sense, their arguments were epochal as they viewed the informal economy on a continuum with the formal economy. Likewise, Sassen (1998) found that informal economies were now also emerging in major cities in developed countries.

The second is a focus on institutions. Hernando de Soto, from his research in Peru, suggests that government intervention through inefficient legislations and institutions prevents the growth of the informal economy, which might in fact possess higher potential for growth than the formal economy (de Soto, 1989). When the costs associated with formalization are prohibitively high, people are forced into informal income generating activities and informal housing to sustain livelihoods. As such, this view advocates deregulation, which has been well received by the neo-classical strands, and further evolves into policies encouraging micro-finance schemes.

The third takes the view that informality is the result of voluntary choices by rational individuals. William Maloney of the World Bank is among the advocates of this view. The fact that they make their argument by comparing the costs and benefits of informality makes their views similar to those of de Soto. However, rather than emphasizing institutional frameworks as bottlenecks, the emphasis is more on the motivations of those that are self-employed or operate micro enterprises, attempting to escape the burdens of social security and taxes (Maloney, 2004).[3]

The differences in emphasis among these perspectives has led to different policy implications as well. While the dichotomy views focused on the survival of the micro self-employed, structuralists targeted micro-producers, traders, and subcontracting workers, and institutionalists and voluntary choice theorists emphasized informal entrepreneurs and enterprises.

In many Asian countries, policies were drafted and implemented in line with the unfolding of such different views on the informal economy. In the 1960s when the negative view was predominant, many of the occupations in the informal economy were the objects for exclusion or elimination. Typical examples include the removal of hawkers and food stalls from the streets in Thailand, Malaysia, and Singapore, or the control of sex-workers under the Sarit regime in Thailand. Policies to support the informal economy only emerged in late 1980s and early 1990s, due to recommendations by the ILO and other UN agencies. As a result, in Thailand, for instance, the terms "informal sector" appeared for the first time in the Seventh National Economic and Social

Development Plan in 1992. The arguments of de Soto also influenced policy makers in favor of deregulation and encouraged policy support to prioritize the establishment of micro-credit schemes.

Nevertheless, concepts such as the informal sector or informal economy remained within a limited group of people, including researchers and the ILO. This situation changed drastically in the 2000s. Many countries redirected their attention to the informal economy and actually implemented policies to address issues related to it. In addition, it also received attention from the wider international community besides the ILO, including the World Band and the Asian Development Bank.

9.2 THE INFORMAL ECONOMY IN ASIA AND ITS ROLES IN THE 21ST CENTURY

9.2.1 Redefining the informal economy under globalization

Despite rapid economic development and industrialization, the informal economy was still widespread in Asia even in the 2000s, against earlier predictions that development would eventually eliminate informality. Informality, particularly in employment, also started to appear in the formal enterprises of developed countries (Standing, 1999). There has been increased awareness that informal employment and work have in fact evolved in various forms in employment and production relationships, involving a wide range of different economic entities.

The unfolding of such phenomena has been attributed to the intensification of global competition. Informality in work and employment is now no longer considered as an issue specific to, or necessarily associated with, underdevelopment. In such a context, the ILO published a report entitled *Decent Work and the Informal Economy* prepared for the International Labour Conference of 2002. This report critically assessed the validity of the definition of the "informal sector," which was introduced 30 years ago by its own Kenya report, mentioned earlier. One of the main points argued was on the sectoral orientation of the term, which implied that informality was specific to certain industries or economic activities, which in turn limited the ability to capture its diversity and complexity (ILO, 2002). Rather, given the spread of informality in employment and production relationships, the term informal economy has increasingly been recognized and used to address this issue.

For the ILO, the problem was that most of the workers in the informal economy were not recognized or protected under the existing regulatory frameworks, thus leaving them vulnerable, deprived of decent work. In response, standards and methodologies were developed to measure the extent of informality, in order to promote decent work in the informal economy.

The following two changes thus took place in the 2000s in relation to the informal economy. The first was the shift from understanding the informal economy from the point of view of a particular industry or economic activity, towards a more comprehensive one encompassing the complexities and diversities of informality. The second was a move away from the view which positioned informality in the context of poverty, towards understanding it as part of the wider dynamics of the macro-economy.

9.2.2 The informal economy in Asia: its size and trends

The Organisation for Economic Co-operation and Development (OECD) published a report entitled *Is Informal Normal?* in the aftermath of the global financial crisis that occurred in the US in 2008 (Jütting and Laiglesia, 2009). Figure 9.1 is reproduced from that report, which suggests that while there had been an increase in per capita GDP in Southeast Asia, this has been accompanied by increased informal employment. So is informality transitory, or has it become the norm?

Table 9.1 summarizes the shares of informal employment according to regions. The share of such workers in East and Southeast Asia in 2009/2010 was a very significant 65%. Country-wise, while some have recorded slight decreases, that for China was still about one-third, and between 40% and 70% for others. The shares of informal employment in Indonesia and China have further shown significant increases in 2016, compared to 2009/2010.

Table 9.2 summarizes the contribution of the informal economy to GDP for selected countries for which data are available. While the data are somewhat outdated, the figure for Asia (including South Asian countries) was estimated at about 31%.

The figures in these tables are based on units as identified according to the ILO's definition. In the past, there had been multiple definitions of informality according to the purpose of analysis: when the focus was on poverty, the units were based on workers and their occupational status; when the focus was on productivity, the units were typically enterprise based. As interest in the informal economy grew, however, the need to develop statistical indicators that were consistent with the System of National Account (SNA) came to be recognized as crucial.

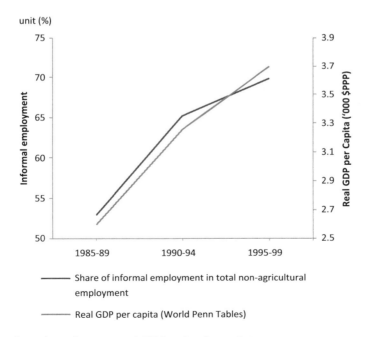

FIGURE 9.1 Informal employment and GDP in Southeast Asia.

Source: Jütting and Laiglesia (2009).

TABLE 9.1 Share of informal employment (non-agricultural employment, %)

Region/Country	Informal employment (2000)	Informal employment (2009/2010)	Informal employment (2016)
Asia	65	–	59
(East and Southeast Asia – except China)	–	65	–
(South Asia)	–	82	–
Indonesia	78	76	80
Philippines	72	70	–
Thailand	51	42	–
China	–	33	54
India	83	84	78
North Africa	48	45	56
Sub-Sahara Africa	72	66	77
Latin America	51	51	49

Source: Regional data for 2000 are from ILO (2002), those for 2009/2010 from Vanek et al. (2014), country data for 2000 and 2009/10 from ILO (2013), and for 2016 from ILO (2018).

Note: "–" denote data not available.

TABLE 9.2 Contribution of the IE to GDP (estimation, %)

Region/Country	The contribution of the IE to GDP (non-agriculture only)
Asia	31
Indonesia (1998)	31
Philippines (1995)	32
Korea (1995)	17
India (1990–1991)	45
North Africa	27
Sub-Sahara Africa	41
Latin America	29

Source: ILO (2002).

Note: IE = Informal Economy.

The new definition is as follows: the informal *sector* is based on the business unit,[4] while informal *employment* focuses on work. Discussions regarding own-account business units and unregistered firms are therefore related to the informal sector, and those related to jobs/work are related to informal employment. *Informal economy*, on the other hand, is a comprehensive concept that incorporates both sector and employment perspectives, whose aim is to understand the structure of the economy. As such, the informal economy can be defined by a matrix with rows to indicate sectors, and columns to indicate employment. The definition based on this matrix is in accordance to that of the SNA during the seventh International Conference of Labour Statisticians held in 2003. The introduction of this matrix has allowed the capturing of the diversities of the informal economy, such as informal employment in formal sector enterprises (such as family workers at formal enterprises) or formal employment in informal sectors (such as formal employment in micro-enterprises classified as informal because of their size).[5]

Governments in Asia have initiated the systematic collection of relevant statistical data on the informal economy. In line with this, the ILO, together with the UN Statistical Institute for Asia and the Pacific (SIAP) and WIEGO, organized a seminar, inviting officials from statistical departments and ministries of labor from 13 countries in Asia (including those from South Asia) in 2015 to discuss progress in each country and share common challenges. Thailand has been publishing the "Formal and Informal Labor Force Market Survey" since 1994, and the "Informal Employment Survey" since 2005. Likewise, Malaysia has also published sector-focused statistical data, the "Informal Sector Survey," since 2009. China has also added relevant variables on the informal economy to its labor market survey in 2015, and the Philippines implemented a pilot program to estimate the share of the informal economy's contribution to total GDP in 2008. However, the estimation of the informal economy using both sectoral and employment data is not easy and remains one of the main common challenges for these governments.

During an academic seminar supported by the World Bank in China in 2010, the results of estimations based on data collected on the informal economy in six major Chinese cities were reported. The study used the ILO's definition matrix, from which it derived four different definitions of informal employment. The first was those who were excluded from social security benefits, including pension, health, and unemployment insurances. The second was those without labor contracts, as stipulated by the Labor Contract Law of 2009. The third and fourth are based on the union and intersection of informal workers based on the first and second definitions, where workers who are informal based on either the first or second definition (union), and those workers to whom both the first and second definition apply, respectively. While the size of the informal economy according to each of the definitions was different, they all exhibited common trends. For example, using the third definition, workers who were informally employed made up 37.2% of total employment. While that number for urban resident workers (as defined by the household registration system) was 29.6%, it was 65.9% for migrant workers (rural resident workers, under the household registration system). Similarly, while 84.1% of those with an urban residency were holding jobs in the formal sector, that share dropped to 54.4% for those with a rural residency. Other findings include the following. The shares of workers in informal employment were particularly high among young workers between the age 16 and 34: 74% in the first definition, and 65% according to the second. Wage levels were about 60% of those with formal employment (Park et al., 2012). Such efforts are intensifying gradually in other countries as well.

9.2.3 Globalization, urbanization, and the dynamism of the informal economy

Globalization and urbanization encourage reproduction of the informal economy, and sometimes, its expansion. It will further grow, change, disappear, and be regenerated, as a result of peoples' responses to cope with, and mitigate, the risks associated with this process (Endo, 2014).

There are several reasons why the informal economy evolves and expands. The first instance is highlighted by the case of motorbike taxis in Bangkok which have emerged because of the city's rapid urbanization and the resulting changes in local service demand. They appeared in the latter half of the 1980s, due to rapid urbanization and lack of infrastructure including public transportation, which led to heavy traffic congestion. It is known that someone living in the outskirts of Bangkok came up with the idea of providing transportation in this niche market. It was reported that there were about 16,000 motorbike taxis in 1988. This number rapidly increased, reaching 110,000 when the registration system was introduced in 2005. With Bangkok developing into a global city, similar types of informal businesses evolved, such as motorbike messenger services. The increase of street vendors is also a response to the increase in urban population.

The second is the expansion of the informal economy due to business cycles and crises. During the Asian financial crisis of 1997, layoffs by formal enterprises occurred in Thailand and Indonesia, which resulted in a rapid increase in the number of workers in self-employment, where entry barriers tended to be low. Likewise, when tens of millions were laid-off in the process of state-owned enterprise reforms in China in the late 1990s, there was an influx of people into the informal economy. The global financial crisis in 2008 triggered a similar response (Horn, 2009). These are results of strategic responses to cope with the idiosyncratic risks in order to protect livelihoods.

The third is an entrepreneurial response due to changes in institutional constraints and competitive environments. One such example can be found in the case of the local market-oriented apparel industry in Vietnam. This happened during the time when Vietnam accelerated the introduction of market mechanisms in its economy in the late 1980s, a program which was induced by the sluggish economic performance of the country's socialist economic planning. Although the establishment of private businesses became possible, the institutions in place were highly in favor of the state-owned, public sector, when Vietnam's financial and distribution systems were quite underdeveloped. Micro and small enterprises nevertheless emerged, which depended on social network based informal inter-firm relationships that allowed complex financial and business transactions to take place, growing into a significant industry. While these economic activities were not captured and recorded in official statistics, they were a significant source of income and sustained the livelihoods of large numbers of families in these localities (Goto, 2013a, 2013b).

On the other hand, changes in competitive environments can also lead to informalization. Thailand's apparel industry had been strong and growing until the early 1990s. However, as the growth rate of wages exceed that of productivity, formal apparel manufacturing firms started to outsource some of their labor intensive functions to informal garment companies, or to increase the amount of irregular work (informal employment) in the formal apparel sector (Goto and Endo, 2014).

9.2.4 The roles and functions of the informal economy

How does the informal economy affect those who make their living out of it? This is a difficult question, precisely because of the diversity and stratification of the jobs and production relationships, as discussed earlier. Regardless of theoretical or methodological differences, there are two common features regarding the positive dimensions of the informal economy. The first relates to the worker's perspective. The informal economy provides the needed work and incomes for the poor, and as such constitutes the "economy for survival." During recessions and major downtrends, it has functioned to buffer the negative effects on the macro-economy. The second relates to the perspective of the enterprise, which suggests that the informal economy is a manifestation of creativity and dynamic entrepreneurship. While the former feature represents an inevitable choice made from necessity, the latter focuses more on local industry growth and entrepreneurial spirits.

Consider the informal economy's relationship with poverty. For the poor, who are disadvantaged or restricted in terms of educational attainment and access to various types of resources, most of the work in the informal economy is important from a livelihoods point of view. These jobs are typically low-paid, unstable, and prone to various types of risks. However, some of those that have been successful in managing risks and expanding their businesses can earn incomes as much as those working in the formal economy.

Its diverse and stratified structure makes it hard to give a simple statement on the potentialities of the informal economy. In informal economies, there are some highly productive sectors that typically require larger investment outlays and sophisticated skills and technology. Because of this, while entry barriers to such sectors are high, they can also be highly profitable. On the other hand, the informal economy expands disproportionately in sectors with lower or no entry barriers, including work such as home-based work or peddling, where productivity tends to be lower, and also are prone to fierce competition. Vicious cycles of poverty happen when people fail to respond to the risks stemming from such increasingly competitive environments or serious business downturns.

The second is from an economic performance perspective, including both the micro- (enterprise) level and the macro-level. Under circumstances of underdeveloped market institutions, as typically observed in developing countries, the informal economy may be a result of rational and strategic behavior of individuals and enterprises. The apparel industry in Vietnam is exactly such an example. The extensive informal industry in Ho Chi Minh City has no doubt contributed to generating local employment as well as possibilities to start businesses as spinoffs from subcontracting arrangements. While in general the informal economy is regarded as of low productivity because the industry exhibits limited scale effects, the smallness of operations may not necessarily prevent high returns. The informal economy constrained because of lack of supporting institutions can, given favorable conditions, be the driver of economic upgrading and promote growth.

The third is its role in social upward mobility. Labor markets in developing countries are often highly imperfect and fragmented according to, for example, educational attainments. In many cases, first generation migrants from rural areas were not able to find a job in the established formal sector. As such, their careers were built within the informal economy. Self-employed work in the informal economy can also be profitable, as in the case of the apparel industry in Vietnam. While the working conditions and stability differ significantly from those in the formal economy, and thus the probability of falling into a poverty trap is higher, it is still possible for workers to find ways into the highly productive sectors in the informal economy. This could help finance the higher education of their children, which enables them to obtain a job in the formal economy. The prospects of upward social mobility in urban cities for second generation migrants were basically provided through the success of first-generation migrants. As such, engagement in the informal economy, from this perspective, has not always been negative (Endo, 2014).

9.3 THE FUTURE OUTLOOK FOR THE INFORMAL ECONOMY AND ITS DILEMMAS

9.3.1 Informality and institutions: taxes, risks, and social protection

There has been a well-known interest in informality since the 2000s, which has prompted active debates. International organization including the ILO, World Bank, ADB, and OECD have published major reports, and discussion of statistical methodologies to systematically collect data is progressing.

The definition by the ILO was an explicit attempt to identify the informal economy in both developing and developed countries. Discussions related to "formalizing the informal economy" are also active. Unlike those in the 1970s where formalization implied the transformation of informality into formal, the discussions now are more broad-based. The focus is on how to keep the positive dimensions of the informal economy and build institutions to reduce vulnerability of those in it. The background and context of these discussions are diverse sets of issues such as middle-income traps, human resource development, and the ageing society, because those in the informal economy live outside formal institutional and legal frameworks. The informal economy may not necessarily shrink in the future, and simulation analysis suggests that the different approaches to the informal economy will lead to significantly different outcomes in terms of how the informal economy will persist (Loayza, 2016). The increase in interest from international organizations could be because of such new findings in research. As regards to formalization, however, the focus is on taxation and social security.

Thailand is an example where clear policies on the informal economy have been implemented. While in the 1990 the government supported the upgrading of the "informal sector" according to advice from international organizations, this did not bear substantial results. However, the Thaksin administration formed in 2001 introduced drastic changes. Thaksin defined self-employed and agricultural workers as "informal economy" (*Setthakit Nokrabob* or "out-of-system economy") and "informal employment" (*Rengaan Nokrabob* or "out-of-system labor"), respectively (while calling the formal ones "in-system"), and conducted a wide-scale survey on the informal economy (Endo, 2014). The data and information were used to design and implement policies such as sectoral specific ones (e.g., the registration system of motorbike taxis), micro-credit schemes, small and medium enterprise development, and support policies.

The administration had two objectives. The first was to identify the informal economy and expand the tax base. By internalizing the informal economy, it could also eradicate the informalities in administrative procedures as well as the illegal activities in it. Although this never materialized, there were ideas to regulate gambling and the sex industry, because of their significant size, which did spark intense discussions.

The second was from a safety net perspective. The Ministry of Labor and Social Welfare started to design social security mechanisms to include self-employed workers and home-based workers, while the Ministry of Finance was considering ways to include informal workers into the pensions system. While a universal health system was introduced to cover the entire population, social security coverage, including pensions and employment insurance, remained at just about 27.5% (ILO, 2004). The underdeveloped state of social security systems is a common challenge across countries in Asia. When the rapidly ageing populations in many Asian societies became one of the focuses of attention, the question of how to bring those self-employed into social security schemes became a key concern for many countries, including China.

The development and extension of social security in developed countries happened as the shares of self-employed workers declined with economic development, and demographic change also occurred accordingly. In contrast, the shares of self-employed workers are still high in many countries in Asia. Asian countries, facing such changes compressed into shorter periods of time, cannot expect to see the economic and institutional development and demographic change happening in an orderly and sequential manner. Yet the provision of social security to the informal economy is a crucial and urgent issue. For example, self-employed workers face not just investment risks; health-related risks also could significantly undermine their businesses. While their positive roles have increasingly been recognized, the risks of displacements by governments in the process of urban redevelopment are high for certain occupations such as street vendors. Real examples of these can be seen in Jakarta, Bangkok, and Ho Chi Minh City, where drastic increase of real estate prices have been recorded.

9.3.2 The new dynamics in the 21st century (1) – the internationalization of the informal economy

Putting aside the question of governments' actual ability to mobilize financial resources and expand social security to the informal economy, if such policies actually were implemented, would the informal economy shrink? The informal economy seems to be, in fact, expanding along with globalization, which is a new trend. Local processes of informalization have now become global, and as new issues have emerged, the above question remains inconclusive, at least for the time being. Some examples merit attention.

The first relates to the evolving micro and small enterprises in the informal economy and their globalizing nature of business. This is unfolding as the boundaries of formality and informality, particularly in middle-income countries, have become increasingly blurred. These firms were assumed to be at the bottom of the economy, where their businesses could only reach highly localized markets with low quality products. Globalization has, however, opened opportunities not just for large corporations, but for some of those micro and small enterprises as well. This has led to a new international business and trade dynamism, which cannot be described by the traditional "developed-developing" hierarchy.

Take the case of the labor-intensive apparel and footwear industry, where the informal sector-oriented value chains that traditionally catered for the local markets are now expanding into the global market. Small- and micro-enterprises in the apparel industries of China, Thailand, and Vietnam now also supply low-end products to niche but growing markets in the Middle East, East Europe, Central Asia, and Africa. These informal enterprises are connected to global value chains differently from those that undertake sub-contracting work in the export-oriented businesses of large, formal corporations to more developed countries.

A related example are the informal commercial networks. One such includes the African merchants procuring various products in Hong Kong and Mainland China, practically connecting African markets to specific industrial clusters in Asia, where both original and imitation products are actively being traded (Ogawa, 2016). A process of "globalization from below" seems to be in motion (Mathews et al., 2012).

9.3.3 The new dynamics in the 21st century (2) – from formal to informal

The OECD report, mentioned earlier, states that while informality was primarily a concern of low-income countries in the 1970s, this has today also become increasingly relevant for middle- and high-income countries.

Informality is now also observed in developed countries such as Japan, which was once considered as a role model of economic development. The issue of focus in Japan is mostly related to the changes in the labor market during the reforms undertaken by the Koizumi administration in the early 2000s, typically manifested in the expansion of irregular employment. This has been particularly observed with female and youth employment and is often associated with poverty. Media reporting on dismissals of irregular workers and "black companies" has become normal. Terms such as "working poor," as first defined in ILO's Kenya report in 1972, is often used to refer to such newly emerging poor (also see Chapter 11).

Irregular workers in developed countries are naturally different from informal workers in developing countries. For instance, in the case of Japan, irregular and temporary workers are officially registered, have proper contracts, and are covered by social security schemes. As such, the progressive informalization in developed countries cannot be treated in the same way as those in developing countries, but several international organizations are putting forward an agenda to put informality issues of developed and developing countries together on the same table. The redefinition of the informal economy by the ILO was an attempt complementing such a move.

Behind this was, first, the issue of the emerging new dimensions of poverty, through increases in irregular employment used by large firms to reduce costs. Second, what underlay this in both developing and developed countries were common factors, such as technological changes and globalization. Third, the informalization of formal employment is now also occurring in middle-income countries. For example, after the Asian financial crisis in 1997, Japanese temporary staffing agency advanced to many middle-income countries in Southeast Asia. Today, it is not uncommon to find large corporations depending on such irregular workers. Increases in formal jobs were once considered as labor market characteristics of developed countries, and economic development was supposed to formalize labor markets in such manners. However, some middle-income countries are already facing informalization through increases in irregular workers.

CONCLUSION

The focus of Asia's miraculous post-war development has always been on the formal economy, while the informal economy was also in operation with diverse, complex, and elusive characteristics. This informal economy was, in fact, for long the source of incomes to build sustainability, and the numbers involved may have exceeded those who operated in the formal economy. The informal economy has been viewed as a symbol of backwardness and underdevelopment. However, it also was, and still is, a social space where people have creatively responded to the risks involved, because of the lack of supporting institutions.

The problems of the informal economy are different from those in the formal economy. The informal economy tends to be much more precarious, and we certainly do not suggest we need more of it. However, an understanding of the Asian economy should also involve an appreciation that the informal economy is wide-spread, and that it is for many in the region practically the last resort to sustain their livelihoods. The creative and innovative responses to the potential risks in the informal economy form another strong strand in the narrative of a dynamic Asian economy.

A challenge in looking at the informal economy is the lack of a clear definition, both conceptional and practical, because of its diversity. The demarcation of formal and informal evolves according to changes in the relationships between the state and society, and between markets and the institutions that govern them. However, because of the need to address some of the issues identified here, definitions and key indicators must be established. Governments have accordingly defined the informal economy in the context of the evolving policy goals of the time.

It may be unrealistic to believe that the informal economy will soon disappear. However, the types of jobs that emerge will also impact what will play out in terms of overall development and of livelihoods of those that are engaged in it. While the informal economy was perceived negatively in early development economics, its importance is significant for the poor and for workers unprotected by formal institutions and without access to important economic resources. As discussed in this chapter, in most developing countries where the formal economy is still limited, the proactive responses of ordinary people in the face of these adversities can still result in new businesses and opportunities, which could further lead to upward social mobility.

On the other hand, the expansion of irregular employment has become a serious social concern for developed countries. This has been regarded as one of the main sources of deteriorating working conditions and insecurity, which could lead to the "race to the bottom." Such informalization of the formal economy is in most cases due to these countries not being able to adjust fully to a changing economic environment amidst declining competitiveness. A re-conception of the informal economy is needed to include developed countries as well.

How would localized responses from the informal economy interact with the challenges emerging from an increasingly globalized Asian economy? What sort of dynamics can we expect to see in the future? How do digitalization and the rise of the platform economy impact the informal economy? While predicting such outcomes is very difficult, it remains clear that new patterns of informality are unfolding in the face of new social challenges determined by evolving economic structures. To correctly understand and design effective policies to mitigate the negative risks associated with the informal economy requires a holistic approach.

BOX 9 Informal residential areas: the functions of "slum" communities from the urban lower-class perspective

Tamaki Endo

What kind of image do you have of "slum" communities? When conducting research in slum communities, people often ask, "Isn't it dangerous?" "Is it clean?" or "What's the sanitation like?" Those who are not familiar with these communities might think of them as "3D" places (the same metaphor used for occupations that are thought of as "dirty, dangerous, and demeaning").

Urban communities, however, are flexible residential spaces which provide multiple functions for residents' needs to adjust and adapt to urban life. Similar to the concept of informality used in occupational aspects, "slum" communities are informal residential areas where people's innovative approaches to coping with the economic and social constraints of daily urban life appear as particular forms in physical and social settings. Spatial arrangements are a result of daily responses to the urban risks and constraints faced by those who are not covered by social security and other supporting systems and are not protected by laws and regulations.

How, then, were communities formed over time? The first challenge faced by new migrants arriving in a city is to secure housing. There is an absolute shortage of low-cost housing in the private housing market. Given budget constraints, the urban lower class cannot afford to purchase a new house on the market. Even on the private rental market, the rent for a one-room apartment often requires more than 50% of monthly income. Thus, the most realistic options for the majority were either staying at the homes of relatives and friends, or to construct shelters on their own. Slums typically increase during the urban expansion period, when large inflows of migrants into cities are observed. Migrants usually seek and settled in undeveloped areas such as wetlands or along railways where no basic infrastructure is available, and construct housing by themselves. Residents can build simple frame houses in as little as ten days.

As mentioned above, these self-constructed communities have multiple functions. First, they are highly flexible residential spaces. In the city, the cost of housing is high and land is scarce compared to rural areas. Thus, a small unit is often shared by two or more generations along with relatives. The self-built housing allows residents to invest in remodeling and improvement of their housing over time, according to their needs and changes in family composition. From the perspective of household accounts, the important feature of the community is that it allows "cumulative investment." In the context of day-to-day financial constraints, households constantly make decisions and prioritize the use of their financial resources according to the family lifecycle (birth, childcare, schooling, and so on). When they can afford housing after they meet other prioritized needs, they gradually invest in residences (Endo, 2014).

Secondly, a community is not only a place to live but also a place to produce and consume. Various economic activities take place in the communities, from vendors, grocery shops, laundries, beauty salons, to repair workshops. For those who work in the informal economy, communities are also places for work.

Third, the community has the function of absorbing the shocks and impacts of urban risks and constraints in urban life. It provides services according to the residents' needs and often functions as a safety net. For example, a resident can sell sweets or food in front of the house from the day after he or she has faced a sudden layoff by an employer. The grocery shops and vendors accept extended credit. One can also buy goods such as medicine, starting from as little as one pill, and alcohol by the glass in the grocery shop. Sometimes, vendors voluntarily provide food to elderly people who live alone and children whose parents return home late. In case of an emergency, some communities run mutual financing associations and/or saving groups within the community.

The residents in the community face several difficulties in life. Their conditions vary and some of them are not necessarily the poorest of the poor. There are large extended families but also single elderly residents. Despite most people being honest hard workers, there are also those who commit crimes. The life of the urban lower class can change sharply day to day as a result of the various urban risks they face. The communities are spaces which provide necessary survival measures for urban life, such as enabling savings on housing costs, the creation of occupations, and mutual support among residents.

Recently, new forms of residential informality have started to appear. For example, in Shanghai, brokers rent a room in a condominium for middle- and upper-class residents and divide the room into 20 units with concrete walls. Each unit is rented out to low-income people. Against the backdrop of a shortage of vacant land and a high threat of eviction in Shanghai, this type of informal group-rented apartment is considered to be a "contemporary slum," and is known as *qunzu*. In Japan, the Mainichi Newspaper also reported in 2013 that many illegally shared rooms with residential arrangements similar to those in Shanghai were found in Tokyo. A typical example was that a room in an apartment was divided into 12 small units, each unit being rented out for around 1,200 yen (about $11) per day. What was interesting were the differences in governments' responses. In Japan, regulations were enforced within a month, but what happened to those evicted is unknown. In contrast, informal settlements in Bangkok and Shanghai are often tolerated until new development plans actually require the use of the occupied land or buildings.

Cities always need the labor of the urban lower class. Services provided in the city, however, tend to prioritize the needs of capital and of well-off residents. The loosely regulated systems and institutional flexibility of middle-income countries allow space for people to practice creative strategies to survive in the city. Even with a well-designed social security system, institutionally tight societies such as Japan, paradoxically create burdens for the urban lower class who are attempting to survive.

NOTES

1 The term "informal economy" has become increasingly popular, replacing the traditional term "informal sector," as discussed later. As this is primarily due to the changes in focus and in priority areas, we will still use the term "informal sector" depending on the context, particularly in the description related to discussion up until the 1990s.
2 WIEGO (Women in Informal Employment: Globalizing and Organizing) is an international network of membership-based organizations (MBOs) of informal workers, individual researchers, and development practitioners (https://www.wiego.org/).
3 Since the 1990 World Development Report, there has been increased focus and emphasis on the urban poor and those in the informal economy by the World Bank. Labor has been regarded as the main asset of the poor, and their productive and efficient use has been prioritized to address issues on economic growth and poverty reduction simultaneously. As the increase of capacity to address the various vulnerabilities and risks would lead to enhanced self-help capabilities, the need to build safety nets has also been encouraged.
4 It should be noted that while the term "informal sector" in the 1970s was a broad-based concept encompassing informality comprehensively, that of today is used in a very limited sense, primarily that denotes an approach to the "informal economy" from a sectoral and establishment (production unit)-based perspective.
5 The definition of the informal economy is multi-dimensional, and can be best expressed by a combination of the types of production units, and occupational status. The production unit comprises the following three types: formal sector enterprises, informal sector enterprises, and households. The "jobs by status in employment" comprise the following five: own account workers (self-employed), employers, un-paid family workers, employees, and members of producers' cooperatives. Except un-paid family workers, four other statuses can be found in both the informal and the formal sector. See Vanek et al. (2004) for details.

REFERENCES

De Soto, Hernando. (1989). *The Other Path*, New York: Harper & Row.
Endo, T. (2014). *Living with Risk: Precarity & Bangkok's Urban Poor*, Singapore: NUS Press associated with Kyoto University Press.
Goto, K. (2013a). "Starting Businesses through Reciprocal Informal Subcontracting: Evidence from the Informal Garment Industry in Ho Chi Minh City" *Journal of International Development*, 25(4), 562–582.
Goto, K. (2013b). "Social Networks, Informal Trade Credit, and Its Effects on Business Growth: Evidence from the Local Garment Trade in Vietnam" *Journal of the Asia Pacific Economy*, 18(3), 382–395.
Goto, K., and T. Endo. (2014) "Upgrading, Relocating, Informalising? Local Strategies in the Era of Globalization: The Thai Garment Industry" *Journal of Contemporary Asia*, 44(1), 1–18.

Harris, J. R. and P. Michael Todaro. (1970). "Migration, Unemployment and Development: A Two-Sector Analysis" *American Economic Review*, 60(1), 126–142.

Hart, K. (1973). "Informal Income Earning Opportunities and Urban Employment in Ghana" *Journal of Modern African Studies*, 11, 61–69.

Horn, Z. E. (2009). "No Cushion to Fall Back On: The Global Economic Crisis and Informal Workers" *Synthesis Report*, Inclusive Cities Project.

ILO. (1972). *Employment, Income, and Equality: A Strategy for Increasing Productive Employment in Kenya*. Geneva: ILO.

———. (2002). *Decent Work and the Informal Economy: Sixth Item on the Agenda*, International Labour Conference 90th Session, Geneva: ILO.

———. (2004). *Thailand Social Security Priority and Needs Survey*, Geneva: ILO.

———. (2013). *Women and Men in the Informal Economy: A Statistical Picture* (second edition), Geneva: ILO.

———. (2018). *Women and Men in the Informal Economy: A Statistical Picture* (third edition), Geneva: ILO.

Jütting, J. P. and J. R. Laiglesia. (2009). *Is Informal Normal? Toward more and better jobs in Developing countries*, Tokyo: OECD.

Lewis, W. A. (1954). "Economic Development with Unlimited Supplies of Labor" *Manchester School of Economic Development and Social Studies*, 22(2), 139–191.

Loayza, N. V. (2016). "Informality in the Process or Development and Growth" *The World Economy*, 39(12), 1856–1916.

Maloney, W. F. (2004). "Informality Revisited" *World Development*, 32(7), 1159–1178.

Mathews, G., G. L. Ribeiro and C. A. Vega (eds.). (2012). *Globalization from Below: The World's Other Economy*, Routledge.

Nakanishi, T. (1991). *Economics of Slums* [*Suramu no Keizaigaku*], Tokyo: Tokyo Daigaku Syuppankai.

Ogawa, S. (2016). *Anthropology of "Living for Today": An Another Form of Capitalist Economy* [*"Sonohi kurasi" no jinruigaku: Mouhitotsu no Shihonsyugi Keizai*], Tokyo: Koubunsya.

Park, A., Y. Wu, and Y. Du. (2012). "Informal Employment in Urban China: Measurement and Implications", *Working Paper* (No. 77737), Washington, DC: World Bank.

Pasuk, P and J. Itoga. (1992). *The Informal Sector in Thai Economic Development*, Tokyo: Institute of Developing Economies.

Portes, A., M. Castells and L. A. Benton (eds.). (1989). *The Informal Economy: Studies in Advanced and Less Developed Countries*, Baltimore: The John Hopkins University Press.

Sassen, S. (1998). *Globalization and its Discontents*, New York: The New Press.

Standing, G. (1999). *Global Labour Flexibility: Seeking Distributive Justice*, London: Macmillan Press.

Todaro, M. P. (1969). "A Model of Labor Migration and Urban Unemployment in Less Developed Countries" *American Economic Review*, 59(1), 138–148.

Vanek, J., et al. (2014). "Statistics on the Informal Economy: Definitions, Regional Estimates & Challenges", *WIEGO Working Paper* (statistics) No. 2, Manchester: WIEGO.

PART IV
Asia at a crossroads

10 Ageing Asia: from demographic dividend to demographic tax

Keiichiro Oizumi and Asei Ito

A typical community service center in China, where many elderly spend their day. Shanghai, China (2011, Photo by Tamaki Endo).

LEARNING GOALS

- Understand the demographic dynamics of Asia.
- Understand how demographic structures affect the economy and society.
- Understand the Asian challenges related to policies pertinent to the ageing society.

INTRODUCTION

Asia was once among the regions with the highest birth rates in the world. The total fertility rate (TFR: number of children a woman gives birth to in her lifetime) was 5.7 during the 1950s and 1960s, well above the then world average of 5.0. However, the current birth rates of many Asian countries have declined to below 2.1, the level required to sustain a given population (a TFR of 2.1 is referred to as the "replacement rate"). Today, Asia is facing the problem of a declining birth rate, further progressing into an ageing society.

Although this decline in birth rates led to the acceleration of an increasingly ageing population, it was also the driving force of economic development, which turned Asia into the growth center of the world. This is because of the sharp rise in the proportion of the working-age population (15–64 years old) during the initial stages of this rapid birth rate decline enabled the region to enjoy a demographic dividend. In order to fully enjoy the demographic dividend, however, it is also necessary to have policies that are in line with such demographic transitions. The presence or absence of such policies will have a significant influence on income levels in the long run.

As the proportion of the working-age population eventually starts to decline, however, the demographic dividend will be lost, and the negative demographic effects on economic growth, called the demographic tax (or burden), will become increasingly apparent. Since Asia is ageing much faster than the rest of the world, establishing an inclusive, sustainable, and fair social security system has become an urgent issue for each of the countries.

10.1 POPULATION GROWTH AND ECONOMIC GROWTH

10.1.1 Rapid population growth

For a long time after World War II, the central issue related to population in developing countries, including those in Asia, was that of overpopulation. The average annual population growth rate in Asia between 1965 and 70 was 2.6%, one of the highest in the world (the world average was 2.1%). At that time, there was strong research interest in looking at the reasons behind the population surge, and its impact on the economy and society. In development economics, Malthus' population principle has often been used to explain population explosion. It assumes that food production increases only arithmetically as "1, 2, 3, 4…" while population increases geometrically as "1, 2, 4, 8…." Malthus' observation was based on the European experience; however, the framework has also been applied to interpret the case of Asia, where the population has snowballed.

Demographic change has traditionally been understood by a conventional demographic transition model consisting of four stages: the initial stage with high birth rate and high death rate; the second stage with high birth rate and middle death rate due to improved nutrition and sanitation; the third stage with middle birth rate and middle death rate due to socio-economic development; then finally, the fourth stage with low birth rate and low death rate (Figure 10.1).

Based on this model, the population surge in Asia was primarily caused by the rapid decrease in the mortality rate during the shift from the first to the second stage. This rapid decline in mortality can be largely attributed to exogenous factors such as the expansion of medical services through support from the international community and improved nutrition. While infant mortality rates decreased rapidly in Asia from the 1950s to the 1970s, its birthrates remained high, which provided the base for a population surge.

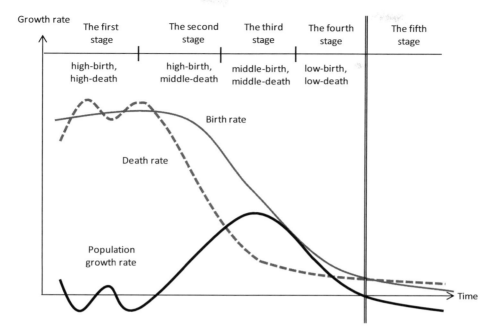

FIGURE 10.1 Demographic transition.

Source: Prepared by the author.

10.1.2 The poverty trap and birth control policies

Rapid population growth due to declines in mortality rates amidst high birth rates was recognized as the main reason that kept developing countries poor. For example, one of the related explanations is the low-income equilibrium trap, which occurs where growth rates of population are higher than those of income (Hayami, 1997; see also Chapter 1). The framework of the vicious circle of poverty proposed by Nurkse (1953) also elaborates on a similar relationship between population and poverty. Furthermore, rapid population increase normally does not accompany increases in savings, resulting in less capital investment. Under such circumstances, a country can be trapped in a vicious circle, making it difficult to escape from poverty.

As such, governments in Asia as well as international organizations have come to recognize the negative effects of population surges on economic and social development. In order to address these issues, birth control measures, including family planning, have been introduced. International organizations such as the World Bank had been focusing on effective implementation of birth control policies for a long time (World Bank, 1984). The most radical and famous of them is China's one-child policy, which directly limited the number of births per family. Similar compulsory birth control measures have also been implemented in South Korea and Thailand.

While the declining birth rate in Asia since the 1980s was a result of such population control measures, socio-economic factors including increased average income, higher women's labor participation rate, spread of the education system, increased numbers of skilled workers, and a rise in urbanization also played major roles. For instance, a higher average income means that women between 15 and 40 years of age have stronger incentives to stay in the workforce. Higher educational attainments and increases in marriage age not only lead to higher income potentials for women, but also indicates higher marginal costs to educate and raise a child. Because of such changes in socio-economic factors and policy interventions, many Asian economies shifted from the "high birth-rate and middle death-rate" stage to the "middle birth-rate and middle death-rate." As a result, a large population cohort emerged in each of the countries with this demographic profile, also referred to as the baby boomer generation.[1] This has led to rapid increases in the working-age population ratio (population of 15- to 64-year-olds/total population) or in the elderly population ratio (population above 65 years old/total population).

10.1.3 Declining birth rates in Asia

Many Asian countries have entered the "low birth and death rate" stage today (the fourth stage in Figure 10.1). Looking at the TFR in 2010–2015, there are ten Asian economies with a figure below 2.1 (the replacement rate), namely Japan, South Korea, Taiwan, Hong Kong, Singapore, China, Thailand, Vietnam, Brunei, and North Korea (Table 10.1). Because birth rates at this stage were assumed to converge around the replacement rate, it fails to fully capture and explain depopulation due to such declining birth rates (Figure 10.1).

It is also important to note that research related to demographic transition has typically been conducted to explain social change in developed countries and may not necessarily capture other important characteristics peculiar to Asia that affect demographic dynamics (Kouno, 2007). As birth rates have generally been decreasing in Asia, the annual average overall population growth rate has also decreased from 2.7% in 1968 (world average 2.1%) to 0.7% in 2015 (1.1%). According to the UN World Population Prospect (medium variant estimation), the Asian population will peak and then start to decline by 2040, while the world population continues to increase during the 21st century primarily due to long-term population growth in Africa and India. This indicates the importance and urgency of examining the ongoing demographic transition in Asia.

10.2 DEMOGRAPHIC DIVIDEND AND DEMOGRAPHIC TAX

10.2.1 What is a demographic dividend?

There are two approaches regarding the impact of population on economic growth: the first focuses on changes in total population size, and the second on changes in population structure (Kato, 2007). In the latter half of the 1990s, there was a growing consensus that changes in the composition of the Asian population were the key attributes that contributed to economic growth (Bloom and Williamson, 1997; Mason, 1997).

The significant baby boomer generation in Asian countries, as mentioned earlier, reflects the process of transitioning into working-age (ranging from 15 to 64 years old), which accompanies sharply rising working-age population ratios, which is referred to as the "demographic dividend." Among the studies that pointed to this was one by Mason (1997),

TABLE 10.1 Total fertility rate (TFR) in Asia

	1950–1955	1980–1985	2010–2015
Asia	5.8	3.8	2.2
Japan	3.0	1.8	1.4
South Korea	5.7	2.2	1.2
Taiwan	6.7	2.2	1.1
Hong Kong	4.4	1.7	1.2
China	6.0	2.6	1.6
North Korea	3.5	2.8	2.0
Mongolia	5.6	5.8	2.8
Brunei	6.9	3.8	1.9
Cambodia	7.0	6.4	2.7
Indonesia	5.5	4.1	2.5
Laos	5.9	6.4	2.9
Malaysia	6.4	4.0	2.1
Myanmar	6.0	4.7	2.3
Philippines	7.4	4.9	3.1
Singapore	6.6	1.7	1.2
Thailand	6.1	3.0	1.5
Vietnam	5.4	4.6	2.0
East Timor	6.4	5.4	5.9
World	5.0	3.6	2.5

Source: UN, World population prospects: 2017 revision.

which suggested that declining birth rates and demographic transitions were both crucial to understanding economic growth and poverty reduction. Bloom and Williamson (1997) applied this idea, which was proposed mainly by demographers, to economics, pointing out that one-third of Asian growth during 1960–1990 can be explained by the demographic dividend. Since then, the concept of a demographic dividend has spread and attracted attention from a wider audience. However, as both Mason and Bloom point out, the demographic dividend is not automatically realized or harnessed; in fact, the effect is influenced by the types and efficacy of the economic policies in place.

10.2.2 The effects of the demographic dividend

Let us examine the mechanism of a demographic dividend using the growth accounting framework. As outlined in Chapter 7, growth accounting attributes the level of output, GDP (Y), to three major factors: labor input (L), capital stock (K), and total factor productivity (A).

Labor input (L) can be calculated by multiplying the size of the labor force population by working hours. Because the ratio of the labor force to the working-age population in a particular country (labor force participation rate) tends to be stable, its long-term change is typically considered to follow the same trend as the working-age population. Although the decline in the birth rate eventually leads to a decline in the working-age population, with a time-lag, the working-age population continues to grow and the potential labor input increases until the working-age population begins to decline. Assuming the labor force participation rate remains constant, the growth rate of the labor force will be the highest when the baby boomers shift reach working age.

The capital stock (K) is a general term for the accumulation of investment that contributes to production activities such as machines, factories, ports, electric power, railways, and roads. The more investment in capital stock, the higher the potential for economic growth. As mentioned, domestic savings, which are the main source of capital stock, will rise due to a decline in the birth rate as follows: (1) an increase in the ratio of the working-age population means an increase in the ratio of the income-earning population to total population, which increases the amount of savings in society as a whole; (2) households can increase their savings because the decrease in the birth rate reduces the financial burden of child-rearing; (3) companies' internal reserves (corporate savings) increase because the abundant labor force keeps wages low; (4) if households start to be self-sustaining, government spending can be diverted away from supporting people's daily expenditures towards supporting infrastructure development. By looking at country-level cross-section data, the domestic savings rate is strongly correlated with the proportion of the working-age population (Figure 10.2). Of course, with the progress of

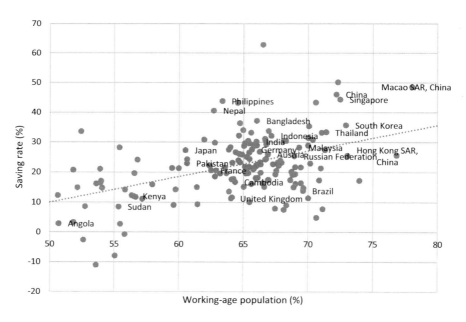

FIGURE 10.2 Working-age and saving rate (2016).

Source: World Bank, World development indicators.

economic globalization, it is possible to raise necessary funds from overseas; however, in developing countries, domestic savings play a major role.

The remaining factor in economic growth is total factor productivity (A), which can be obtained as a residual that cannot be explained by either labor or capital stock inputs. As such, this would include not only progresses in production technology, but also a wide range of other contributors such as education systems that would affect human resource development, the introduction of efficient business management models, and the development of laws and systems. In Asia, the fall in birth rate has contributed to the spread of primary education. According to the World Bank's report entitled *The East Asian Miracle* (World Bank, 1993), the spread of primary education has been one of the key factors in achieving high growth in Asia, and this was possible due to the decline in the birth rate. Furthermore, the spread of primary education has attracted foreign companies to transfer technology to the local economy. This productivity improvement is also supported by the shift of labor from primary to secondary industries and tertiary industries, and the migration of population from rural areas to urban areas (see Chapters 6 and 8).

10.2.3 Economic policies that are consistent with the demographic transition

An increase in the working-age population ratio does not necessarily promote economic growth. Without so-called demographic-friendly policies, the effects can hardly be achieved. Some such compatible policies can be found in the experiences of South Korea and Taiwan, which have been able to utilize their demographic dividends most effectively in Asia.

The first effect of the demographic dividend is the increase of labor input. In the 1970s, the South Korean and Taiwanese governments converted their previous import substitution industrialization policies into export-oriented industrialization ones in order to generate employment for their young labor forces including baby boomers (see Chapter 2). The two governments utilized the young labor force for the production and export of labor-intensive products such as textiles and clothing, which became the drivers of rapid economic growth.

The second effect works through the rise of domestic savings rates. Higher savings rates enable economies to promote the development of capital-intensive industries such as steel and petrochemicals, by effectively utilizing domestic funds. In this process, financial institutions that allocate domestic savings to such productive sectors play important roles. In the 1980s, the ratio of the working-age to total population in South Korea and Taiwan exceeded 60%, supporting high saving rates exceeding 30% of GDP. With these funds, South Korea and Taiwan have been able to make enormous investments that enabled the transformation of their economic structure towards high-tech industries such as heavy chemicals, automobiles, electronics, and electric products.

Finally, as economic development progresses, institutions to support business, such as legal frameworks and accounting systems become established, and advancements in education systems will also sustain growth through productivity improvements. For this to occur, constant efforts at the government, enterprise, and individual levels are needed. For the government, upgrading of its education system from primary to secondary and beyond is the key. For companies, carrying out R&D to promote technological innovation is crucial. In South Korea, for example, more than 80% of high school graduates enter university, and its companies are among the most active in R&D, the expenditures on which are the highest among the Organisation for Economic Development and Co-operation (OECD) countries, reaching 4% of GDP in 2014. These have been the foundations on which South Korea and Taiwan have managed to shift and upgrade their economies, driven by high-tech industries such as automobiles and electronics, at the time the demographic dividend was in effect.

In contrast, countries such as China and Thailand were not able to make full use of their demographic dividends. In China, the industrial sector could not fully absorb the baby boomer generation as priority was given to the development of heavy industries (capital-intensive industries) under the planned economy regime, where the activities of private enterprises were severely restricted until the end of the 1970s (see Chapter 3). Labor migration from rural to urban areas was also strictly controlled through the household registration system. In Thailand, the lack of infrastructure and the underdeveloped nature of the education system restricted the full employment of its abundant working-age population. It was only after the mid-1990s that China and Thailand started to take full advantage of their young labor forces through the promotion of labor-intensive industries. Figure 10.3 shows the trends of agricultural employment and the working-age population ratio from 1980 to 2015. This indicates that when the working-age population ratio had reached its peak in China and Thailand, agricultural employment was still at approximately 30%, a much higher ratio compared to Japan and South Korea.

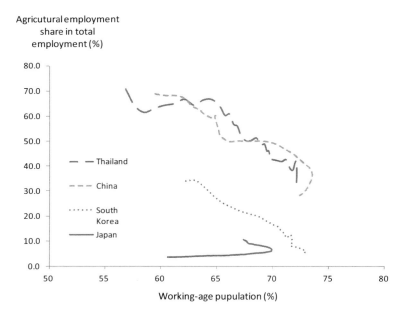

FIGURE 10.3 Agricultural employment ratio and working-age population (1980–2015).

Source: World development indicators.

10.2.4 From demographic dividend to demographic tax

The demographic dividend operates only for a limited period. While there is no clear way to define the period of demographic dividend, we assume that it takes place as long as the working-age population ratio continues to increase (Table 10.2).

According to this criterion, Japan's period of demographic dividend ended in 1992. Likewise, those of South Korea, Taiwan, Hong Kong, Singapore, China, Thailand, and Vietnam had all come to an end by 2015. As discussed earlier, however, we have assumed a constant labor force participation ratio, but the period of demographic dividend could be further expanded by increasing this ratio. For example, even though the working-age population in Vietnam has already peaked, there is still a massive amount of surplus labor in the rural areas, and thus there is still significant room to raise the labor force participation ratio by mobilizing and absorbing such labor into productive sectors.

Nevertheless, the labor input and domestic savings rate will decrease along with economic development, resulting in declining working-age population ratios in the long run. This is often referred to as demographic tax (or burden).

According to Table 10.2, in 2016, Japan and Asian NIEs including South Korea and Taiwan had successfully made the shift to high-income countries by the time their working-age population ratio peaked, while China, Thailand, and Vietnam remain at middle-income levels. The growing concern about a situation of "growing old before getting rich" reflects this situation in China (Cai, 2016). In order to reduce the negative effects of the demographic tax, it is important to improve the employment rate of elderly people and women as well as of foreign workers (see Chapter 6 for international labor mobility). Productivity improvements and innovation can also contribute to solving the problems. In the case of Japan, Yoshikawa (2016) argues that a depopulation and ageing demographic profile could lead to a potentially higher per capita capital stock, which could further induce innovation. However, it is questionable whether innovation can be accelerated in an ageing society, offsetting the negative effects of declining birth rates and evolving issues with an ageing population. A declining birthrate and an ageing population will increase the median population age, which could lead to fewer innovations since these tend to be driven by younger generations with more up-to-date knowledge and skillsets, higher aspirations, and higher mobility.

10.3 AGEING AND SOCIAL SECURITY

10.3.1 The rapid increase of the ageing rate

The demographic tax has multi-dimensional effects. When the demographic dividend ends, the burden (costs) to support an ageing society in terms of medical care and pensions will increase rapidly. It is noteworthy that, compared to the dividend, whose effects are largely on the production-side, the burden is mostly related to the spending-side, and comes into effect at a surprising speed (Oizumi, 2013).

Longer life expectancies also come into play and should be taken into consideration. Average life spans in Asia rose significantly after World War II. Initially, increased life expectancies were caused by the decrease in infant mortality, but in recent years, "longevity," which is the increase of life expectancy of the elderly, has been the main

TABLE 10.2 Demographic dividend and ageing-population ratio in Asia

	Demographic dividend period Start	Demographic dividend period End	Per capita GDP (USD) 2016	Average life expectancy (1950–1955)	Average life expectancy (2010–2015)	Ageing population ratio (2015)	The year ageing population ratio exceed 7%	The year ageing population ratio exceed 14%	The year ageing population ratio to be doubled
Asia	1966	2010				9.7	2000	2027	27
Japan	1930–1935	1992	38,917	62.8	83.3	26.0	1971	1995	24
South Korea	1962	2013	27,539	47.9	81.4	13.0	2000	2018	18
Taiwan	1962	2014	22,453	58.2	79.3	12.3	1994	2018	24
Hong Kong	1961	2010	43,528	63.2	83.4	15.2	1983	2013	30
China	1966	2010	8,113	43.8	75.7	9.7	2001	2025	24
North Korea	1971	2020	–	37.6	70.8	9.7	2004	2033	29
Mongolia	1974	2010	3,660	43.2	68.5	3.9	2030	2054	24
Brunei	1965	2019	26,424	58.3	76.7	4.4	2025	2037	12
Cambodia	1966	2044	1,230	40.3	67.6	4.1	2032	2056	24
Indonesia	1971	2030	3,604	43.5	68.6	5.1	2025	2050	25
Laos	1983	2045	1,925	40.9	65.4	3.9	2038	2058	20
Malaysia	1964	2019	9,360	54.8	74.7	5.9	2021	2046	25
Myanmar	1967	2026	1,269	36.1	66.0	5.3	2023	2056	33
Philippines	1964	2054	2,924	55.4	68.6	4.6	2032	2069	37
Singapore	1963	2010	52,961	60.2	82.3	11.7	1999	2019	20
Thailand	1969	2010	5,899	50.8	74.6	10.6	2002	2022	20
Vietnam	1968	2013	2,173	53.5	75.6	6.7	2017	2034	17
East Timor	2001	2073	2,102	30.0	67.7	3.5	2066	2089	23
World	**1967**	**2012**		47.0	70.8	8.3	2002	2040	38

Source: UN, World population prospects: 2017 revision, IMF, World Economic Outlook.

Note: The start of the demographic dividend refers the year the working-age population ratio started increase, while the dividend end with the working-age population ratio peaks.

contributor in many economies. For example, life expectancy at age 60 increased from 14 years in 1950–1955 to 21 years in 2010–2015 for Asia as a whole. The extension of life expectancy means that Asia has escaped from a state of poverty that threatens the life of infants and reached a society where the elderly can enjoy healthy lives, which is arguably one of the greatest achievements of post-war Asian economic development.

In 2015, nevertheless, the ageing rate of Asia (the ratio of 65 years old and above in the total population) was 9.7%, already exceeding the global average of 8.3%. The elderly population in Asia reached 221.7 million, accounting for 36.2% of those of the world. Its ageing rate will be 15.8% in 2030 (when the world average is estimated to be 11.7%), and the elderly population will increase to 309.6 million.

While the level of ageing is different in each of the countries in Asia, it is important to note that the speed of ageing has been much faster than the Western experience. Table 10.2 also shows the estimated years to make the transition from an *ageing society*, with an elderly population ratio of 7%, to an *aged society*, where the elderly population ratio exceeds 14%. As of 2015, Japan and Hong Kong are the only countries/economies whose elderly population ratio exceeded 14%. According to the author's calculation based on the UN World Population Prospect (medium variant estimate), Japan's elderly population exceeded 7% in 1971, and reached 14% in 1995. In other words, it took Japan 24 years to transform from an ageing society to an aged society. The number of years for this to happen was 115 for France, 85 years for Sweden, 47 years for England, and 40 years for Germany. Japan's ageing speed is exceptional compared to these developed countries. However, as Table 10.2 demonstrates, the speed of many Asian countries is even faster than that of Japan. For example, it took only 18 years for South Korea to become an aged society, which is six years shorter than Japan.

Given this rapidly ageing demography, the challenge for Asian economies is to design and implement a social security system to support the elderly. As Japan's experience shows, the fiscal burden to support a universal social security system designed under a young demographic profile will inevitably increase along with an ageing population. In Japan, the ratio of social security benefits out of total national income increased from 5.8% in 1970 to 29.6% in 2015. Of these benefits, over 70% are elderly related, which is causing serious pressures on other social security and public spending (Data from National Institute of Population and Social Security Research, Japan). It is difficult to implement a similar scheme in Asian countries where fiscal resources are much more limited, and therefore a significantly more cost-effective social security system with a smaller fiscal resource base will be needed.

Another important issue is the domestic regional variance in the ageing of the population. Table 10.3 shows the trend of elderly population rates by province using the Chinese population census. As of 2000, Shanghai had the highest ageing rate, largely due to the level of economic development, resulting in a TFR of 0.8, which was the lowest in China. However, Shanghai's ranking in terms of the elderly population ratio has declined in the following decade; from 11.5% in 2000 to 10.1% in 2010. This is not because of the recovery of the birthrate in Shanghai. Instead, it was the result of migration of youth from other regions into Shanghai. As a result, in areas where young people are moving out, ageing is advancing much more rapidly, causing a "hollowing-out" problem in other provinces. The ageing rate of Chongqing, where a significant proportion of its youth has migrated to Guangdong Province, has risen sharply from 8.0% in 2000

TABLE 10.3 Top 10 regions with highest ageing ratio in China

		2000					2010		
		Total	Urban	Rural			Total	Urban	Rural
1	Shanghai	11.5	11.3	12.6	1	Chongqing	11.7	9.3	14.5
2	Zhejiang	8.9	7.2	10.6	2	Sichuan	10.9	9.0	12.3
3	Jiangsu	8.8	7.5	9.8	3	Jiangsu	10.9	9.1	13.6
4	Beijing	8.4	8.4	8.4	4	Liaoning	10.3	10.3	10.3
5	Tianjin	8.4	8.6	8.0	5	Anhui	10.2	8.5	11.5
6	Shandong	8.1	6.6	9.1	6	Shanghai	10.1	9.9	12.1
7	Chongqing	8.0	7.7	8.2	7	Shandong	9.8	8.2	11.5
8	Liaoning	7.9	8.0	7.8	8	Hunan	9.8	8.1	11.0
9	Anhui	7.6	6.7	7.9	9	Zhejiang	9.3	7.1	13.0
10	Sichuan	7.6	6.8	7.8	10	Guangxi	9.2	7.5	10.4
	National	7.1	6.4	7.5		National	8.6	7.8	10.1

Source: China population survey 2000 and 2010.

to 11.7% in 2010. Furthermore, the ageing rates of the rural areas in Chongqing City have soared from 8.2% to 14.5% during the same period. The number of years required to double the ratio of elderly to the population in these rural areas was about 12 years, which is twice the speed that of Japan.

In the middle-income countries of Asia, ageing in rural areas with low-income levels is accelerating, and is a rapidly evolving issue. How to support the lives of the elderly in these locations is an important agenda if a sustainable future is to be built (Cai et al., 2012).

10.3.2 The current status of social security policies in Asia

Establishing inclusive and sustainable social security systems is among the most pressing issues for a rapidly ageing Asia. Although the focus and coverage of social security systems varies according to differences in economic and social conditions, political systems, culture, and customs in each of the Asian countries, its development roughly follows three stages. In the first stage, a scheme for civil servants and military personnel is established. Next, a social security system (mostly insurance schemes) for employees of private enterprises is developed. Finally, the system is expanded to include self-employed and agricultural workers, and universal social security is completed. Table 10.4 describes each stages of the social security system in Asia in relation to demographic conditions and the degree of urbanization.

The first stage is the social security system in low-income countries with high birth rates and high youth population ratios. Laos, Cambodia, and Myanmar belong to this stage. The coverage of the social security systems in these countries is limited to civil servants and military personnel, and the next policy goal is to extend the system to employees of private enterprises.

TABLE 10.4 Stages of social security in Asia

	Social security		Stage of economic development		Demographic status	
	Coverage	Agenda	Income level	Industrial structure	Population structure	Urbanization
Stage 1 Laos, Cambodia, Myanmar	Only civil servants (including military personnel)	Expanding the coverage to private employees	Low	Primary industry dominated	Declining birth-rate	Rural-based society
Stage 2 Vietnam, Philippines, Indonesia	Civil servants and employees in private companies	Expanding the coverage to self-employed and agricultural workers	Lower-middle	Process of industrialization	Rapid decline in birth-rate	Beginning of urbanization
Stage 3 Malaysia, Thailand, China	Expanding to self-employed and agricultural workers	How to achieve universal coverage	Upper-middle	Secondary industry dominated	Start ageing	Beginning of mega-regionalization
Stage 4 Japan, South Korea, Taiwan, Singapore	Universal coverage	How to prepare financial resource and to achieve a fair distribution	High	Tertiary industry dominated	Ageing and depopulation	Urban-based society

Source: Prepared by author.

The second stage is the social security system in the countries where industrialization has progressed, including the Philippines, Indonesia, and Vietnam. At this stage, the social security system is centered on insurance schemes covering both civil servants and private enterprises. In these countries, the working-age population is rapidly increasing, creating a strong need for labor-related insurance and safety nets such as work accident insurance and unemployment insurance. The next policy agenda is to extend coverage of social security systems to the self-employed and agricultural workers.

The third is where the economy develops the capacity to establish a social security system covering much wider social groups. China, Thailand, and Malaysia are now in the process of setting up a universal social security system. When self-employed workers and agricultural workers are covered by the system, coordination between the existing social security system and a new one becomes urgent. Because the issue of ageing becomes important, economies have to accommodate the increasing need for pension and health care systems.

Finally, the fourth stage is where the entire economy is covered by a social security system. Japan, South Korea, Taiwan, and Singapore are examples which have completed the establishment of universal social security systems. However, with ageing further accelerating, there still remain issues to be addressed. These include challenges to reduce the financial burden, to maintain fairness among systems according to the type of industry and employment, and to guarantee fairness between generations (see Chapter 11).

10.3.3 The agendas of promoting social security policies in Asia

Support from international organizations has also encouraged the development of social security systems in Asia. Until the 1990s, international organizations promoted social security-related agendas as complementary components of economic structural reform programs, such as the introduction of unemployment insurance and various social safety nets. In the 21st century, influenced by the Millennium Development Goals (MDGs) of the United Nations, social protection for socially vulnerable groups such as women, children, the elderly, and disabled people has become an important agenda. Efforts to support developing countries intensified with the adoption of the Sustainable Development Goals (SDGs) in 2015. Since the SDGs put an inclusive society as their overarching goal, international organizations have started supporting the establishment of a social security system covering everyone regardless of the stage of economic and social development.

Changes in political regimes also motivate governments to accelerate the development of social security systems. In South Korea, the democratization that occurred in the late 1990s was a driving force for the rapid development of the country's social security system. The development of its national social security system promoted under the Kim Dae Jung administration was referred to as "the ultra-fast expansion of the welfare state" (Kim, 2008). In China and Thailand, the development of their social security systems is articulated as a national duty in their constitutions, which is currently in progress. The expansion of the social security system for low-income people has become a common pledge in any election campaign in Asia today.

Problems, however, remain in many Asian countries. In the mid-1990s, the World Bank proposed a multi-layer model of social security systems for developing countries, which consists of a first tier "public pension scheme (pay-as-you-go)," a second tier "forced funding scheme," and a third tier "arbitrary funding scheme" (World Bank, 1994). However, it became increasingly clear that too many of those countries lacked financial resources to fund the schemes. A fourth tier called "family and community support" was proposed accordingly, which suggests the involvement of local communities to support the elderly and low-income people, in addition to a national basic pension system (Holzmann and Hinz, 2005).

Developing countries, including those in Asia, are still struggling toward establishing such a sustainable pension scheme to this day. An obvious obstacle is the limitation of financial resources to secure the level of benefits. With large income disparities, if the same level of pension payments and medical services for civil servants, military workers, and employees in private enterprises are extended and applied to self-employed workers and agricultural workers, it would compromise sustainability because of increased financial expenditures. In fact, in China, Thailand, and Malaysia, where the governments are considering the development of a universal social security system, the pension payments for self-employed workers and agricultural workers are set at significantly lower levels than those for civil servants, which makes it hardly possible to even sustain daily life with the benefits alone.

To establish an inclusive social security system, it is necessary to revitalize the local or regional communities that complements the public social security system. There are a number of community concepts in Asia that provide certain community level services such as the "*dong*" in South Korea, "*shequ*" in China, and "*tambon*" in Thailand. In South Korea, a unique activity called "beautiful neighbor" is being implemented. This initiative, led by welfare centers in each local district, opens shops that can provide meals, stationery, and hairdressing services as well distribute coupons to elderly people free of charge. Elderly people who use these coupons provide services for those shops or participate as local volunteers in return (Kim et al., 2017).

In promoting community welfare and employment of the elderly, an increase in government spending as the population ages is unavoidable. Many Asian countries have undertaken tax reform in recent years, including the implementation of an inheritance tax in Thailand and the introduction of a consumption tax in Malaysia. In middle-income countries with large income gaps, the financial resources would have to come mainly from urban residents and high- and middle-income groups. It would not be easy to reach a broad-based public consensus on the introduction of new taxes or raising the ongoing tax rate. In this respect, the addressing the demographic tax problem is not just an economic issue but has strong political dimensions as well. A government will be required to put forward convincing arguments for tax reforms on which a national consensus can be built, while identifying the distributional consequences such as who benefits, who does not, to what extent, who supports whom and why. Inclusive public discussions must be encouraged and promoted, through transparent and accountable political processes to achieve such a goal.

CONCLUSION

As one of the countries where ageing has progressed most intensively in the world, Japan is expected to contribute to addressing the related issues in Asia. As of 2016, the Japan International Cooperation Agency (JICA) has already provided support for such issues to China, Thailand, Malaysia, Indonesia, and Mongolia. The Ministry of Health, Labor, and Welfare of Japan is also leading discussions related to ageing based on the concept of "Active Ageing" in Asia. In addition, many Japanese companies have started to see "Ageing Asia" as an opportunity to expand businesses into nursing care services. However, Japan is also still in search for a viable prescription to be applied for its own ageing society.

As shown in the example of South Korea, Asian countries are also intensifying their efforts towards addressing the issues relevant to the ageing society through public as well as private and community level interventions. It is interesting to note that countries are also starting to introduce information and communication technology (ICT) such as smartphones, tablet personal computers, and robots to solve the related problems, which allow easier monitoring, through the Internet, of health and other conditions of elderly parents living separately. There are increased potentialities for countries such as China where the ICT sector is rapidly evolving, to develop telemedicine and remote care technologies to address issues of the ageing society. Given such a dynamically changing regional industrial landscape, developed countries like Japan and South Korea will need to work with other Asian economies to jointly address the issue, rather than just act as technology providers. Sharing the fruits of growth through economic integration is not enough; Asian countries must now solve social problems together as well. As Asia continues to make its shift from demographic dividend towards demographic tax, new forms of international cooperation and initiatives will become necessary.

BOX 10 Who are the "elderly people"?

Keiichiro Oizumi

Conventionally, the elderly population is defined as those 65 years of age and above. However, there is no clear and consistent global definition for this. Reports and analysis of the UN often treat people older than 60 as elderly, reflecting the situation and circumstances of many developing economies. The fact is that the definition of the elderly varies from country to country. For example, China and Thailand follow the UN criteria of those above 60 years of age, whereas in countries like Japan and South Korea the threshold is typically 65 years old and above.

Changing the definition of the elderly changes the landscape of society. If we use 60 years old as the definition, the elderly population in Asia in 2015 is 328.7 million and the ageing rate reaches 14.6%, which suggests that the entire region has already entered into the stage of an "aged society." The "elderly" population will increase by 113 million people, and the ratio will be five percentage points higher than in the case of the 65-year-old criteria.

On the other hand, some countries are raising the age threshold to reflect the improvement of health conditions and workability of the elderly in their country. In Japan, the Japan Geriatrics Society issued a report in January 2017 proposing that people over 75 years old should be considered "elderly," 65- to 74-year-old as "semi-elderly", and those who are 90 and above as "super elderly" (Japan Geriatrics Society, 2017).

If we adopt the definition of elderly as those at the age of 75 and above, the elderly population in Asia in 2015 would be 81.5 million, and the ageing rate 3.6%. These numbers are 134 million less and 6.0 points lower than the 65 years old criteria, respectively. By modifying the definition of the elderly, the demographic dividend and tax also change. The definition should of course reflect the reality and its purpose. In order to fully enjoy the current long life expectancy, promoting employment opportunities for the elderly will be important, which requires the creation of an environment in which the elderly can work. The elderly would play important roles not only as workers, but also as leaders in social activities,

> particularly in community-based activities. The realization of such an "ageing" society where the elderly actively participate in economic and social activities, without degrading their quality of life, has been emerging as a global trend. An ageing society is not a problem, but rather a reflection of a better society where longevity has become possible. To achieve a truly prosperous elderly society, the imagination and actions of all are needed.

NOTE

1 Note, therefore, that this chapter uses "baby boomer" in a wider sense than the term is used in many Western countries such as the United Kingdom, where it refers only to people born during the baby boom in the years immediately following World War II.

REFERENCES

Bloom, David, and Jeffrey Williamson. (1997). "Demographic Transitions and Economic Miracles in Emerging Asia," NBER Working Paper No. 6268.

Cai, Fang. (2016). *China's Economic Growth Prospects: From Demographic Dividend to Reform Dividend*. Cheltenham, UK: Edward Elgar.

Cai, Fang, John Giles, Philip O'Keefe, and Dewen Wang. (2012). *The Elderly and Old Age Support in Rural China: Challenges and Prospects*. Washington: The World Bank.

Hayami, Yujiro. (1997). *Development Economics: From the Poverty to the Wealth of Nations*. Oxford, UK; New York: Clarendon Press.

Holzmann, Robert, and Richard Hinz. (2005). *Old Age Income Support in the 21st Century: An International Perspective on Pension Systems and Reform*. Washington: The World Bank.

Japan Geriatrics Society. (2017). *Koureisya no Teigi to Kubun ni kansuru Nihon Rounenngakkai/Nihon Rounennigakkai Koureisha ni kansuru Teigikentou Wakingu Gurupu karano Teigen (Gaiyou)* [A Proposal for a Definition and Distinction on Elderly from the Japan Geriatrics Society (summary)], https://jpn-geriat-soc.or.jp/proposal/pdf/definition_01.pdf

Kato, Hisakazu. (2007). *Jinkou Keizaigaku* [*Demographic Economics*]. Tokyo: Nikkei Publishing.

Kim, Sung Won. (2008). *Kohatsu Fukushi Kokkaron: Hikaku no nakano Kankoku to Higashi Ajia* [*Late-comer Welfare State: Korea and East Asia in* Comparative Perspective]. Tokyo: University of Tokyo Press.

Kim, Sung Won, Keiichiro Oizumi, and Akiko Matsue (eds.). (2017). *Ajia niokeru Koureisya no Shakaihosyou: Jizoku Kanou na Fukushi Syakai wo Motomete* [*Social Security for Elderly People in Asia: Toward a Sustainable Welfare Society*]. Tokyo: Akashi Publishing.

Kouno, Shigemi. (2007). *Jinkougaku heno Shotai: Shoushi Koureika ha Dokomade Kaimei Saretaka* [*An Introduction to Demography: What Do We Know about Low Birthrate and Ageing*]. Tokyo: Chuou Koron Shinsha.

Mason, Andrew. (1997). "Population and the Asian Economic Miracle," *Asia Pacific Population & Policy*, No. 43.

Nurkse, Ragnar. (1953). *Problems of Capital Formation in Underdeveloped Countries*. Oxford: Oxford University Press.

Oizumi, Keiichiro. (2013). *Ageing in Asia: When the Structure of Prosperity Changes*. Tokyo: Oriental Life Insurance Cultural Development Center.

World Bank. (1984). *World Development Report 1984*. Washington: The World Bank; Oxford: Oxford University Press.

World Bank. (1993). *The East Asian Miracle: Economic Growth and Public Policy*, New York: Oxford University Press.

World Bank. (1994). *Averting the Old Age Crisis: Policies to Protect Old and Promote Growth*. Washington: The World Bank.

Yoshikawa, Hiroshi. (2016). *Jinkou to Nihon Keizai: Choju, inobesyon, keizaiseicho* [*Population and Japanese Economy: Longevity, Innovation, and Economic Growth*]. Tokyo: Chuou Kouron Shinsya.

11 Unequalizing Asia: from poverty to inequality

Kunio Urakawa and Tamaki Endo

Cartoon about the 2011 flooding in Thailand, which appeared in the English newspaper *The Nation*. The inner city of Bangkok was protected at the expense of its suburbs and rural areas. The cartoon shows intensifying class conflict.

Source: Stephff, October 2011 *The Nation*.

LEARNING GOALS

- Understanding the recent situation of poverty and inequality and their changes over time.
- Understanding mechanisms and factors in rising inequality in Asia.
- Discussing the social issues Asian countries are facing and future prospects of rising inequality.

INTRODUCTION

After World War II, Asia's population living in absolute poverty – those living at or below the poverty line[1] – steadily decreased. As described in Chapter 1, *The East Asian Miracle* of the World Bank (1993) lauded the rapid "economic growth with equity" prevailing in Asia until the 1990s, which achieved high growth with reductions in poverty and inequality.

However, despite the swift recovery from the 1997 financial crisis and the economic prosperity which followed, economic disparities (gaps in income and assets) among individuals and households have been growing considerably since the 2000s. Excessive inequality negatively affects public health, levels of education, and public security. Rising inequality is therefore becoming a policy issue of concern for the governments of Asian countries. Public awareness has also been growing. A report by the Asian Development Bank (ADB) stated that technological progress, globalization, and market-oriented reforms, which have been the key drivers of Asia's rapid economic growth, are also the basic forces behind rising inequality in many countries (ADB, 2012, p. 12). Others argue that popular responses to greater inequality are underpinning the rise of populist governments and political instability in countries such as Thailand and the Philippines.

Unlike developed countries, middle-income and developing countries that have experienced compressed development and social change have yet to develop adequate social security systems such as pensions, medical insurance, and other welfare programs. Without such safety nets being established, their demographic structures are changing rapidly, manifested in declining birthrates and ageing populations (see Chapter 10).

Japan, which achieved economic development earlier than other countries in Asia, has long been regarded as a country of high equality. Since the 1990s, however, growing inequality has come to represent a social issue there as well. Poverty (particularly relative poverty)[2] issues have also become increasingly apparent, drawing public attention. Trends in Japan have preceded those in other Asian countries. As such, they are suggestive of how various factors such as demographic change and casualization of employment attributable to globalization, likely affect inequality. In fact, the trend of growing inequality due to an ageing population is also attracting attention from middle-income countries.

This chapter presents analyses of recent trends and key factors in poverty and inequality in Asian countries today. It particularly focuses on the shifts of emphasis from poverty to inequality and then recently, from inequality back to poverty. The chapter also presents an examination of policy debates and responses taken as possible solutions. The next section provides an overview of trends in poverty and inequality in Asia after World War II. Then, it introduces the Kuznets hypothesis and other related arguments. The second section presents trends of inequality since the 2000s and their mechanisms of growth using the examples of Japan, China, and the ASEAN countries. The third section discusses the future outlook.

11.1 FROM POVERTY TO INEQUALITY

11.1.1 "The East Asian Miracle" and poverty reduction in Asia up to the early 1990s

Asia is known as a region which achieved remarkable growth and poverty reduction in the decades immediately following the end of World War II. Figure 11.1 shows the

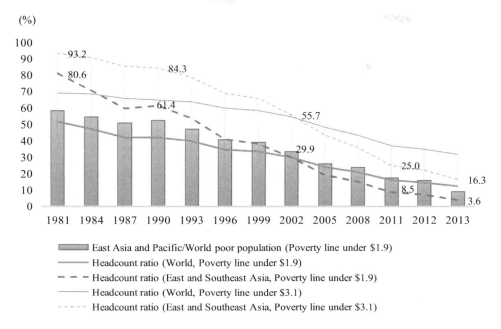

FIGURE 11.1 Poverty headcount ratio in East and Southeast Asia (2011 PPP).

Source: The World Bank, PovcalNet (accessed on October 10th, 2017).

Note: The data of 10 countries of East and Southeast Asia are used (Japan and NIEs countries are not included. North Korea's data is not available). For the ratio of poor population to the world, aggregated data of "East Asia and Pacific" (19 countries) is used.

changes in poverty rates as defined by the World Bank. The population living in poverty at a subsistence level income of $1.9 per day or less has decreased significantly from 80.6% in 1981 to below 30.0% in the 2000s, then to only 3.6% by 2013. The ratio of the population living in poverty was higher in Asia than the world average for a long time. This has, however, been reversed in the 2000s as Asia has made significant progress in poverty reduction.

Asia's global share of the number of those living in poverty has also decreased. 58.9% of the world's poor were living in the East Asia and Pacific Region in 1981, which decreased to 9.3% by 2013 (poverty line of $1.9 per day). During the same period, Asia's share of the global population changed only from 37.6% to 32.9%.

The World Bank referred to the way in which Asia achieved rapid growth with equity as the "Asian miracle." Their report compared the levels of inequality and per capita real GDP growth during 1965–1989 among 40 countries. It identified only seven economies that had achieved high growth while reducing inequality, which were all in Asia (World Bank, 1993, pp. 29–30). This result presented a stark contrast to the performance of Latin America during the same period.

Nevertheless, this started to change in the late 1990s. Inequality in Latin America had started to decline, while that in Asia was increasing (Kanbur et al., 2014). While the poverty rate also rose in the wake of the financial crisis in 1997, this was a temporary phenomenon and it declined again soon after. However, the rise of income inequality and relative poverty has shown no downward trend, and as such is regarded as one of the major issues of concern.

11.1.2 Rising inequality in Asia

The 2012 annual report of the ADB entitled *Confronting Rising Inequality in Asia* specifically focused on issues related to inequality. According to the report, of the 28 countries in Asia for which comparative data were available for the 1990s and 2000s, 11 (accounting for about 82% of developing Asia's population in 2010) reported rising inequalities in per capita expenditures or income, as measured by the Gini coefficient (data also included South and Central Asia, ADB [2012], p. 38). The report suggested that had growth been more equal, this would have lifted an additional 240 million, or 6.5% of the region's population, out of poverty (Kanbur et al., 2014, p. 6).

Table 11.1 presents the changes in the Gini coefficients of Asian countries since the 1980s.[3] First, it is apparent that the Gini coefficient is increasing in middle-income countries such as China and Indonesia. Malaysia and Thailand show a slight decline, but their levels of inequality still remain high, with a Gini coefficient between 0.4 and 0.5. Second, regarding China and Indonesia, for which rural and urban Gini coefficients are available, the urban Gini coefficients have been higher than those for rural areas. Third, for high-income countries such as Japan and South Korea, the Gini coefficients since the 2000s has been stable, while there was a significant increase during the 1980s and 1990s for Japan. It should be noted that the figures for Japan are not based on initial incomes but based on incomes post-redistribution. As we will discuss in Section 11.2, the Gini coefficient in initial income before redistribution has continued to increase in recent years. Fourth, regarding lower-middle income countries, inequality in Laos has been rising since the 2000s, although that of Cambodia is showing a decline.

As will be explained in a later section, each government often calculates and publishes their own estimations for policy planning purposes. While there may be discrepancies between estimations by the international organizations and by governments, they tend to show similar trends. These differences could derive from, for example, whether they use per capita income or expenditure to calculate the coefficients. It could also be due to the difference of whether the data provided to international organizations from national statistical offices were raw-data or stratified group data.

Figure 11.2 shows the quantile ratio of income distribution. In middle-income countries, the income shares of the top 20% (5th quantile) are around 46–51%. The share of this group for Japan was lower, at about 40%, suggesting that its redistribution policies have been relatively effective. The share of the bottom 20% (1st quantile) have been the smallest in China and Malaysia, with a share of 5%.

11.1.3 The Kuznets hypothesis and Asia

The Kuznets hypothesis is probably the most popular framework pertinent to discussions on the relationship between economic development and income inequality. Kuznets pointed out in his seminal paper entitled "Economic Growth and Income Inequality,"

TABLE 11.1 Changes in Gini coefficient of Asian countries

	China (Urban)	China (Rural)	Malaysia	Thailand	Indonesia (Urban)	Indonesia (Rural)	The Philippines	Laos	Cambodia	Japan (Income after redistribution)	South Korea
1981	0.18	0.25		0.45						0.31	
1984	0.18	0.27	0.49		0.33	0.29				0.34	
1987	0.20	0.29	0.47		0.33	0.28				0.34	
1990	0.26	0.31		0.45	0.35	0.26				0.36	0.30
1991							0.44				0.29
1992			0.48	0.48				0.34			0.28
1993	0.28	0.32			0.35					0.37	0.28
1994				0.43			0.43		0.38		0.29
1995			0.49								0.28
1996	0.29	0.34		0.43	0.38	0.28				0.36	0.29
1997			0.49				0.46	0.35			0.28
1998				0.41	0.34	0.26					0.32
1999	0.32	0.35		0.43	0.35	0.25				0.38	0.32
2000				0.43	0.32	0.24	0.46				0.32
2001					0.32	0.24					0.31
2002	0.33	0.38		0.42	0.34	0.26		0.35		0.38	
2003					0.34	0.25	0.44				

(Continued)

	China (Urban)	China (Rural)	Malaysia	Thailand	Indonesia (Urban)	Indonesia (Rural)	The Philippines	Laos	Cambodia	Japan (Income after redistribution)	South Korea
2004			0.46	0.43	0.34	0.27			0.35		
2005	0.35	0.36			0.34	0.28				0.39	
2006				0.42	0.36	0.29	0.44				0.31
2007			0.46	0.40	0.37	0.30		0.37	0.41		0.31
2008	0.35	0.39		0.40	0.37	0.30			0.35	0.38	0.31
2009			0.46	0.40	0.37	0.30	0.43		0.35		0.31
2010	0.36	0.41		0.39	0.38	0.32			0.33		0.31
2011	0.36	0.39		0.37	0.42	0.34			0.32	0.38	0.31
2012	0.35	0.40		0.39	0.42	0.33	0.43	0.38	0.31		0.31
2013	0.37	0.34		0.38	0.43	0.32					0.30
2014					0.43	0.32				0.38	0.30

Source: Made from the World Bank, PovcalNet. For Japan, official data from the survey of income after redistribution conducted by Ministry of Health, Labor and Welfare (MHLW). For Korean data before 2002 is quoted from Kaku (2004), and since 2006, database of OECD is used (accessed 2017/8/25 http://stats.oecd.org/).

Note:
1 The estimate of China and Indonesia in ProvcalNet is mostly separated to urban/rural. The Gini index of whole country is available for the following years: China, 2008 (0.43), 2012 (0.42); Indonesia, 2013 (0.39).
2 The estimation of the World Bank uses data of socioeconomic surveys provided by each governments. The condition of data provided differs among countries. Some countries changed provision of data from grouped stratified data to raw data. Recent data provided are as follows: China (urban and rural, income data in 1980s and stratified expenditure since 1990s), Malaysia (income, raw data), Thailand (expenditure, raw data), Indonesia (urban and rural, expenditure, raw data), Philippine (income and expenditure, raw data, in this table, expenditure data is used), Laos (expenditure, raw data), Cambodia (expenditure, raw data). In case of Japan and South Korea, income (raw data) is used for the analysis.

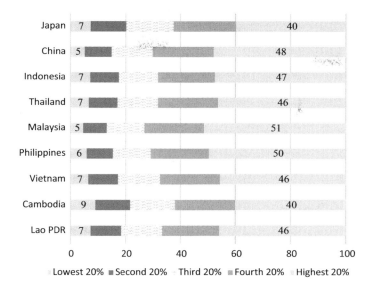

FIGURE 11.2 Income share by quantile income class (around 2010).

Source: Made from Poverty and Equity Databank and PovcalNet, World Bank (accessed on April 24th, 2017).

Note: Year of data is as follow: Japan (2008), Malaysia (2009), Indonesia (2013), and rest of the countries (2012).

that developed countries such as the United States, England, and Germany historically experienced increasing inequality in the early phases of economic growth, followed by a trend shift towards declining inequality. For instance, reduction in income inequality in England was observed from the 1890s, and in the United States and Germany from the 1920s (Kuznets, 1955). Kuznets attributed the factors underlying these trends to industrialization and urbanization, which was accomplished through the reallocation of capital and labor from low-productivity sectors (agricultural sector) to high-productivity sectors (industrial sector).

As the Kuznets's hypothesis describes, capital investment in the industrial sector, accompanied by labor migration from rural to urban areas, has been widely observed in the early stages of economic development. Consequently, the economy's average income level increases at the same time as regional and household income inequalities also increase. However, when the flow of labor from agriculture to industry settles, then labor supply in urban areas increase. At this stage, declining income inequality is observed. This inverted U-shape relation between income levels and inequality is what later economists designated as the "Kuznets curve" or "Kuznets hypothesis" (Figure 11.3).

Whether the Kuznets curve applies in cases of other countries has long been an interest of many development economists. In practice, however, obtaining country level time series data is not easy. Therefore, GDP per capita (purchasing power parity) data of some selected countries and the associated Gini coefficients are used to examine whether the levels and inequality of income exhibit inverted-U patterns as described

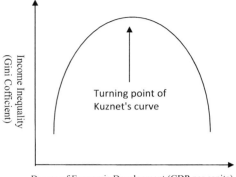

FIGURE 11.3 Kuznets curve.
Source: Prepared by author.

by Kuznets's hypothesis. Robert Barro, for instance, used the data of 92 countries and found that inequality increased in the early stages of economic development but then started to shrink (Barro, 2008).

Palma, on the other hand, argues that there is no empirical evidence that supports Kuznets's hypothesis. She stated that a crucially important characteristic of recent inequality is "homogeneity in the middle vs. heterogeneity in the tails," with "centripetal" movement in terms of the income share of the middle class, and income polarization at the very top and bottom of income classes. Irrespective of regional differences, three common dynamics are observed in most countries: a dominant and growing share of the rich, marginalization of the poor, and a stable and homogeneous middle class (Palma, 2011). Abdullah et al. also tested Kuznets' hypothesis using the data of eight countries in Southeast Asia and concluded that there was some evidence in relation to urbanization but no evidence to support such relationships with respect to non-agricultural employment. Moreover, their survey of related studies shows that only 5 out of 13 papers presented evidence to support Kuznets's hypothesis (Abdullah et al., 2015, p. 2).

In recent years, some empirical research has put more emphasis on looking into the patterns between the two variables rather than assessing whether the relationship is in fact in the form of an inverted-U shape. For example, some research using panel data of Organisation for Economic Co-operation and Development (OECD) member countries between the early 1960s and the late 1990s has revealed a U-shaped relationship between income per capita and inequality, instead of an inverted-U one. Because most of the OECD countries have already completed their transitions in economic structure from agriculture to industry, it would not be surprising that one fails to find an inverted-U relationship, which was based on the 19th and early 20th century experiences of the West (Galbraith, 2012).

There has also been increased interest since the 1990s in looking at the issue from a reverse causality perspective: how would income inequality, in turn, affect economic development (e.g., the growth rate of GDP per capita). For example, Barro (1999) suggests that income equality in Asia had positive effects on growth, similar to primary education enrollments.

11.2 BACKGROUND AND CAUSES OF INCREASED INCOME INEQUALITY: CASES FROM ASIAN COUNTRIES

11.2.1 Why is income inequality increasing in Asia?

Why is inequality growing in many countries and economies in Asia? Ravi Kanbur and others of the ADB have argued that the key drivers of the recent inequality in Asia include globalization, technological changes, and market-oriented reforms. In other words, they claim that the same factors that contributed to economic development have also boosted income inequality. They assert that three biases, or heterogeneity in returns, cause inequality in income distribution. First is the higher returns to capital than to labor (decreasing labor share of income), second is higher returns to skilled than unskilled workers (increasing skill premium), and the third is higher returns to residents of urban and coastal areas where more infrastructure has been developed, compared to those living in rural and inland areas (spatial inequality).

The ADB suggested that spatial inequality explained 30–50%, and skill premium due to technological changes 25–35% of the income inequality in Asia (ADB, 2012; Kanbur et al., 2014). In addition, while the recent decline in the labor shares of developed countries has been highlighted in various studies, labor shares in the ASEAN countries have been initially lower than those in developed countries. Pasuk Phongpaichit argues that this low level of labor shares of income has created the foundation for an unequal society in Asia (Pasuk and Baker, 2016).

Some attribute the growing inequality since the 2000s to increased job instability, because of expansions in irregular employment (Suehiro, 2014). Since the beginning of the 1990s, the proportion of dispatched and contract workers has risen in Japan and South Korea due to deregulation in labor market policies. Similar phenomena have also been observed in middle-income countries since the 1997 Asian financial crisis.

The following sections present cases of inequality in Japan, China, and ASEAN countries such as Thailand and Indonesia, with focuses on the main trends and their underlying factors.

11.2.2 The case of Japan

Regarding inequality, Japan leads Asia in terms of research output. It has long been thought that Japan's post-war economic development led to a highly equal society, often referred to as a "100-million middle class" society. The share of respondents who considered their own living standard as "middle class" in the Public Opinion Survey Related to People's Lifestyles, conducted by the Cabinet Office, exceeded 80% in the mid-1960s, and reached nearly 90% in the 1970s (Hashimoto, 2009). In the 1990s, however, income and asset inequality began to grow (Tachibanaki, 1998). Today, Japan's Gini coefficient has risen above the OECD average.

Figure 11.4A portrays changes in income inequality in Japan that occurred between 1961 and 2013. Income inequality for both the initial income before redistribution (income earned from economic activities in the market) and the income after redistribution rose considerably, particularly during the 1980s and the 1990s. However, although the Gini coefficient of initial income continued to increase consistently during the 2000s, that of the redistributed income has remained mostly unchanged.

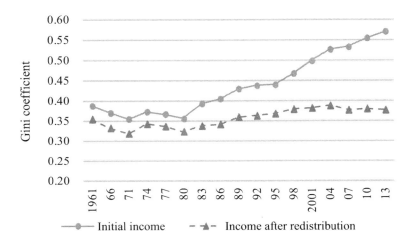

FIGURE 11.4A Income inequality in Japan (1961–2013).

Source: Referring Tanabe and Suzuki (2013), data is from the survey of the redistributed income of the MHLW.

Note: Gini coefficient of Figure 11.4A is calculated by using equivalent income of households with adjusted number of household members.

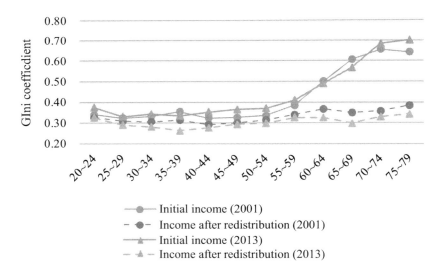

FIGURE 11.4B Gini coefficient by householder's age group (equivalent income).

Source: Referring Tanabe and Suzuki (2013), data is from the survey of the redistributed income of the MHLW.

Note: Gini coefficient of Figure 11.4B is calculated by using equivalent income of households with adjusted number of household members.

The causes of increased inequality in Japan include, first, the effects of an ageing population (Ohtake, 2005). Figure 11.4B shows different Gini coefficients by age group of household members in 2001 and 2013. The figure demonstrates that income inequality is greater for households in elderly groups than for those of the working-age generation. Therefore, an increase of the share of this high-age group among the total population, for whom the income inequality had originally been large, leads to an increase in the Gini coefficient of the entire economy. Ohtake suggested that approximately 24% of the increase in inequality between 1980 and 1992 can be explained by the ageing factor (Ohtake, 2005). It is noteworthy that the increase in inequality is not a consequence of an aged society per se, but of high-income inequality among elderly people in Japan. In many OECD countries, the Gini coefficient of the working generation is, in fact, higher than that of the elderly generation (Forster and d'Ercole, 2005).[4]

One of the reasons for the wide income inequality among elderly households in Japan is poverty in parts of that age group. This is manifested by the fact that a significant number of low-income households qualify for welfare benefits. According to the National Survey on Public Assistance Recipients of the Ministry of Health, Labor, and Welfare (MHLW), approximately half of recent welfare benefit recipients are households headed by the elderly. Although the number of protected elderly households remained mostly constant at approximately 200,000 households until the first half of the 1990s, it began to rise in the latter half of the 1990s, reaching approximately 750,000 households by 2014. The share of poor households is particularly high among single-person elderly households.

The second factor is related to the changes in the forms of employment, and increased wage gaps among workers associated with these changes. Since the collapse of the bubble economy in the 1990s, many companies have strived to reduce costs by shifting employment practices away from the traditional permanent contracts and seniority systems towards irregular employment. The share of workers whose first job is in the regular employment category has been consistently decreasing. As of 2016, irregular employment accounted for 37.5% of all workers (22.1% of male employees and 55.9% of female employees, respectively). According to an MHLW survey, the wage level of workers under irregular employment contracts was 65.8, when the average wage of regular employment was 100. The ratios were 67.4 for men and 72.0 for women, respectively. Although wage gaps between regular and irregular employment have been decreasing gradually since the mid-2000s, the disparity remains larger than those of other OECD countries (JILPT, 2017). Another characteristic is the high proportion of irregular workers among young people in recent years. The percentage of irregular employment in the first jobs of high-school graduates is 35.6% for men and 50.4% for women. These shares for university graduates aged 22–24 is 29.8% for men and 28.2% for women.

The third cause of inequality is the limited redistribution effects compared to other countries at similar income levels: the differences in Gini coefficients before and after redistribution was much smaller in Japan than the OECD average during the first half of the 2010s. The redistribution effects through taxation have been particularly low. Japan's social security expenditures for families as a percentage of its GDP are also lower than those in other countries (OECD, 2015). These are also the main causes of the disparities among elderly people and poor households, as discussed earlier.

In addition to the three causes presented above, other factors have also been pointed out, including changes in households structures such as an increase in single-person households and a decrease in three-generation households, skill-biased technological change such as the information revolution, weakening of the Douglas–Arisawa Law,[5] and financial deregulation (Ohtake, 2005; Tachibanaki and Urakawa, 2006). Furthermore, interregional migration related to, for instance, college admission, employment, and job changes exert long-term effects on economic disparities among different regions and generations.

11.2.3 The case of China

Until the 1980s, China showed very low inequality: its Gini coefficient remained at approximately 0.1–0.2 (Table 11.1). Income inequality began to grow after the launch of reform and opening-up policies. In 2013, the National Bureau of Statistics of China calculated the country's nationwide Gini coefficients retroactively to 2003 using income data. According to the government estimate, the Gini coefficient was highest in 2008 at 0.49. While this started to decline, it remained at 0.47 in 2013, implying China is a country with particularly high inequality among Asian countries.

The industrialization strategy of China, which prioritized the development of coastal areas, accelerated income inequality. Reforms to promote economic transition towards a market-based system and increased wage gaps are also seen as causes of increasing inequality. Since the mid-1980s, when the emphasis of reforms shifted to urban areas, large influxes of foreign capital into coastal areas have caused interregional disparities in economic development. During the latter half of the 1990s, a large number of workers were dismissed under state-owned enterprise (SOE) reforms, while the incomes of managers and specialists working for private-sector companies and privatized SOEs increased (Marukawa, 2013).

Spatial inequality and wage gaps, which are regarded as major sources of inequality in China, are intricately connected to the further widening of income inequality. As described in Chapter 3, major interregional disparities have evolved since the 1980s between the rapidly developing coastal areas and the stagnating inland areas. The Theil index (an indicator of inequality),[6] estimated from regional income data from the China Statistical Yearbook, increased from 0.02 to 0.06 during the 1990s. Much of this rise could be attributed to the relative gains of just one province (Guangdong) and two cities (Shanghai and Beijing), with a much more gradual development of other regions (Galbraith, 2012, p. 236). The increased interregional economic disparity also contributed to the growth of income and wage inequalities between households in urban areas and those in rural areas.

The rise of interregional disparities, however, began to slow down in the 2000s. Since the latter half of the 2000s, the Theil index had been at around 0.08, which is not necessarily low, but has remained more or less constant. This seems to be associated with issues of migration from inland to coastal areas and wage levels in manufacturing, particularly the coastal areas in the south of China. Initially, most workers moving from rural and inland areas gained employment in the coastal manufacturing sector as their pathways into urban areas. The wage levels in this sector, however, had been relatively low; in fact, average manufacturing sector wages in coastal provinces were only just above the national average (Galbraith, 2012). Factors contributing to important changes in labor demand center on rapidly rising demand for China's exports in the 2000s, which increased 382% (in US dollar) from $249,203 million in 2000 to $1,201,647 million in 2009 (see wits.worldbank.org).

In late 2000s, wages started to rise in China's coastal areas where export production is concentrated, and wages in inland areas started to rise as well. Although the argument of whether the Chinese economy has passed a Lewis turning point has not been settled (see also Chapter 3), this also induced changes in the understanding of the underlying mechanisms of increased interregional disparity (Li and Sicular, 2014). In other words, inequality among provinces exemplified by wage gaps between inland and coastal areas seems to have remained unchanged or may actually have been decreasing slightly since around the 2000s.

In contrast to interprovincial disparities, inequality within provinces (gaps among industrial sectors in a province) continued to expand in the 2000s. Inequality was particularly apparent in the urban areas of coastal regions. A major cause of increased disparity is related to the growth of the service sector. Banks and other financial institutions continued to grow primarily in urban areas such as Beijing, Shanghai, and Guangdong, generating employment and increasing wages. The new information technology (IT) industry developed rapidly too. A case study of Beijing during 2004–2007 suggests that approximately 75% of the increase in inequality can be attributed to three out of 22 industries – banking, finance, and information technologies (IT industry) (Galbraith, 2012, p. 240). Workers in these industries are primarily from urban areas with strong academic backgrounds, typically with university degrees. As wages increase in these industries very rapidly, the Gini coefficients of the urban areas will in general rise. This is because while mega cities such as Shanghai are experiencing a striking increase of the wealthy and middle classes, they are also attracting larger numbers of rural migrant workers, as discussed in Chapter 8. The household registration system (*hukou*) peculiar to China encourages this tendency. Rural migrant workers are restricted in terms of employment opportunities compared to city residents. The access of migrants to social security programs is also limited.

Finally, as in Japan, the ageing population is starting to influence inequality in China as well. A study using the same methodology as that used by Ohtake (2005) for Japan showed that, although rising inequality within the same generation explains approximately 60% of inequality growth in the 2000s, ageing also accounted for 10% of this increase in China (Zhang and Xiang, 2014). Redistribution through taxation and social security systems, as well as pension schemes, remain inadequate in China. As such, the ageing of the population could play out to exacerbate intergenerational inequality, and that among the elderly, more intensively compared to Japan.[7] According to a 2013 report, only 24% of the elderly who responded to a survey selected "pensions" as their major source of income, while the share for "family support" was 41%, and 29% for "income from labor" (Japan External Trade Organization, Beijing Office 2013).

11.2.4 The case of ASEAN

Among ASEAN countries, especially in the ASEAN 4, inequality has risen, as in other Asian countries. As Table 11.1 shows, the Gini coefficients of Malaysia and the Philippines have been constantly high. Indonesia is also showing a rising tendency, with a Gini coefficient in urban areas now exceeding 0.4. In Thailand, the Gini coefficient from the World Bank's database is showing slight improvement. However, according to the Thai government's estimation, it was still as high as 0.47 in 2013 (NESDB, 2015). Reduction of inequality remains a key policy priority.

While these countries achieved great reduction of absolute poverty along with rapid economic growth, the fruits of economic development were not equally shared among different social classes and regions. For example, the income share of the top 20%

increased, and the top 1% and 5% showed particularly high income growth (Kanbur et al., 2014). Studies also show that concentration of asset holding by households in higher income groups represents an even more striking trend. In the case of Thailand, the Gini coefficient for assets is 0.66. If limited to financial assets, it is as high as 0.85 (Pasuk and Baker eds., 2016). Likewise, a highly influential OXFAM report suggests that Indonesia has the sixth worst inequality of wealth (financial and non-financial assets) in the world. According to the report, 49% of total assets belonged to the top 1%. The wealth of the four richest billionaires in Indonesia ($25 billion) is reported to be greater than that of the poorest 40% (about 100 million people) of the country combined ($24 billion) (OXFAM, 2017).

Similar to other Asian countries, the key drivers of rising inequality are identified as globalization, trade and financial liberalization, and spatial inequality. The ADB's study of Indonesia, the Philippines, and Vietnam show that the urban–rural income gap has contributed approximately 20% of overall inequality in the three Southeast Asian countries (Kanbur et al., 2014). Concentration in mega regions in these countries is important as well (see Chapter 8). Inequality within the cities, in addition to interregional inequality, has also been growing. For example, an analysis of inequality in expenditures in Indonesia in 2013 shows that the contribution of intra-regional inequality has been greater than that of inter-regional inequality (Yusef et al., 2014). Thailand also shows a growing trend of inequality within cities, whereas the Gini coefficient at the national level has started to ease slightly. Indeed, Bangkok's Gini coefficient has been rising to reach 0.51 (national 0.48) in 2011 (NESDB, 2015).

Another important driver of inequality that is attracting wide attention is the rising skill premium due to differences in educational attainment and occupations. The ADB report, described above, suggests significant contribution of education to inequality, ranging from 46% in Thailand (2005) to 18% in Vietnam (2008), calculated by expenditure. The report warns of a growing trend prevailing since the 2000s (Kanbur et al., 2014). Figures 11.5A and B show college enrollment rates by household income quartile, and the differences in wage levels by educational backgrounds in Thailand, respectively. As to college enrollment, the gap between the bottom 25% and top 25% is significant and is further expanding from 24 percentage points (1986) to 50% points (2009). Wage inequality among different educational groups is also apparent. The gaps between the "completed tertiary" group and others are large. A strong correlation between a parent's income and the educational attainment of their children is often reported in other countries as well. In addition, the number of educational institutions also differs according to regions. Universities and colleges tend to especially concentrate in certain urban areas, which contributes to inequality of opportunity. Rising skill premiums that occur through differences of educational attainment and occupations are very likely contributing to exacerbate disparities and promote labor immobility.

Finally, it is important to point out that ageing is a potential driving force of rising inequality in the future in ASEAN countries, as is the case already in Japan and China (see also Chapter 10). For example, only 5% of survey respondents were depending on "pensions" as their main sources of income in 2014, while those for "family support" and "labor income" were 41% and 34%, respectively (NSO, 2014). Vulnerable social security systems and disparities in asset holdings are expected to affect the quality of life after retirement greatly for all groups, except for those in higher income groups who can

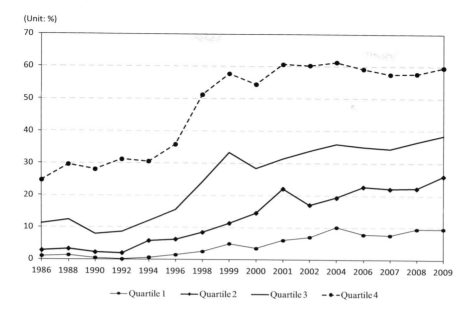

FIGURE 11.5A College enrollment rate by household income quartile.
Source: Pasuk and Baker (2016, p. 45).

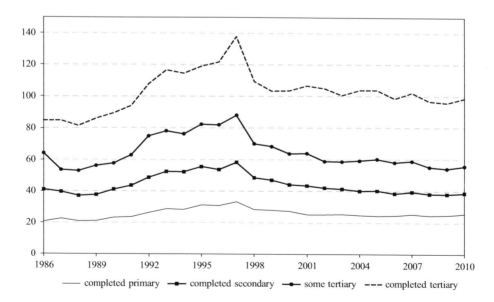

FIGURE 11.5B Real hourly wage by educational group.
Source: Pasuk and Baker (2016, p. 48).
Note: Unit is baht at 2009 prices.

support their livelihoods with their own assets. This trend is already apparent in South Korea because of compressed development. In South Korea, only 6.2% of the elderly were relying on pensions, out of those who are dependent on a single-income source (68.1% of total, in 2010) (Kim, 2017). Its poverty rate for elderly people was the highest among OECD countries.

11.3 POLICY RESPONSES OF ASIAN COUNTRIES AND FUTURE OUTLOOK

11.3.1 Growing public concern about Asian income inequality, and countermeasures

Many Asian countries have begun to look into the issue of income inequality since the 2000s. In 2004, the Chinese government announced its goal of building a "Harmonious Society," which emphasizes the promotion of both economic growth and equality. Similar initiatives include the "One Malaysia" of Malaysia and the "Sufficiency Economy" of Thailand. Indonesia and the Philippines have both adopted a policy goal of "inclusive growth" in their five-year national plans. Indonesia has in particular set specific numerical targets for reducing its national Gini coefficient from 0.41 in 2013 to 0.36 by 2019. Behind such movements are worries about increasing inequality, but other factors such as the rise of populism and political instability have also contributed to such trends.

In modern economics, economic growth and equality (through redistribution policies) have long been regarded as tradeoffs. There have been arguments in recent years, however, that these two can be complementary, and mutually reinforcing. International institutions have published reports with similar conclusions (Ostry et al., 2014; OECD, 2015; World Bank, 2016; UNDP, 2013; Berg, 2015, UNESCO, 2016). The common message of the ADB, International Monetary Fund (IMF), and World Bank is that excessive inequality can generate disincentives for economic development, which leads to the inclusive growth concept.

It should be noted that the meaning and definition of "inclusive," however, vary among the advocates. Some argue that the share of the middle class in an economy should be increased, while others assert that specific emphasis should be assigned to raising the incomes of low-income groups. Others advocate that economic opportunities created by economic growth should be equally open and accessible to all (UNDP, 2013). Policy priorities and specific instruments are also likely to vary, depending on how one defines "inclusive." Organizations such as the United Nations Development Programme (UNDP) and the International Labour Organization (ILO) tend to emphasize the importance of looking at inequality from a broader perspective that extends into social and political dimensions, in addition to the traditional tangible aspects such as income levels. They have been arguing in recent years that correcting horizontal inequalities (disparities that arise irrespective of income class, such as gender and ethnicity) is also important for building a fair and stable society, in line with the Sustainable Development Goals (SDGs) of the United Nations.

11.3.2 Policy responses and prospects for middle-income countries

Promoting competitiveness and equality simultaneously is a challenging task, particularly for middle-income countries. Compressed development has exposed these countries to these highly complex issues, while social security systems remain vulnerable under limited fiscal resources (also see Chapter 8). Prioritizing competitive strategies may exacerbate the underlying causes of increased inequality.

Thailand, for instance, has been gradually abolishing measures to correct interregional inequalities such as investment incentive policies for rural areas since the 2010s, and has been encouraging investments in mega regions to increase the country's global competitiveness. Similar policy shifts are observed in other countries too, through measures such as corporate tax cuts to attract multinational companies. Such policies, however, may lead to increased spatial inequality.

Regarding interregional wage inequality, basic neoclassical economic theory has suggested the need to minimize government intervention. If workers have freedom of movement, labor will shift naturally from low-wage to high-wage regions, which is likely to reduce interregional wage gaps through demand-and-supply balances. In some cases, however, such reallocation of labor does not occur automatically. Unless governments take active measures, interregional inequality can worsen (Myrdal, 1957).

In China, increased employment opportunities and wage growth in inland areas that have been occurring in recent years have mitigated the disparities with the country's coastal areas. As explained earlier, however, interregional gaps in opportunities for employment in high-productive industrial sectors in which wages are high, and for education and training, remain large. As discussed in the preceding section, disparities attributable to skill premiums and educational background are linked to spatial inequality, which cannot be resolved easily without the adoption of some corrective measures.

Moreover, as concerns about the concentration of assets in the upper classes, and about inequality of opportunities, increase, vulnerable social security systems are progressively seen as urgent problems. Rising inequality is not only due to external factors such as globalization and technological progress, but also to internal factors such as domestic institutions and policies. Therefore, there are arguments supporting appropriate interventions in redistributive policies to correct inequalities in order to further encourage economic development. In fact, many OECD countries including Japan have reduced inequalities through such policies. The difference in Gini coefficients between the initial and redistributed incomes of middle-income countries, however, has indicated little change. The UNDP estimates that in China the Gini coefficient– before and after redistribution - changed only for 6% from 0.42 to 0.40 in the latter half the 2000s. In Indonesia, the change was just for 2% from 0.39 to 0.38, while that for Malaysia was only 1% in the value of the Gini coefficient. In Thailand, the Gini coefficient has remained unchanged (UNDP, 2013). During the same period, redistribution effect has been observed in Japan for 18% (from 0.370 to 0.305) and Singapore for 18% (from 0.504 to 0.413). As a response, these middle-income countries are now considering and experimenting with the extension of pensions and other social security systems to include the self-employed and agricultural workers (also see Chapter 10). A large disparity in assets also hinders social mobility and solidifies social stratification. Even tax policies such as the imposition of inheritance taxes and asset taxes have been included in the scope of discussion. Nevertheless, reaching consensus on these policies is not simple (also see Box 11). How governments balances conflicting policy orientation and responds to them are keys to achieving future social stability.

11.3.3 Policy responses and prospects in a high-income country: case of Japan

As reviewed in the preceding section, the growth of income inequality in Japan peaked in the 2000s and began to show a levelling off in terms of redistributed income. The background of such changes, however, is that the share of the low-income class increased in Japan's income distribution. In other words, downward trend in income for the entire society has been observed (Oshio and Urakawa, 2008).

As described earlier, however, current redistribution policies such as pension and medical insurance programs are certainly contributing to the reduction of inequality and poverty even in such a difficult situation when compared to other Asian countries, albeit at a lower level than the OECD average. These efforts have been most effective for elderly people. While Japan's Gini coefficient for initial income has been rising consistently since the 2000s, that of redistributed income has remained generally unchanged. One of the reasons for this trend is the increase in the percentage of elderly people receiving public pension and medical benefits in the total population (see Figure 11.4A).

Attention must be paid to the fact that income transfer among different generations will become difficult with declining birthrates and ageing populations. In recent years, the risk of poverty has been increasing not only for the elderly, but also for the young and middle-aged groups. A heavier emphasis on intra-generational redistribution as opposed to income transfers between generations will be important to improve the efficacy of redistribution policies. Furthermore, differences in social insurance coverage and welfare benefits between regular and irregular workers are significant, even between those working for the same company. The percentage of employment insurance coverage of regular workers, for instance, was 92.4%, while that of part-time employees was 60.6%, and that of temporary workers such as day laborers was only 19.4% in 2014. Safety nets remain inadequate for workers who are exposed to high risks such as unemployment, health issues, and poverty.

Developed countries such as Japan, which have led the process of economic development in Asia, are now facing trends of decreasing incomes and evolving relative poverty because of the "informalization" of employment, as discussed in Chapter 9. Alternative mutual support functions offered by families, communities, and localities are also much weaker compared to those of less developed countries. While improving public-based social services and establishing effective redistribution policies remain important, creative solutions that utilize and combines private initiatives and locally based welfare systems with the existing ones should be sought.

CONCLUSION

Development economists have long argued how economic growth, poverty, and inequality interact. The initial stages of industrialization in Asia occurred when most of the countries were still poor, and thus economic growth was achieved by utilizing their abundant and cheap domestic labor forces. The development of basic social infrastructure including the provision of primary education and basic sanitation contributed to alleviating absolute poverty. It also allowed the mobilization of the low-cost, high-quality labor force which supported Asia's phenomenal industrialization process, the so-called "East Asian miracle." However, the fruits of industrialization were not shared equally among people in different regions and social classes.

The growth of income inequality in Asia is probably also drawing great attention because of the escalating frustration with vested interests and the resulting political instability. Unlike the times during which most people were poor and able to tolerate dissatisfaction to some degree, individual needs and values are now much more diverse. The poor and middle class are raising their voices on social media, through political movements, and in various other ways. Such social changes have compelled the governments of many countries to take notice of the problems arising from inequality.

Complex factors converge to increase income inequality. The mechanisms of growing inequality described in this chapter include changes in spatial inequality caused by changes in industrial structure, changes in population and household structures, changes in the distribution of capital and labor income share because of globalization, changes in the forms of employment, and inadequate redistribution policies. As discussed in this chapter, if the factors that enabled compressed economic development also facilitated inequality, then correcting the inequality cannot be expected to be simple. If no measures are taken to address excessive economic disparities, then the dissatisfaction of the poor who have now become "active voters with voices" cannot be contained. In a society where inequality, not absolute poverty, is the issue, the key is whether a path to social upward mobility is open. The questions that one should ask when considering the future prospects of Asia are whether social mobility is occurring, or conversely, whether the tendency to solidify stratification is increasing. If various choices are defined strongly by structural factors or unequal opportunities, rather than as the result of the voluntary actions of individuals or households, then the sense of despair in society may be difficult to overcome.

While efforts at "inclusive growth" and "no one left behind" are loudly announced everywhere, the specific details of such policies must be examined more carefully. Many Asian countries have long prioritized economic growth over other policies. The Japanese management method which achieved the continuous improvements in efficiency that supported the country's post-war economic development was spread internationally by the term "Kaizen." At the same time, the term "Karoshi," or death from overwork, has also come to be known internationally as well. Such development models must now be re-examined, with emphasis not only on the quantitative dimensions of growth, but also on the qualitative aspects of development, which should be the cornerstone for a more sustainable and prosperous Asia.

BOX 11 Inequality and democracy

Wataru Kusaka

There is a fundamental contradiction between democracy based on the ideal of equality, and capitalism that reproduces inequalities. Developed countries were able to "solve" this tension by utilizing increased revenue to expand redistribution and to include the poor into the system during their time of rapid economic development. Nowadays, however, under the hegemonic neoliberalism that prioritizes free market competition over tax increases and welfare, welfare states have been disappearing in some developed countries whereas the implementation of comprehensive welfare programs has not been affordable in developing countries. Thus, the conflict between democracy and capitalism has come to the fore as a serious common challenge for many countries in terms of how they can practice democracy in societies with widening inequality.

Growing inequality deepens social divisions and foments antagonism between groups. In the process, the poor become hostile not only to the rich but also towards migrants and foreigners. Meanwhile, the middle class, forced to compete in the labor market under great stress, become exasperated with the poor whom they view as largely dependent on politicians' hand-outs or welfare. Yet, considering diversity among countries, it is not clear whether this widening inequality contributes to a deepening of democracy by strengthening voices demanding equality, or damages it by escalating social antagonism. Several factors can be identified that have an impact on the way inequality affects democracy.

The first factor relates to what kinds of "we/they" antagonism could be constructed by people's frustration over inequality. On the one hand, widening inequality can worsen the "division of the nation" by strengthening conflict not only along class lines but also ethnic or religious divisions. On the other hand, economic dissatisfaction can also strengthen nationalism calling for "solidarity of the nation" through exclusion of foreigners, corrupt officials, and criminals. Such discourses of antagonism would spontaneously erupt from societies or be intentionally created by ambitious politicians.

Second, to what extent do social divisions cross or overlap? Where multiple divisions such as class, ethnicity, religion, and region complexly cross each other and constitute a mosaic-like society, any of the single divisions could escalate into serious antagonism since individuals simultaneously belong to multiple social groups. In contrast, where multiple divisions overlap, stronger and more divisive antagonistic relationships are likely to be formed.

Another factor relates to whether antagonism among groups is recognized as a conflict over the distribution of interests or over morality, a definition of good and evil. Conflicts over interests can be mediated through an adjustment of resource distribution. However, moral antagonisms tend to set up others as enemies to be destroyed; thereby threatening the plurality of democracy, which is premised on coexistence and competition among diverse groups (Kusaka, 2017).

The last factor pertains to the strength of democratic institutions. Where political parties and congress appropriately represent interests of social groups and mediate conflict among them in the process of policy making, inequality is more likely to be redressed. However, inequality may cause political instability in cases where particular social groups do not have political parties representing their interests, or a populist leader without an institutionalized political party holds power, or the party system is unstable.

Representative cases of how inequality destabilized and disrupted democracy can be found in the Philippines and Thailand in the 2000s, where the electoral victory of populists, Joseph Estrada and Thaksin Shinawatra, owing to support from the poor, triggered massive reactionary demonstrations among the urban middle class. This opposition denied the legitimacy of the popular electoral results. As of 2020, Thailand has yet to practice a free popular election without control by the military. In contrast, in South Korea and Taiwan in the 2010s, discontent with widening inequality became a factor that facilitated leftist-liberal parties' gaining of power. The different strengths of democratic institutions among these countries may partially explain the differing outcomes.

In multi-ethnic Indonesia, multi-social divisions commonly cross, but resentment against rich Chinese Indonesians amid the economic crisis in the late Suharto era foregrounded divisions of ethnicity and class to make them overlap, which triggered riots against Chinese Indonesians in Jakarta 1998. Moreover, against the backdrop of recent Islamization, religious issues can link the overlapping divisions of ethnicity and class. In 2016, a governor of Jakarta who is a Christian Chinese Indonesian was ousted by popular demonstrations in the name of Islam. In Malaysia, political institutions that share power among Malay, Chinese, and Indian ethnic groups have functioned to maintain ethnic harmony. However, the United Malays National Organization, which held power and ruled for 60 years until 2018, promoted Islamization in order to appeal to conservative Malays and to arrest declining support. This strategy caused damage to the consensus on multi-ethnic harmony. Evidently, Islamization in both countries depoliticizes the issue of inequality by highlighting religious morality as a focal point of politics.

There are also cases where increasing inequality occurs with the rise of a nationalism that constructs and demonizes "enemies of the nation" such as foreigners, corrupt officials, and criminals. Ambitious politicians capitalize on such discourses to further their power. In Japan, nationalist feelings against neighbors in East Asia have bolstered the Liberal Democratic Party's popularity under the leadership of Prime Minister Shinzo Abe. The Communist Party of China headed by Xi Jinping, and the military regime in Thailand, utilize strict anti-corruption initiatives against corrupt officials to gain support from society, which is also helpful to depoliticize the issues of inequality and democratization. President Rodrigo Duterte in the Philippines, who has implemented the war on drugs that has killed, according to the police, at least 7,000 drug users and dealers, enjoys support from almost 80% of the nation.

As argued above, widening inequality tends to escalate a variety of antagonism in societies and imposes stress on democracies. In order to resist this dangerous trend and make democracy sustainable and meaningful, it is important to create a politics of *agonism* (Mouffe, 2005), in which conflicting forces with different moralities engage in a struggle with mutual respect, not a politics of antagonism in which forces aim to exclude and destroy others in order to enhance their own popularity.

NOTES

1 Absolute poverty represents a level below which an individual or household is unable to subsist or maintain a minimum standard of living. Primarily, governments of developing countries and international organizations have led the measurement of absolute poverty. In the 1990 World Development Report, the World Bank defined the sustained consumption level of one US dollar a day as a criterion for absolute poverty. Considering changes in prices, the World Bank subsequently proposed the absolute poverty criterion of 1.90 US dollars a day (equivalent to the purchasing power parity of 2011, revised October 2015).
2 Relative poverty defines poverty through comparison based on society-wide distribution of income and consumption. International comparative statistics of the EU and OECD, for example, use standards for poverty such as the median (60% or 50%) of disposable income (equivalent disposable income) of households, with numbers of members adjusted.
3 The Gini coefficient is a widely used measure of economic inequality, primarily reflecting the distributions of income and consumption (expenditures). For the Gini coefficient, which takes a value of from 0 to 1, greater inequality produces a value closer to 1. Understanding income distribution in emerging countries (and some developed ones too) is not straightforward. Income, particularly of high-income groups, is often underestimated.
4 An analysis based on nine OECD member countries in the 1990s indicated Gini coefficients of the working generation for seven countries (Canada, Finland, Germany, Italy, the Netherlands, Sweden, and the U.K.) other than Japan and the U.S. as approximately 7% higher than the national Gini coefficient.
5 This law states that a negative relation exists between the household head income and the spouse employment rate.
6 The Theil index is a statistic used to measure economic inequality. The Theil index measures how the population is away from the egalitarian state of everyone having the same income, by using the income share of each individual or of each household as a weight. It is characterized by the ability to decompose an inequality level into multiple sub-groups.
7 In China, the "Three Nos" in urban areas and the "Five Guarantees" in rural areas are used for poor elderly people. The "Three Nos" are applicable to old people who have no ability to work, no income, and no one legally required to support them. The "Five Guarantees" stipulate that old persons are eligible to receive five social security services (food, clothing, housing, medical care, and funeral assistance) as a

relief program for rural poor people beginning in the 1950s. Uzuhashi et al. (2012) present additional details about the transition and issues related to social security systems for elderly people in China.

REFERENCES

Abdullah, A. J., Doucouliagos, H. and Manning, E. (2015). "Is there a Kuznets process in southeast Asia?" *The Singapore Economic Review*, 60(2), 1–22.

Asian Development Bank. (2012). *Confronting rising inequality in Asia: Asian Development Outlook 2012*, Asian Development Bank.

Barro, R. J. (1999). "Inequality, Growth and Investment" NBER Working Paper, 7038, 1–52.

Barro, R. J. (2008). "Inequality and growth revisited," Working Paper Series on Regional Economic Integration No. 11, Asian Development Bank.

Berg, J. (2015) *Labour Markets, Institutions and Inequality*, ILO.

Förster, M. F. and Mira d'Ercole, M. (2005). "Trends in income distribution and poverty in OECD countries over the second half of the 1990s," OECD Social, Employment and Migration Working Papers No. 22. OECD Publishing, 1–79.

Galbraith, James K. (2012). *Inequality and Instability: A Study of the World Economy just before the Great Crisis*, Oxford University Press.

Hashimoto, Kenji. (2009). *Postwar History of Inequality: Japan's hierarchical society* [Kakusa no sengoshi: Kaisou shakai nihon no rirekisyo], Kawade Press. [In Japanese].

Japan External Trade Organization, Beijing Office. (2013). *The Research Report on Industry for Elderly in China* [Chugoku koureisya sangyou tyousa houkokusyo], Beijing Office, JETRO [in Japanese].

Japan Institute for Labor Policy and Training (JILPT) (ed.). (2017). *Data book of International Labor Statistics 2017*, Japan Institute for Labor Policy and Training.

Kaku, Yanchun. (2004). "The IMF system and social policy in South Korea," [IMF taisei to kankoku no shakai seisaku], *The Review of Comparative Social Security Research*, 146, 32–42.

Kanbur, R., Rhee, C. and Zhuang, J. (eds.). (2014). *Inequality in Asia and the Pacific*, Asian Development Bank and Routledge.

Kim, Sung-won. (2017). "Korea: Ageing and increase of longevity risk [Kankoku: Jinkou no koureika to takamaru choju risuku," in Suehiro, Akira, and Oizumi, K. (eds.), *Social transformation of East Asia: Societal view from population census data* [Higashi Asia no syakaihendou: Jinkou sensus ga kataru sekai], Nagoya University Press [in Japanese].

Kusaka, Wataru. (2017). *Moral Politics in the Philippines: Inequality, Democracy and the Urban Poor*. Kyoto University Press and Singapore University Press.

Kuznets, S. (1955). "Economic growth and income inequality," *American Economic Review*, 45(1), 1–28.

Li, S and T. Sicular. (2014). "The distribution of household income in China: Inequality, poverty and policies," *The China Quarterly*, 217, 1-41.

Marukawa, Tomoo. (2013). *Contemporary Chinese Economy* [Gendai Chugoku Keizai], Yuhikaku [in Japanese].

Mouffe, Chantal. (2005). *On the Political*. Routledge.

Myrdal, G. (1957). *Economic Theory and Under Developed Regions*, Gerald Duckworth & Co. Ltd.

NESDB. (2015). "Report on Situation of Poverty and Inequality in Thailand 2013 [Rai-ngan kan Wikhro Sathanakan kwaam Yaak jon lae kwaam Leuam lam nai Prathet Thai 2013]," NESDB. [in Thai].

NSO. (2014). *The 2014 Survey of the Older Persons in Thailand*, NSO and Ministry of Information and Communication Technology.

OECD. (2015). *In It Together: Why less inequality benefits all*, OECD.

Ohtake, Fumio. (2005). Inequality in Japan [Nihon no hubyoudo]. Tokyo: Nippon Keizai Shinbun Press [in Japanese].

Oshio, T. and Urakawa, K. (2008). "The trend of poverty and redistribution policies in the first half of the 2000s [Nisen nendai zenhan no hinkonka no keikou to saibunpai seisaku]," *The Quarterly of Social Security Research* [Kikan Shakai Hosho Kenkyu], 44(3), 278–290, [in Japanese].

Ostry, J.D., Berg, A, and Tsangarides, C.G. (2014). "Redistribution, Inequality, and Growth," IMF Staff Discussion Note.

OXFAM. (2017). "Toward a more equal Indonesia," OXFAM briefing paper, OXFAM.

Palma, Jose Gabriel. (2011). "Homogeneous middles vs. heterogeneous tails, and the end of the 'Inverted-U': The share of the rich is what it's all about," Working Papers in Economic (CWPE) No. 1111.

Pasuk, Phongpaichit, and Baker, C. (eds.). (2016). *Unequal Thailand: Aspects of Income, Wealth and Power*, NUS Press.

Suehiro, Akira. (2014). *Economics of Emerging Asia* [Shinkou ajia keizairon], Iwanami Shoten [in Japanese].

Tachibanaki, Toshiaki. (1998). *Economic Inequality in Japan: Examining from income and asset* [Nihon no kakusa: syotoku to sisan kara kangaeru], Iwanami Shoten [in Japanese].

Tachibanaki, T., and Urakawa, K. (2006) *A Study of Poverty in Japan* [Nihon no hinkon kenkyu], Tokyo University Press [in Japanese].

Tanabe, Kazutoshi and Suzuki, T. (2013). "The trend of inequality from various Japanese goverment's income surveys," [Tashurui no syotoku chosa wo mochiita wagakuni no shotoku kakusa no doko no kensho] *Keizai-Kenkyu*, 64(2), 119–131 [in Japanese].

UNDP. (2013). *Humanity Divided: Confronting Inequality in Developing Countries*, UNDP.

UNESCO. (2016). *World Social Science Report Challenging Inequalities: Pathways to a Just World*, ISSC, IDS and UNESCO.

Uzuhashi, T., Yu, Y., and Xu, S. (eds.). (2012). *The Socially Disadvantaged and Social Security in China: Light and Shadow of the Reform and Open Policies* [Chugoku no jyakusyasou to syakaihosyo: Kaikakukaihou no hikari to kage], Akashi Shoten [in Japanese].

World Bank. (1993). *East Asian Miracle: Economic growth and public policy*, World Bank and Oxford University Press.

World Bank. (2016). *Taking on Inequality: Poverty and Shared Prosperity*, World Bank.

Yusef, A., et al. (2014). "Twenty Years of Expenditure Inequality in Indonesia, 1993–2013," *Bulletin of Indonesian Economic Studies*, 50(2), 243–254.

Zhang, J. and Xiang, J. (2014). "How ageing and intergeneration disparity influence consumption inequality in China," *China and World Economy*, 22(3), 79–100.

12 Environmentally challenged Asia: in the context of backwardness and diversity

Fumikazu Ubukata

Strait obscured by haze; degraded mountains (left: China mainland from Macau, right: Sarawak, Malaysia. Photo by Fumikazu Ubukata).

LEARNING GOALS

- To recognize environmental problems as a threat to the Asian economy, and to develop the view of "environmentally challenged Asia."
- To understand the relationships between economic growth and environmental problems, including their causes and mechanisms.
- To consider Asian environmental problems from the viewpoints of backwardness and the diversity of issues, and to understand implications for the differentiation of changing processes and their consequences.

INTRODUCTION

The Asian economy has been developing rapidly for the past several decades. Its speed exceeded even the rapid economic development in Japan during the 1960s, let alone that of the western countries. This can be seen as a "compressed economic development" process.

However, this rapid economic development has created various social problems, among which environmental problems are typical instances. In Japan, serious environmental pollution became one of the most pertinent social problems during the rapid economic growth of the 1960s. After some initial reluctance, Japan finally began to address these issues in the 1970s. The outline of this story seems somewhat similar to the current situations experienced in other Asian countries. Do they implement the same responses as Japan, or do they follow their own courses of action?

This chapter focuses on the process both of development and of coping with environmental issues, as these processes accommodate the social peculiarities of Asia or other regions. For instance, the well-known concept of "internalization" of externalities is often regarded as a key concept in the economic literature as an approach to solving environmental problems. This is based on an economic theory in which the market fails to allocate resources efficiently when the market experiences an externality.[1] Many interactions in nature, such as carbon sequestration/release and water purification/pollution, are sources of externalities as they occur outside the economic system. It is therefore important to "internalize" these interactions into the economic system through processes of taxation/subsidy, direct negotiation, and establishment of a "new" market that regards the environment as "goods" and "services."

These theoretical measures, however, are challenged by various barriers, most of which come from social and natural peculiarities that are region/country specific. These barriers impact what externalities are identified and how we internalize them. Examining policy formation and implementation processes can elucidate how these barriers can be overcome or how they impede planning from above.

Since the 1990s, much research has dealt with such processes addressing environmental problems in Asia. Most of these studies, however, focus on particular problems in particular countries, which may overlook the variety of issues and interrelationships among them. This is a crucial point as the internationalization/globalization of environmental problems has become increasingly important since the 2000s. Thus, environmental problems in Asia should also be viewed as such.

This chapter explains the emergence and coping processes for various environmental problems in Asia. It does so from two interrelated contexts: backwardness and the diversity of issues. It further provides additional insights by introducing a case study of the pulp and paper industry in Southeast Asia in order to understand the current status of changing processes.

12.1 ENVIRONMENTAL PROBLEMS IN ASIA AND THEIR CHARACTERISTICS

12.1.1 The duality of backwardness and the diversity of environmental issues

The first important viewpoint when we consider Asian environmental problems is that of backwardness. According to Terao (2015), Asian environmental problems are characterized by "dual backwardness." One of these is "late-comer public policy," whereby environmental problems emerged as additional agendas to pre-existing industrial and political settings. The other is "economic backwardness," where their commitment to developmentalism has impeded a quick response to the problems. How this "dual backwardness" has affected the formation and implementation of environmental policy is one of the chief arguments when considering the future of Asian environmental problems, even though many Asian countries have already started to accelerate mitigation measures.

The second viewpoint is related to the diversity of problems and points of issue. Quite naturally, Asian environmental problems are diverse, including air pollution, water pollution, increase in solid waste, loss of biodiversity, desertification, and climate change. Of them, problems like climate change are recently emerging problems that were not recognized at the time of Japan's rapid economic development.

The diversity of natural and social environments in Asia also contributes to the diversity of environmental problems. First, the region includes countries with different stages of economic development. This may differentiate the problems, ranging from those due to poverty or low technology to those caused by excess supply. Second, from the Mongolian desert to the Indonesian rainforest, the Asian natural environment is extremely diverse. Moreover, the very same natural phenomena may sometimes be understood through the viewpoints of situated social and political contexts in different countries. Thus, questions regarding how and by whom a natural phenomenon is regarded as a political issue are matters of social scientific discovery.

How do these diversities affect ongoing environmental measures in Asian countries, especially where they are said to be "backward"? As pointed out above, many current descriptions of Asian environmental problems, apart from general reviews and introductory ones, are spread over countries/regions and academic fields. The academic divide is especially conspicuous. For instance, the so-called "brown agenda (environmental pollution and wastes)" and "green agenda (depletion and degradation of natural and ecological resources)" stand in different academic fields and represent different sections in governmental administration. Few efforts have been made to understand them using a common framework.

To further assist readers in effectively imagining the above-mentioned diversity of environmental problems, the Chapter briefly describes two cases: air pollution in China and forest depletion in Indonesia. Each represents the brown and green agenda, respectively.

12.1.2 Environmental pollution and destruction: some examples

12.1.2.1 Air pollution in China

It is well known that the problem of air pollution among the mega cities in China, such as Beijing, is serious. The extent and the area of actual pollution, however, are far more serious than we imagine. The root causes of the pollution are also too complex to find a simple solution.

According to Chiashi (2015), most of the cities that have serious annual average exposure to PM2.5 are in Hebei province. This is because the province, which is located near Beijing and Tianjin, has become one of the largest centers of heavy industry. Hence, air polluters became concentrated in the area during the process of Chinese economic development. In China, the dependence on coal as an energy source is still high; and since coal produces smoke, it is one of the reasons why air pollution is taken seriously. In addition, coal is not an efficient source of energy, and is also regarded as a major source of CO_2 emissions, which can exacerbate global climate change (China is already the largest greenhouse gas (GHG) emitter in the world).

Serious damage is reported not only in urban and peri-urban areas, but in inland rural areas as well. This is partly due to the use of coal heating by rural households during winter. Air pollution has also affected people's health. Some reports show that the average life expectancy in northern China was more than five years shorter than that in southern China in the 1990s (National Geographic, 2013). Moreover, some areas are facing "compounded pollutions" that continue to be affected not only by the atmosphere but also by other pollutants such as those in water and food (Fukushima, 2013).

Reflecting on these realities, the national government recently strengthened its environmental measures, such as tighter regulations and monitoring, including stronger penalties for violators. The government has also started the introduction of a nationwide emissions trading system since the end of 2017 (World Bank and Ecofys, 2018). Some point out that an environmental restructuring of the society and economy is taking place in China (Mol, 2006), and that this transformation has achieved some success (He et al., 2012). Despite these national level commitments, however, the progress is slow in the areas most affected by serious pollutions. The pro-development political economic relationship between provincial level governments and companies has impeded effective implementation (Chiashi, 2015).

12.1.2.2 Forest depletion in Indonesia

Indonesia has the largest tropical forests in Asia. The forests in this country are famous for their high biodiversity, such as orangutans, tigers, and wild elephants. In addition, the peat swamp forests in the lowland areas of the Sumatra and Kalimantan islands accumulate huge underground carbon stocks, which are quite important for the global commons.

Despite their importance, the Indonesian forests have been rapidly depleting for several decades. According to World Bank statistics, the forest coverage rate in Indonesia decreased from 65.4% in 1990 to 50.2% in 2015.[2] This means more than 270 thousand hectares of forest have been lost over the past 25 years.

The underlying causes of such a rapid deforestation process is a complex combination of timber harvesting by the timber industry, plantation developments by the pulp and paper industry and the oil palm industry, government-initiated immigration projects, villagers' agricultural use, forest fires, and so on. Similar to the Chinese air pollution case, the political economy is quite an important factor. Especially during the Suharto regime (1967–1998), the famous developmental dictatorship regime led by President Suharto, forest industry played a central role in the rent seeking activities of his cronies and military officers, and provided for huge "off-budget" spending by the regime (Ascher, 1999). More recently, rapid plantation development has accelerated deforestation, causing haze problems in neighboring countries (see the discussion in later section).

While vested interests prevail, the customary rights of local villagers who have traditionally lived in the forests have been largely neglected. Some were violently deprived of their customary rights over forest use for the sake of development or conservation projects. After the collapse of the Suharto regime, some of these angry villagers violently occupied the forests, resulting in further social confusion and deforestation. Since the 2000s, political decentralization and a commitment to international environmental agendas under the democratic government have been changing forest management in a more inclusive way. The way forward, however, is still a difficult path.

The above two cases are prime examples of famous environmental problems in contemporary Asia. Readers may now grasp the importance of understanding the element of diversity when addressing environmental challenges. In fact, as we can see from the "composite" cases in subsequent sections, the distinction between "brown" and "green" is not so clear, and sometimes these agendas are interrelated with each other. In addition, both have common characteristics in terms of "dual backwardness" with regards to environmental policy as a result of "catch-up" style economic development under the political commitments of developmentalism. Therefore, the next section looks at Asian environmental problems considering their relationship to economic development.

12.2 ECONOMIC DEVELOPMENT AND ENVIRONMENTAL PROBLEMS

12.2.1 The environmental Kuznets curve

The environmental Kuznets curve is one of the best-known concepts explaining the relationship between economic development and environmental problems (Figure 12.1). This presents the hypothesis that the state of environmental problems traces an inverse U-shaped curve as the economy grows. If true, a country may experience serious environmental problems in the midst of economic development, but the problems will dissipate after a later stage of development is reached.

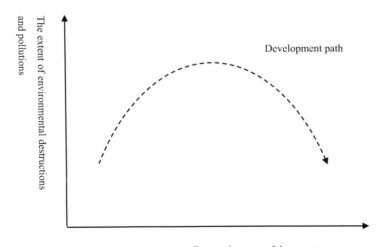

FIGURE 12.1 Environmental Kuznets curve.

Source: The author.

From a macro perspective, there are two possible reasons explaining why this occurs. The first reason is the change in industrial structure. It is well known that economic development entails a change in the dominant economic activities, shifting from agriculture/forestry/fishery to manufacturing, and from manufacturing to service industries. Of these phases, the second (the manufacturing-dominated stage) entails the highest environmental risks.

The second reason is the change in people's preferences. In advanced economies, the environment as "goods"[3] get scarce enough to shift people's preferences into environment-friendly ones. Companies react to these preferences through the market, and citizens and NGOs engage in environmental movements or lobby to protect the environment; and finally, environment-friendly politicians and parties emerge. These socio-political changes provide larger opportunities for technological and institutional change, such as the emergence of environmental regulations, taxation, and innovations.

These explanations represent "single-track" understandings of environmental reform that are mainly based on western experiences. If they prove suitable for understanding the future of Asian countries, following "sustainable industrialization" paths that seek to lower the peak of the inverse U-shaped curve may prove advantageous. This allows for the "backwardness" in these countries to effectively draw on western and Japanese experiences and technological support.

12.2.2 The environmental Kuznets curve in Asia

This is, however, a general case, indicating just one of the possible paths that can be used to construct environment-friendly societies or economies. Regarding this hypothesis, what kind of realities can we find from the data in Asian countries? First, let us work from a macro perspective using the World Bank's Open Data (World Development Indicators). Here we use CO_2 emissions and exposure of PM2.5 as representative of a "brown" agenda, while using forest covers (percent of land area) for the "green" agenda.

Figures 12.2 and 12.3 show the relationships between per capita real gross domestic product (GDP) and CO_2 emissions per 100 US dollars of GDP, and between per capita real GDP and per capita CO_2 emissions, respectively. At first glance, the former generally follows an inverse U-shaped trend (though the variance is large), while the latter follows an increasing trend (though the increase of the rate is declining). In this case we can support the environmental Kuznets curve in terms of environmental efficiency (the former), but not in terms of per capita emissions (the latter). However, the CO_2 emissions here do not include emissions from land use change, for which the estimates are quite ambiguous. This can be crucial in data estimation; for instance, it is said that Indonesia, where a large area of peat swamp forest has been destroyed, may be the third largest CO_2 emitter in the world if the emissions from land use are included (Fogarty, 2015).

Figure 12.4 indicates the case of PM2.5 exposure. From this figure, we cannot identify as clear relationships as for CO_2 emissions. We may find some relationships among some countries, for example, increasing trends between Myanmar and China, and among Cambodia, Laos, and Vietnam. In these countries air pollution is still becoming increasingly severe. We may also find the countries nearby to Singapore following

Environmentally challenged Asia 239

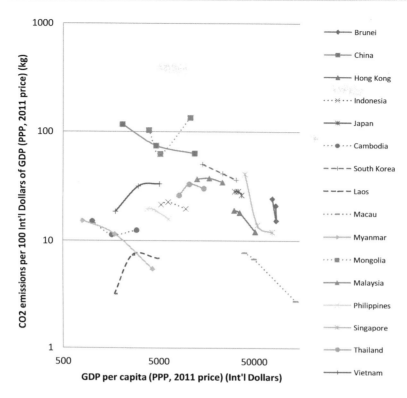

FIGURE 12.2 Economic development and CO_2 emission per 100 US dollars of GDP in Asia (1993–2013).

Source: The World Bank Open Data (World Development Indicators).

Note: Both horizontal and vertical axes have exponential scales. For all the countries except Brunei, the trajectories move from left to right as time passes. Each dot in a country's trajectory indicates the points of 1993, 2003, and 2013 from left to right, respectively.

similar trajectories. This is probably due to the patterns of haze situations, which are discussed later. In short, we may partially identify some relationships from this figure though the overall trajectory is not clear.

Now we may consider the "green" agenda. Figure 12.5 shows the case when considering the forest cover. Here, a U-shaped curve is regarded as the environmental Kuznets curve (Mather, 1990). This figure, however, fails to show any type of trend associated with economic development. The country differences are too large to specify overall relationships. For instance, rapid deforestation is obvious in countries like Cambodia and Myanmar, while forest covers are rising in Vietnam, which is at a similar level of economic development. The "no trend" figures remain unchanged when considering forest areas per capita. The only trend that can be identified, is that the forest areas remain stable in high GDP countries, but we have to remember the fact that these countries, such as in Brunei, Japan, and South Korea, have small national territories. This stability may be due to their small size, indicating that their trends may be due to geographical considerations, rather than the result of economic development.

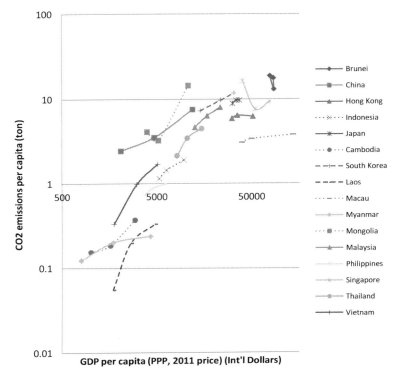

FIGURE 12.3 Economic development and per capita CO_2 emission in Asia (1993–2013).

Source: The World Bank Open Data (World Development Indicators).

Note: See Figure 12.2.

Additionally, forest data are notorious for their ambiguity in definition, given that the figures are themselves of low credibility. For instance, in Figure 12.5 the forest cover in Laos suddenly shifts to an increasing trend during the 2000s. Under the definition of forest in the Food and Agricultural Organization (FAO) data, a source for the World Bank database, forest is defined as land that is occupied by trees with higher than five meters of cover over more than 10% of canopy cover.[4] The official statistics in Laos, however, do not apply this definition. In Laos, forest is defined as requiring more than 20% of canopy cover. The application of this stricter definition affects the official forest covers in Laos, which show a continuous decline.

12.2.3 The environmental Kuznets curve and issues of focus

What then can we learn from these simple analyses? The first point relates to the large variation in country-wise data. It is only when considering CO_2 emissions that certain overall trends are obvious, and only CO_2 emissions per 100 dollars of GDP demonstrate a trend that is consistent with the environmental Kuznets curve. For the others, we have to look more carefully at future trends using individual country data.

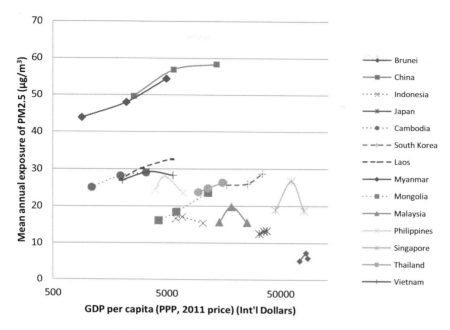

FIGURE 12.4 Economic development and annual exposure of PM2.5 (1995–2015).

Source: The World Bank Open Data (World Development Indicators).

Note: Horizontal axis has an exponential scale. For all the countries except Brunei, the trajectories move from left to right as time passes. Each dot in a country's trajectory indicates the points of 1995, 2005, and 2015 from left to right, respectively.

The second point concerns the differences among the issues. For instance, variation among the countries is smaller when considering CO_2 emissions, but is too large to distinguish any trend for the forest covers. The case of PM2.5 may be in-between that of CO_2 emissions and the forest cover.

The third point concerns the differences in data credibility. Data for forest areas and CO_2 emissions from land use change are not so credible due to ambiguous definitions or difficulties in estimation. This is in contrast to CO_2 emissions from non-land use sources, which can be estimated with more reliability by utilizing energy consumption and economic statistics.

We can thus conclude that the validity of the environmental Kuznets curve depends on how, what, and on which country we focus, especially when considering the "green" agenda, where trends tend to be more area-specific (thus harder to generalize) and harder to quantify (thus harder for science to deal with). In consequence, by using only macro-level data and analysis, we cannot go any further. We have to take meso-level and micro-level approaches to examine the possibilities for environmental measures and actions in Asia, which rest at a crossroads for the creation of a sustainable society. Then how do these differences among regions and issues emerge for processes involving environmental policy making and implementation? We now explain the case of the pulp and paper industry in Southeast Asia, an industry that includes both "green" and "brown" agendas, in order to examine differences in the policy processes.

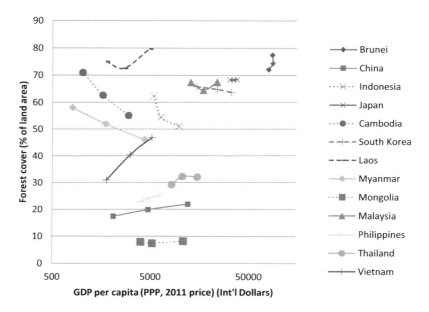

FIGURE 12.5 Economic development and forest cover (1993–2013).

Source: The World Bank Open Data (World Development Indicators).

Note: Horizontal axis has an exponential scale. For all the countries except Brunei (above to below), the trajectories move from left to right as time passes. Each dot in a country's trajectory indicates the points of 1993, 2003, and 2013 from left to right, respectively.

12.3 THE KEY ARGUMENTS AND THE PROCESSES OF CHANGE

12.3.1 The pulp and paper industry in Southeast Asia[5]

The pulp and paper industry in Southeast Asia started to develop during the late 1980s, utilizing the rich forest resources in the region. Especially in Indonesia, currently one of the world's major producing countries, factories with huge production capacities began operations during the 1990s. In addition to Indonesia, Thailand is also important in the regional industry.

The expansion of the pulp and paper industry in both countries has caused serious environmental impacts, including two major issues. One of them is the issue of chlorine compounds (especially elemental chlorine), including dioxin, in the process of pulping and breaching. Since these compounds are toxic, there were concerns not only for air and water pollution discharged, but also on the impact on consumers' health if these substances remained in the products.

Another issue is forest destruction through the procurement of raw materials for these products. The industry requires a huge amount of raw material and using the timber from natural forests and forest plantations provides a large part of this. This actually accompanied by not only environmental but also social issues. In Southeast Asia, the procurement of raw materials has caused land conflicts between the pulp and paper companies and local villagers since the late 1980s.

12.3.1.1 "De-chlorination" and the introduction of chlorine-free pulp

The first issue, the use of chlorine compounds in production, emerged in the late 1980s when dioxin, a highly toxic substance, was linked to the pulp and paper industry in western countries. By the 1990s international NGOs, such as Greenpeace, launched an anti-chlorine campaign. As a result, consumer groups, government officials, and company engineers from various countries came to address the issue despite their differences in standpoints. As a result, the issue of "de-chlorination" of paper spread worldwide, through the mobilization of many people and financial resources.

In Southeast Asia, this problem resulted in the additional issue of the existing forest land and the resource conflicts that the industry had already faced. International NGOs included local NGOs in Indonesia and Thailand in their networks and mobilized them to demand tighter regulations and even to stop production by some companies. This successfully created a political atmosphere where society allowed for the industry to be monitored beyond the domestic laws and regulations.

As a result, Southeast Asian governments started policies to promote "de-chlorination" efforts, and companies started to consider the introduction and development of related technology. Reflecting upon this issue, Northern European companies researched the development of chlorine-free bleached pulp, such as ECF (elementally chlorine free) and TCF (totally chlorine free), in the early 1990s. Southeast Asian companies, especially the large companies which were new to production at the time, started to utilize these technologies and also tried their own methods to control the use of chlorine.

12.3.1.2 Forest destruction and procurement of raw material

Then how have the measures to halt deforestation by the pulp and paper companies developed? During the 1990s, many private companies had entered the pulp and paper productions in Southeast Asia. Their first choice for raw material procurement was to exploit forest resources or establish forest plantations in the land they had rights to. Because forestland is considered state property in most Southeast Asian countries, the companies exploited forests in their concessions, which were granted the right to exploit resources or utilize forestland under long-term lease agreements. These areas, however, in many cases included the land under customary land use by local villagers due to the ambiguous rights of land and resource use. This ambiguity has caused serious land conflicts with local villagers, and at the same time companies have been severely blamed for deforestation by both domestic and international NGOs, claiming that their forest exploitation and plantation development caused ecological disturbances.

Reflecting on these situations, different measures were taken in Thailand and Indonesia. In Thailand, the government started to lease degraded national forest reserves to the pulp and paper companies, from the 1980s, in order to develop forest plantations. This policy sparked severe criticisms because it was accompanied by the eviction of local villagers. Faced by the protests, the government had to restrict forest leases to private companies. At the same time, the companies also shifted their focus to procuring raw materials by purchasing them from farmers and started implementing small-scale contract tree farming schemes. This strategic shift from forest leasing to farm forestry drastically decreased new land and forest conflicts caused by the industry.

In Indonesia, on the other hand, the powerful Suharto regime had severely repressed social movements. It was not until after the 1997–1998 Indonesian economic crisis and the subsequent fall of the Suharto regime that huge protests in regard to these forest land conflicts began in earnest. In addition, the economic crisis seriously impacted the industry. As the companies had incurred huge overseas debts in order to invest in their factories, the devaluation of the Indonesian Rupiah made it impossible to service their accumulated foreign debt. Many troubled companies, however, were thought too big to fail. Under the International Monetary Fund's structural adjustment program, most of these companies were bailed out, retained concessions and production facilities, and continued operations while restructuring management (Barr, 2001).

Because of their overcapacity and the existence of competitive crops such as oil palm and rubber, the Thai-style solution of promoting farm forestry was not considered in Indonesia. After the 2000s, and especially after the Yudhoyono regime (2004–2014), pressures by the Norwegian government, international NGOs, and western companies in the downstream supply chain helped the Indonesian companies and the government to strengthen measures to tackle deforestation as well as to uphold local villagers' customary rights (so called *adat*). The actual measures on the ground, however, largely depend on the companies, leaving the problem far from a total solution.

12.3.1.3 Common points and differences

Let us now consider the common points and differences of the processes to know how to cope with the above two issues in the Southeast Asian pulp and paper industry. One notable common point is the dependence on foreign actors. In both cases, foreign actors, such as northern European companies and international NGOs, played some key roles in agenda setting. The dependence was higher in the "de-chlorination" campaign than for any other raw material issue, while in Indonesia after the 2000s foreign actors also became influential in the latter. This foreign dependence represents the nature of "backwardness" in Asian environmental policy measures.

Now let us consider the differences. In the issue of "de-chlorination," concerns of the western consumer groups were reflected in the actions of the international NGOs, whose campaigns urged companies and government agencies to take technological and policy measures. Though dependent on the European consumers and NGOs, this relatively smooth process is what the environmental Kuznets curve assumes.

In the issue of raw materials, however, the pathways for a solution are not that smooth, owing to fewer technological contributions and a higher local involvement. In Thailand, which has a lower total production capacity in the industry, the government and companies utilized the political opportunities of the early 1990s, and successfully shifted their production base for raw materials into farmers' production. Indonesian companies had no such options, leaving the status quo intact until the 2000s.

Put in a simple way, the above discussion indicates that the Southeast Asian pulp and paper industry has taken effective measures in the "brown" agenda, while it has faced difficulties in the "green" agenda. In the former, people tend to hold pressing concerns because pollution directly leads to an increase of health problems; the issue also appeals to global citizens in the globalized economy. There is larger room for technological solutions to control pollutants. On the other hand, in the latter, the problem is basically local; people in the global economy have less concern over their survival (except those directly affected in the field). There are fewer possibilities for technological solutions, making time-consuming discussions and negotiations with stakeholders a more important matter.

The above-mentioned implications in the pulp and paper industry are consistent with those from analyses in the previous section on the environmental Kuznets curve in Asia; the "green" agenda is more area-specific and harder to quantify. Of course, this may be somewhat oversimplified; as shown in the previous section, the local politico-economic factors concerning Chinese air pollution prevented a change to the situation. Other possibilities include, at least in theory, the development of technology and production systems using non-timber raw materials in the pulp and paper industry. It is important, however, to emphasize that the environmental issues or agendas, being "brown" or "green," can affect the processes for change and their effectiveness, along with global trends and area-specific contexts.

Asian countries, especially those that are called middle-income countries, are at the crossroads in terms of the environmental Kuznets curve. In order to "curve" the problems, their "backwardness" allows them to learn a lot from western experiences. We have to recognize, however, that what they are facing is rather different from what the western countries and Japan experienced. The typical examples of this include cross-borderization/globalization and the increasing complexity of the issues. Below, haze pollution in Singapore is introduced as one of these "new" problems.

12.3.2 Cross-borderization and the increasing complexity of the issue: haze pollution around Singapore

When we go to Singapore, we sometimes experience foggy weather, to the extent that we cannot see skyscrapers in the city. This is the haze pollution that bothers many Singaporeans. The haze affects the daily life of Singaporeans, and some even suffer from respiratory diseases. The reason for the haze is the forest fires on the other side of the Strait of Malacca where there is the Sumatran island of Indonesia. Though variable year by year, the haze from the forest fires is carried by the wind and spreads across the Malay Peninsula, causing serious air pollution. Because of its cross-border aspect, it has become an international issue in which many ASEAN countries get involved (Nguitragool, 2011).

Plantation development and peat swamps are considered to be major backgrounds for forest fires. On the island of Sumatra, forests have been rapidly depleted since the 1990s for the plantation development for the pulp and paper industry and palm oil industry. Plantation development sometimes is accompanied by burning of the fields, and the fire occasionally spreads to a large area. Especially in the peat swamp areas, forest fires cause fatal damage to peat, a large carbon stock that has accumulated over millions of years. In the peat swamp areas, plantation development also requires the construction of drainage systems. This makes peat dry and highly flammable, causing even the smallest mishandling of a cigarette to ignite a serious forest fire, releasing carbon into the air for long periods of time.

The measures attempting to tackle this problem have been going through the following process. Following the widespread forest burning of 1997, ASEAN has sought the development of a regional action plan, including measures to monitor, prevent, deter, and mitigate forest burning. These initiatives bore fruit, resulting in the ASEAN Agreement on Transboundary Haze Pollution in 2002. Based on the previous measures, it also gave legal force under international law (Jones, 2006). Indonesia, however, has been reluctant to ratify the agreement. The agreement lacked specific provision for a system of enforcement and deterrence, probably due to the influence of powerful business interests (*ibid*).

In 2013, the issue suddenly progressed. Since the haze pollution in Singapore was quite severe that year, in August 2014 Singapore's congress passed the Transboundary Haze Pollution Act 2014 (Tan, 2015). This act generally attributes civil and criminal liabilities to companies and individuals who are directly or indirectly related to haze pollution in Singapore regardless of national boundaries. Though this is a domestic law, it was epoch-making because it asserted legitimacy to be applicable to individuals and organizations outside the national territory. Such a "hard line" approach by the Singapore government delivered a strong signal to the Indonesian government and companies. After this move, the Indonesian government ratified the ASEAN agreement (Soeriaatmadja, 2014), and banned new development in the peat area as of 2015.

Many points of this issue are unique. First, its cross-border nature limits the availability of policy options for a single government. Second, it has the dual characteristics of encompassing both "green" (forest fire) and "brown" (air pollution) agendas. In reference to the actions taken by the Indonesian government, such issues may be highlighted by various actors at the international level as a means of enhancing policy priorities and possibilities that develop changing processes. As in the typical "green" agenda, however, it may also make effective action difficult due to the involvement of complex local politico-economic factors and fewer technological options. This is exemplified by the limitations on the actual application of the Transboundary Haze Pollution Act (Tan, 2015). Forest fires in Sumatra are a complex issue that not only involve companies but also many local villagers. It is therefore very hard to control, and more than anything, it is impossible for the Singapore government to bring all these cases to court.

CONCLUSION

This chapter has tried to synthesize an understanding of Asian environmental problems from the viewpoints of "backwardness" and the diversity of the issues. The "compressed economic development" which Asian countries experienced brought about the phenomenon of "dual backwardness" in the implementation of environmental measures and actions. This creates a dependence on other public policies and is accompanied by slow responses to emerging problems. As various environmental problems have emerged, however, Asian countries have been forced to recognize these issues, and to start taking effective measures and actions. In this sense, it might be said that the "Asian economic model" was environmentally challenged, and in its aim of moving toward a "sustainable path," it may reap the advantages of backwardness by lowering the peak of the environmental Kuznets curve.

As explained above, however, Asian environmental problems have a variety of characteristics and raise complex issues, so sometimes these countries may not benefit as much from the advantages of backwardness as the environmental Kuznets curve suggests; this is particularly evident in "green" agenda scenarios, where the known solutions are not necessarily applicable since the issues are largely area-specific and provide little room for technological solutions. In such cases the chances for reform will be slim if foreign actors only provide well-known solutions without understanding area-specific contexts. The existing "sustainable development" approach, which maintains a commitment to developmentalism along with its politico-economic structures, may not be able to take the necessary steps acceptably. It is necessary that we not only consider developing legal systems and technological innovations, but also accommodate area-specific measures and actions based on people's participation and inclusion of various social sectors.

Also, recently emerging cross-borderization and increasing complexity of the issues make environmental actions more complicated and difficult to manage. As the haze pollution problem suggests, however, these characteristics may affect the interests of international actors, making the issues of high priority, and leave possibilities for decisive action. In order to realize these possibilities, it is necessary that we go beyond academic, sectoral, and professional divides to achieve a comprehensive understanding of the issues, as well as of locally based persistent initiatives. We need to understand the diversity of the issues and take collaborative action that includes various people who view them from different standpoints.

It is said that our 21st century is the century of the environment. As in the enactment of The Paris Agreement under the United Nations Framework Convention on Climate Change (UNFCCC) and the adoptions of Sustainable Development Goals (SDGs) in the United Nations, all countries are required to engage in some environmental actions for global society. Taking some environmental actions means reforming social, economic, and political systems. Such changes in a rapidly developing Asia will affect not only the Asian economy but also the future of the world.

BOX 12 The ambitious attempts of Asian governments to "internalize" externalities

Fumikazu Ubukata

In developing countries, including those in Asia, their backwardness sometimes leads them to introduce the newest policy initiatives from global discussions. One typical example is market initiatives to regard the environment as "goods" and "services," such as emission trade systems (ETS) and payment for environmental services (PES: also known as payment for ecosystem services).

The former, being famous for the EU's scheme (EU Emissions Trading System: EU ETS), is a system to reduce total emissions of environmentally harmful substances, including GHG, while allowing emission trade among companies on the basis of allocating them emission rights. In Asia, China started the process of introducing a national emission trade system in 2017, after some pilot applications in major cities. The latter regards various benefits from the natural environment as "environmental (or ecosystem) services," and promotes payments from service users to providers in exchange for maintaining the service flows. In addition to the famous Costa Rican example, in Asia, Vietnam introduced such a nationwide scheme in 2010.

As explained in this chapter, these "market" initiatives for controlling environment are based on the classical theoretical remedy of "internalizing" the externalities. At a glance, some may think that these schemes may have a decentralized structure because they are "market-oriented," but it is not necessarily the case. As these are politically created market schemes, their institutional designs and implementation process, including who aims for what, and how it works, are crucial. In many such schemes, as a result, the role of the state becomes large, and political factors seriously affect their performance. Readers should ask why, in Asia, China and Vietnam are among the pioneer countries introducing these schemes.

NOTES

1. An unintended and uncompensated loss or gain in the welfare of one party resulting from an activity by another (Daly and Farley, 2004, p. 433).
2. World Bank, World Development Indicators. https://datacatalog.worldbank.org/dataset/world-development-indicators.
3. They are regarded as luxury goods whose demand increases more than income increases.
4. Cultivated lands, city parks, and gardens are excluded from the definition.
5. This subsection is mainly based on Ubukata (2009) and Sonnenfeld (2002).

REFERENCES

Ascher, W. (1999). *Why Governments Waste Natural Resources: Policy Failures in Developing Countries*. Baltimore: Johns Hopkins University Press.

Barr, C. (2001). *Banking on Sustainability: Structural Adjustment and Forestry Reform in Post-Suharto Indonesia*. Washington, DC and Bogor: WWF and CIFOR. http://www.cifor.org/publications/pdf_files/books/cbarr/banking.pdf (June 13, 2016).

Chiashi, A. (2015). *Chugoku Kankyo Osen no Seiji Keizai gaku* [Political Economy of Environmental Pollutions in China]. Kyoto: Showado.

Daly, H.E. and Farley, J. (2004). *Ecological Economics: Principles and Applications*. Washington, DC: Island Press.

Fogarty, D. (2015). "Indonesia set to be world's No. 3 air polluter", *The Straits Times*, October 18. https://www.straitstimes.com/asia/se-asia/indonesia-set-to-be-worlds-no-3-air-polluter (May 31, 2019).

Fukushima, K. (2013). *Chugoku Fukugou Osen no Shotai* [Uncovering the Compounded Pollutions in China]. Tokyo: Fusosya.

He, G., Lu, Y., Mol, A.P.J., and Beckers, T. (2012). "Changes and Challenges: China's Environmental Management in Transition", *Environmental Development* 3, 25–38.

Jones, D. S. (2006). "ASEAN and Transboundary Haze Pollution in Southeast Asia", *Asia Europe Journal* 4, 431–446.

Mather, A. S. (1990). *Global Forest Resources*, London: Pinter Publishers.

Mol, A. P. J. (2006). "Environment and Modernity in Transitional China: Frontiers of Ecological Modernization", *Development and Change* 37(1), 29–56.

National Geographic. (July 8, 2013). Coal-Burning Shortens Lives in China, *New Study Shows*. https://news.nationalgeographic.com/news/energy/2013/07/130708-coal-burning-shortens-lives-in-china/ (June 3, 2019).

Nguitragool, P. (2011). *Environmental Cooperation in Southeast Asia: ASEAN's Regime for Transboundary Haze Pollution*. Abingdon: Routledge.

Soeriaatmadja, W. (2014). "S'pore welcomes Jakarta's move to ratify haze pact", *The Straits Times*, September 17. https://www.straitstimes.com/asia/se-asia/singapore-welcomes-jakartas-move-to-ratify-haze-pact (May 31, 2019).

Sonnenfeld, D. A. (2002). "Social Movement and Ecological Modernization: The Transformation of Pulp and Paper Manufacturing," *Development and Change* 33, 1–27.

Tan, A. K.J. (2015). *The 'Haze' Crisis in Southeast Asia: Assessing Singapore's Transboundary Haze Pollution Act 2014*. Working Paper 2015/002, Singapore: Faculty of Law, National University of Singapore.

Terao, T. (2015). "Keizai Kaihatsu Katei ni Okeru Shigen-Kankyo Seisaku no Keisei: Futatsu no "Kohatsusei" ga Motarasu Mono [The Formation Process of Resource and Environmental Policy: Dilemma of "Late-comer" Public Policy Formation with Economic Backwardness]", in Terao, T. (ed.), *Kohatsusei no Politikusu: Shigen, Kankyo Seisaku no Keisei Katei* [Politics of the Environment: The Formation of "late-comer" Public Policy]. Chiba: IDE-JETRO. pp. 3–42.

The World Bank and Ecofys. (2018). *State and Trends of Carbon Pricing 2018*. The World Bank. https://openknowledge.worldbank.org/handle/10986/29687 (May 31, 2019).

Ubukata, F. (2009). *Getting Villagers Involved in the System: The Politics, Economics and Ecology of Production Relations in the Thai Pulp Industry*. Kyoto: Center for Southeast Asian Studies, Kyoto University.

Conclusion: competing Asia, co-existing Asia

Kenta Goto, Tamaki Endo, Asei Ito, and Keiichiro Oizumi

INTRODUCTION: IS THE 21ST CENTURY AN "ASIAN CENTURY?"

It has been a while since the 21st century has been referred to as the "Asian century." What used to be a poor region has now evolved into a vibrant growth center of the global economy. Having established itself as the "world's factory," Asia – particularly East and Southeast Asia – is now on par with the developed regions of Europe and North America in terms of investment and innovative capabilities. However, this book has also made extensive reference to other equally real aspects of Asia, where it continues to struggle to meet both persisting as well as emerging challenges. The 21st century may well be the "Asian century," but it will also be one in which different dynamics, both positive and negative, interact and unfold at multi-dimensional levels. Asia's past performance, current achievements, and future prospects are difficult to comprehend solely from any one particular perspective. Writing a book like this in the face of such dynamic settings requires explicit recognition of the complexities that arise from such entangling micro and macro level phenomena, and the interrelationships between these that shape future trajectories.

The point of entry for investigation into the Asian economy in the 20th century used to be almost always about growth and development, primarily because of the initial extensive poverty and stagnation that permeated the region. However, as development started to take root, lifting many out of poverty and putting Asian economies on a fast track towards industrialization, Asia suddenly became the focus of attention. Its phenomenal region-wide economic development, which was once heralded as a "miracle," quickly labelled Asia as a "success case." The region was, of course, not immune from problems, of which the financial crisis of 1997 was among the most severe. While it experienced significant difficulties following the 1997 crisis, its macroeconomic recovery was nevertheless unexpectedly rapid, regaining growth momentum to once again lead regional and global growth. There have been, however, fundamental differences with the past in the underlying factors that drive the Asian economy further into the 21st century.

As discussed in Part I of this book, Asia is now a major player as a producer, consumer, recipient of investment, and investor. One of the crucial differences that divides this century from the previous one is the overwhelming significance of China, which has been a major catalyst for a much of the drastic change that we see today in the Asian economy.

Specifically, many countries in Asia were, during the catch-up phase, dependent on developed countries outside the region for capital and intermediate goods, funds (investments), technology, and information. Innovation originating from Asia is, as mentioned, now becoming active, and the rise of its market has made it become a prime target for businesses. Such fundamental and qualitative changes have further prompted and enhanced quantitative expansions of the Asian economy globally, which in turn are further inducing qualitative changes.

The traditional approach to the study of the Asian economy was primarily country based. However, considering these interrelated complexities, such an approach would fail to capture the essence underlying the dynamics of the Asian economy. The limitations of such a nation-state based approach stem from the following two issues. The first is related to the increasing roles enterprises and cities play in the organization of the contemporary Asian economy, particularly in the configuration of international production and distribution networks. These have led to multi-layered connections, linking different dimensions of Asia. The second is the compressed development processes that have led to drastic changes in development patterns. The following sections will attempt to interpret the Asian economic dynamics with focuses on "connectivity" and "compressed development."

C.1 THE ASIAN ECONOMY IN AN ERA OF INTERNATIONAL CONNECTIVITY

Countries in Asia have started to connect at various levels, within the region and beyond. This is the result of the increased international mobility of goods, funds, people, and information. Part II of this book (Borderless Asia) has particularly discussed such cross-border flows in great detail, which serve as the basis of ongoing Asian dynamism. It is this increasing connectivity that lies at the heart of the Asian economy of this century.

The various types of interconnectedness that continue to shape Asia evolved from the strategic behavior of individuals and corporations attempting to dynamically maximize utilities or profits. While such *de-facto* mechanisms have been key to connectivity, they have also occurred within a *de-jure* context that made establishing linkages increasingly easy.

As discussed in Chapters 2 and 4, one of the most important features of globalization and economic integration is the expanding and deepening global value chains that are progressing most intensively in Asia. Trade and investment liberalization in the 20th century was, needless to say, crucial to the development of these global value chains. However, the defining factor was the rapidly diffusing internet and related technologies reaching literally into every corner of Asia, which significantly reduced service link costs. The latest news from London or Chicago can now be accessed instantly from Laos or Cambodia at virtually zero marginal cost. This is of course not limited to countries in Asia, but the multinational enterprises that configure value chains across the region have utilized this new infrastructure actively and strategically, which has led to the current complex and sophisticated forms of regional economic integration. This in turn has further prompted intra-regional mobility of goods, services, and factors of production. It was such *de-facto* dynamics that led to the ongoing expansion and deepening of international connectedness, which also strengthened information, infrastructure, and human networks beyond borders.

In this process, cities have evolved as major nodes in global value chains, connecting and agglomerating the fragmented processes and functions that are highly dispersed geographically. Growth strategies must now inevitably include scenarios to increase the connectivity of cities, as successful economic upgrading necessarily entails processes and functions that are of higher value-added. Such cities often stand out from other regions within the country, in many cases to an extent that they can exercise much stronger political influence at the overall nation-state level, and also exert influence over Asian economic dynamism.

The Asian economy in the 21st century can no longer be understood, or its essence be captured, by treating it as a collection of individual countries. It is crucial to look at the forms and characteristics of these connections, as well as the nodes, to understand it as an organically evolving system. The assessment of current challenges as well as future outlooks can no longer be analyzed or assessed from an individual country perspective – it should be interpreted in a wider regional context.

C.2 COMPRESSED DEVELOPMENT AND REGIONAL CHALLENGES

The growth characteristics of Asia in the 21st century have also changed drastically from those of the 20th century. Regional development in the previous century occurred systematically according to the flying geese model, where intra-regional structural transformation followed a particular hierarchical pattern based on income levels. "Compressed development" is a useful concept to understand what underpins such a change.

Rapid economic development in Asia has been presenting those countries with the associated challenges related to industrial and social changes, which in the past unfolded and were observed primarily in developed countries. The time-frame within which these events progressed has also shortened significantly, and hence the expression "compressed." In the 20th century, "compressed development" meant that developing countries were catching up rapidly on more developed ones by harnessing the "latecomer's advantage." In the 21st century, however, developing countries are no longer just catching-up, but in some cases are "leap-frogging" to go ahead of those that previously were running in front of them. At the same time, social issues and problems like those observed in more developed countries have been emerging in late-coming, developing countries in Asia too.

With respect to the leap-frogging on the economy side, there have been cases in which local firms in Asia have achieved successful upgrading in a very short time, as the case of the Taiwanese PC industry indicates. This was achieved by complementarities between the strategies of firms from both advanced and developing countries, as well as the division of labor among these firms according to fragmentation dynamics. As discussed in Chapter 7, leap-frogging has occurred particularly in relation to digitized technologies, where the growth and future potentialities of innovation have become significant in Asia. The economic order of Asia is now increasingly multi-polar and can no longer be described in relation to the levels of development. Unlike in the past, the Asian economy is led not just by corporations or investors from developed countries, but also by those from developing countries. Accelerated digitalization and "servicification" of the economy will further induce such multi-polarizing trends.

From a more social perspective, changes have been taken place at the same time as the systems to address the associated challenges have remained premature. Parts III and IV of this book both discussed key issues and the associated risks in relation to those emerging issues caused by compressed development.

For example, the emergence and rapid growth of mega cities is one of such leap-frogging phenomena observed in almost all of the countries in Asia. The central areas of these mega cities resemble those of the mega cities in more developed countries; the life-styles of those living in Bangkok are much closer to those in Singapore or Seoul than to those in secondary cities such as Chiang Mai or other rural areas. When these cities can successfully trigger agglomeration (Chapter 7) and increasing returns dynamics (Chapter 8), there is a good chance that this could pave the way for local innovation. On the other hand, the development of such cities could also exacerbate common issues such as informalization, growing inequality, and environmental problems.

The social problems that were once unique to developed countries have started to appear in middle-income countries as well. Ageing populations have, for instance, evolved as a major social issue in the late 1990s in Japan; however, this is also a potential issue for other countries as well, where in Korea and soon in China the speed of ageing is expected to surpass that of Japan, as discussed in Chapter 10. This could present these countries with much more difficult problems, primarily because, unlike Japan, social security systems are not fully available there yet. Similar issues have arisen with respect to rising inequality and environmental problems. The fact that most governments in Asia are financially constrained makes these issues even more difficult to address.

C.3 THE FUTURE OUTLOOK FOR THE ASIAN ECONOMY – COMPETING AND CO-EXISTING

The ability to enhance competitiveness within mutually dependent, symbiotic relationships determines the possibilities of sustainable development in the Asian economy. Upgrading of core competences as defined through international fragmentation dynamics is the key tactic of a grand strategy where collective efficiency underlies competitiveness in 21st century globalization. Deepening connectivity as such, on the other hand, will also further induce socio-economic interdependence at the regional level, which trends will only be enforced as multinational enterprises and cities increase their positions as key nodes in global value chains.

Given these evolving dynamics, the roles of nation states have also undergone transformations particularly to ensure sustainability in their future development trajectories.

Most of the countries and economies in Asia gained independence from colonialism after World War II. The key challenges to these countries in the wake of independence were related to state-building, in which addressing poverty issues through economic development was key. Import substituting industrialization and export promotion policies were actively pursued with the aim of advancing the competitiveness of their own industries. State leadership was crucial particularly in deciding target sectors ("picking the winners") to be promoted with high priority.

Japan is one such country that achieved post-war growth through these active, state-led industrial policies, through which it has successfully transformed its economic structure from labor intensive towards capital intensive activities, and ultimately towards technology and knowledge intensive ones during the course of rapid economic growth. The time when all of the production processes were contained within a country's borders has gone, however, and international comparative advantages are determined based on the economics of fragmented processes and functions. The prospects of inclusion in global value chains, and the development trajectories of firms and local industries, are now entirely dependent on the strategic decisions of lead firms that configure these value chains, in which nation states play only limited roles. In addition, these lead firms are typically foreign firms.

While this book has emphasized the centrality of the multinational enterprises led "*de-facto*" integration in Asia, it does not intend to downplay the important roles of nation states in this process. One of the main reasons why MNEs were able to lead regional economic integration is because governments in this region guaranteed a relatively free and safe international economic environment. The provision of economic and social infrastructure such as ports, roads, electricity, legal frameworks, and education systems were solely catered for by nation states, all of which contributed to strengthening and deepening cross-border connectivity. The fact that no massive military conflict has broken out since the end of the Vietnam War should also be remembered as one major factor behind regional prosperity. Nation states were indispensable actors in the provision of such "public goods."

However, the roles of states, and the contents of "public goods" provided, are also rapidly shifting into new dimensions. In addition to the provision of direct support to industries through, for instance, granting preferential treatment and encouraging investments in R&D, policies that promote building "social capabilities" to connect to "others" beyond borders will become important in the future.

Increased connectivity, however, may also transmit negative effects through these networks. Financial crises or natural disasters influence remote places through these connections almost instantly. Increased international mobility of people could also lead to the spread of infectious diseases, terrorism, and criminal activities. The ability of states to manage these evolving risks will become crucial in the near future.

One of the biggest concerns in relation to increased connectivity is to ensure that the fruits of growth are distributed more equally among the domestic populace. As discussed in Chapters 8 and 11, growing income inequality is among the most worrisome symptoms that may compromise the sustainability of the Asian economy. Growth in one part of the economy does not automatically trickle down to the periphery and the marginalized. While the spread of the internet and related technologies have connected people through the cyberspace, their livelihoods are still embedded in physical localities. When increased connectivity intensifies competition, this may put even those living in remote areas at greater risk. People who are affected by these risks tend to suffer for a much longer period. For instance, the Korean government in 2013 announced a rescue package for those who were still suffering with debt repayments related to the financial crisis of 1997. The 16 years that had elapsed since then were still not enough for many to recover fully from the Asian crisis. New roles of nation states should include the better management of the evolving risks due to increased connectivity, and the building of resilient societies. The realization of a sustainable and prosperous Asia is highly dependent on how nations can promote inclusive and participatory development processes and suggest roadmaps to co-exist.

In connection to this, one of the important issues, which is not fully addressed in this book, is related to international/regional governance: how should countries in Asia respond *collectively* to those newly emerging challenges that expand and deepen beyond borders? What sort of regional, or global governance mechanisms would be most effective and acceptable, in which connectivity plays out in win-win outcomes for all? These could be new and exciting areas on which future research efforts are awaited.

CONCLUSION: JAPAN IN THE 21ST CENTURY ASIA

Japan is at the crossroads; its position in Asia is drastically changing, reflecting the larger dynamics of Asia in the 21st century. Asia's post-war development was, to some extent, led by Japan. Prior to the publication of *The East Asian Miracle* in 1993, Japan was the focus when it came to discussions related to the Asian economy. One of such examples is *Japan as Number One: Lessons for America*, by Harvard University sociologist Ezra Vogel, published in 1979 (Vogel, 1979). The post-war era from the 1950s to the latter part of the 1980s was in fact "Japan's era."

As the world entered the 21st century, however, Japan's leadership position in some of the key industries underwent significant changes. For example, when the Japanese car manufacturer Nissan experienced severe hardships in the late 1990s, it resulted in a bailout by the French automotive giant Renault. In electronics, some of the leading electronics companies such as Sharp and Toshiba Lifestyle Products and Services Corporation (the white goods division of Toshiba) were acquired by Taiwan's Hong Hai Precision (Foxconn) and China's Midea in the 2010s, respectively.

Mergers and Acquisitions (M&A) of domestic companies by foreign ones are a major form of foreign direct investment (FDI). While Japan has been one of the most prominent global investors, its inbound FDI remains quite limited. The Japanese government, as a response, has stepped-up efforts to attract more FDI; however, most major M&A projects have been received with much negative publicity. Nevertheless, as dynamics of the Asian economy are underpinned by key factors such as "compressed development" and "connectivity," such phenomena are natural outcomes of rational decision making, and thus inevitable. A new strategic framework will become crucial, acknowledging, and accommodating the evolving factors that underlie the dynamics of the Asian economy.

Reflecting these changes, Japan needs to urgently re-consider the way it has been connecting to others in Asia, which should entail a fundamental shift from a unidirectional towards a bidirectional approach. This is most likely a social capability issue. Japan's closedness is often referred to as a major bottleneck hampering the operations of potential foreign investors. The *keiretsu*, an exclusive and rigid inter-firm set of relationships are typical examples. These "Japanese ways of doing businesses" may have been effective when Japan was coordinating value chains by applying its own management systems, leading economic growth in Asia. However, there could come a time when such traditional, Japan-centered approaches reach their limits, and could actually be detrimental to promoting the further growth of the Japanese economy. Japan must better understand that it is also part of a dynamically connecting and evolving Asia.

From such a perspective, the implication for Asia is that these new types of social capabilities would have to encompass bolstering connectivity at both the individual as well as the broader community levels in order to embrace diversity, while effectively managing the risks involved to maximize positive returns. To achieve this, governments, as the executive branches of nation states, should go beyond the provision of physical infrastructure, and invest in developing human capabilities which facilitate better connectivity with "others."

In the 21st-century Asian economy, co-existing through symbiotic relationships will be the key. New challenges will emerge, for which the solutions must be provided by future generations such as some of the readers of this book. Challenges typically can lead to new opportunities, if addressed wisely through collective efforts.

REFERENCE

Vogel, Ezra F. (1979). *Japan as Number One: Lessons for America*, Cambridge, MA: Harvard University Press.

Index

Note: **Bold** page numbers refer to tables; *italic* page numbers refer to figures and page numbers followed by "n" denote endnotes.

Abdullah, A. J. 216
Abe, Shinzo 229
absolute poverty 210, 221, 227, 230n1
Accumulated-Debt Problem 92, 96
ADB *see* Asian Development Bank (ADB)
ad-hoc status-quo policy 121
AFTA *see* ASEAN Free Trade Area (AFTA)
aged society 201, 206, 219
ageing rate 199, 201–202, **202**
ageing society 22, 134, 163, 180, 192, 199, 201, 207
agglomeration 57, 98, 134, 138, 156
agricultural employment ratio 198, *198*
agricultural workers 130, 180, 202, 203, 205, 225
AIIB *see* Asian Infrastructure Investment Bank (AIIB)
air pollution, in China 235–236
Alibaba 63, 142, 166
Ali-Yrkkö, Jyrki 97n4
antagonism 228–230
anti-chlorine campaign 243
apparel industry 74, 77; export-oriented 75, 178; Thailand('s) 178; opportunities and challenges of 90; Vietnam(ese) 70, 74–75, 86–87, 93–94, 178, 179, 182
artificial intelligence (AI) 124, 139, 141, 144
ASEAN *see* Association of Southeast Asian Nations (ASEAN)
ASEAN Agreement on Transboundary Haze Pollution (2002) 246
ASEAN-China economic cooperation framework 42
ASEAN-China Free Trade Agreement (ACFTA) 42
ASEAN Economic Community (AEC) 29–30, 42, 122
ASEAN Free Trade Area (AFTA) 29, 41
ASEAN-Korea Free Trade Agreement 42

Asia: declining birth rates in 194, **195**; economic growth in 19, 42; economic integration in 5, 29, 30; economic order of 253; economic relations and interdependencies within 23; environmental Kuznets curve in 238–240, *239–242*; export-oriented growth in 32; foreign capital and 94–95; foreign population in 115, *116*, **116**, 117; global capital and financial environment and 100–101; in global trade evolution 30–31, **31**; income inequality in 217; industrialization in 19, 82–85; international migration in 109–110 (*see also* international migration); intra-regional trade in 37, *38*; Kuznets hypothesis and 212, 215–216, *216*; as major regional market 40–41; policy challenges for 102–104; population growth in 110; post-war reconstruction of 14–15; poverty reduction in 210–212, *211*; rise of 82; rising inequality in 212, **213–214,** *215*; risks and opportunities in middle-income 22; social protection policies in 202–204, **203**; stagnation and underdevelopment in 15–16; structural changes of capital flows in 98, *99*, 100; sustained growth in 22
Asian century 2, 130, 147, 250–251
Asian Development Bank (ADB) 2, 41, 92, 102, 157, 174, 210, 217, 222
Asian Drama: An Inquiry into the Poverty of Nations (Myrdal) 16
Asian economy 1, 5–9, 23; characteristics of **2–4,** *2–5*; era of international connectivity 251–252; future outlook for 253–255; from historical perspective 24–25; miracle and crisis of 20
Asian entrepreneurs, in Silicon Valley 124–125
Asian Financial Cooperation 103–104

Index

Asian financial crisis 13, 19, 23, 87–88, 95–97, 100, 106, 133, 178, 182, 250; East Asia, success story 18–19; financial system reform 102–103; neoclassical era 19–20; in Southeast Asia 88; in Thailand 29; to WTO 35–37
Asian Four Tigers 16
Asian Infrastructure Investment Bank (AIIB) 63, 102
Asianizing Asia 28–30, 35, 40, 72, 84
Asian monetary cooperation 103–104
Asian Newly Industrializing Economies (Asian NIEs) 13, 16, 17, 22, 23, 49, 71, 83, 84, 112, 134; and catch-up industrialization 130–131; export-oriented growth 20; export-oriented industrial pattern of 143; industrialization patterns in 18, 56; rise of 31–32
Asian production network 21, 54–56, **55**
Asian regional FTAs 41–42
Association of Southeast Asian Nations (ASEAN) 29, 41, 151, 221; centrality of 41–42; and China trade relationships 37; free movement of high-skilled workers 122–123; income inequality in 221–222, 223, 224; international migration 112–113; into regional triangular trade structure 34
authoritarian 18, 23, 60, 142

backwardness 238, 247; advantage of 17; and environmental issues 234–235
Bakrie Group 98
balance of payment 95; capital flows and 89–91
Balassa, Bela 18, 44
Bandung Conference 14
Barro, Robert 216
beautiful neighbor activity 205
Belt and Road Initiative (BRI) 59, 63, 102
bilateral FTAs 30
bilateral trade agreements 42
birth control policies 193–194
birth rates, decline in 192, 194, **195**
Bloom, David 195
bond market development 103–104
brain circulation, in Silicon Valley 124–125
Bretton Woods system 91
Broad Economic Categories (BEC) classification 45
brown agenda 235, 237, 238, 241, 245, 246
buyer-driven value chains 73–75

capital 88; Asian financial crisis 95–97; challenges 101–102; demand for 114; distribution of 227; financial environment and Asia 100–101; migrant workers and 114; structural change in 2000 97–100
capital flows: in Asia, structural changes of 98, 99, 100; and balance of payments 89–91, 90; for Thailand 98, 99

capitalism 228, crony capitalism 35, state capitalism 59, mass capitalism 60
capital mobility 91–95
capital stock 88, 92, 196, 197, 199
capital transactions 89; inflow and outflow of foreign funds 90
Castells, Manuel 173
catch-up industrialization 1, 5, 19, 34, 42–43, 130–134, 144, 237; primary and secondary education 134
cheap labor 17, 36, 53, 74, 77, 143, 164–165
Chiang Kai-shek 18
Chiang Mai Initiative (CMI) 20, 103–104
Chiashi, A. 235
China: accession to WTO 35–37, 41–42, 55; ageing ratio in 201, **202**; air pollution in 235–236; as assembly factory 54–56, **55**; in Asian and global economy 57–59; characteristics and limitations of planned economy 50–52, 51; demographic dividends 198; distance and income disparity in 117, 119; economic growth of 36–37, 49, 49, 51, 51, 60–62, 61, 133–134; economic transition toward market economy 52–53, 53; employment opportunities in 225; female migrants from 118, 119; Five Guarantees in 230n7; fixed exchange rate policy 107n1; GDP in 54; Gini coefficient of 220; income inequality in 220–221; industrial clusters in 138–139; industrial development based on domestic market 56; industrialization in coastal region of 56–57; industrial sector of 198; informal economy in 177; innovation policy in 141–142; Lewis turning point argument 56–57; national emission trade system 248; one-child policy 193; opening-up policy 53–54; production networks, and regional economic integration 20–22; rapid urbanization in 148; regional and global economy 18; regional division of labor 37, 38; research and development of 58, 136; rise of 2, 20–22; short-term credit transaction 107; state capitalism and mass capitalism in 59–60; Three Nos in 230n7; trade policies of 42; unicorn companies in 145; urban inflow in 154; urbanization rate in 166; as the workshop of the world 54
China threat 21, 36–37
chlorine-free pulp 243
City Cluster Development report 157
civil war 52, 94
cluster theory 157
CMI *see* Chiang Mai Initiative (CMI)
Coastal Region Opening Strategy 54
CO_2 emission 238, 239, 240, 240–241
Cold War 14, 15, 41, 49
collective-owned enterprises 53
Communist Party of China (CPC) 59–60, 229
compounded pollutions 235

compressed development 4, 158, 210, 225, 252–253
compressed economic development 227, 233, 247
compressed urbanization 150, 161, 163
connectivity 63, 87, 157, 251–256
conventional demographic transition model 192
corporate social responsibility (CSR) 96–97
Council of Mutual Economic Assistance (COMECON) framework 87
cross-borderization 245–247
cross-border movements 110
cross-border trade 72, 73
Cultural Revolution 51
cumulative investment 184
currency: foreign 20, 71, 90–91, 94–96; GDP growth rates 3, **4**; management of 91; supply and demand of 90; Thai Baht 19, 95, 96
currency cooperation framework 104
currency mismatch 104
current transaction 89–90

Davis, Kingsley 151
Decent Work 96, 97
de-chlorination 243, 244
Dedrick, Jason 93
de-facto economic integration 5, 6, 21, 23, 29, 30, 44, 250, 252, 254; and global value chains 35–41; opportunities, and challenges 41–44, **43**
deforestation process 236–237
de-jure economic integration 5. 6. 21, 23, 29, 41, 42, 44, 251
democracy 228–230
demographic dividend 131, 138, 194–197, *196, 197,* 199; and ageing-population ratio 199, *200,* 206
demographic-friendly policies 197
demographic tax 192, 199, 205, 206
demographic transition 192, *193,* 194; economic policies with 197–198, *198*
Deng Xiaoping 52, 54
dependency theory 15, 23
Detert, Neal 97n4
developmentalism 18, 48, 235, 237, 247
digital divide 138
digital hardware products, exports of 70
digitalization 7, 134, 144, 183, 253: of economy 137, 144; investments in 136–138, *137*
disguised unemployment 171
Doi Moi policy 75, 83
dollar–yen exchange rate 33
domestic economy 14, 31, 46, 57, 89–91, 94, 95, 100, 121
domestic market 31, 54, 75, 90, 145; expansion of 22, 72, 84; industrial development based on 56, 78; substantial potentialities of 50

double mismatch 104
Douglass, Michael 157
dual backwardness 234–235, 237, 247
duration mismatch 104
Duterte, Rodrigo 229

East Asian Economic Community 44
East Asian Miracle 1, 18–20, 24, 35, 134, 197, 210–212, *211,* 227, 255
East Asia: economy in 58; exports of 82; labor force in 24–25; success story of 18–19
e-commerce (EC) 40, 63, 142, 144, 166
economic crisis 19–21, 229, 244
economic development 154, 158; and CO_2 emission 238, *239, 240,* 240–241; defined as 151; and environmental problems 237–242; patterns of 154; and PM2.5 exposure 238, 241, *241;* through urban sector 171
economic disparity 15, 153–154, 159, 210
economic growth 32, 224; after Asian financial crisis 133–134; in Asia 19, 42; of China 36–37, 49, *49,* 133–134; declining birth rates 194, **195**; innovation in 134–139; issues on 186n3; of Korea 131; in post-war Asia 29; poverty trap and birth control policies 193–194; rapid population growth 192, *193;* role of capital in 88, *89;* rural-urban migration and 151; of Thailand 133–134; total factor productivity in 197
economic integration 30, 251–252; of ASEAN 122; forms of 44; process of 82
Economic Partnership Agreements (EPAs) 42
Economic Planning Institute of South Korea 18
economic takeoff theory 15
elderly population 201, 206–207
electronic products, production locations for **55,** 55–56
electronics industry 58, 125, 138, 139
emerging Asia 20–22
emission trade systems (ETS) 248
employment: agricultural 198; casualization 210; informal 175, *175,* 176, **176,** 177, 180; in informal economy 4, 171–172; labor and 84, 85; irregular 182, 183, 217, 219; of migrant workers 120–123; source of 8; in Thailand 72, 120
employment permit system 121
environmental Kuznets curve *237,* 237–238, 247; in Asia 238–240, *239–242;* and issues of focus 240–241
environmental pollution 235–237
environmental problems 234, 247; backwardness and environmental issues diversity 234–235; economic development and 237–242; environmental pollution and destruction 235–237
EPAs *see* Economic Partnership Agreements (EPAs)
e-pay 166

equality 8, 224–226
equity financing 105, 106
Estrada, Joseph 229
EU crisis 29
Euro-centric historical views 24
Europe: decline in economic performance 29; large scale monetary in 101–102
European Economic Community (EEC) 41
European Union (EU) 29; intra-regional trade in 37, *38*
export: in Asia 30–31, **31**; from China 37; commodities of 82, **83**; of digital hardware products 82; in East Asia 82; shares to US 32, *33*; of textile products 32
export-oriented industrialization 17, 23, 54, 120, 133, 197
export processing zones (EPZs) 31, 148, 154

Factory Asia 22, 69–70, 83–84
FDI-based foreign companies 98
financial channels 105–107
financial factors, Asian Financial Crisis 19–20
financial intermediation 106–107
financial sector 20, 60, 96–98, 100–105
financial system reform 102–103, 105, 107n4
Five Guarantees 230n7
fixed exchange rate system 91, 92, 95, 96
floating exchange rate system 95
Flying Geese Model 19, 21, 34, 252
flying geese pattern *35*, 36, 43, 75, 87, 252; domestic 57
foreign capital 104–105; and Asia 94–95; inflow of 100; *see also* international capital flows
foreign currency 20, 71, 90–91, 94–96
foreign direct investment (FDI) 21, 31, 33, 40, 59, 71–72, 89, 98, 138, 143, 154, 255
foreign exchange regimes 96
foreign exchange reserves 95, 107n3
Foreign Labor Act (1978) 120
foreign labor, demand and supply of 112–113, 115, 121
foreign migrant workers 162
foreign population: in Singapore and Hong Kong 118, **120**; trends of 115, *116*, **116**, 117; *see also* international migration
forest depletion, in Indonesia 236–237
forest destruction 243–244
forest fires 245–246
Formal and Informal Labor Force Market Survey 177
formal economy 8, 170, 173, 179, 180, 183
formal employment 177; informalization of 182, 183
fourth-generation (4G) communication infrastructure 137, 138
fragmentation 73, 83, 156, 253; theory 39, *39*, 85

free markets 50–51
free trade agreements (FTAs) 5, 21, 29; in Asia 41; geographical expansion of 44

Geertz, Clifford 16
General Agreement on Tariffs and Trade (GATT) 29, 41
General Agreement on Trade in Services (GATS) 41
geographic distance, international migration 113
Gereffi, Gary 73, 74
Germany: Industry 4.0 plan 141, 143; Kuznets hypothesis 215
Gerschenkron, Alexander 17
getting old before getting rich phenomenon 60–62
Gini coefficient 212, **213–214**, 224, 230n3, 230n4; of China 220; of Japan *218*, 218–219, 229; of Malaysia 221; of Thailand 221–222, 225
global financial crisis (2008) 13–14, 59, 60, 101, 141, 178
globalization 1, 7, 8, 13, 18, 20, 23, 44, 49, 70, 154, 155, 157, 164, 173, 181, 197, 210, 217, 222, 225, 227, 245, 251–252, 253; of environment 234; of informal economy 177–178; informal economy redefining under 174; process of 82
global manufacturing hub 2, 81
Global Positioning Systems (GPS) 138
global production networks, era of 72–73
global value chains (GVCs) 17, 35–41, 44, 82, 140, 251–254; and corporate social responsibility 84–85; implications from framework 81–83; industrial clusters and mega-cities in 156–157; local industries and firms in 74–75; mega-cities 148, *155*, 155–156; mega-regions evolution 157–158; perspectives of 73–74; proliferation of 83; Taiwanese notebook PC industry 78–80; Vietnamese apparel industry 74–78
Going Global program 59
Go-Jek 145
gold-dollar dual standard regime 91
The Great Divergence (Pomeranz) 24
Great East Japan Earthquake (2011) 21
Great Leap Forward 51
green agenda 235, 237–239, 241, 245–247
gross domestic product (GDP) 131, *133*; of Asia 40; of Asian economy **2–4,** 2–5; of China 54; expenditure compositions of Thailand and Indonesia **97,** 97–98; of Japan 49
gross regional product (GRP) per capita *155*, 155–156
growth accounting 131, **132,** 133, *133*, 195
Gulden, Timothy 158

Hara, Kakuten 15
hard line approach 246
Harmonious Society 224
Harmonized Commodity Description and Coding Systems (HS) classification 45
Harris–Todaro model 151, 171
haze pollution 245–246
Haze Pollution Act (2014) 246
Heckscher-Ohlin model 37, 70, 72
Helleiner, Gerald 17
high-income country 44 ; policy responses and prospects in 226
high-skilled workers, free movement of 122–123
home-based work 179
home-based workers 170, 181
Hong Kong: African merchants in 182; elderly population in 201; female migrants from 118, *119*, **120**; foreign population in 115, *116*, **116**, 117, 118, **120**; urbanization rate in 148
household registration system 153, 154, 177, 198, 221
human capital 18, 52, 89, 123, 134–136, **135,** *136*, 140, 157, 161
Human Society 25
100-million middle class society 217

ILO *see* International Labour Organization (ILO)
import: in Asia 30–31, **31**, 40; China 37, 40, 56; commodities of Taiwan and South Korea 70, **71**; SITC classification 45
import-inducing export structures 20, 23
import substitution industrialization (ISI) 15, 31, 254
income distribution 212, *215*, 217, 226
income inequality: in ASEAN 221–222, *223*, *224*, 254; in Asia 217; in China 220–221; growth of 227; in Japan 217–219, *218*, 226
India: brain circulation 125; economy of 1; entrepreneurs and engineers 124; industrialization in 24, 25; foreign population in 112; FTA with 42
Indonesia: financial system reform 103; forest depletion in 236–237; forest destruction 244; GDP expenditure compositions of **97,** 97–98; inequality in 222; informal economy in 178; multi-ethnic 229
Indonesian Rupiah 19
industrial clusters 138–139, 155; in global value chains 156–157
industrialization 17, 148, 250; in Asia 19; in Asian NIEs 31–32; of China 220; and cities as production centers 154–155; in coastal region of China 56–57; of developing countries 16; era of foreign direct investment (1980) 71–72; era of global production networks (2000) 72–73; era of international trade (1970) 70; initial stages of 227; in Japan and India 25; pattern of 56; primary and secondary education 134; social security system 203
industrial products, shares of 33, *34*
Industrial Revolution 24
industrial sector: capital investment in 215; of China 198
Industrial Training and Technical Internship Program 123
inequality 210; and democracy 228–230; in Latin America 211–212; of opportunity 222; rise of 212, **213–214,** *215*
informal economy 22, 130, 151, 169–170, 186n1, 186n5; birth and views of 171–172; defined as 170; dichotomy approach 172–174; employment in 4; expansion of 178; from formal to informal 182; globalization, urbanization, and dynamism of 177–178; ILO 170, 172, 180; informality and institutions 180–181; internationalization of 181–182; positive dimensions of 179; problems of 183; redefining under globalization 174; relationship with poverty 179; roles and functions of 178–180; size and trends of *175*, 175–177, **176**
informal employment 175, *175*, **176,** 177, 180
informality 170, 173–175, 180–185, 186n4
informalization 4, 178, 181, 226, 253; of formal employment 182, 183
informal residential areas 184–185
informal sector 171, 172, 176, 186n1, 186n4
information and communication technology (ICT) 205–206
information technology (IT) industry 221
innovation 2, 7, 22, 23, 58, 62, 84, 96, 114, 124, 129–130, 134–135, 138–145, 156, 158, 198–199, 238, 247, 251; human capital and research and development 134–136, **135,** *136*; industrial clusters and networks 138–139; investments 136–138, *137*
innovation-centered growth 22
innovation policy: China 141–142; foundations of 140–141, *140*; Thailand 142–144
input-induced growth structure 20
institutional factors, Asian Financial Crisis 20
institutional/organizational approach 18–19
institution-based integration 29
inter-industry trade 21
internalization, of externalities 234, 248
international capital flows: and balance of payments 89–91, *90*; changes in 92, *93*, *94*; and growth 88–89, *89*; post-war monetary and financial order and capital mobility 91–95; *see also* foreign capital
international capital mobility 88, 95
International Conference of Labour Statisticians 177

international division of labor 5, 7, 16–19, 20, 21, 23, 37, 39–40, 49, 53, 70, 81, 84, 156
internationalization 63, 102, 234; of informal economy 181–182
International Labour Organization (ILO) 84, 85, 170, 172, 180, 224
international migration: benefits and costs of 113–114; changes in labor demand 117–118, *119*, **120**; demand and supply of foreign labor 112–113; distance and income disparity roles in 117, *118*, *119*; feminization in 117–118, *119*, **120**; trends in *111*, 111–112, **112**; *see also* foreign population
International Monetary Fund (IMF) 91, 97, 102, 244
international NGOs 243, 244
international outsourcing 72; growth of 73
international transactions 89
international vertical division of labor 39, 39–40
interprovincial disparities 221
interregional disparities, rise of 220
inter-regional inequality 158–161, *159*, *160*, 161, **165**
interregional wage inequality 225
intra-Asian trade 21, 24, 62
intra-industry trade 21; industrialization and expansion of 72
intra-regional division of labor 37
intra-regional export 35, *36*
intra-regional trade 30, 42, 72, 104; in Asia 37, *38*; in European Union 37, *38*; in NAFTA 37, *38*; structure of 34
investment 88–89; in IT capital and digitalization 136–138, *137*; liberalization of 122; repayment for 91
irregular employment 182, 183, 217, 219
irregular workers 182
ISI *see* import substitution industrialization (ISI)
IT capital investments 136–138, *137*
Itoga, J. 172

Japan: ageing in 201; apparel industry 75; Asian consumer markets 164–166, **165**; economic development 210; economic growth 30; economic partnership 42, **43**; environmental pollution 234; female migrants from 118, *119*; foreign population in 115, *116*, 117; GDP in 49; Gini coefficient of *218*, 218–219, 226; income inequality in 217–219, *218*, 226; industrial clusters in 138, *139*; industrialization in 25; industrialization patterns of 106; industrial structures changes in 32; international competitiveness of 34–35, *35*; manufacturing sector to ASEAN countries 33; post-war reconstruction of 14–15, 254; poverty in 219; regional and systemic growth 1; research and development of 136; rise of 29; social challenges 22; trade policies of 42; in 21st century Asia 255–256; unicorn companies in 145; urbanization rate in 148
Japan Bank for International Cooperation (JBIC) 21, 164
Japan International Cooperation Agency (JICA) 205

Kanbur, Ravi 217
Kenya: ILO Employment mission 171; informal sector in 174; report 174, 182
Khanthanavit, Anya 107n4
knowledge-intensive functions, apparel industry 77
Komiya, Ryutaro 52
Korean War 52
Krugman, Paul 20, 131, 133
Kuznets hypothesis 212, 215–216, *216*

labor 88, 186n3; income distribution of 227; re-allocation of 110; share of income 217; shortages of 121
Labor Contract Law (2009) 177
labor demand 114, 121, 220; in Asia 115; changes in 117–118, *119*, **120**; role of 113
labor force 24–25, 57, 164, 196–199, 227; participation rate 196
labor-intensive industry 19, 25, 34–35, *35*, 122
labor market 56–57, 110, 114, 124, 171, 179, 182; structural change in 56–57
labor migration 109–110, 198, 215
land finance 62
lead firm 75, 77, 81, 254
leap-frogging 43, 252
Lee Hsien Loong 144
Lehman shock 101, 104
Lewis, Arthur 56–57, 151, 171
Lewis turning point 56–57, 220
liberalization: economic 54; of international labor migration 123–124; investment 122, 251; policies 29; trade 3, 41–42, 122, 251
life expectancy 199, 201
low-income equilibrium trap 16, 193

macro-economy 170, 174, 179
Made in China 2025 plan 141–142
Maddison, Angus 24
Malaysia: distance and income disparity in 117, *119*; exports commodities of 70, **71**; female migrants from 118, *119*; fixed exchange rate policy 107n1; foreign population in 115, *116*, 117; Gini coefficients of 221
Maloney, William 173
Malthus 192
Mao Zedong 50–52
market-friendly approach 18
Marshall Plan 92
Marukawa, Tomoo 60

Mason, Andrew 194
mass entrepreneurship and innovation initiative 142
matrix 176–177
mega-cities 6, 22, 148, 150, 155, *155*, 155–156, 164, 166n1, 221, 235; challenges of 161–162; emergence and rapid growth of 253; in global value chains 156–157
mega-regions 6, 148, 150, 161; evolution of 157–158; and inter-regional inequalities 158–161, *159,* *160,* 161, **165**; socio-political risks and policy dilemmas in *162,* 162–163
micro-organizational finance systems, issues in 105–107
middle-income countries 163, 164, 182, 185, 245; ageing in 202; income distribution of 212, *215*; policy responses and prospects for 225–230
middle income group 156
middle-income trap 2, 22, 44, 62, 78, 130–134, 141, 142, 162, 163, 180
migrant workers: and capital 114; in China 154; demand and supply of 115, 123; high-skilled 122; inflow of 114; language training for 121; outcomes for 114; unskilled 120
Millennium Development Goals (MDGs) 22, 204
mobile payment systems 58
modern economics 224
modularization 39, 40, 80
mortality rates 192
multinational enterprises (MNEs) 3, 17, 29, 72, 84, 148, 154, 155, 163
Multinational Enterprises and Social Policy (MNE Declaration) 96
Myanmar: FDI to 72; secondary education in 134; workers from 120–121
Myrdal, Gunnar: *Asian Drama: An Inquiry into the Poverty of Nations* 16

Nakanishi, T. 172
National Economic and Social Development Plan: Seventh (1992) 173–174; of Thailand (2001–2006) 143; 3rd 154
national emission trade system 248
neoclassical approach 18
neoliberalism 173, 228
Newly Industrializing Countries (NICs) 16, 48
Newly Industrializing Economies (NIEs) *see* Asian Newly Industrializing Economies (Asian NIEs)
Nikkei China Related Stock 50 index 58
non-IT capital investments 137
North American Free Trade Agreement (NAFTA) 30, 37, *38,* 41
North–South problem 15
notebook PC industry, Taiwan 78–81; distribution of value 81–82; upgrading in value chains 80–81
Nurkse, Ragnar 193

Ohtake, Fumio 221
opening-up policy 35, 53–54, 154, 220
Organisation for Economic Co-operation and Development (OECD) 15, 175, 182, 198, 216
outward economic growth strategies 17
outward-looking growth policy 16
over-urbanization 148, 150–153, **152,** *153*; policies to 153–154

Palma, Jose Gabriel 216
The Paris Agreement 247
Park Chung-hee 18
Pasuk, P. 172
patron–client relationships 172
payment for environmental services (PES) 248
People's Communes 50, 52
People's Republic of China (PRC) 50, 52, 59
Philippines: debt moratorium 94; typhoons hit 162; Gini coefficients 221
planned economy, China 50–52, *51*
plantation development 236, 243, 246
Plaza Accord 32–35, *34–36,* 54, 72, 94, 143
PM2.5 exposure 238, 241, *241*
Pomeranz, Kenneth: *The Great Divergence* 24
population growth 8, 16, 110, 115, 131, 150, 151, 192–194
Porter, Michael 157
post-war Asia, economic growth in 29, 48
post-war East Asian industrialization 24
post-war export pessimism theory 17
post-war monetary, capital flows 91–95
poverty 1, 13, 210, 250; in Asia 15; and birth control policies 193–194; informal economy relationship with 179; issues on 186n3; in Japan 219; reduction of 210–212, *211*
Prebisch, Raul 15
primate cities 148, 150–153, **152,** *153,* 158
private enterprises 53, 60, 198
producer-driven value chains 73
product architecture 43, 73, 79
public awareness 210
public goods 254
pull factors: international migration 114; in Thailand and Korea for migrant labor 120–122; urbanization 155
pulp and paper industry, in Southeast Asia 242–243; common points and differences 244–245; de-chlorination and chlorine-free pulp 243; forest destruction and raw material procurement 243–244
push factors, international migration 113, 123; urbanization 155

race to the bottom 183
rapid economic development 170, 234, 252
rapid economic growth 234
rapid population growth 192, 193, *193*

rapid urbanization 148, 151, 154
raw material procurement 243–244
RCEP *see* Regional Comprehensive Economic Partnership (RCEP)
real economy factors, Asian Financial Crisis 20
reform and opening-up, China 49–50, 52–54, 59–60, 220
Regional Comprehensive Economic Partnership (RCEP) 30, 44
regional development 252–253
regional division of labor, in production, and horizontal trade 37, *38*
regional economic order 35, 43, 44
regional economic integration 44
regional FTAs 30
regular employment contracts 219
relative poverty 210, 212, 226, 230n2
research and development (R&D) 55, 83, 134–136, **135,** *136,* 140–141, 157
Research Institute of Economy, Trade and Industry (RIETI) 37
residential informality 185
RIETI-TID database 46
risks, informality 180–181
Rostow, Walt 15
rural-urban migration 151, 154, 171, 173

Salim Group 98
Sarit Thanarat 18
Sassen, Saskia 156, 173
savings/investment rate 16, *196,* 197
Second World War *see* World War II
self-constructed communities 184
self-employed work 179
self-employed workers 170, 180, 181, 202–205, 225
shared poverty 16
short-term capital 94, 96, 101
short-term credit transaction 107
Silicon Valley 139, 145, brain circulation and Asian entrepreneurs in 124–125
Silk Road Economic Belt 59, 63
Silk Road Fund 63
Singapore: female migrants from 118, *119,* **120**; foreign population in 115, *116,* 117, 118, **120**; haze pollution 245–246; high-skilled workers 123; international migration 113, 117; urbanization rate in 148
Sino-Japanese war 52
skill premium 217, 222, 225
slum communities 151, 161; from urban lower-class perspective 184–185
small and medium enterprises (SMEs), in Korea 121
smart hardware 145
smart nation vision 144

socialist economic planning system 50
social protection: informality 180–181; policies 202–204, **203**
social security 4, 22, 163, 170, 180, 184, 192, 201, 202–204, **203,** 219, 221, 225, 253
social upward mobility 179, 227
socio-economic factors 193–194
solvency problem 91, 98
Sonnenfeld, D. A. 248n5
de Soto, Hernando 173, 174
Southeast Asia 13; Asian financial crisis in 88; financial regulators in 107n2; GDP in 175, *175;* industrial clusters in 138; informal employment in 176, *175;* pulp and paper industry in 242–243; unicorn companies in 145; urbanization rate in 148
South Korea: birth control measures in 193; demographic transition 198; economic growth of 131; exports commodities of 70, **71**; financial system reform 103; foreign population in 115; government as intermediary 121–122; income inequality in 224; industrial clusters in 139; industrialization patterns of 106; inequality in 229; research and development of 136; small and medium enterprises in 121; trade policies of 42; unicorn companies in 145; urbanization rate in 148
Soviet Union 14, 41, 50, 52, 75
spatial economics 138, 157
spatial inequality 217, 220, 225, 227
Special Economic Zones (SEZs) 53–54
stagnation 1, 13; growing Asia emergence 16–17; post-war reconstruction of Japan and Asia 14–15; and underdevelopment in Asia 15–16
Standard International Trade Classification (SITC) 45
State-owned Asset Supervision and Administration Commission (SASAC) 60
state-owned enterprises (SOEs) 50, 53, 60, 77, 220
status-quo policy 120–121
structural adjustment program 92, 244
sub-prime loan problem of 2008–2009 29
substantial income disparity 111
Suehiro, Akira 19
sufficiency economy 143, 224
Sugihara, Kaoru 24, 25
Suharto (President) 236, 237, 244
supporting industry 98, 138, 156–57
sustainable development approach 247
Sustainable Development Goals (SDGs) 22, 204, 224, 247
systemic dynamics 19
System of National Accounts (SNA) 45

Taiwan(ese): companies 55; exports commodities of 70, **71**; high-tech communities in 125; Hsinchu 138; industrial clusters in 139; inequality in 229; PC industry 74, 78–79, 81, v83
Taiwan Semiconductor Manufacturing Company (TSMC) 138
taxes, informality 180–181
Terao, T. 234
textile products, export of 32
TFP *see* total factor productivity (TFP)
TFR *see* total fertility rate (TFR)
Thai Baht 19, 95, 96
Thailand: Asian financial crisis in 29; birth control measures in 193; capital flows for 98, 99; demand-driven *status-quo* policy 120–121; demographic dividends 198; distance and income disparity in 117, 118; economic disparities in 153–154; economic growth of 95, 133–134; exports commodities of 70, **71**; female migrants from 118, 119; financial crisis in 35; financial system reform 103; foreign population in 115, 116, 117; forest destruction 244; Formal and Informal Labor Force Market Survey 177; GDP expenditure compositions of **97,** 97–98; Gini coefficient of 221–222, 225; GRPs per-capita for 158–159, 159; informal economy in 178, 180; inheritance tax in 205; innovation policy in 142–144; international migration 113; interregional inequalities 225; IT capital investments in 137; population and slum communities in 151–153, 153; population pyramid in 159, 160, 166n2
Thailand 4.0 143
Thaksin Shinawatra 143, 180, 229
Theil index 220, 230n6
3rd National Economic and Social Development Plan 154
Three Nos 230n7
total factor productivity (TFP) 131, 195, 197
total fertility rate (TFR) 191–192, 194, **195**
trade: between China and ASEAN 37; cross-border 72; global-level agreement on 41; liberalization of 41, 122; in parts and components 21
trade policies, of Japan, China, and Korea 42
Trade-Related Aspects of Intellectual Property Rights (TRIPS) principles 41
trade-related databases 45–46
Transboundary Haze Pollution Act 246
Trump; Administration 44, 142
TSMC *see* Taiwan Semiconductor Manufacturing Company (TSMC)
20-year National Strategy 143
21st Century Maritime Silk Road 59, 63
two-sector model 151, 171

UN Comtrade Database 45
unemployment 151, 171–172, 177, 226
unicorn companies 139, 145
United Malays National Organization 229
United Nations Development Programme (UNDP) 224, 225
United Nations Framework Convention on Climate Change (UNFCCC) 247
United States (US): decline in economic performance 29; in economic growth of Asia 32, 33; financial crisis in 88; financial sector in 100; high-tech communities in 125; industrial clusters in 139; Kuznets hypothesis 215; large scale monetary in 101–102
United States–Mexico–Canada Agreement (USMCA) 41
universal social security system 201, 203–205
unlimited supply of labor 56–57
UN Statistical Institute for Asia and the Pacific (SIAP) 177
Upgrading 44, 78, 80, 106, 134, 144, 179, 197, 252: defined as 74; in value chains 81–83; urban communities 184
urbanization 6, 129, 134, 147–149, 194, 202, 215; challenges and prospects for 158–166; in global value chains 155–158; industrialization and cities as production centers 154–155; of informal economy 177–178; mega-regions evolution 157–158; over-urbanization and primate cities 150–153, **152,** 153; policies to over-urbanization 153–154; trends in 149, 149–150, 150
urbanization rate 148, 149, 149, 150, 151, **152**
urban population, in Asia 147, 149, 149, 150
urban sector 57; informal economy in 171
US–China trade dispute 141–142
USMCA *see* United States–Mexico–Canada Agreement
US–Vietnam Bilateral Trade Agreement (BTA) 89
Uzuhashi, T. 231n7

Vietnam: apparel industry in 74–75, 178, 179; development point of view 95; informal economy in 178; IT capital investments in 137
Vogel, Ezra F. 49, 255
voluntary export restraints (VERs) 32
vulnerable social security systems 222, 225

wage gaps 219–221, 225
wage workers 170
Watanabe, Toshio 28, 29
Williamson, Jeffrey 195
WIPO *see* World Intellectual Property Organization (WIPO)
Women in Informal Employment: Globalizing & Organizing (WIEGO) 173, 177, 186n2

working-age population 57, 62, 130, 192, 194, 196, *196*, 198, *198*, 199, *200*
working poor 172, 182
work-permit systems 120
World Bank 48, 92, 97, 102, 103, 110, 137, 156, 174, 193, 197, 210, 211, 240
World Intellectual Property Organization (WIPO) 139
world's factory 2, 21, 36, 81, 250
World Trade Organization (WTO) 21, 29, 41–42, 46, 50; China accession to 36, 55, 62; financial crisis and China's accession 35–37, 41–42
World War II 1, 13–14, 24–25, 30, 91, 104, 148, 150, 171, 192, 199, 207n1, 210, 254

Xiaomi ecosystem 145
Xi Jinping 59, 60, 229
Xing, Yuqing 97n4

Yoshikawa, Hiroshi 199